The First Summer People

THE THOUSAND ISLANDS 1650–1910

The First Summer People

THE THOUSAND ISLANDS 1650–1910

Susan Weston Smith

A BOSTON MILLS PRESS BOOK

CANADIAN CATALOGUING IN PUBLICATION DATA

Smith, Susan, 1944 —
The first summer people: the Thousand Islands
1650–1910

Includes bibliographical references and index.
ISBN 1-55046-037-4

1. Thousand Islands (N.Y. and Ont.) — History.
I. Title.

F127.T5S65 1993 974.7'58 C93-093681-7

First published in 1993 by
Stoddart Publishing Co. Limited
34 Lesmill Road
Toronto, Ontario
Canada M3B 2T6
(416) 445-3333

A BOSTON MILLS PRESS BOOK
The Boston Mills Press
132 Main Street
Erin, Ontario
N0B 1T0

Winners of the Heritage Canada Communications Award

American Association for State and Local History Award Winner

Design by Gillian Stead
Typesetting by Justified Type Inc., Guelph
Printed in Canada

The publisher gratefully acknowledges the support of the Canada Council, Ontario Ministry of Culture and Communications, Ontario Arts Council and Ontario Publishing Centre in the development of writing and publishing in Canada.

This one is for Smith

CONTENTS

Who were the "Island Indians" pictured in William Bartlett's engravings? Why did they leave? Where did they go? — Collection of the author

PREFACE

Tour-boat captains taking travellers through the picturesque Thousand Islands in the St. Lawrence River relate fascinating tales about particular sites — like romantic Boldt Castle on Heart Island — but information about the bigger picture is more elusive. Who named the region the Thousand Islands? Why would anyone call an island Deathdealer or Bloodletter? Who were the "Island Indians" pictured in William Bartlett's celebrated engravings of the islands? Why does the boundary line between Canada and the United States zigzag through the island waterway? And most important: who were the first Thousand Islanders? Finding answers to these questions led me to gather material for this book.

Perhaps I should begin by describing what the book does *not* contain. It is not a complete history of the Canadian or the American region of the upper St. Lawrence River known as the Thousand Islands. Nor does it give complete histories of islands. It will provide an overall understanding of who settled the islands, who fought for them, who lived on them and who first bought them. No modern ownership information is given, and only the names of those who purchased the islands prior to 1910, for the most part, are recorded.

The thrill in research is finding a missing piece of information that is startling. Several times in researching the Thousand Islands, I was fortunate to find a book, an article or a map that provided this thrill and often led to other discoveries.

In the summer of 1988 I visited the British Hydrographic Department archives in Taunton, England. After a day of reviewing Canadian maps I was discouraged. I could not find some Canadian charts that I knew were there because I had seen photocopies given to Canada by Britain and deposited in the National Archives of Canada (NAC, formerly the Public Archives of Canada). These Canadian charts were first engraved and printed in 1828, and I wanted to see the originals.

Then, just one hour before I was to catch my train to London, I listened to a presentation given by the chief archivist to a group of British schoolchildren (not nearly as attentive as I was). In describing the system of printing charts and explaining what an important service the British Hydrographic Department has performed for the Royal Navy and merchant fleets around the world, the archivist brought forth a leather-bound record book crumbling with age. "This is the first record book," the archivist explained. "The first charts ever printed are recorded in this book." I nearly jumped across the table, for I knew the surveys in Canada were some of the earliest completed by the British Hydrographic service.

As soon as the youngsters left the room I gingerly opened the book and there it was: *Canadian Lakes, 1815–18*. Our charts!

In minutes I was sitting at a chart table while the archivist unrolled Capt. William FitzWilliam Owen's hand-drawn map, dated 1816. It is beautifully coloured and beautifully drawn. To the archivist's knowledge, it had not been unrolled for several decades, perhaps not for "over a century." It was Captain Owen who named the Thousand Islands — more than 250 of them.

The names jumped out at me as I stared at the map. Puzzles were solved. Some fifty island names on the charts had never been transferred to the engraving plates and therefore had never been seen.

At one point I yelled — to my embarrassment — because I finally understood why Aubrey Island, now part of the St. Lawrence Islands National Park (Admiralty Islands), was called Porter on Owen's engraved charts. I had long since given up hope of finding a member of the British Admiralty with the name of Porter in 1816. Suddenly I realized that Owen had commemorated "the porter," the man in the office who carried the charts and equipment! The only problem had been that the word *the* had been left off the printed chart. Owen also named islands after "the Clerks" and "the Messengers." Within an hour I had my answers and 255 island names. In Part II is an account of Owen's work as a surveyor and in assigning names to the islands, to be found under the headings for Historic Name.

I found the second most exciting source of answers to island questions in a file in the Jefferson County Historical Society Museum in Watertown, New York. A cardboard-covered notebook filled with pencilled entries of island sales turned out, to my delight, to be a record of dozens of deed transactions for the American Thousand Islands. There was no name in the book to identify its owner, but the notes, with useful marginalia, had been kept over several years. One page recorded sales of panes of glass, which indicated that the book had belonged to Andrew Cornwall, co-owner of an island and one-time employee in a glass factory in Redwood, New York. Cornwall's meticulous entries on the island sales was an essential key to the history of the Thousand Islands. Much of the material quoted in my American section comes from his notebook.

More fruitful days were spent in libraries: in the National Archives of Canada; in the United States Archives in Washington, D. C.; the many libraries and museums in the Thousand Islands region. In 1975 I received my first writing contract for the St. Lawrence Islands National Park, for *A History of Recreation in the Thousand Islands*, and then in 1982 I completed another contract for Parks Canada, Eastern Ontario Region. Each led me to conduct more than fifty personal interviews. All this has provided the answers to most of my questions.

ACKNOWLEDGMENTS

As a professional-development officer for a university, I write hundreds of thank-you letters a year, a simple task compared to thanking the hundreds of islanders and the many librarians who have helped me complete this project.

I had invaluable help and encouragement from friends and family. Betty Corson, a Kingston editor, greatly facilitated the writing process, and Elizabeth Goodfellow provided the typing skills and good spirit to get me through a lengthy manuscript. Members of Parks Canada, St. Lawrence Island National Park (Mallorytown), provided photographs and reference material, as did John Nalon, president of Gananoque Historical Society, and Phoebe Triffon, a curator with the Thousand Islands Antique Boat Museum, Clayton. I also appreciated the support of librarians from the Gananoque Public Library, the Jefferson County Historical Society, the Holland Library (Alexandria Bay), the Clayton Library, and other local libraries in Kingston, Ontario, and in Ogdensburg, Canton and Watertown, New York.

I am grateful, too, to the staff of the New York Public Library, the Library of Congress and the United States Archives in Washington, D.C., as well as the National Archives of Canada, in Ottawa.

I also thank all the islanders and mainlanders who helped by answering my questions, granting interviews and providing family histories and island information.

I owe a special debt to Helen Wright Greuter of Washington, D.C., a summer islander on Sagastaweka Island. Her professional advice, encouragement and friendship helped me complete my task.

I would like to thank Ken Deedy, president of the Thousand Islands Land Trust, who supplied a trunkful of photographs and memorabilia; many of his photos appear in this book. He also provided me with motivation. And I thank Blu Mackintosh for pointing me in the right direction towards John Denison, Boston Mills Press, and more importantly, to managing editor Noel Hudson and designer Gillian Stead.

Finally, I have dedicated this book to Smith. Eliot D.W. Smith, my husband of twenty-seven years, died while crossing to our island on our hovercraft in December 1989. He would be proud to see this manuscript complete, for he loved the mighty St. Lawrence River more than most. Beginning in 1971, we toured the river from spring to fall with our children, Donald and Janet. Together we became islanders. Eliot knew the many bays and channels that I have described, and he took me through all of them. He also provided much love and support during years of research. To my Smith and our children I offer my deepest thanks.

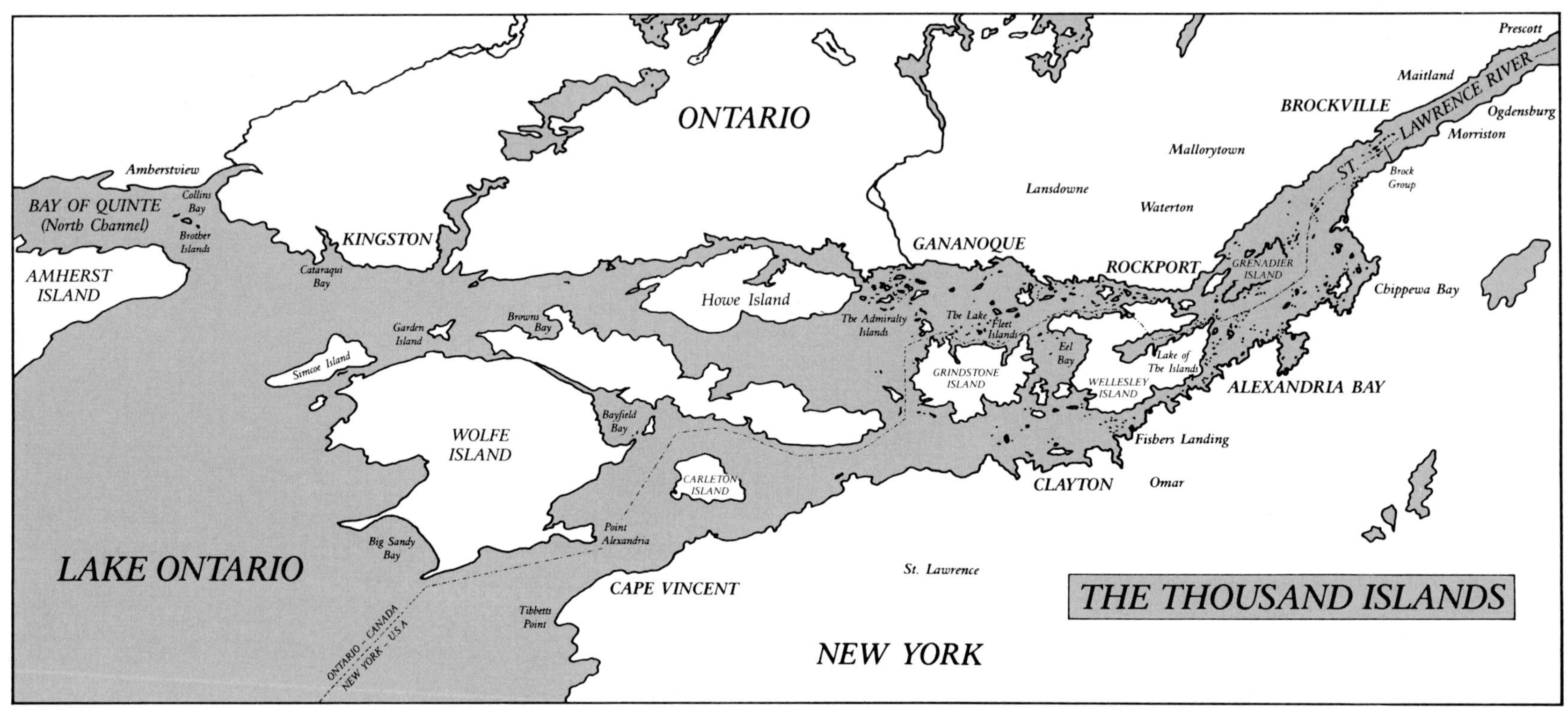
THE THOUSAND ISLANDS
ONTARIO
LAKE ONTARIO
NEW YORK
Amherstview
BAY OF QUINTE
(North Channel)
Collins Bay
Brother Islands
AMHERST ISLAND
KINGSTON
Cataraqui Bay
Garden Island
Simcoe Island
Browns Bay
Howe Island
WOLFE ISLAND
Bayfield Bay
CARLETON ISLAND
Big Sandy Bay
Point Alexandria
CAPE VINCENT
Tibbetts Point
ONTARIO - CANADA
NEW YORK - U.S.A.
GANANOQUE
The Admiralty Islands
The Lake Fleet Islands
GRINDSTONE ISLAND
Eel Bay
WELLESLEY ISLAND
Lake of The Islands
CLAYTON
Fishers Landing
Omar
St. Lawrence
ROCKPORT
GRENADIER ISLAND
ALEXANDRIA BAY
Chippewa Bay
Lansdowne
Waterton
Mallorytown
BROCKVILLE
Maitland
Prescott
Ogdensburg
Morriston
Brock Group
ST. LAWRENCE RIVER

HOW TO READ THIS BOOK

PART I

The Historical Review

The historical review begins with the white man's discovery of the Thousand Islands in the 1650s and moves through two and a half centuries. The story is told in chronological order, allowing the reader to see the development of island life from the beginning of settlement until the "Golden Era," when the islands became popular with wealthy Canadian and American city folk. The review ends when the islands were sold for use as summer retreats about 1912; thus, modern ownership information is excluded.

PART II

Island Descriptions

Almost nine hundred islands are listed in geographical order, not alphabetical order. This approach was taken so the reader may consider the islands in groups (i.e., Admiralty Islands or Alexandria Bay islands). For the most part, the islands are recorded from west to east, beginning at the eastern end of Howe Island and going downriver to Brockville in Canadian territory, and going from Grindstone Island downriver to Morristown in American. No information is given for the city of Kingston, or for Wolfe Island and Howe Island: these two islands are separate townships and have histories of their own.

The Canadian Islands

The history of Canadian island ownership was relatively easy to uncover. Because the islands were considered aboriginal land and were under the aegis of the Department of Indian Affairs, early data are housed in the National Archives of Canada in Records Group 10. Although the Thousand Islands files are dispersed among other reserve lands across Canada, the finding aids are concise and material can be found with minimal effort. Three surveys recorded the islands: John McNaughton's of 1862, Charles Unwin's of 1874, and Walter Beatty's, published in 1894. All three are included in this book. Modern Canadian island names are taken from *The Plan of Canadian Islands in the River St. Lawrence*, 1987, T.I.A.R.A., Blu Mackintosh, editor.

The American Islands

Ownership and development of the American islands proved much more difficult to trace. Islands were sold as private land, first in groups and later individually. Several county histories and community publications (see Bibliography) contain valuable information, but for the most part a researcher is limited to using newspaper articles for personal information. It is difficult to check these sources for accuracy, and mistakes have often been perpetuated. Rather than exclude the American islands completely, I have combined information from my own research, newspaper clippings and material provided by Hazel Simpson McMane, Alexandria Bay historian. Any errors and omissions in the book are my own.

Island names are recorded as they generally appear on the Canadian and New York State county maps. Those islands for which little or no information was available have been excluded from the text.

Susan W. Smith
Sagastaweka Island
Gananoque, Ontario
Summer 1992

PART I

THE HISTORICAL REVIEW

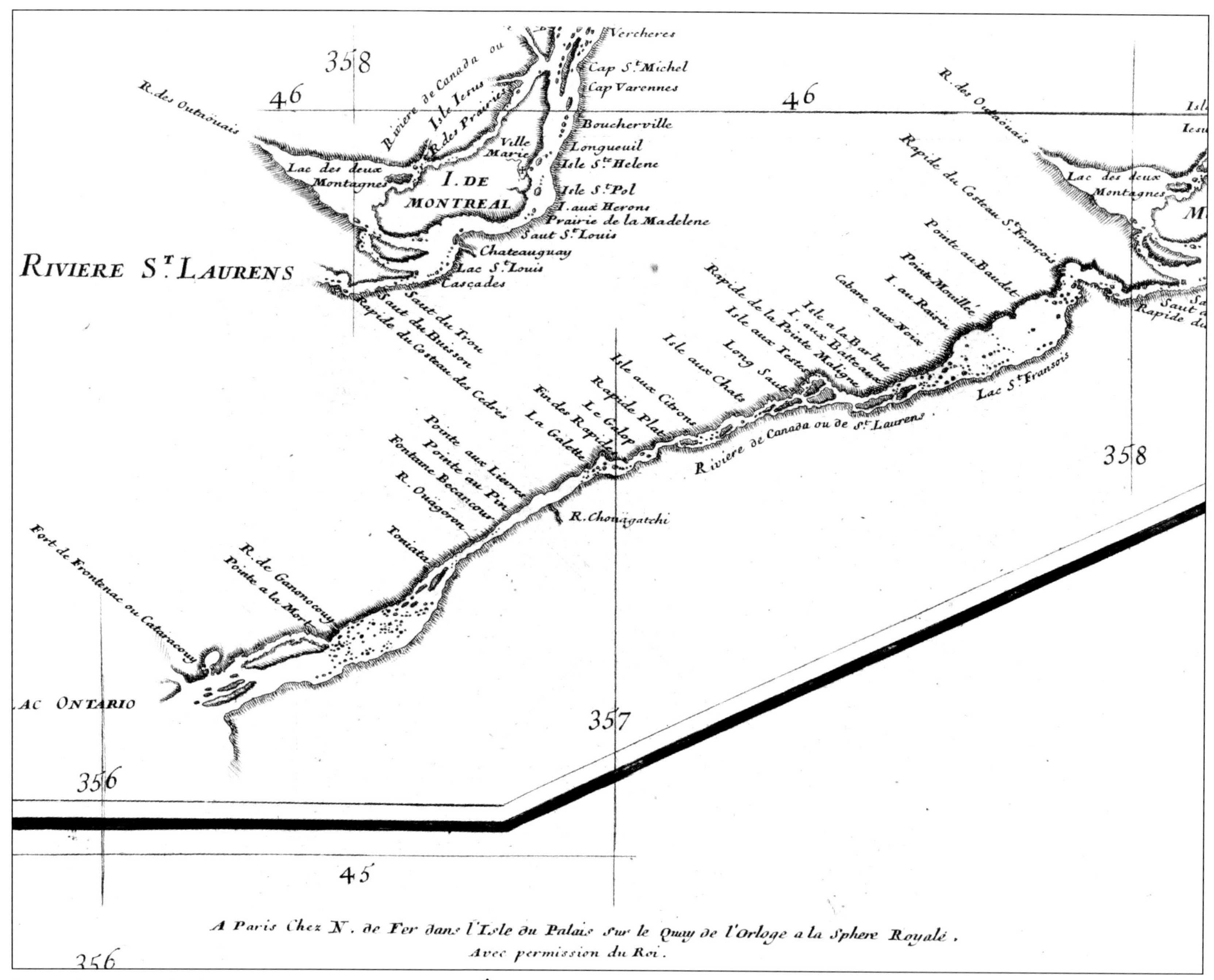

Jean Deshayes, a royal hydrographer, named the region Les Mille Îles. — McGill University Archives, Association of Canadian Maps, facsimile 81,1715

1 DISCOVERERS AND EXPLORERS
1650–1760

More than three hundred years ago Daniel de Remy, Sieur de Courcelle, the governor of New France, described the Thousand Islands in the upper St. Lawrence River as a "melancholy abode." He even went so far as to say there was "nothing agreeable about the islands other than their multitude."

He discovered the region after making his way up the treacherous rapids between the tiny villages of Montreal and Quebec and the great lake that was described by his native pilots. Courcelle was more interested in going farther west than in enjoying the scenery. He wrote in his journal that he found "an infinity of little islands which are at the entrance of the lake, in such great number and in such variety that the most experienced Iroquois Pilots sometimes lose themselves there. . . ." Luckily, those who followed viewed the Thousand Islands in a different way.

The first recorded information about the Thousand Islands is found in printed journals written three centuries ago by passing coureurs de bois (independent fur traders), missionaries and French government officials. Since that time historians have tried to identify places and pinpoint locations of specific areas from the early descriptions, but because of the great number of islands it is almost impossible to give exact locations. It is safe to say that several islands and mainland points were visited by these voyageurs.

In 1672 the legendary Louis de Buade, Comte de Frontenac, was appointed governor of New France, and the following year he made a journey through the Thousand Islands. Frontenac camped on an island "about a league-and-a-half from Ontondiata, where the eel fishery begins." He made a good day's journey and, "having passed all that vast group of islands with which the river is spangled," camped at a point above the Gananoque River called Onnondakoui by the natives.

In July of that year Frontenac entered the superb natural harbour at Cataraqui (now Kingston) at the head of four squadrons of canoes carrying brightly clad French forces and Huron allies. He and his officers, their guns at the ready, rode in a flat-bottomed bateau decorated with pennants, followed by two barges laden with tools and supplies. They came to meet the most famous French explorer of his time, René-Robert Cavelier, Sieur de La Salle, who had founded Cataraqui in May. La Salle brought accounts of vast spaces and untold riches in furs in the wilderness; Frontenac recounted the steady growth of the French colony.

René-Robert Cavelier, Sieur de La Salle.
— Jno. Haddock, *A Souvenir, The Thousand Islands of the St. Lawrence River,* 1895

Louis de Buade, Comte de Frontenac. — National Archives of Canada C3934

The two men agreed that the new settlement must become an outpost of the fur trade and of the French empire in North America, and together they built Fort Frontenac at the source of the St. Lawrence River.

La Salle returned to France and won King Louis XIV's approval for a land grant that included the fort and an area approximately 13 kilometres (8 miles) to the east and west and 3 kilometres (2 miles) inland. He also received Île Tonti (now Amherst Island) to the west and the islands lying off Cataraqui: Grande Île (now Wolfe Island), Île Cauchois (also spelled Cochois, supposedly named after James Cauchois, one of La Salle's river pilots; now Howe Island), as well as several smaller islands — but at a cost. He was obliged to pay for building the fort and also had to maintain a garrison and establish a French colony around the fort. Another responsibility included helping to civilize the natives who camped nearby. Religion was an important priority in this Catholic country, so La Salle also had to promise to build a church and support one or more Recollet priests.

However, La Salle was an explorer rather than a landowner, and he received the king's patent for the right to explore the country and find a passage to Mexico in the south, as well as the right to trade for furs in the far-off lands and the right to build forts along the route. He left his fort near the Thousand Islands to continue his explorations.

The next few years saw many sailors travel through the Thousand Islands. Passage was still difficult, but tradition has it that enterprising French-Canadian boatmen, called voyageurs, marked a channel through the labyrinth by planting French poplars, a fast-growing tree, along the route. Clearings were made and used as "pipe stops," or places to rest and light a pipe. The boatmen's routine of stopping every two hours led to a method of identifying locations by describing them as one or two "pipes."

Most boatmen used the north channel through the waterway, hugging the Canadian shore. As they passed through Le Petit Detroit, a small channel between Tar Island and Grenadier Island, they received a form of baptism. Each new boatman had to wade across what he thought was a shallow channel. The peals of laughter and the boatman's first swimming lesson taught him otherwise. The territory west of this spot was considered *pays sauvage*, or wilderness.

It was unwise for river travellers to explore the waterway, for there were hundreds of bays and channels, many of which led to dead ends and marshlands. One diary explained that it was necessary to "turn very short to enter the Bay of Corbeau [Halsteads Bay], which is large and fine, passing Isle au Citron [Gordon Island], which is a good league in length. It is fine and well wooded."

The voyageurs travelled in 40-foot-long flat-bottomed bateaux. The crew of twenty-five sang as they paddled, keeping a rhythm with the oars hitting the water. They quickly learned to appreciate the calm waters and tranquillity of the Thousand Islands, knowing of the dangers that lay ahead. If they were going west, they had to cross the vast open waters of Lake Ontario; in the other direction, they had treacherous rapids to navigate downriver.

But when the mouth of the Great Lake is reached, the navigation is easy, when the waters are tranquil, becoming insensibly wider at first; then about two-thirds, next one half and finally out of sight [of land]; especially after one has passed an infinity of little islands which are at the entrance of the Lake, in such great number and in such a variety that the most experienced Iroquois Pilots sometimes lose themselves there, and experience considerable difficulty in distinguishing the course to be steered, in the confusion and as it were in the labyrinth formed by the islands, which otherwise have nothing agreeable beyond their multitude. For these are only huge rocks rising out the water, covered merely by moss, or a few spruce or other stunted wood whose roots spring from the clefts of the rocks which can supply no other aliment or moisture to these barren trees than what the rains furnish them.

After leaving this melancholy abode, the Lake is discovered appearing like unto a sea without islands or bounds, where barks and ships can sail in all safety; so that the communication would be easy between all the French colonies that would be established on the borders of the Great Lake which is more than a hundred leagues long by thirty to forty wide.

O'Callaghan and J.R. Brodhead. *Documents Relating to the Colonial History of the State of New York*. Albany, 1855. Vol. IV, 45.

Peace was shattered in New France after Frontenac was recalled to France in 1682. His successor as governor, Joseph Antoine Le Febvre de La Barre, set out from Montreal in 1684, leading an expedition against the Iroquois. His troops had a miserable voyage up the river, encountering mosquitoes and contracting a malarial fever. Many died en route to and from the islands.

Jean Deshayes, a royal hydrographer, sent by the French king to chart the colony's shoreline, gave the region its name: Les Mille Îles, or the Thousand Islands. He and other prominent men of science furnished valuable surveys and hydrographic drawings of the vast territory of New France. The Sansons family, headed by Nicholas and his sons Guillaume and Adrien, began publishing maps of North America in Paris as early as 1650, using information gathered by the Jesuit missionaries and explorers to locate various geographical points. The map they published in 1656 was the first to use the name Lake Ontario; it was known in New France as Lac de St. Louis.

Deshayes was over fifty years old when he left France on his first trip to the New World. During the summer of 1687, he made his way up the St. Lawrence River with a new governor of New France, Jacques-René de Brisay, Marquis de Denonville. But Deshayes was frail, suffering from poor health, and became so ill on the voyage to Cataraqui that the crew thought he would not survive. Fortunately, he managed to complete the journey, for his sketches are the first accurate charts of the St. Lawrence River shoreline between Quebec City and Lake Ontario, and they were used by other mapmakers for many years.

Like Frontenac's first trip to Cataraqui, Denonville's trek west in June 1687 was also impressive. He led almost eight hundred French troops, nine hundred Canadian militia, coureurs de bois and four hundred Hurons on an expedition against the Iroquois. Reports had been received that there were "several Iroquois" fishing in the Thousand Islands and living on the mainland on the south shore in what is now called Chippewa Bay. The governor sent word that they should be detained, but by then the small band had made their way to Cataraqui. Denonville and his troops camped in the islands for two days, resting after the tough voyage up the rapids. When they arrived at Cataraqui, they learned that an officer, Champigny, had proceeded ahead and invited the neighbouring Iroquois to a feast, hoping to capture them before they had the opportunity to warn their brethren that the French were coming.

Champigny was supposed to invite the Iroquois who lived in the Bay of Quinte, but his scouts claimed that the small band could not be found. Instead, they rounded up the local inhabitants and took them to Fort Frontenac — including the small band who lived on an island known as Ontoniata (now considered Tar Island or the mainland at Cook's Point). The total number of prisoners included 51 warriors and more than 150 women and children. The scouts tortured, wounded and killed many of the warriors. "They were tied to posts in the fort by the neck, hands, feet, in such a way that they could not lie down, or drive away the hordes of mosquitoes, and a number of Indians, who were Christian converts, were amusing themselves by burning the fingers of the unfortunates in the bowls of their pipes."

The prisoners who survived were sent to Quebec; many were baptized and given to Christian missions, while the others were placed on board a ship and sent to France to serve as galley slaves.

Denonville and his men left Cataraqui in July and headed west to meet a contingent of French at the mouth of the Genessee River. They combined forces and marched on Seneca villages in the area. Although the native residents had fled, the white men proceeded to destroy their crops and burn their shelters. Denonville returned to Quebec after rebuilding La Salle's fort at the mouth of the Niagara River.

Soon afterwards, the Iroquois began to terrorize French settlements in retaliation, and French ships on Lake Ontario were no longer considered safe. Hoping to forestall more native attacks against the settlers, Denonville wrote to the king, requesting the return of the prisoners he had captured at Fort Frontenac the year before. Even though the king had ordered that the natives be well treated, Denonville worried that "if ill treatment has caused them all to die, — for they are people who easily fall into dejection, and who die of it, — and if none of them come back, I do not know at all whether we can persuade these barbarians not to attack us again."

When the French gained the support of the Algonquins, the Iroquois had turned to the English. The English, only too glad to capitalize on the wrath of the Iroquois, encouraged them to retaliate. This led to more attacks against the white settlers, who lived within stockades and dared not venture outside to tend their fields.

What had started as a probable victory for Denonville and the French ended in dissatisfaction, for not only were the French settlers suffering, but so did the lucrative fur trade. Even the Thousand Islands felt the results of the tensions. One journal records that Father Millet, a former missionary to the Oneidas and chaplain at Fort Frontenac, was captured near the fort. He was bound and carried to an island "about six miles below" at a place that was used to build canoes. He was stripped and forced to "sing for the amusement of his captors, and tortured." The next day he was taken downriver to the Point la Morte (near the east end of Howe Island and Sheriff's Point). It was very hot and when he complained of sunstroke, a "squaw" presented him with a "kind of English hat." They continued to drift downriver through the islands, making plans to attack, for they were the same band responsible for the historic Lachine Massacre, during which more than twenty habitants were tortured and killed. The band stopped at Atoniata (probably Grenadier or Tar Island) and stayed there for three days to hunt and fish. Father Millet was sure he was to be killed, but he understood their language and learned that he was to be sent across the river to the Oneida headquarters. He was adopted by the Oneidas and lived with them until 1694.

In an attempt to establish peace, the king reappointed Frontenac as governor. When he returned to New France, he discovered that Denonville, fearing further repercussions by the Iroquois, had ordered Fort Frontenac to be destroyed. In an attempt to stop Denonville from carrying out his plan and ending any hope of maintaining a trading post there, Frontenac sent three hundred of his men towards Cataraqui. They were only a few miles west of Montreal when they met Denonville's men returning from their assignment.

Much to Frontenac's dismay, the men reported that they had "set fire to everything in the fort that would burn, sunk the three vessels belonging to it, thrown the cannon into the lake, mined the walls and bastions, and left matches burning in the powder magazine; and, further, that when they were five leagues on their way to Montreal a dull and distant explosion told them that the mines had sprung." Luckily for the French, the Iroquois galley slaves were returned — thirteen in all, "clad in French attire." They came back to Canada on the same ship as Frontenac and, rather than remaining hostile to the French, they became ambassadors, helping Frontenac gain peace with the warring natives. Still convinced of the need for trade, the governor ordered his men to rebuild Fort Frontenac, which, although damaged by Denonville's men, was not completely destroyed.

Count Frontenac made peace with the Iroquois in 1701. By this date they had all but vanished from the north shore of the St. Lawrence River, and for the next fifty years the fort and its surrounding countryside enjoyed a long period of quiet. Meanwhile exploration, settlement and fur trading led to further growth, and further struggle between France and Britain for supremacy in the New World.

For six months each year the river provided a water highway to the west. In 1720–21 Father Charlevoix, a Jesuit priest, travelled up the river, and from his journals we learn that he stopped at Toniata (which he spelled Tonihata and refers to Grenadier Island) and visited with an Iroquois known by the name of "Quaker." This man was very friendly and welcomed his visitor with food and hospitality. He had assembled a small band of eighteen to twenty families on the island, tended his garden and dressed like the French. Charlevoix, eager to take advantage of the beautiful weather, declined the invitation to linger, and he and his party continued on through the Thousand Islands. He described his passage up the river: "I had still thirteen leagues to Catarocoui; the weather was fine, and the night very clear, which induced me to embark at three o'clock in the morning. We passed through the midst of a kind of archipelago, which they call *Mille Isles*. I believe there are about five hundred. When we had passed these, we had a league and a half to reach Catarocoui. The river is more open, and at least half a league wide; then we leave upon the right three great bays, very deep, and the fort is built in the third."

In 1754 the British living to the south in the colonies realized that the French were continually encroaching on their territories to the west. The English had already established the Hudson's Bay Company in the Far North, and both countries felt the tremendous economic pressures of the fur trade. When both sides felt they had the advantage, a war, known as the French and Indian War, began. The struggle began in 1754, and in the beginning the French were the victors. The Marquis de Montcalm, who was appointed commander in the field in 1756, took three thousand men from Fort Frontenac to Fort Ontario (Oswego, N.Y.) and captured it. He took 1,700 prisoners, destroyed the British fort and gained control of Lake Ontario. The following year he laid siege to Fort Henry (Lake George), and 2,500 British surrendered within a week. In July 1758 Montcalm led over three thousand troops from Fort Frontenac across the river again and defeated the British forces of over six thousand regulars and nine thousand militia at Ticonderoga. But a month later British Lieut.-Col. John Bradstreet, with three thousand men, captured Fort Frontenac.

He not only captured the fort and its troops but systematically destroyed the provisions and the environs. He captured "110 men, some Women, Children and Indians," but most were allowed to return to Quebec. Bradstreet even stopped long enough to write a pass for the commander, M. Noyen, to "shew" should he be stopped en route to Quebec.

Before sailing back across Lake Ontario, Bradstreet's men set fire to Fort Frontenac, the surrounding houses and the vessels in the harbour. One account states that "in and about the fort we found sixty pieces of cannon, sixteen mortars, and six brass patterraras [small brass guns], all which were effectually destroyed and render'd unfit for use". For a second time Fort Frontenac was left in ruins.

The French under Montcalm suffered a great defeat again in September 1759, when a British army under Gen. James Wolfe sailed up the St. Lawrence River to Quebec. The ten-minute battle on the Plains of Abraham was decisive: the British won, but both Wolfe and Montcalm lost their lives on the battlefield.

The final expedition to end the war began in the summer of 1760, when ten thousand troops, including seven hundred native allies, assembled under the command of a British general, Jeffrey Amherst. The forces travelled down the St. Lawrence in seventy-two whale boats, about 170 bateaux and two armed vessels, the *Onondaga* and the *Mohawk*. Their destination was the fort at La Présentation (now Ogdensberg), and then on to Montreal.

Imagine the sight of such a flotilla of boats and men travelling down the river. The voyage was not an easy one. After entering the river, Amherst was frustrated by the maze of islands. He complained that it took the very best Iroquois pilots to choose the right course, and even then mistakes were made.

One mistake has been glorified in the history of the Thousand Islands — the story of the Lost Channel. The saga began when the *Mohawk* and the *Onondaga* and the entire fleet started their voyage down the south channel through the islands. As they passed Isle aux Chevreuil (now Carleton Island) they discovered a bateau "loaded with French soldiers put off." Captain Loring of the *Onondaga* knew that they were on the watch for the English and would soon notify the French fort at Oswegatchie, so he signalled to the *Mohawk* that he was going to chase the French bateau, hoping to capture it quickly. What followed was an exciting passage through the islands, crossing from the safe, more direct route on the south shore to the maze of islands near present-day Ivy Lea. Not only did he arrive after dark, but he was also ambushed by "arrows and musketry" from the surrounding islands. Worried that the whole flotilla would fall victim to the ambush, Loring instructed Coxswain Terry and a crew to take one of the ship's "quarter boats" and row back to warn the *Mohawk*. Loring then turned his guns on the enemy, who evidently jumped into their waiting boats and paddled to safety behind other islands. Loring then had another boat lowered from the deck and sent the crew off to find a safe passage out of the maze. Then the *Onondaga* anchored and waited for Coxswain Terry's return. After a time Loring sent an ensign off in a boat to look for the missing crew. This crew got lost rowing around the islands; they could find neither Terry nor the channel from which they had set out. They finally managed to return to the *Onondaga* and named the area "the River of the Lost Channel." Coxswain Terry had indeed disappeared. He never made it to the *Mohawk* and never returned to the *Onondaga*.

In August 1760 Lord Amherst and his flotilla reached Fort Lévis, east of Prescott, and forced it to surrender. He reached Montreal on September 6; it was lightly defended by two thousand French troops, and two days later the governor of New France surrendered to Amherst.

With the destruction of Fort Frontenac, and then the final British march east and the capture of Fort Lévis and Montreal, the Thousand Islands reverted to a quiet refuge and hunting ground for the natives. It is likely that some of the original French families who lived outside the palisades of the fort remained in the region. Some may have ventured through the islands during the summer months, but there are no records to substantiate this. More likely it was the brave fur traders who remained the only white men to take advantage of the islands each summer, but merely stopping at a "pipe stop" for a short rest.

For the next twenty-five years the land around Fort Frontenac was virtually abandoned. Two decades later another military post was established — not on the mainland but on an island.

2 THE FORT ON CARLETON ISLAND
1778–1783

"This is by far the more advantageous site for a fort!" exclaimed Lieut. William Twiss, Royal Engineer, as he finished rowing around Buck Island, located in the south channel separating the mainland and Grande Island (Wolfe Island). It was August 8, 1778, and Twiss remembered the instructions of his commander, Sir Frederick Haldimand: "I will rely upon your Judgement about the situation to be fixed . . . to find the place most capable of defence and most convenient for answering the purpose of protecting the vessels we send and the other craft we build."

Twiss and Capt. Thomas Aubrey arrived in the Thousand Islands from Montreal with Haldimand's orders. With them were several detachments of soldiers and a number of carpenters and blacksmiths eager to establish a naval station because the British were fighting a war against the young rebel army of the Thirteen Colonies.

Before deciding to build on Buck Island, Twiss and his men surveyed the site of the old Fort Frontenac on the mainland at Cataraqui. There were seven points of comparison between the two sites. Neither site was capable of defending the entrance to Lake Ontario because the river was too wide, and a decision had to be made to defend one of the two channels through the Thousand Islands. Twiss decided that the island site was better for the simple reason that it was an sland and was located in the "easiest Passage which any Boats can approach by." Twiss also decided that the 2-acre island was "sufficient to supply the Garrison with Vegetables." Buck Island also had two defendable harbours that provided protection from the west winds. Cataraqui, on the other hand, had a windswept harbour and was considered "sickly from a nauseous swamp at the head of the Bay." "Cataraqui is not favourable for building vessels as there is no good timber near it, and none can be had without bringing it a great distance," stated Twiss in his correspondence. Yes, the island site was much better, and thirty days later construction was under way.

Buck Island, a convenient "pipe stop" and trading post, was well known to those who travelled through the Thousand Islands. The British changed its name to Carleton Island, after Sir Guy Carleton, former governor-general of Lower Canada as well as the former commander of the British forces. The fort itself was named after Frederick Haldimand.

The American army made the decision in the summer of 1779 to move into native country along

Sir Frederick Haldimand, Governor of the Province of Quebec, 1773. — National Archives of Canada C3221

Sir Guy Carleton.
— Metropolitan Toronto Reference Library, J. Ross Robertson Collection T16567

what is today the corridor of upper New York State, Pennsylvania and Ohio. Their "scorched earth" policy of destroying the orchards and crops of settled natives ensured retaliation. Many of the subsequent raids originated on Carleton Island, where native war parties formed to head south. The island went on alert when Mississauga scouting parties in the Mohawk Valley returned with word that the Americans were building up strength. More guards were stationed at the east end of the island. Haldimand sent instructions to reinforce the site, and as a further precaution the island was "reconnoitred" every morning before the gates were opened. The soldiers also cut down all the brush and trees surrounding the fort so that the lookouts would have a clearer and wider view.

At the same time it was necessary to use small gunboats to escort the bateaux that brought supplies from Quebec. The passage through the Thousand Islands was considered the most dangerous. In addition, the shipwrights were busy building vessels capable of reinforcing the British naval strength on Lake Ontario.

Throughout the summer of 1780 native war parties, led by British officers, carried out raids and attacks to the south. The Americans retaliated by destroying a large portion of the Mohawk settlements. By the time winter came, the Iroquois were given the choice of settling either on Carleton Island or at the base at Niagara. Most took the western option, but several families remained at Carleton. Among these was Molly Brant, the widow of Sir William Johnson, British superintendent of Indian Affairs and Joseph Brant's sister. Brant (Thayendanagea) had been educated by Sir William Johnson. He became chief of the Six Nations.

Molly Brant assumed a leadership role among her people. One passage in government correspondence described her influence: "Their common good behaviour is in a great measure to be ascribed to Miss Molly Brant's influence over them, which is far superior to that of all their Chiefs put together."

The workmen continued their building efforts. At one time there were some seven hundred men stationed on Carleton Island. A blockhouse was built to guard the harbour, the naval stores and the new ships being constructed. It was also recommended that a trench or ditch be dug around the fort, but the excavation proved complicated because of the limestone cliffs and the composition of the island. A requisition of "thirty barrels of powder and six dozen potfires: Half a Potfire is used every day at present for blowing the Ditch of the Fort." It took more than four months to dig the trench with an average rate of "about twelve inches an hour." It was about 5 feet deep and in some places as much as 24 feet wide.

Finally, in August 1781, the fort and its surrounding gully were finished. During the following winter disaster struck as a fire swept through the shipbuilding barracks. All the sails and rigging were lost.

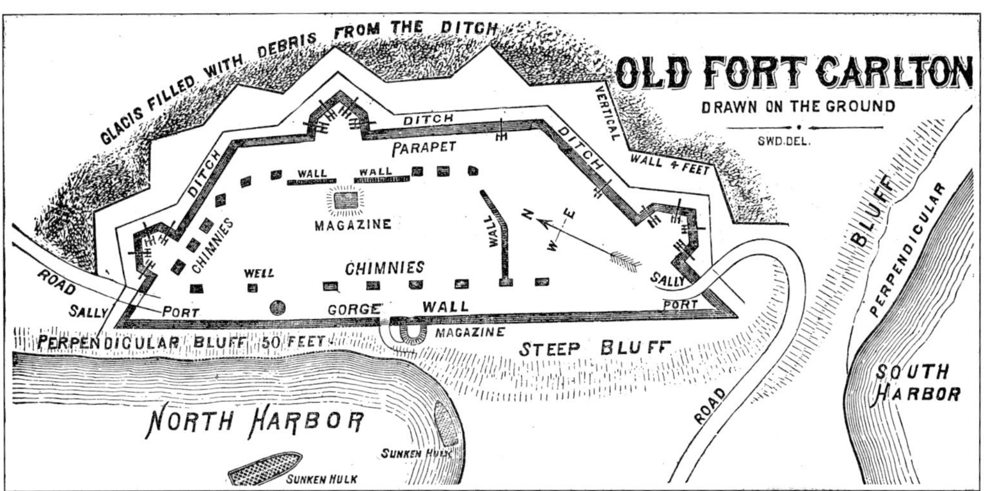

The drawing of Old Fort Carlton [sic] *shows the layout of the fort with its parapet and ditch.*
— Jno. Haddock, *A Souvenir, The Thousand Islands of the St. Lawrence River*, 1895

Then, in April 1783, the commanders received word that a peace treaty had been signed and all work and construction were to stop.

A problem of jurisdiction developed when the Treaty of Paris designated an international boundary line between British North America and the new United States. This line was to run through the middle of the Great Lakes and down the middle of the St. Lawrence River to the forty-fifth degree of latitude and then east to the Atlantic Ocean. If this boundary line were enforced, Carleton Island, an important British fort, would fall in United States waters!

At the same time there was another problem. The British had to find land for the loyal British subjects, who wanted to remain faithful and therefore made their way north, away from the newly formed United States. These men and women, called United Empire Loyalists, needed a refuge from their hostile home towns. There were also an estimated two thousand Mohawks, under the leadership of Joseph Brant, who wanted to settle north of the border. They had remained

Joseph Brant, Thayendanegea, Mohawk chief. — Metropolitan Toronto Reference Library T 31859

loyal to the British through two wars, first conquering the French in 1755 and then being defeated in the American Revolution.

Years earlier, the British, in order to keep peace and foster friendship with native bands, formulated a land policy that guaranteed no land would be taken from the bands without proper surrenders and/or payments. So before the Mohawks or the United Empire Loyalists could settle, the mainland had to be purchased or surrendered.

Where to settle was the next question. Survey parties again visited the site of Fort Frontenac at Cataraqui, and it was quickly agreed that the old fort could again become a land base. When the British questioned Mohawk chief Brant about the need to purchase the land occupied by the Mississaugas, Brant replied that no surrenders were needed because all the land on both the north and south shores of the St. Lawrence River and Lake Ontario had once belonged to his ancestors and were therefore already Mohawk, or Iroquois, territory.

In one way Brant was right. Long before the white man discovered the upper St. Lawrence, the area had been considered debatable ground between the Algonquins and the Iroquois. At the time the French discovered and named the region, the Iroquois had gained superiority and were the dominant group. During the ensuing years, great numbers of Iroquois lost their lives either in wars with the French and with other native groups, or from fatal epidemics. They gradually moved south into upper New York State, and by the mid-1700s the Iroquois had all but disappeared from the north shore of Lake Ontario. When this happened, groups of Algonquins or Ojibwa (also called Chippewa) hunted and fished in the old Iroquois territory as far east as the Thousand Islands. They were known by the French and later by the English as "Mississaugas."

In order to settle the question of ownership of the Canadian mainland, the Mississaugas were summoned to Carleton Island and persuaded to make a land surrender. A Loyalist officer, Capt. William Crawford, who fought beside the Mississaugas in raids during the Revolution, negotiated the surrender of land from the Thousand Islands west to the Bay of Quinte. The northern boundary extended back as "far as man can travel in a day." The Mississaugas received "as much coarse red cloth as will make but a dozen coats and as many laced hats . . . ." They also received guns, powder and ammunition. Unfortunately there is no surviving signed surrender for this transaction, and the only reference we have is through recorded British correspondence.

This Carleton Island surrender gave the Crown the right to the land west of the Thousand Islands, but the land east to Lachine (Quebec) was still claimed by the Iroquois. So Captain Crawford summoned the Iroquois Onondaga chiefs from St. Regis (near Cornwall, Ontario) to gain another surrender on the north shore, from Pointe Baudet (near the Quebec border) on the north side of Lake St. Francis up to the mouth of the Gananoque River. Again, no deed survives and there is no mention of the islands. Therefore, in both cases we can assume all the islands remained in the ownership of the Mississaugas or the St. Regis band.

The process of settling the waiting Mohawk tribes and the loyal British could now begin. Plans were made to move the military installations on Carleton Island to the mainland on secure British territory. Surveyors found the abandoned Fort Frontenac at Cataraqui in better condition than expected, and soon supplies and even buildings were moved. At the same time surveyors laid out townships along the north shore of the St. Lawrence River and west of Fort Frontenac to the Bay of Quinte.

The crumbling chimneys on Carleton Island in the late 1800s.
— Jno. Haddock, *A Souvenir, The Thousand Islands of the St. Lawrence River*, 1895

Thus, only five years after Lieutenant Twiss chose the 2-square-mile island as the proud headquarters for a British naval station, Carleton Island's military importance was over. Although it was no longer considered to be in Canada, the British were reluctant to abandon their strategic position in the river. The actual land ownership was decided in 1795 with the signing of Jay's Treaty, but the Americans never occupied the island. Instead, a small British garrison remained the only residents until the War of 1812.

The land surrenders negotiated on Carleton Island ensured that more travellers would make their way through the Thousand Islands. Some would remain to inhabit the north shore.

John Graves Simcoe, first governor of Upper Canada.
— Metropolitan Toronto Reference Library, J. Ross Robertson Collection T 14946

3 SETTLEMENT OF THE CANADIAN SHORE
1783–1812

"Capt. Justice Sherwood left Montreal in September 1783 with eleven men. It took them two weeks to make the journey west to the Thousand Islands, but during that time they made an extensive survey of the land along the north shore of the St. Lawrence River, gathering information about the land, its timber and its water sources. Along the way small survey parties travelled inland, describing some of the land as the "best quality they ever saw." They arrived at the Thousand Islands on September 30, and their one-sentence description ensured that little interest would be taken in this rocky section of the north shore: "We arrived at Carleton Island, there is a vast number of islands between Oswagatchie and this place, but in general, they appear to be barren rocks, excepting one called Granadier [*sic*] Island, which appears to be fine Land."

As a result, the north shore through the Thousand Islands was not settled nearly as quickly as the land to the east or to the west.

The first lieutenant-governor of Upper Canada was John Graves Simcoe. He inaugurated his administration by establishing rules for granting free land to the many hundreds of Loyalists waiting to settle. Townships were 10-mile-square sections in the interior and 9- to 12-mile-square sections along the shoreline of rivers and lakes. A farm lot was 200 acres.

Not all the land was to be given or granted. The Protestant clergy and the Crown each reserved one-seventh of each township. These "reserves" were never allocated in one section of the township but rather divided much like a checkerboard throughout each area. Although normally the land grants could not exceed 200 acres, there was a provision that allowed petitioners to increase the grant to as much as 1,000 acres at the discretion of the lieutenant-governor.

Those who were to receive this free land had to show that they were able to clear and work the land. They also had to declare their loyalty to the "King in His Parliament as the supreme Legislature of his Province." The grants were given in various sizes according to the recipient's military rank. Field officers received 1,000 acres, captains received 700 acres and every subaltern, staff or warrant officer received 500 acres. Noncommissioned officers received 200 acres, and every private received 100 acres. Fifty acres were given for every member in a family. Land was also awarded to those who

Colonel Joel Stone was the founder of the settlement at Gananoque.
— Metropolitan Toronto Reference Library, J. Ross Robertson Collection T 15506

had suffered loss of property in the newly formed United States after the war.

Although the system was advantageous to the officers and military men, the actual allocation of lots was quite fair. The surveyors drew large maps of the townships. The number of each lot was placed in a hat. On the day of allocation the Loyalists had the luck of the draw in deciding where they would spend their first years in Canada.

Col. Joel Stone was the founder of the settlement at Gananoque. He arrived in Canada about 1789 as a United Empire Loyalist from Connecticut, first settling in Cornwall. He applied for a land grant there but discovered that the best land was taken. Disappointed, he left Cornwall and travelled west, where there was available land.

Tradition states that the bateau carrying Stone pulled into the point on the west bank of the Gananoque River, and he hoisted a white handkerchief on a pole to signal for help or recognition. Two Mississaugas saw the signal and paddled in a canoe to the point from a small island to the west, which was soon known as "Little Island" (later called Ormiston's Island and today known as Cunningham). There, Stone met a French-Canadian trader, John Carey, who was trading among the Mississaugas and passing boatmen.

A few days later Stone ventured to the mainland and surveyed the mouth of the river. He discovered a waterfall and immediately saw the potential for a mill. He petitioned the government for a grant of free land — grants like those given to other Loyalists — to include both the east and west banks of the river.

Unfortunately for Joel Stone, he got part of his wish but Sir John Johnson, the government's Indian superintendent, petitioned for the same land, and he was an important person. Johnson became a Loyalist when he was knighted in 1765 by the King of England. He and his father, William, owned over 170,000 acres in the Mohawk Valley, but at the start of the American Revolution he was forced to leave his home and escape to Montreal. He immediately formed his first battalion, known as the King's Royal Regiment of New York. For a time after the end of the war he was in charge of settling the first United Empire Loyalists in Canada. In 1782 he was appointed superintendent general and inspector general of Indian Affairs, a position he retained until his death in 1830.

Johnson probably lost more land than any of the Loyalists who fled their homes. Therefore, he felt he had a right to petition for several land grants throughout Canada, including the seigneury near Montreal and several acres of land in Kingston (now the site of many businesses in downtown Kingston, including the Hôtel Dieu Hospital). He also wanted Grande Island (Wolfe Island) and Isle Cochoy (Howe Island) but was satisfied with the latter when he learned that Wolfe Island was already considered private land. In reality he never received the patent for Howe Island and as a result was bound and determined to have land at the mouth of the Gananoque River, which had recently been named River Thames by Lieutenant-Governor Simcoe.

While Johnson was trying to gain the patents to Howe Island, Stone learned that his petition for the land on either side of the Gananoque River was being contested. He wrote several letters explaining that he had made his application before Johnson, to no avail.

Johnson also wrote letters explaining that Stone was taking timber from Howe Island, which he now considered to "be worth little now as the greatest part of the Timber has now been cut by Mr. Stone, and others encouraged by him, saying I have no title to it. A stop should certainly be put to such depredation, whether I get it or not, of which I can have no doubt, after what has been done. I am only surprised with what face it can be withheld from me for so long."

After deliberation, the land commissioners divided the Gananoque River in halves. Sir John agreed to accept 1,000 acres on the west bank if his grant also included two islands lying opposite the town, known as the Nut Islands. The commission agreed and he received patent for Isle au Blé d'Inde (Corn Island) and Nut Island (Hay Island). He also received the grants for Howe Island and Amherst Island, near Kingston.

Sir John Johnson received a patent for the east bank of the Gananoque River, L'Ile au Blé d'Inde (Corn Island) and Nut Island (Hay Island), off the small settlement of Gananoque.
— J. De Peyster, Col. A.S., Artist, National Archives of Canada C 2847

Although Johnson never lived on his property, he did visit the area at one time, and when he met Stone he offered him 1,000 acres on Tonti (Amherst Island), near Kingston. But Stone did not consider that a good investment and declined the offer.

After Joel Stone received a patent for the west bank, he had the land surveyed and marked. One of his first business partners was John Carey, whom he had met on his first day in the region. Together they built a tavern (described by Mrs. Simcoe on a voyage through the islands as

"Carey's house, which was so dirty a house that we pitched the tent"). They traded with the island natives and catered to the passing boatmen by offering ale, King's biscuit, and a lesser quality navy biscuit. Stone went on to become one of the most important landowners and entrepreneurs of the region.

As the years passed, some land sections along the north shore of the St. Lawrence River were settled, farmland cleared and log cabins built. One of the first landowners along the north shore east of Gananoque was Oliver Landon, who came from Litchfield, Connecticut. He arrived after a recorded "twenty-one day" journey from Cornwall to the east, through the wilderness in a carriage pulled by a span of horses. This was a remarkable feat, considering that there were no roads and much dense forest to pass through.

The Mallory family also settled on the river front. First Enock and his brother Jeremiah received land grants near today's La Rue Mills. Jeremiah traded or sold his grant to William La Rue (known as Billa). Then another Mallory settled at what is now known as Mallorytown Landing and eventually moved farther inland to Mallorytown. The mill sites were the most valuable, and La Rue soon decided to dam the small creek that ran through his property to the St. Lawrence. In a ravine close to the mouth of the river he built his mill. Other mills were subsequently built farther downriver.

The first permanent settler in Elizabethtown (Brockville) was Thomas Sherwood. As early as 1874 he settled there, on a lot located about 2 miles east of present-day Brockville. It could be said there were three founding families in Brockville: those of Daniel Jones, Charles Jones (not related) and William Buell. There was no real village, only a creek and a clearing along the river. William Buell arrived in 1785 and built the first house. He, like Joel Stone, is well recognized for his contribution in settling the region. He donated several acres of land to the county. The courthouse and the site of the churches surrounding Courthouse Square in downtown Brockville are on his land. Daniel Jones, another important pioneer in the region, built a sawmill on the land next to Buell's. Charles Jones was born in 1781 and came to Canada with his father, Ephraim Jones, who settled in Augusta, a few miles to the east. He married Mary Stuart, the daughter of the first Church of England minister in Upper Canada.

Because of the importance of the various founding fathers of the tiny village that began to grow in the first decade of the 1800s, there was a controversy as to what its name should be. Charles Jones considered Charleston and William Buell wanted Williamstown. Tradition says for a time it was known as Snarlingtown, but the matter was settled when the town was officially named after Sir Isaac Brock, then commander of His Majesty's troops in Upper Canada.

A road was finally laid out between Kingston and Brockville. It began as a tree-lined path that was later widened for wagon traffic. Because of the marshlands and swamps along the water's edge and the number of creeks, the road was set several miles inland. Joel Stone provided a ferry service across the Gananoque River in 1801, and petitioned the government to help in building the first bridge. By far the most convenient and comfortable way to travel was by water. Bateaux and large scows, called Durham boats, brought hundreds of settlers west to a new frontier.

We can thank Lieutenant-Governor Simcoe's wife, Elizabeth, for her diaries and drawings, through which we now know more about the Thousand Islands. While stationed in Canada the Simcoes travelled through the islands between Montreal and the western settlements several times. Mrs. Simcoe first described the islands in June 1792. They travelled in a bateaux, which was the only form of transportation. More than once Mrs. Simcoe exclaimed that she needed a great deal of courage to entrust her life and the lives of their children to the crewmen and the dangers of the water journey.

Accommodations were also unsuitable, as this description shows: "Friday, June 29. We came to so miserable a house where we were to lodge tonight, within a league of Grenadier Island, that we preferred pitching a tent for ourselves, letting the children sleep in the boat, and left the house for a gentleman. While the tent was pitching, I fished and caught a small perch. Many people carry trolling lines, or lines which run out of a small fishing wheel or pulley lying out of the stern in their boat, and catch abundance of black bass and other fish all the way up the St. Lawrence." The next day they reached the "river Gananoqui," and it was here they found John Carey's house and again found the rooms so "dirty" that they again pitched a tent.

Two years later Mrs. Simcoe once more travelled through the islands, this time on her way east to Lower Canada's Montreal and Quebec. On this visit she stayed at "Fairfield's house," described as being "close to the mill at Gananoqui." On the following day she continued her voyage, arriving in the dark at "Capt. Cowan's opposite Oswegatchie. Here I had a large room with six windows in it."

Elizabeth Simcoe left us her diaries and drawings.

— Metropolitan Toronto Reference Library, J. Ross Robertson Collection T16542.

— Elizabeth Simcoe, Artist, National Archives of Canada C 13917

Mrs. Simcoe returned to Upper Canada in the winter, and the only road was along the north side of the St. Lawrence River. She met her husband in Cornwall, and after spending a few days in that town they travelled to Kingston. There had been a storm a few days before and the trails were covered with several feet of newly fallen snow. Although cautioned not to proceed on their journey, the Simcoes persisted. The description of the journey shows that the lieutenant-governor and his wife were strong-minded and tenacious. The road conditions forced their driver to turn out onto the ice for much of the journey through the Thousand Islands. This, too, proved to be dangerous:

> When we arrived at Carey's we heard that Mr. Forsyth had lost both his horses three days ago at the mouth of the Gananowui [*sic*], by keeping too far from the shore; they saved the carriole by cutting the traces, but neither he nor his companions were dexterous enough to save the horses. The people of the States are particularly expert in saving horses from drowning; they travel with ropes, which they fasten round the horses' necks if they fall into the water; pulling it stops their breath, and then they float and can be pulled out; then they take off the rope as quickly as possible, and the horse travels on as well as before. . . .
>
> When the Governor Simcoe was driven . . . to Detroit he carried these "choke ropes", and had occasion to use them. A "choke rope", or check band, is a small strap of rope or leather by which the bridle is fastened around the neck of a horse.

In 1796 the Simcoes made their last journey through the islands on their way to Montreal and Quebec for their departure to England. Mrs. Simcoe's final description relates a pleasant experience and a fitting way to remember the Thousand Islands. They stopped on an island a few miles past Gananoque. Mrs. Simcoe named the island "Isle au trippe," "from gathering *trippe de roche* on the rocks. It is a kind of liverwort plant good for diseases of liver, which the Canadians going to the Grande Portage boil and eat on very hungry days, but it is bitter and not wholesome." They also stopped at another spot: "I called it 'Bass Island' [this turned out to be the mainland], for the number of black bass I saw swimming in shallow water near the shore. We supped at ten, the stars shining unusually bright. We placed the beds on the trunks in one of the bateau, which was covered with sail cloth over the awning. We slept extremely well and so cool that we determined to keep that bateau so fitted up for the rest of the voyage rather than go into houses, now the Governor is so unwell, and suffers from the heat, besides the fresh breeze on the water kept away the mosquitos."

Wind came up on their last day and caused them some difficulty. The last passage in Mrs. Simcoe's diary describes the islands lying off of Brockville: "Passed Toniata Isles and the river of that name, then the Isles au Baril, on one of which we landed. The wind and sea so high we had difficulty in turning the Point, from the whence we had a pretty view of the Islands."

We can see from Mrs. Simcoe's diary and other history books that only the names of those whose lives and accomplishments were considered noteworthy are mentioned. It is safe to say there were many settlers whose contributions to clearing the rocky cliffs along the river are long forgotten.

Many stayed for only a few short years, moving on to more settled areas as time went on.

Imagine the anticipation of these Loyalists as they rowed along the St. Lawrence River. They probably travelled up the river with twenty other bateaux, each carrying passengers, provisions, tools and livestock. At their stop the new settlers would gather their belongings and disembark on the shore, watching the fleet continue west towards the Bateau Channel and Kingston. They had received enough clothes for a year or two, as well as food, provisions and seeds for crops. They would have been careful to unpack their tools, a gun and ammunition for hunting, and an axe for felling trees and splitting wood. Some were lucky enough to be given a cow or an ox. They fashioned a shelter out of the trees and began to clear the land to plant crops. On warm evenings, after the toil of the day, they surely dropped a line into the water to catch fish and gazed out at the islands, imagining the time when they could build a small boat to explore the many bays and channels of the Thousand Islands.

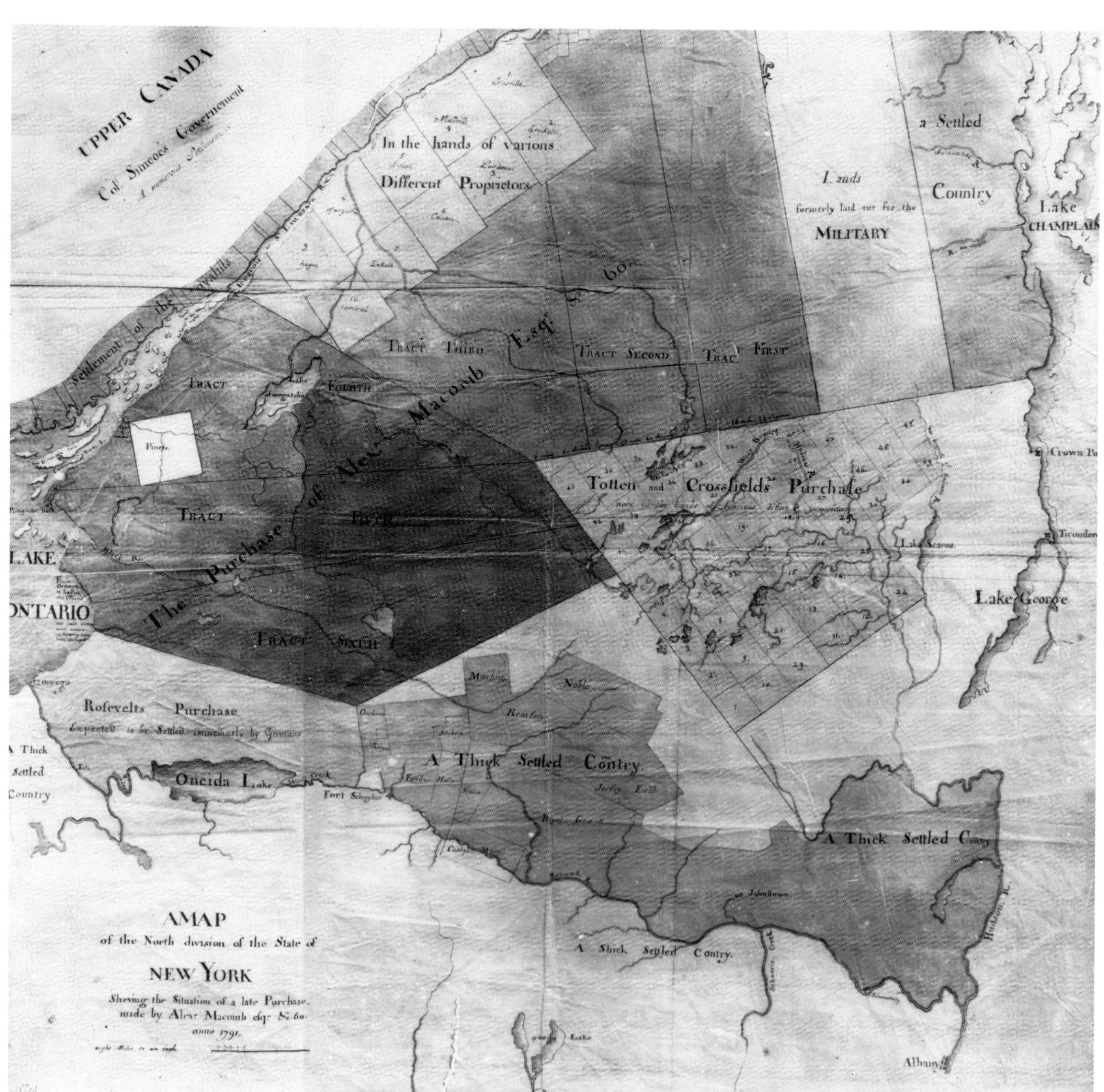

Macomb's purchase included the Thousand Islands.

— National Archives of Canada, National Map Collection, NMC 51744

4 SETTLEMENT OF THE AMERICAN SHORE
1790–1812

"Alexander Macomb saw the Thousand Islands several times before he made a bid to purchase them in 1792. Macomb, born in 1748, came to America with his parents from Northern Ireland and settled in Albany, New York. He moved to Detroit to begin his business career, and by the time he was thirty he was a prosperous fur trader, often travelling back and forth through the Great Lakes and the Thousand Islands. One night while he was camping on Carleton Island, his canoe and all his supplies were stolen by some natives. "Mr. Macomb had his silver works stolen out of the boats at Carleton Island by Indians, but pursuing them, got the best part of them back. . . ."

It is hard to believe that Macomb and others passing through the islands would consider the region valuable, for it was certainly a wilderness. But at the same time that the Loyalists were settling on the north shore, New York State officials were eager to settle their side of the river. Oneida land claims in New York were settled soon after the Revolution, allowing the New York government to establish the ten 100-square-mile townships called the Ten Towns of the St. Lawrence. Five towns were surveyed along the south shore of the St. Lawrence from Massena west to Hammond (near Chippewa Bay), and five immediately behind these. The state originally planned to sell lots to individuals, thus forming a strong settlement on the American bank. Instead, land commissioners encouraged the sale of large tracts to single buyers, who in turn were supposed to burden the cost of development in selling the lands. When this happened, wealthy New York speculators were touched by "land fever."

About 1790 Macomb moved his family to New York City, where he moved among the wealthy. The dignified home he built there was later used as the Presidential mansion by George Washington, the new president of the United States, when he and his wife, Martha, moved to New York, then the capital of the United States. Macomb met his future land partners, Daniel McCormick and William Constable, at the St. Patrick's Society, an organization formed to help Irish immigrants who were flocking to New York in pursuit of a better life.

The three partners, struck by land fever, petitioned the state land commissioners for the purchase of almost 3.5 million acres of land. The sale was known as the Great Macomb Purchase. It included the Ten Towns along the St. Lawrence, the greater part of Franklin County, nearly all of St. Lawrence County, all of Jefferson and Lewis counties and part of Oswego County. The sale also included the "waste and unappropriated land comprised within the bounds herein aftermentioned, all the islands belonging to the State in from the said lands. . . ." After deliberation the final land patent excluded "Carleton Island and an island called Long Sault, in the river, as well as a six square mile reservation for the St. Regis Indians" (near Cornwall, Ontario). He paid what was considered even in that time a "ridiculous price of eight cents an acre"!

Unfortunately, Macomb speculated in several losing ventures and eventually lost his property during one of the first economic depressions in the United States. In fact, he was put in debtors' prison. In time he was released and tried to regain some of his former prestige. He eventually left New York City and moved to Georgetown, in Washington, D.C., where he died in 1831.

Although we do not know if Macomb ever returned to the islands to spend any time or to enjoy his valuable purchase, we do know that he was indirectly responsible for bringing settlement to the south shore and eventually to the Thousand Islands. When Macomb went bankrupt, William Constable, Macomb's former partner, was left with the task of selling the land. Constable went to France in 1792. The French Revolution had begun, and he thought he could persuade wealthy nobility to leave France and settle in upper New York State. It was not a preposterous idea: after all, over one thousand aristocrats and royalists had been killed by the mobs.

One of his first contacts was Jacques Le Ray de Chaumont and his son, James. Jacques Le Ray had been sympathetic to the struggling Americans during the Revolution and had financed the young army. When the war was over, the new nation owed Le Ray more than two million francs. Unable to collect the money, Le Ray sent James to America as his representative.

The young man fitted quickly into New York society. He was familiar with American ways because Benjamin Franklin had stayed in the Le Rays' chateau while he was in France soliciting financial and military help during the Revolution, and again when he was negotiating peace as one of the appointed U.S. commissioners. Franklin in fact had taught English to James.

Le Ray lived in the United States for five years, and by the time he returned to France he had received partial payment from Congress on the debt to his father. He had become an American citizen, he had acquired an American wife, and he, too was touched by land fever.

When William Constable told James Le Ray, whom he had met two years before, about his plan to sell land in upper New York State, James introduced him to his bother-in-law, Paul Chassanis. Chassanis purchased 210,000 acres of the old Macomb tract (roughly part of Jefferson County between Rome and Watertown, and between the Black River and Lake Ontario). The tract was known as Castorland.

Chassanis and his partners had wonderful plans for their new purchase. They wanted to clear the land, build roads and sell lots to settlers; they also wanted to grow crops and cultivate vineyards and orchards. However, only twenty families crossed the ocean from France to Castorland. The harsh weather conditions, the difficult transportation and the unsuitability of the pioneer way of life for these aristocratic Frenchmen made existence in the wilderness almost unbearable.

In 1798 the New York legislature rescinded permission for French citizens to hold property in the state, and arrangements were made to have all the French-owned property transferred to James Le Ray, who was an American citizen. During the French Revolution James Le Ray — although not an aristocrat but a wealthy businessman — had been in danger. Once, when he left the country, he learned that his father had been arrested as an émigré. He rushed back to Chaumont and pleaded for his father's release. Anticipating the senior Le Ray's arrest, the family had already turned all land holdings to James. As a result a resolution was passed:

> Because of the excellent letter of recommendation that he and his wife have, and because said citizen has an old certificate of naturalization antedating the Revolution, and by his own oath taken in 1788 has become an American citizen, and also because his properties acquired at Chaumont have been free from any feudal or seigneurial stain, it is resolved: Jacques (James) Donatien Le Ray, student and friend of the immortal Franklin, and fellow-citizen of the French Republic's allies in North America, is and he remains under protection of the law and of all loyal Frenchmen, and his chattels and estates are given safe keeping and safety.

James and his wife, Grace Coxe, took up residence in France until the end of the century, when his wife became ill and wanted to return to the United States. He sent her back with his good friend Gouverneur Morris, who had just finished serving as ambassador to France. James soon followed, and probably through Morris's encouragement he began to take an interest in his vast upper New York State land holdings. One of his first land sales was to a group of Quakers who purchased 10,000 acres of land and settled the small village of Philadelphia in Jefferson County.

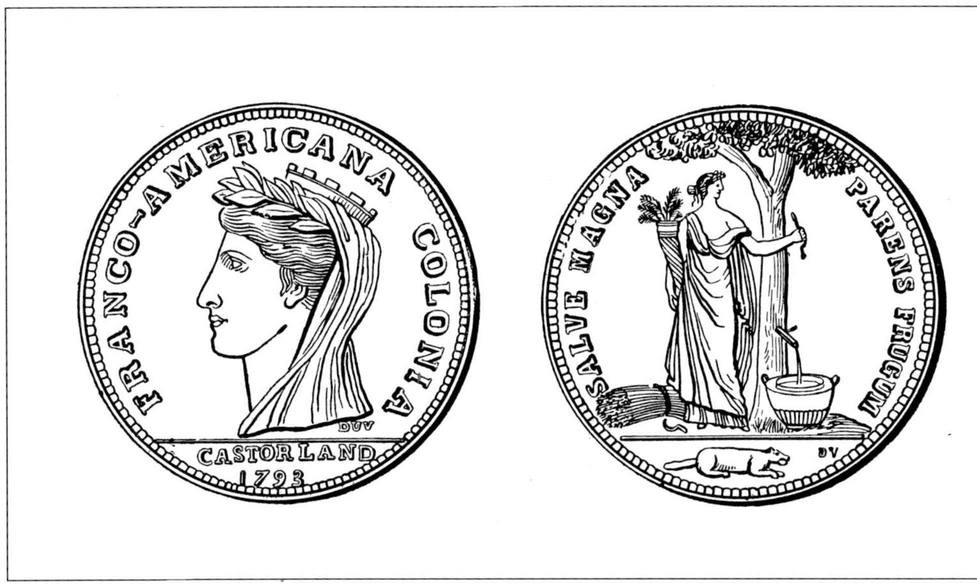

Medal issued by the Chassnais Franco-American Land Company.
— Jno. Haddock, *A Souvenir, The Thousand Islands of the St. Lawrence River*, 1895

When James Le Ray visited the North Country with his friend Morris he must have been impressed, because he returned to France and sent instructions to build a house on his land so that he could bring his family back to North America. He asked Morris to oversee his land holdings, which were still a wilderness. By then nearly all the residents in the early settlement of Castorland had long since departed and the land was left to the occasional passing trader or timber thief. The house that Le Ray commissioned was built at LeRaysville, which is now on the site of Fort Drum, a United States military base. It was considered to be one of the grandest mansions in the North Country, complete with a basement and a chapel. Le Ray obviously wanted to continue living the same lifestyle he was accustomed to in France, taking little regard for the wilderness that surrounded him for hundreds of miles. A biographer writes that his household included "his personal priest, his physician, a corps of engineers and surveyors, and a large number of slaves." He travelled around the wild countryside in a carriage pulled by six horses and flanked by uniformed footmen!

Le Ray instructed the engineers and surveyors to assist in building roads — to improve transportation from one settlement to another and even to the river. The first road was laid out in 1801 and ran between the small settlement at Philadelphia to a small bay on the St. Lawrence River, a location that Le Ray named after his son Alexander: Alexandria Bay.

For the next sixteen years Le Ray fostered settlement in Jefferson County. He sold and leased hundreds of acres to his fellow Frenchmen. He laid out towns and villages, and even donated land for churches. (He gave an additional 100 acres to the Quakers at Philadelphia to build their church.) He also lent his name and those of his family to towns and other villages: Le Ray and Chaumont to commemorate his family, Cape Vincent after his eldest son, Vincent, and Teresa after his daughter. He even named a town after his dog, Plessis! This time, settlement prospered.

Life along the St. Lawrence River, and in particular among the Thousand Islands, was quiet. Although Alexander Macomb had included the islands in his land purchase, they were excluded in the final patents. The government was unwilling to make the delineation between American and Canadian islands until the boundary line was set, so the islands remained unsold.

The first recorded U.S. land survey took place in 1798 when Benjamin and Moses Wright surveyed the Great Macomb Purchase. The men were supposed to travel by water along the northern boundary in bateaux, and expected to meet a second survey party at French Creek (now Clayton). The second group were to come north through the woods. They missed each other, and from their description we learn that a log cabin had been built at French Creek some years earlier. They took this apart and made a raft to float downriver towards another rendezvous near St. Regis. A few miles below the creek they discovered "Canadian Timber Thieves" cutting logs along the U.S. shoreline — evidence that the south side of the St. Lawrence was abandoned and ripe for the plunder of the valuable timber.

Over the next decade small groups of settlers made their way to Jefferson and St. Lawrence counties. The town of Hammond (Chippewa Bay), was named after Ahijah Hammond, who was the brother-in-law of David A. Ogden, purchaser of a large portion of St. Lawrence County. Hammond was a speculator who had never lived in the region, preferring to remain in New York. The first white man to reside in the town was William McNeill, described as a hermit who lived and hunted and fished in Chippewa Bay. A clearing was made in the summer of 1812.

Morristown, first called Morrisville, was laid out opposite the small Canadian village of Elizabethtown (Brockville). It was first settled in 1804 after being surveyed by Jacob Brown, who later achieved the rank of colonel in the United States Army. David Ford was the land agent, and neighbours included Arnold Smith, who kept a public house, and Thomas Hill.

Clayton, another Le Ray village, was originally settled to discourage timber thieves from cutting and absconding with easily accessible timber along the banks of French Creek and the Thousand Islands.

In 1801 the Le Ray land agents hired a man named Bartlet to run a ferry service to Gananoque, but it ran only for a brief time. In fact, legend has it that Bartlet set his small cabin on fire one night and left by its glowing light! (An indication that life was lonely for south shore residents.)

A sawmill was erected on Wheeler Creek in 1803. Then, a few months before the War of 1812, a lumber company was formed. Woodiah Hubbard, from nearby Champion, and a Canadian partner cut timber.

The only real village at this early date was established at Cape Vincent, originally called Gravelly Point but later changed to honour Le Ray's eldest son. Vincent designed the village, and in 1809 hired Eber Kelsey to work with twenty men to clear a 50-acre tract along the river. The site was chosen because it was so close to Kingston. It was clear that a ferry service could easily run between Cape Vincent, Carleton Island, Grande Island (Wolfe Island) and Kingston, Upper Canada.

The men built a wharf, a "block dwelling house," and barns. At the same time Richard M. Esselstyne built a store and started a trading service. A doctor from Vermont, Avery Ainsworth, followed, providing the first medical services in the vicinity. As early as 1808 the ferry service began, as did contact with the bustling town of Kingston.

Lumber brought residents. When the logging in the immediate area was completed, they turned west and imported almost two hundred thousand logs from Western New York.

In 1807 the Embargo Act was proclaimed by the United States. It was designed to forbid trading between the United States and other countries. It was not popular with most of the citizens of the United States and certainly not in the Thousand Islands. One of the greatest revenue-making crops in the North Country was potash. A ton of ash could fetch as much as much as $200 to $300 in Montreal. Soon smuggling lanes were established, all leading to the Thousand Islands and the tranquil and secluded waters of the islands' bays and channels. These same bays and channels would soon become a battleground.

The Blockhouse at Brockville. — William Denny, Artist, National Archives of Canada C452

5 THE THOUSAND ISLANDS AND THE WAR OF 1812

The first prisoners taken in the War of 1812 in the Thousand Islands were "a single sergeant, three invalid soldiers and two women." They were all that formed the British garrison on Carleton Island!

When the United States declared war on Britain, Abner Hubbard and two friends living near Clayton decided that they should capture this small garrison. It was hardly a glorious victory, and even a surprise to the American military. Col. Jacob Brown wrote: "Some of our people, without orders and in fact without consulting with any person in the service, captured the little garrison on Carleton Island, and the prisoners are now on their way to Sackets Harbor." (This name appears with various spellings: Sackets or Sacketts; Harbor or Harbour.)

The declaration of war was unpopular with both Canadian and American Thousand Islands residents. The reasons for the lack of enthusiasm were different for each side.

Problems first developed in 1807 when President Thomas Jefferson declared the Embargo Act in an attempt to protect American ships from British impressment gangs and from attacks by the French. The embargo was intended to limit exports from the United States and thus deprive foreign countries of American goods. Instead, it caused economic hardships for the American citizens. Some of the first Americans to defy the embargo were the citizens of upper New York State, for whom the selling price of potash was too much of a temptation. Before long, a black market was established in the North Country and especially in the Thousand Islands. Smuggling lanes were laid out between Watertown and the St. Lawrence River, with the outlet to the river near today's Fisher's Landing. United States patrol boats were supposed to keep watch.

Canadian officials did not want war either. They realized that Canada's border, stretching from the Atlantic coast to Lake Superior, would be impossible to defend. England was also financially committed to the Peninsular Wars against Napoleonic France. But when the U.S. Congress passed a resolution in favour of war, the upper St. Lawrence River became a war zone, and families saw brothers living on opposite sides of the river become enemies.

The Thousand Islands should have been discussed often in the strategy tents of both nations, for securing the island waterway could have helped to win the war for either country. The islands and their channels provided excellent cover for secret attacks — as they had for black-market activities. The St. Lawrence was the lifeline of the British troops. If the Americans had cut off the entrance to this water highway leading west from the ports of Montreal and Quebec, it would not have taken long before the western forts and towns surrendered. But there were only a few skirmishes in the islands, and suffice it to say that the stories in history books written on both sides of the river show that the turbulent two years could have been far worse. However, both British and American military and naval officials spent much of their time planning strategic or tactical activities involving the large naval stations on Lake Ontario at Kingston and at Sackets Harbor and points west.

Kingston was the main depot for Upper Canada throughout the war. The civilian population in Kingston before the war was fifteen hundred, and there were approximately five hundred military men stationed in the vicinity. During the war the military and naval population swelled to more than five thousand, while the local population quickly rose to two thousand civilians. This caused great shortages of food and supplies; what could not be found locally had to be purchased and transported from Quebec and from England.

The Provincial Marine was officially responsible for the naval services on the lakes after war was declared. They were administered by the Quartermaster General's Department. Their commanders agreed that the number of boats and the number of trained crews were dismal. It took almost two weeks for a supply-laden bateau to make its way from Lachine to Kingston, and it cost the military fifty-four shillings a hundredweight. The roads were also poor. As one traveller described the road between Brockville and Kingston: "six miles above Brockville the woods commence; the roads here are unpleasant, long stretches of corduroy bridges over the swamps and low grounds, bridges remarkably solid, some long and lofty, span creeks and fairly-wide rivers." Therefore, if for no other reason than time and cost, the importance of moving supplies from the seaports of Montreal and Quebec westward was a priority.

The British took an early command of the naval forces in the region a month after war was declared. They discovered six American merchant vessels making their way west from Ogdensburg to Lake Ontario. Two were captured and the others retreated to Ogdensburg, a U.S. military installation. The British blockaded the river and would have succeeded in keeping the vessels in port had the British commander, Sir George Prevost, not agreed to a temporary truce with the Americans. Consequently, the merchant ships made their way back to Sackets Harbor, where they were promptly outfitted for war.

Although the Provincial Marine had succeeded in their first encounter in the Thousand Islands, they were not as successful in an attack, described by some as "half-hearted" on July 19, 1812, at Sackets Harbor, the other main U.S. installation.

In 1801 Augustus Sackett, a land speculator, had purchased a parcel of land in upper New York State. When he visited the land he realized he had chosen a part of the shoreline on Lake Ontario that provided an ideal harbour for ships. He also found tall timber, which was later used for shipbuilding and the timber trade. When war was declared, there were only twenty houses in the village of Sackets Harbor, but the number of houses and barracks quickly multiplied in order to house the estimated fifteen thousand U.S. troops stationed there soon after.

The attack on Sackets Harbor began after an American captain sighted the British fleet approaching from Kingston. He placed his ship broadside to the entrance, allowing nine guns to face the British. He took the remaining guns off the ship and placed them onshore. Although the British ships were all placed near the harbour entrance, they were too far away for their gunfire to cause much damage. At the same time the poorly equipped U.S. troops could not take advantage of the situation because they had the wrong size cannonballs! A smart soldier suggested wrapping the small balls in carpet to fit the cannon, but most of the shot fell short of their targets, too.

Suddenly one of the British cannonballs landed on a cliff. Another alert soldier rushed over and swooped it up, carried it gingerly to the big "old Sow" cannon, loaded her up and fired. The British cannonball hit the British ship, causing its commander to signal a retreat. "At this," wrote American General Jacob Brown, "the band on shore struck up the national tune of Yankee Doodle, and the troops, who had through the whole affaire behaved like veterans, sent up their cheers of victory."

The next raid was back in Canadian territory. General Brown wrote to the governor, explaining that when he thought the forces at Sackets Harbor were at their lightest, it would be wise to have "fitted out a secret expedition under the command of Captain Benjamin Forsyth" to attack the small Canadian village of Gananoque because they were sure to find a great cache of ammunition — something that was badly needed by both armies. He was also convinced that such an attack would frighten the Canadian residents.

United States General Jacob Brown.
— Metropolitan Toronto Reference Library, T 31861

On September 20, 1812, Captain Forsyth landed his force of "ninty-five" in daylight 2 miles west of Gananoque, at Sheriff's Point (also known as Lindsay's Point). When he was three-quarters of a mile away from the village, he fired at two approaching horsemen, "one of whom was probably shot, the other fled to the village." When Forsyth's men arrived at Gananoque they found the enemy, 110 strong, "drawn up on order of battle." There was a barrage of gunfire, but the shots were sent over Forsyth's head. Without firing a shot, Forsyth and his men ran towards the enemy, who turned and crossed the town's bridge. Forsyth realized how prudent this was and immediately "broke up" the bridge. Forsyth did not say how many of the Canadian enemy were killed, but Brown estimated that from ten to fifteen lost their lives. Forsyth's small group captured twelve prisoners, "3000 ball cartridges and 41 muskets." They found 150 barrels of provisions, but because the men did not have empty boats to carry away the loot, they set it on fire.

Brown praised his men and stated quite clearly that "private property was held sacred." He also concluded that the men in the American militia were "poor" and many would not survive the winter because they had no proper clothing. He wanted the government to raise the pay of the these brave soldiers. "I can not believe that these men would leave me; it would grieve me if they should; but it is a stain upon our national character, that the citizen soldier of this country should be worse paid and provided for, than any other class among us."

On the other side of the river, the Canadian version views the attack in a different light. Thad. W.H. Leavitt, in his 1879 *History of Leeds and Grenville Counties*, states that Forsyth took the village peaceably. "They surrounded the residence of Col. Stone, but failed to find him. Hearing some person moving upstairs, one of the soldiers fired in that direction. The ball took effect in the hip of Mrs. Stone, making a severe, but not dangerous, wound. Imagining that they had killed the Col. they immediately departed." Leavitt scoffs at the Forsyth's reports of destroying the government stores. He evidently interviewed a senior resident who remembered the attack and claimed that "the stores consisted of half an ox, and some old blankets and bed ticks, all of which were burned by the valiant Yankees."

Leavitt also reports that only one man was wounded and there were no deaths. Another tale that has been passed down proudly by the townspeople of Gananoque is the story that Mrs. Stone threw her gold into a barrel of soap, and it was "thus saved from the enemy."

The second Forsyth strike was in Brockville in February 1813. This time troops came from Morristown across the frozen river, getting a local resident to lead them because the ice could be treacherous. They broke into the jail and freed all prisoners but one — a convicted murderer. The men took back muskets, rifles and casks of ammunition. They also captured more than forty Canadians, some of them prominent citizens of the town, who were taken to Ogdensburg and later released.

A second, and equally uneventful, battle against Sackets Harbor was launched in May 1813. Sir George Prevost set sail for the harbour, but the winds were against him. They were so light that it took the fleet much longer than usual to cross the lake. The ships could not manoeuvre into the best position for battle, and as a result they left with a few naval stores and some 150 prisoners. Hardly a decisive battle.

Later in the spring of 1813, the British Navy came to Kingston. Sir James Lucas Yeo was appointed commodore and commander-in-chief of His Majesty's Ships and Vessels on the Lakes of Canada.

It has been said that if the British Admiralty had held the war with the United States in more esteem, Yeo would not have been appointed and a more senior officer would have been given the command. Nevertheless, he arrived in Kingston by water in a regular river bateau. This was probably fortunate because he learned firsthand how

Diary of an Officer

My Quarters at Cananocoui — On the 27th of July, Major Heriot and three companies of the Voltigeurs were ordered to Fort George. On the 29th I was sent to Cananocoui, in command of a *select* detachment made up of the culls of the corps — the old, the halt, the incapables, the cripples — in short, an assorted lot of *invalids*. Voltigeurs invalids! These words coupled together are contradictory, bizarre and non-sense, I admit, but such was the case, and, to cap the joke, my redoubt was dubbed the Hospital!

Cananocoui is pretty and quite a picturesque spot — good fishing, good sport, nothing to do — all these things are delectable yet time hangs heavy. I am weary and unhappy as any can well be. I am consumed with "ennui." Colonel S— [Stone], Captain H., and D., a tavern-keeper are the swells of the place. I keep myself to my miserable quarters, and do not associate with these great people. Like the good Lafontaine of old, I sleep part of the day and do nothing the rest; hunting and fishing is devoid of attractions for me. Would that some of my friends drift this way. Nothing easier. Batteaux start from Montreal every day, and, when with me, should they be overtaken by "ennui," opportunities of return are just as plenty.

Shall I tell of the many attractions of my quarters? (1) My four poster consists of four rough planks, nailed to four uprights; and can accommodate six with ease; (2) My room has two large window sashes — my kitchen the same — but being fond of an abundance of fresh air, I have not provided the sashes with panes, there it can never be said "who breaks the glasses pays" for there are none; (3) To close my quarters I would need four doors, the kitchen door is stowed away in the garret — it has no hinges, two others have their panels knocked out; the fourth consists of the frame only; (4) The walls are throughout of a rich, smoky, brown colour; they are not hung with costly goblins [*sic*] tapestry, but the delicate webs of my friends the spiders festoon the ceiling; nor are there artistic paintings — such decorations are not in fashion in Cananocoui; preference is shown in my apartments for drawings in chalk or coal, representing various fantastic creatures — related to the mammoth perhaps; their prototypes certainly antedated the deluge. Now come and see for yourself if I have not told you the truth, all the truth, and nothing but the truth, about the attractions of my quarters in far-famed Cananocoui . . .

Written during the War of 1812, Jacques Viger's journal, translated from French by J.L.H. Neilson as "Diary of an Officer in the War of 1812–14," *Queen's Quarterly*, Vol. 2, 1894–95, 318–28, Vol. 3, 1895–96, 23–30.

Sir James Lucas Yeo, commodore and commander-in-chief of His Majesty's Ships and Vessels on the Lakes of Canada.

— Metropolitan Toronto Reference Library, J. Ross Robertson Collection, T15241

vulnerable the vessels were in the river — not only because the rapids were treacherous but also because the islands provided the cover for enemy patrols. As a result Yeo issued an order: "No bateaux should ever be allowed to leave Prescott without an escort, nor should a division of gun boats [*sic*] ever be allowed to remain long here, but immediately on arrival sent back to Prescott for another convoy."

At first the "gunboat" was the vessel that was used on both sides of the river. It was capable of carrying supplies; it could be sailed in wind and, more important, rowed; it could also easily make its way in shallow waters. The crew consisted of an officer, thirty seamen and forty regulars armed with "pistols, cutlasses, tomahawks and boarding pikes." Gunboats ranged in size from nearly 50 to 60 feet in length and from 8 to 16 feet in width.

The British Navy gave the "Gunboat Establishment" great importance, and the men assigned to the gunboat fleet were some of the most respected naval men to serve in the North American station. Blockhouses constructed at Brockville, on Bridge Island near Mallorytown Landing, and in Gananoque allowed guards to keep track of river travel. They were simply constructed buildings of stone and square timbers. The upper storeys were built with an overhang of 18 inches. Both storeys had "loopholes" for muskets. There were also portholes in the upper level. Stockades surrounded the blockhouses. With the loopholes and portholes letting in the winter winds, and fireplaces smoking incessantly, life in the blockhouses was almost unbearable.

Each blockhouse detachment included a fleet of three gunboats that provided protection for the bateaux bringing supplies up the St. Lawrence between Montreal and Kingston.

Yeo also brought sailors to Kingston, including Capt. Richard O'Connor, whom Yeo often placed in charge. Some of the original Provincial Marine officers remained in service, but many were demoted when the British Navy arrived. Nevertheless the change in command ensured a stronger naval presence on the Great Lakes.

Yeo wrote often to the British Admiralty, requesting larger ships and better-trained men. He said there had been too many "pressed Americans, infirmed old men, and boys in the drafts hitherto dispatched to Kingston." He also needed more skilled artisans and builders, as well as supplies to equip the naval yards. The only thing he didn't need was wood — which the Canadas had plenty of!

The first two ships Yeo had built were frigates: the *Prince Regent* (fifty-six guns) and the *Princess Charlotte* (forty-two guns). A third ship, the *Psyche*, was actually built in England and brought in pieces to Montreal, then carried upriver to Kingston — a tremendous task.

In the summer of 1813 the Americans licensed two privateers to begin patrolling in the Thousand Islands. Privateers were privately owned and commanded vessels that roamed the oceans and the inland waterways, attacking enemy shipping. They had to be licensed or granted permission to do so. The *Neptune* and the *Fox* were the two that were granted permission to ambush convoys travelling through the waterway with supplies. The first attack was a success, the privateers capturing supplies destined for Kingston. But British gunboats soon gave chase. They followed the Americans to Goose Bay, below Alexandria Bay. They made their way up Cranberry Creek until they could go no farther because the Americans had felled trees in their path. As the British ships slowed to a stop, they were ambushed and had to withdraw, losing several troops. But the Americans were not fully the winners. As they made their way back to Sackets Harbor, the privateers ran into the British *Earl of Moira*, and in the end had to sink their own ships, and their bounty, in order to escape being captured.

As the shipbuilding race continued, drydocks in Sackets Harbor soon rivalled those in Kingston. Records show that in order to build three ships, they needed "600 ships carpenters, 60 ship joiners, 60 pairs cross-cutters, 120 sawyers, 15 carriage makers, 1 armorer and 5 tin men." Most of the supplies had to be brought from the Atlantic states, causing severe transportation problems. Unlike the British, who had only the St. Lawrence River on which to transport goods and supplies, and who were constantly on the alert for enemy ambushes, the Americans had to rely on the American Oswego and Mohawk rivers as transportation routes. Their problems were different because their roads were in poor shape and in many cases non-existent. Colonel Brown once complained that it took his men more than ten days to travel a mere 80 miles. But finally, in November 1813, the Americans were ready to move against Montreal, hoping to cut the British army by half, leaving the western part of the country abandoned.

Engagement in the Thousand Islands.

— Coke Smyth, Artist, National Archives of Canada C1029

Thus, early in the month, United States Gen. James Wilkinson assembled six thousand troops on Grenadier Island in Lake Ontario, and moved the

Isaac Chauncey, Esq. was the U.S. Navy commodore.
— Metropolitan Toronto Reference Library, J. Ross Robertson Collection, T15206

whole fleet down the river in three hundred boats. Wilkinson hoped he could travel unnoticed down the river, but as soon as the British realized the number of troops that were ready to move, they alerted Kingston, thinking that was where the army was heading. Lieut. Col. Joseph W. Morrison was told to watch the enemy.

The American flotilla began to travel downriver on November 5, led by "Bill" Johnston, who two decades later led another navy in battle in the St. Lawrence during the Patriots' War of 1837–38. Morrison followed close behind. Wilkinson's troops eventually landed on Canadian soil at Crysler Farm, with the British in hot pursuit. The American loss of the battle that followed on November 11 was a turning point in the war; it followed the American army's defeat at Châteauguay, Quebec, on October 26. Wilkinson, hearing the news from Châteauguay, withdrew to the American shore and abandoned his drive to capture Montreal.

During the last year of the war, the Sackets Harbor and Kingston shipyards raced to build the largest and greatest number of ships. Each side refused to engage in a major naval battle until it felt it had naval supremacy.

Finally, in September 1814, the British launched the *St. Lawrence*, built by John Dennis, a master shipwright. This three-deck wooden ship was the largest of its kind; it had taken only months to build. It weighed 2,230 tons and carried more than one hundred guns. It took a crew of 837 officers, seamen and marines. The *St. Lawrence* sailed on its maiden voyage with 150 other ships across Lake Ontario to Niagara. The news travelled quickly, and the American commodore, Isaac Chauncey, soon learned that the *St. Lawrence* could "blow any two of his largest ships out of the water." Kingston and the British had won the shipbuilding race, but the *St. Lawrence* never fired her guns in battle.

The British had attacked Oswego and were planning a major battle on Lake Ontario when the war ended with the signing of the Treaty of Ghent on December 24, 1814. On the same day, back in Kingston, Yeo planned to launch his other warship, the *Psyche*. But there was too much ice in the river, and he had to wait for a thaw, which came on January 3. It took almost three months before Yeo heard of the official end of the war with the signing of the treaty. Because of the distance between Ghent and the North American stations, news of the signing came too late to prevent the fighting of the battle of New Orleans in January 1815 — a battle that was won by the

The St. Lawrence, *the largest ship of its kind, carried a crew of 837 seamen.*

— Metropolitan Toronto Reference Library, J. Ross Robertson Collection T15243

Thad. W.H. Leavitt described an incident from the War of 1812 in his *History of Leeds and Grenville Counties*, published in 1879.

An Incident During the War of 1812

Among the most active of the Loyalists during the War were the Grant brothers. One of them, Lieutenant Grant, and Captain Reuben Sherwood, were [*sic*] employed along the frontier in the Secret Service. On one occasion, Grant and Sherwood were up among the Thousand Islands prospecting, having with them a force of nine men, when they ascertained that the Americans were building a block house at Gravelly Point. Leaving their men on an island, they proceeded in a small boat, and landed a short distance below the point, in the woods. Sherwood proposed to Grant that they should take the entire party prisoners. Proceeding through the woods, they came suddenly upon the militiamen who, with muskets lying on the ground, were preparing the timber for the block house. The Americans were astonished at the appearance of two British officers in full uniform. Sherwood, in a loud voice, called out, "what are you doing here," and in the same breath demanded to be shown to headquarters. Turning at the same time to Grant, he said, "consider these men prisoners, and if one of them attempts to pick up a musket give the signal to the Indians, but don't do so unless absolutely necessary." Sherwood then proceeded to the Major's headquarters, near at hand, and demanded his sword, which was promptly surrendered, that officer laboring under the belief that he was surrounded by a band of Indians, who only waited for a signal to rush upon and scalp every Yankee. Sherwood then proceeded to parole the men one by one, for the remainder of the war, despatching them by circuitous route for their homes. The Major was marched down to the boat, where great was his surprise to find that he had been outwitted by shrewd Canadians, and that only two officers were necessary to capture a score of armed Americans. He was taken to Prescott, where he was afterwards exchanged for Colonel Carley, who had been taken prisoner in their midnight raid upon Brockville.

Americans. After all that, very little change occurred in the territories of both Canada and the United States.

The end of the war signalled a new beginning for Upper Canada. Almost in a post-mortem, the Canadian government officials began to see the problems that could occur if there was ever another war. They could never again rely on the St. Lawrence River as an only supply route. A new plan was developing to link Kingston with Montreal through a series of lakes and rivers, to the north, and many of the Royal Engineers who served in the War of 1812 were soon put to work surveying and engineering the construction of a great waterway. It was the first Rideau Canal and it opened in 1832, an engineering feat still much admired today.

In addition, many of the officers and men who served in the army and the navy were given land and encouraged to settle in Canada. Much of the industry that had been developed to supply the war effort could now be geared for peacetime manufacturing. The St. Lawrence River also began to transport more immigrants who were seeking a new life in Upper Canada.

On the American side, life was also returning to normal. The young men who had served in the militia in Sackets Harbor were quick to return to their homes. In the small villages on the banks of the St. Lawrence, some of the shipwrights who had worked so hard to build warships were now ready to build merchant ships to ply the waterway. At the same time the Erie Canal, from Albany to Buffalo, was being built to open transportation to new markets and land to the west. Things were changing quickly for upstate New York. And finally, with the end of the war, Americans and Canadians living on either side of the Thousand Islands became neighbours again.

6 CAPT. WILLIAM FITZWILLIAM OWEN AND THE FIRST SURVEY, 1815–1817

The British Admiralty summoned hydrographer Capt. William FitzWilliam Owen to Kingston in June 1815. Owen and his surveyors are long forgotten, but their hydrographic survey, still considered quite accurate, gave some of the first names to the islands — many still in use today.

Shortly after the War of 1812, William's brother, Sir Edward Campbell Rich Owen, became commodore and commander-in-chief of His Majesty's ships on the Great Lakes. The cost of keeping the British Navy in full service at Kingston after the end of the war was great, so the first and most important task assigned to Edward Owen was to "wind down the yards, disperse the naval forces and expatriate the seamen but not below a level that would hazard the security of the Canadas." The Admiralty also wanted a proper survey of the waterways in order to decide the boundary line between the United States and Canada and to designate important military areas. To carry out these surveys the British Admiralty chose Edward's brother, Capt. William FitzWilliam Owen.

Captain Owen arrived in Kingston in May 1815. Soon after, Sir Edward issued official instructions that described the importance of doing a survey of

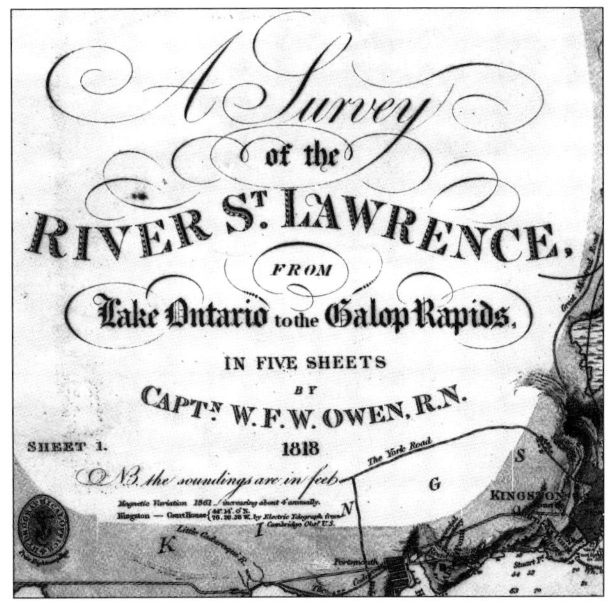

— National Archives of Canada V12 EC Series 2, Sheet 1, 1863

the St. Lawrence River from the Galop Rapids "through the Lake of the Thousand Islands as well as the three lakes: Ontario, Erie and Huron." He also appointed two assistant surveyors, Lieut. Alexander Vidal and Master John Harris, to help his brother.

The first survey of the Thousand Islands began in the winter of 1816, when ice was thick and "handling the frozen lines made the task

Historic Island Names

"It is exasperating," said Capt. William FitzWilliam Owen as he sat in front of his surveyors' notes, deciphering the many triangles and drawings. "Much confusion arises in very important records and transactions, from the same name being attached to different places and from the same place being designated by different names."

There must be a better way to distinguish the islands of this section of the St. Lawrence River, he thought, a way to describe the islands and the passages that are safe for the King's Navy and the supply ships travelling west or east. Reviewing the charts, Owen wrote a memorandum to his officers and to the British Admiralty in London. A simple yet decisive plan was dated May 1815.

This was the beginning of the master plan to designate the hundreds of islands in the section of the upper St. Lawrence River. Owen began at Lake Ontario and moved east downriver to Brockville, choosing the names of prominent figures for major islands and dealing with the surrounding small islands as groups, naming them as well. He changed Wells Island to Wellesley Island, Grindstone Island to Gore Island, and Hickory Island to Francis Isles. The Nut Isles, described as Admiralty Isles from Gananoqui (*sic*) eastward, became Crokers Isles. Islands located between Gore and Wellington islands were called Barrows Isles. The islands east of Bathurst Island (Grenadier) and near Brockville became the Brock Isles.

Owen's charts with soundings and names were carefully recorded by draftsman Lieut. George Cranfield. Eventually they were sent to England and used by the engravers in 1828 for printing.

The final names, drawn on or beside the islands, followed the original Owen plan with some variations. If you study the charts you cannot help being intrigued by the systematic approach given to naming each section of the islands.

How did Captain Owen choose island names with such precision and so few inconsistencies? Some of the answers can be found in published biographies, but finding the members of the British Navy and Army who are commemorated so prominently on the Owen charts is more difficult. The task was made much easier by a 1909 publication at the Royal Canadian Military Institute. Written and edited by L. Homfray Irving, the *Officers of the British Forces in Canada During the War of 1812* lists most of the forces involved in the war. Included in this is the list of the Indian Department and the various chiefs who sided with the British. Irving not only names the officers and divisions, but in the footnotes we find many biographical references to those commemorated on Owen's charts.

Another good reference to the names of islands is James White's 1910 edition of *Place Names in the Thousand Islands*. Unfortunately, many references are incorrect. His work, however, is reasonably good and gives excellent leads to finding the correct names.

Many Canadian street names bear the same names as islands. This may not be unusual, but history tells us that these streets were named on city maps long after 1815 and for far greater deeds. A typical example is Sydenham, who was only a lowly employee of the Treasury Department at the time of the survey but was appointed Governor General of Canada in 1839.

Owen's final charts divided the islands into thirteen groups. Some of these are easy to research. As soon as the Admiralty hydrographers began charting the high seas they prudently honoured the "home office" or those responsible for sending supplies and approving salaries. For this reason Admiralty officials were commemorated all over the world, especially during this era in British history when the navy and the Admiralty Office sent hydrographers and explorers in pursuit of discovery. In the Thousand Islands, the Admiralty Islands, near Gananoque, and the Treasury Chambers, near Rockport, followed this tradition.

Surveyors knew how essential the survey vessels and equipment were to the safety of the men. Naming the islands in the Lake Fleet, opposite the town of Gananoque, was an opportunity to acknowledge the vessels and their crews.

Many of the naval officers who were in the War of 1812 still served on the Great Lakes at the time of the survey, so the Navy Islands, west of Ivy Lea, offered an opportunity to honour the heroes and officers of the Royal Navy. The same was accomplished for army officers, with over 18 islands in the Brock Isles, opposite Brockville. In Chippewa Bay, the Indian allies were remembered. Seven natives who had fought and sided with the British during the war were honoured.

The islands off present-day Alexandria Bay were called the Old Friends. They were the ships that Owen served on before coming to the Great Lakes in 1815. The Summerland Group served to recognize the hydrographers responsible to Owen for the surveys.

The group known as the Amateur Islands was probably named in jest, as it commemorates many who served in the Royal Engineers and not in the Royal Navy — "amateurs" in the navy's opinion. Captain Owen and the draftsman must have enjoyed the banter that was exchanged between the regiments serving in Kingston. Many of those listed in the Amateurs were members of the 70th Foot Regiment, which arrived in Kingston in 1814, near the end of the War of 1812. Several of these men were discharged at the same time as Lieutenant Cranfield. They could have travelled back to England on the same transport ship, the *Vittoria*. It is also conceivable that

Sir Arthur Wellesley, the Duke of Wellington.
— *Wellington & Waterloo*, Major Arthur Griffiths, published by George Newnes, Limited, 1898

Cranfield worked on the drawings while on board ship and chose to honour his shipmates!

The largest group to be honoured were the officers who had fought in the Peninsular War with Arthur Wellesley, Duke of Wellington: over fifty-four soldiers' names were assigned to Canadian and American islands surrounding Wellesley Island. Owen, Cranfield and his surveyors would have had a hard time knowing who deserved mention on the charts. The Peninsular War was fought between 1808-1814 and the Hundred Days War, which occurred after Napoleon escaped from the Isle of Elba and began his second siege, ended with the famous Battle of Waterloo in 1815. These battles were still fresh on the minds of the British public, but modern researchers may wonder how the team naming the islands knew who was important.

Perhaps the answer lies in the dusty volumes of *The Gentleman's Magazine*, first published in 1731 by an English printer. This monthly collection of essays and articles taken from other printed sources and published as a magazine was popular at the time of Captain Owen's survey.

The *Gentlemen's Magazine* contained original poetry, fiction and a review of events in London and around the world. The editor often published war dispatches sent to London from battlefields around the world. Also included was a section of the "Gazette, &c. Promotions, Eccl. Preferments [Church of England appointments] and Obituary Notices." This is where we find a clue to the island names.

It is conceivable that Captain Owen brought several copies of the magazine with him from England, or he and his brother ordered them to be sent with other supplies from home. The magazines from 1814 to 1817, the year before he was sent to Canada and then while he was stationed in Kingston, include several references to promotions from "Whitehall, London." The list shows the same names as the islands, and often in the same order as they appear on the charts.

Other issues of the magazine list Foreign Office and Admiralty appointments. Some names that appeared in certain months were not used as island names, which leads us to assume that not all magazine issues made their way across the ocean.

Historians also credit the naming of the Thousand Islands to Henry Wolsey Bayfield, the naval officer who succeeded Captain Owen as chief surveyor when Owen was recalled to England in 1817. Bayfield was certainly involved, because his name appears on the first sheet of the survey: a large bay on the south side of Wolfe Island is called Bayfield Bay and shoals on the north side commemorate him as well. Bayfield worked in London at the Hydrographic Office in 1828, when the charts were engraved and published. He probably chose the final names to be included on the engraved charts and decided which names would be left off.

Over the decades many of the Owen island names have remained in use, while others never appeared on charts. Some of the Owen names were changed soon after an island was sold. This is especially true in the American sector, where local residents never saw the offical Admiralty charts and soon gave family or descriptive names to their islands.

Captain William FitzWilliam Owen, British Admiralty hydrographer, wrote the plan to name the islands for his survey in 1816. — National Archives of Canada C2590

insurmountable." After the survey party lost its horses through the ice and had to rescue Captain Owen and his men from drowning, they postponed their work and returned to Kingston and their winter headquarters, known as the hydrographer's house. Here Captain Owen taught his young crew the mathematical equations involved in surveying. The house was comfortable and served as both classroom and quarters for the surveyors. John Harris was married and his wife, Amelia, took charge of the housekeeping during the winter months. She also became an assistant hydrographer. Years later, when the surveyors corresponded, they often referred to that winter "with a thousand pleasing recollections" (see Part II, Hydrographers).

In March 1816 Captain Owen began a six-week survey of the river from Jones Creek (near Mallorytown) west to the Bay of Quinte. The weather had improved, but the ice still supported the men and their equipment.

In the summer Vidal and Harris began another survey of the river, from Brockville west to Kingston. Special care was taken in this area because the surveyors thought the final boundary line between the United States and Canada would be drawn on their maps. They worked quickly and sent their preliminary sketches to Kingston and the hydrographer's house. There, Amelia transcribed the drawings to charts, taking care to piece papers together to make the sheets large enough to display the drawings. Captain Owen stressed the importance of placing every island in its exact location.

Hydrography was a new science. During the Thousand Islands survey the men experimented with rockets. Captain Owen sent one group of surveyors to Grindstone Island and another out into Lake Ontario. Both groups watched for rockets fired from Kingston, then recorded the exact time by chronometer and the exact angle by sextant. The information they sent Captain Owen showed their position on the chart. Many of the methods developed by Captain Owen when he was in Kingston helped future surveys not only in North America but around the world.

Captain Owen turned his attention to Lake Ontario after the Thousand Islands survey and recruited a young naval lieutenant, Henry Wolsey Bayfield. Bayfield had joined the Royal Navy in 1806, when he was eleven, and after the War of 1812 he became a lieutenant. Captain Owen liked the young man, saw that his penmanship was neat and legible, and felt that he would be an ideal student. Captain Owen arranged for Bayfield to help on the survey of Lake Ontario on board the sloop *Star* and taught the young man the fundamentals of surveying.

All through the winter of 1816–17 the surveyors worked on Lake Ontario, taking measurements through the ice. They compiled twelve detailed area maps of "specific geographic landmarks." Next came the surveys of Lake Erie, the east coast of Lake Huron, Lake Michigan and the Niagara and Trent river systems.

Comdr. Edward Owen was recalled to England after spending only six months in Kingston. The recall coincided with the absence of Sir Robert Hall, Kingston's naval commissioner. Therefore Capt. William FitzWilliam Owen took charge of the complete naval operations under the title "Senior Officer and Acting Commissioner of His Majesty's Navy in the Canadas." This responsibility proved to be a difficult task because he dealt not only with the survey but also with the management of the shipyards.

Admiral Henry Wolsey Bayfield was taught the fundamentals of surveying by Captain William FitzWilliam Owen.

— Metropolitan Toronto Reference Library, J. Ross Robertson Collection T15489

Eventually Captain Owen wrote to the Admiralty and asked for a leave of absence, and soon after, the Admiralty decided to close the hydrographic department in Canada. By the time Owen received his recall instructions, he had finished his work with "only the tidying up to do." The Admiralty then left Henry Bayfield in charge of completing the hydrographic mandate, which included surveying Lake Erie and Lake Huron (see Part II, Historic Name sections).

In 1828 the Canadian Lakes series of Admiralty charts was published. In fact, it was one of the first series to be engraved and circulated. The charts not only located the islands geographically, but they also described shoals, marshlands, rocks, the direction of currents, and the topographical view of trees and brush growing on the shores. Several channels were named, as were points of land on islands and on the mainland.

The 1828 charts were corrected and published again in 1861. Both series are remarkably accurate; many of the depth soundings are the same today. The shapes of the islands and their number are not correct, but the surveyors were not making a strict topographic chart and therefore only drew the islands from a visual perspective.

The charts were supposed to be used to set the boundary line between Canada and the United States, but they never were. In 1818 a new boundary commission was appointed and another survey of the river began.

7 CREATING THE INTERNATIONAL BOUNDARY LINE, 1818

The first boundary in the Thousand Islands was defined in the Treaty of 1783 as a line "along the middle of said river into Lake Ontario, through the middle of said lake until it strikes the communication by water between the lake and Lake Erie. . . ."

When the Treaty of Ghent was signed to end the War of 1812, both sides expressed doubt about the location of "the middle of the said River, Lakes and Water communications and where certain islands lying in the same were within the Dominions of His Britannic Majesty, or of the Unites States." Article IV of the treaty stated that two commissioners were to be appointed and that they should determine who owned which islands.

John Ogilvie was appointed commissioner for Great Britain; Peter B. Porter of New York State was the American representative. When Ogilvie died soon after the commission began their work, he was replaced by Anthony Barclay. Two agents were also appointed: John Hale was the British agent, Samuel Hawkins the American agent. Joseph Delafield was appointed assistant to Hawkins and in 1821 replaced him. The agents' responsibility was to "argue" on behalf of their respective countries. David P. Adams was the principal surveyor; one of his assistants was William Bird.

David Thompson was appointed "astronomer royal" and Alexander Stevenson was clerk and assistant secretary for the Canadian team.

It took several years for the commission to complete the survey to western Ontario, Lake of the Woods and Lake Superior. The commissioners began their work at a meeting held in Albany, New York, on November 18, 1816.

In a letter David Thompson described the problems that were caused by the islands:

> When the survey was undertaken to decide the place of the above boundary line, several important questions arose not contemplated in the Treaty; among which was the middle of the River is a line equidistant from both banks of the River, this line would often intersect islands, which would give a boundary line on land, under circumstances very inconvenient to each Power, especially on civil and criminal processes, illicit trade, etc. etc. It was therefore determined that to whatever Power the greater part of an intersected island should belong, that power should have the whole of the island.

Major Joseph Delafield.
— Illustration from McElroy, Robert and Riggs, Thomas, editors, *The Unfortified Boundary: A Diary of the First Survey of the Canadian Boundary Line from St. Regis to the Lake of the Woods, By Major Joseph Delafield*

Another problem arose when the British stated that they wanted Wolfe Island. They were afraid that if the island was given to the United States, it could be fortified and used to bombard the British fortifications at Kingston. To settle the issue, the British gave up Grand Island in the Niagara River as well as Barnhart Island near Cornwall. The commissioners also agreed that the boundary line should be 100 yards from the shore of all islands. If there was not that much room, then the line was to run exactly in the middle between the two shores. For this reason the International Boundary runs in a zigzag fashion through the maze of islands.

David Thompson and Joseph Delafield left documents that record the actual survey through the Thousand Islands. The Thompson papers are housed in the Ontario Archives, and today Thompson is considered one of Canada's finest geographers. He was born in 1770, and when he was fourteen came to Canada as an employee of the Hudson's Bay Company. He was a fur trader, explorer, astronomer and surveyor. Thompson was also the first white man to travel down the Columbia River from its source to the Pacific Ocean. Wherever he went he took sightings and drew maps, and when he left the Northwest he prepared a map that was used for several decades as the basis for western maps. When he came east he first lived near Montreal and later settled in Williamstown, east of Cornwall. As chief surveyor for the commission, he signed the finished maps. His work was never recognized in his lifetime, and he died in poverty near Montreal in 1857.

In the 1940s a journal was found and privately published by the family of the American agent, Joseph Delafield. It describes in detail the survey of the St. Lawrence and the whole distance of the Boundary Commission's work.

Joseph Delafield was born in New York City in 1790. As a young man he studied law, but after a serious illness he decided to "look about for some out-of-doors occupation." He was fascinated by natural history and became a well-known geologist. In 1817, when the Boundary Commission began its work, Delafield volunteered to join the team as assistant agent, believing that the commission would cover territory that would prove to be rich in minerals and wildlife.

Unlike Owen's survey, this project was plagued by petty jealousies and bickering. Although peace

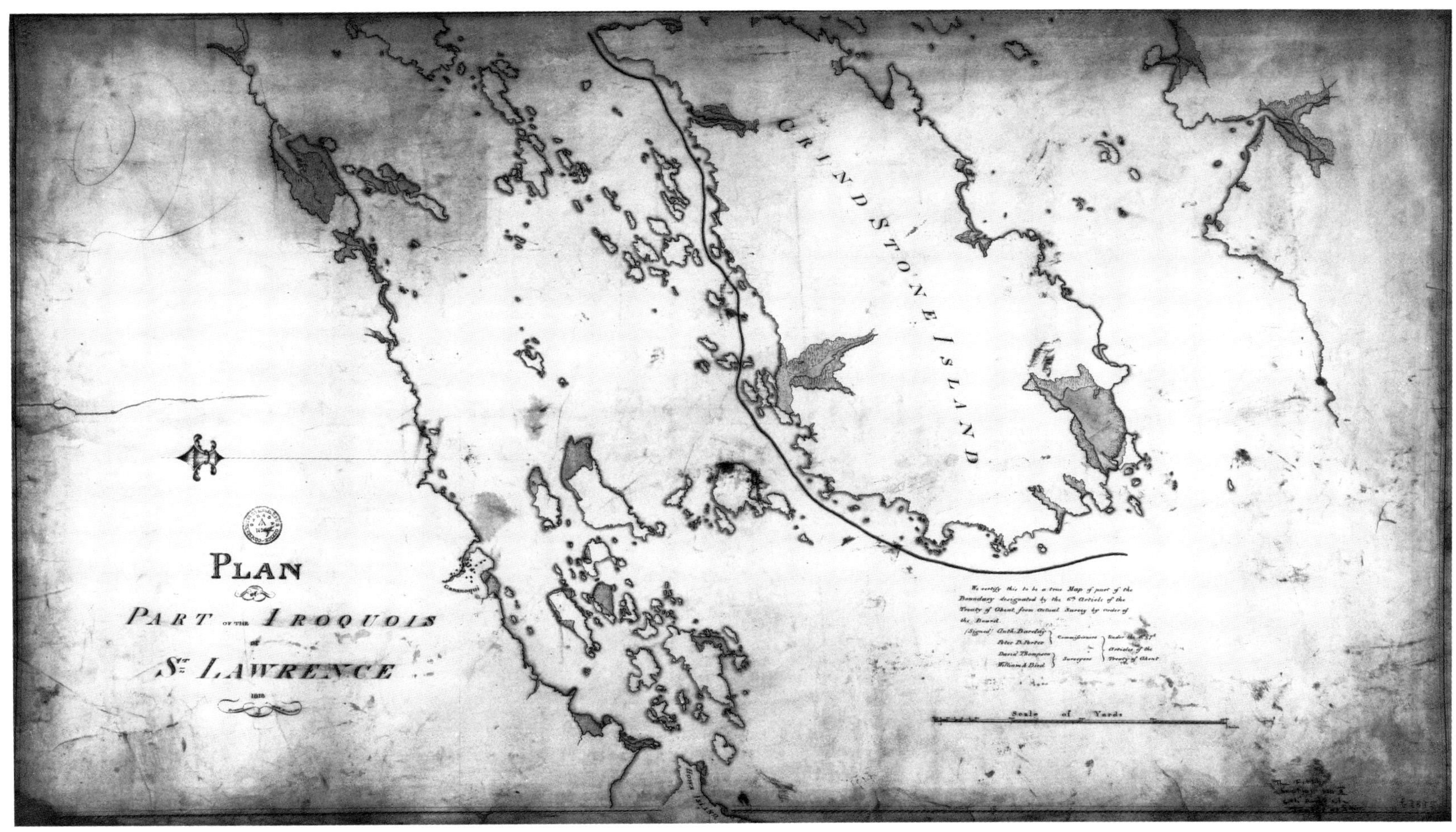

Survey of the Thousand Islands.
— National Archives of Canada, National Map Collection, NMC 16862

had been negotiated four years before, political feelings following the War of 1812 still ran high on both sides of the river. The very nature of the International Boundary Commission was one of arbitration. Neither side had gained any territory on the St. Lawrence River during the war, so determining where the line would fall should have been easy.

At the beginning of the survey, near Cornwall, the line was drawn down the middle of the river, so the squabbles were over personalities, not politics. For instance, the American commissioner, Porter, and the American agent, Hawkins, disagreed over their importance and their powers under the treaty. The Americans made disparaging remarks about the British; they thought that they "had established themselves in a very superior style, in both respects, their encampments and their number and that of the British commissioners fall far short in their arrangement."

The survey in the Thousand Islands began in front of Brockville and Morristown in July 1818. Delafield set up the American camp on an island at the head of the Brockville Narrows (probably Myers Island). The Canadian surveyors set up camp on the opposite shore.

Near Cornwall, both the British and American surveyors mapped the same 40-mile section of the river. This proved cumbersome and a waste of time because there was little argument where the line should be drawn. As a result the commissioners changed the procedures and divided the river into "equal and alternate sections." The Americans plotted the river from Brockville to Grindstone Island. The Canadian headquarters were on Howe Island, and Thompson was responsible for the survey from Grindstone Island west to Kingston and Lake Ontario. This ensured fast work, and it was estimated that the survey crew could cover a distance of 250 miles each season.

American William Bird did most of the survey work around Wellesley Island. David Thompson took the American charts as soon as they were completed and kept in close contact with Delafield. From their correspondence we can see that they respected each other, although Delafield often criticized Thompson's work for its inaccuracies.

Delafield was impressed with the wildlife on the islands. He saw deer, porcupines, minks and otters. He collected geological information by gathering samples of granite and quartz for his collection. He noted the difference between the two shores. The Canadian shoreline from Cornwall to Brockville was almost completely cleared and farmed, while the American side was virtually a wilderness. Delafield was also impressed with the islands as a whole, which he referred to as Mille Îles.

In August, Delafield moved his camp to a "small island opposite Wells Island [Wellesley Island] in the center of this channel looking up the narrows 8 or 10 miles." When Bird began the survey on the north side of Wellesley Island, he complained because the work was "extremely laborious and tedious owing to the increased number of islands."

Grindstone Island was noted as being cleared by "Wells under Indian Title," and "Gannanauque" (*sic*) had "about a dozen houses," as well as an excellent sawmill belonging to a "Yankee" by the name of McDonald.

Towards the end of August they explored both the main shore and Grindstone Island for a new campsite and chose the south side of Grindstone Island, near its head. "It is well sheltered in from the S.W. winds by a grove of pine trees, has a good harbour for our boats on its N.E. side and is otherwise desirable."

The survey of the Thousand Islands was completed by the end of September, and the survey teams disbanded for the winter, making plans to resume work in the spring.

Three years later, in June 1822, the boundary commissioners signed their agreement and the islands became officially Canadian or American. This set the stage for island ownership, which until then, on the American shore, had been considered state land and was still in dispute. On the Canadian shore the islands were considered aboriginal land, but now the land was officially in Canadian territory.

8 SQUATTERS AND MISSISSAUGAS ON THE CANADIAN ISLANDS, 1820–1856

A survey of the islands in 1822 described the island residents: "A few Indians reside in the islands which are thickly scattered in the river St. Lawrence opposite to the townships of Younge, Leeds and Lansdowne in this district; but they are too unimportant to be of consequence in our estimate of population, even if their numbers could have been ascertained."

From 1810 to 1830, these "unimportant inhabitants" known as the Mississauga or Island Indians, began leaving the Thousand Islands, and their departure signalled changes in the region. The natives probably got along very well with their white neighbours, and it is safe to say that it was not white men themselves who drove the natives off the islands, but rather it was as a consequence of the white men's industrious timber-cutting.

Since before the War of 1812 timber had been harvested from the islands to build the lumber rafts that were sent downriver to Montreal and Quebec to be sold. William Wells was one of the first to cut timber from the islands. He was born in the United States but left to join other Loyalists in Upper Canada. He received a land grant near Mallorytown and began clearing the land; later he sold that land and settled on a large farm below Brockville. Wells hired local woodsmen to clear timber from the shoreline of the St. Lawrence and the Thousand Islands. The large trees were chopped, worked into square logs or staves, then pushed into the river and lashed together. There was great skill in building these rafts. Because the oak timbers were heavy and difficult to float, the first task was cutting layers of pine or other light wood that floated easily. Then every section, called a dram, was carefully lashed together to ensure that the rafts could withstand the pounding as they made their way down the river though the treacherous rapids below Prescott.

Employers like Wells chose hardy woodchoppers to work the islands, men who were systematic in their cutting, concentrating on the easiest locations. This meant the largest islands, like Grindstone, Wells (now Wellesley) and Le Roux (now Hill Island), were cleared first. The woodsmen would set up camp at a central point and then cut a swath through the bush in a circle until all the large lumber was gone. Once the largest stands of trees were removed, the lumbermen moved farther inland. Two communities became headquarters for the industry: Cape Vincent in the United States, and Garden Island, off the town of Kingston, in Canada

The Frontenac *was the first steamboat to appear on Lake Ontario.*

— Toronto Metropolitan Reference Library T16098

By the beginning of the 1820s the islands had changed in appearance. But in the next few years even greater changes were to occur. One invention that had the greatest impact on development in the Thousand Islands was the steamboat. The first one to appear on Lake Ontario was the *Frontenac*, built in 1816 at Ernestown on the Bay of Quinte. The *Frontenac* was 170 feet long and had two paddle-wheels, each of which measured 40 feet in circumference.

Soon afterwards Henry Gilderslieve, an American, came to Kingston and built another ship, the *Queen Charlotte*, and in Sackets Harbor across Lake Ontario, Eri Lusher and Charles Smyth obtained the rights from Robert Fulton to build a steamship that they christened the *Ontario*.

The novelty of seeing these steam-driven ships arrive in harbour caused great excitement. All of a sudden there was a means of transportation that did not depend on the weather. These ships could ply the river from the time the ice went out in the spring until the river froze again almost nine months later. Large crowds appeared at the town wharf as soon as the steam whistle blew. Bookings were taken for overnight trips. The accommodations on the *Ontario* were described as "excellent, as no pains or expense has been spared by her owners, in her construction or equipment."

The steamships' boilers had an insatiable appetite for wood. Where did the wood come from? The islands, of course. Soon men who could not find local employment discovered they could cut down the smaller trees growing on the islands and exchange them for goods and food at wood stations along the river. Thus, in a short decade, the appearance of the islands changed drastically. It was not long before industrious woodsmen had cleared the islands of virtually all their trees, and what was left was brush and bare rocks and cliffs. This mass clearing discouraged wildlife, and without the wildlife and the trees for shelter, native families moved westward to the Bay of Quinte.

In 1822 a group of Methodist missionaries came to Kingston to convert the Mississaugas to Christianity. Two men helped to record this era of history: William Case and Peter Jones. Jones was the son of a Welshman and an Ojibwa chief's daughter, and through his journals, including *Life and Journals of Kah-Ke-Wa-Quo-Na-By*, we learn about the Thousand Islands aboriginals.

A permanent settlement for the mission was found on Grape Island in the Bay of Quinte, and some of the first natives to live at the mission came from the Thousand Islands. They built a church and a school to give the children an "English education." The missionaries persuaded the band to "abandon their nomadic habit" and turn to "agricultural and mechanical pursuits." Coincidently, the land they leased from local white men was land previously surrendered in 1783 by the ancestors of these same native families on Carleton Island.

Over fifteen Mississaugas signed an indenture with local residents at Belleville in October 1826. They did not have to pay rent, but they were not allowed to "cut down or destroy the trees or underbrush except so much as may be required to be cleared away for the purpose of cultivating or for building for ourselves, or for fencing our clearings."

During the winter of 1827, more native families made their way to the Grape Island mission. By July of the following year, the same families who had been destitute and starving on the islands and in mainland camps now owned teams of oxen and tools and lived in log houses. Interestingly, it was the Methodist Church in the United States that provided money for these buildings and improvements.

The mission prospered. Both adults and children adopted a new way of life. Some young men taught at other native communities. The only problem was the size of the mission. When it grew to more than 150 members, smaller islands had to be leased in the bay.

Early in 1828 the band approached the government to ask for a land grant on the mainland. Peter Jones accompanied John Sunday, the spokesman chosen to make an appeal. These two native leaders met first with the Reverend John Strachan of the Anglican Church. Jones reported: "He was friendly, and made some enquiries about the general fate of the Indians, and requested me to give him in writing a short statement of the condition of the Belleville and Rice Lake Indians, which I promised to do." At eleven o'clock the same day they appeared at Government House in Kingston but were kept waiting for two hours. They met with an impressive group: "the Governor's secretary, Dr. Strachan, the Attorney General and another official."

Reverend Peter Jones, Kah-Ke-Wa-Quo-Na-By.
— Metropolitan Toronto Reference Library T31049

Reverend John Sunday, Shahwandais.
— Metropolitan Toronto Reference Library T16049

> To our astonishment, we were now informed by Dr. Strachan, that the Governor did not feel disposed to assist the Indians so long as they remained under the instruction of their present teachers, who were not responsible to Government for any of their proceedings and instruction, he was therefore unwilling to give them any encouragement. But should the Natives come under the superintendence of the Established Church, then the government would assist them as far as laid in their power. When stating their reasons for wishing us to come under the teaching of the Church of England, the Dr. and Attorney General said, that the Indians were considered by the Government to be under the war department, and therefore it was necessary that they should be under their instruction; and that another reason was, that it would make the missionary establishments more permanent; whereas at present they were liable to fluctuation the only resource of the Methodists being that of subscriptions. It was also proposed to my brother and me, that if we would assist them in this undertaking, and come under their directions, our salaries should be increased, and we should have access to the contemplated college.

Jones and Sunday were bitterly disappointed and returned to the waiting chiefs to report the dismal news. "Then all our labours have been in vain with our great father the Governor," said the chiefs. Sunday said simply, "We have heretofore made out to live from year to year even when we were sinners, and shall not the Great Spirit whom we now serve take care of us, and preserve us from all harm." Jones agreed with Sunday and suggested that they leave it to "God in prayer."

Jones returned to see Dr. Strachan again two days later, on Friday, February 1. He brought his report and was again asked to bring the band over to the Church of England. Strachan "then told me that the Government would accomplish their design [whether] my brother John and I were willing or not, but added that if they had our assistance it could be accomplished sooner."

The idea of moving to a larger reserve was abandoned and the families living on the rented islands in the Bay of Quinte remained there until 1836. At the annual conference of the Wesleyan Methodist Church in Belleville, eight years after the request for a reserve had been made, the government announced that a new reserve in the township of Alnwick on Rice Lake was available to the Grape Island mission. By 1837 the mission was moved to the reserve, called Aldersville. From then on the band was known as the Alnwick Band of Mississauga Indians.

So, for more than a century, the Mississaugas, who had lived, fished and hunted in and along Lake Ontario and on the St. Lawrence River in the Thousand Islands, left the waterway. However, though they moved to Rice Lake, many miles inland, they retained ownership of the Thousand Islands, returning each summer to collect rent on their island leases. Matters stayed the same for the next two decades.

In June 1856, twenty years after moving, the band met again. This time they signed a surrender, Number 77, which gave the Crown (in the name of Queen Victoria) "those islands lying in the Bay of Quinte, on Lake Ontario, in Weller's Bay and in the River St. Lawrence" — as well as points and parcels of land considered Mississauga property on the mainland. The terms stipulated that the Crown held the land in trust and when "sold or otherwise disposed of," the principal was "safely funded and the interest accruing therefrom to be paid annually" to the band and their descendants "for all time to come." The Thousand Islands were now under the control of the government.

As soon as the Mississaugas left the islands, white settlers replaced them. In 1823 Hay Island, which was once owned by Sir John Johnson, was purchased by the McDonalds of Gananoque and cleared by Peter Pelow. Charles Pécor, a Frenchman, lived on Forsyth Island. Others lived on nearby islands as well. In the winter some boarded up their huts and went back to families in Quebec or went inland looking for work in the lumber camps.

SURRENDER NO. 77

Know all Men by these Presents that we, the undersigned, John Sunday, John Simpson, Jacob Sunday, John Pigeon, Joseph Skunk, Thomas Frasure and James Indian, Chiefs and Principal Members of that portion of the Mississauga Tribe of Indians formerly living on "Grape Island," in Lake Ontario, but now settled and residing in the Township of Alwick, in the Newcastle District, Province of Canada, in general council assembled, as well for ourselves as for each and every member of that portion of the Mississauga Tribe of Indians to which we belong or form a part, for the consideration hereinafter mentioned and stipulated, do hereby freely, fully and voluntarily surrender, convey and forever quit claim to Our Most Gracious Sovereign Lady Queen Victoria and Her successors, in trust, to be sold or otherwise disposed of, to the best advantage for ourselves and our descendants forever, all and singular those islands lying and situated [*sic*] in the "Bay of Quinte" on Lake Ontario. Weller's Bay and in the River St. Lawrence; and also, all points and parcels of land claimed by us on the mainland which have not heretofore been ceded to the Crown, save and except the land claimed and now occupied by our tribe in the said Township of Alwick; the principal arising from such sales to be safely funded and the interest accruing therefrom to be paid annually to us and our said descendants for all time to come.

This instrument must be immediately submitted for the consideration of our Great Father the Governor General, and unless His Excellency is pleased to approve of the foregoing arrangement, it must be and remain null and void to all intents and purposes.

In Witness whereof, we have hereunto set our hands, seals and totems at our village in Alwick, this nineteenth day of June, A.D. one thousand eight hundred fifty six.

Signed and sealed in our presence, after having Been read and fully explained to the Council, John S. Grafton.

John Sunday (Totem)
John Simpson (Totem)
Jacob Sunday (Totem)
John Pigeon (Totem)
Joseph Skunk (Totem)
Thomas Frasure (Totem)
James Indian (Totem)

Canada, Indian Treaties and Surrenders, From 1680–1890 in 2 Volumes, 1891. Vol. 1, facsimile edition, Toronto: Coles Publishing Co., 1971.

An early painting of the islands which shows the second-growth trees and vegetation.
— National Archives of Canada C37204

Daniel Howe lived on McDonald Island in the 1820s. He not only cleared the land, but he also built a "sheban," or cabin, on the south side, where he supplied local residents with "high wines" brought in from the United States. In 1829 he, too, sold the island to the McDonalds of Gananoque, who started a hog farm on the island (see Part II, the Admiralty Islands). They killed and dressed as many as 150 hogs in a single year. However, the enterprise proved unprofitable and ended by the mid-1830s.

During the same year Lindsay and Bostwick islands were farmed. Henry Campbell, a butcher from Gananoque, leased Campbell Island (now called Sagastaweka Island). William Tidd was one of the first settlers on the island now called Tremont Park. Others lived on islands in the Navy Islands and the Lake Fleet. James Macdonald, a lighthouse keeper, lived with his family on St. Lawrence Island (now known as Sugar Island, the Lake Fleet).

Farther downriver, Hill, Grenadier, Tar and Club islands had the best farmland in the area. Families began settling there in the 1840s. Many had come from the United States and began cultivating the land for crops and planting orchards.

In 1847 Francis Kerky leased Mudlunta Island (a native word for Half Moon) from the "Chipway Tribe" (*sic*) or, as they were officially known, the Alnwick Band. The lease, dated June 2, 1847, is signed by band members Jacob Storms, John Storms and John Simpson. Kerky and his family could live on the island "as long as the grass grows and the water runs for the sum of five shillings yearly." The band representatives and Kerky made their marks beside their names. The rent was probably paid once a year when the members arrived in their canoes, dressed in a combination of native and white men's clothing. Mrs. Kerky must have invited them to share a meal or sit for a while, looking at the view from the island, which was located close to Gananoque.

Francis Kerky and his wife were typical of the early island residents. Most white men were considered squatters, but in reality many negotiated leases with the Mississaugas and held signed quit-claims that were recognized as legal documents. Most were poor fishermen, boatmen or woodcutters. Many could not afford to buy working land on the mainland and were happy to squat on an island. Their only responsibility was to make a living fishing or raising a small crop to keep their families. Some, like Kerky, were visited by the Mississaugas to collect the year's rent. It was life on the river.

Not only were the islands changing, but so were

The Gananoque Mill, painted in 1839 by H.F. Anslie.
— National Archives of Canada C520

the villages on the mainland, too. Brockville had a population of five hundred in 1821. During the next decade this number more than doubled, so that by the 1830s it was one of the few hamlets boasting a population more than 1,200. By then the village had churches, a school and a newspaper. Local families used several islands in the Brockville Narrows for hunting and fishing camps.

In 1843 Thomas Darling built a wood station, Darlingside, on the bank of the St. Lawrence. It served as a general store specializing in tea. The Darlings also served as bankers for the region, supplying mortgage funds to local farmers and settlers. The general store was beautifully designed. Unlike most construction in the area, it was Georgian style and displayed finely carved wood trim and facing boards.

Upriver, in Gananoque, industrial activities began. Most of the early building had taken place on Stone's land grant, on the west bank of the Gananoque River, but in 1824 Joel Stone's son-in-law Charles McDonald and his brother John bought old Sir John Johnson's land grant on the east bank for $4 an acre. They cleared the land and laid out streets. They also built the largest flour mill of its time in Upper Canada, supplying about one-quarter of all the flour that was sent to Montreal. The grain to supply the mill arrived in schooners from the West, and bateaux and Durham boats carried the flour downriver. The

The Darlingside Tea Company label.
— Private collection, R. Wallace, Darlingside, Ontario

capacity of the mill was 250 barrels a day. The mill, which was five storeys high, was powered by two large "wheels" that were directly geared to run three giant granite millstones.

The McDonalds ground the grain and installed the most up-to-date equipment for handling, weighing, cleaning and packing the flour. They built a large warehouse on the riverbank to store the barrels before shipment. The Gananoque Mill give out "due bills," which were the first paper money in the region.

During the 1850s the flour business in Ontario began to fail, probably owing to a combination of railroad construction, a boll weevil attack and competition from other mills that were being built in Toronto and Montreal with more modern equipment. The mill was eventually converted into the Globe Works, and a group of small businesses occupied the building, including a pin factory, a spoon factory and a clothes-wringer manufacturer. The Skinner Company made scythes and saddle hardware on the site for many years. The building was destroyed by fire in 1881.

In addition to the flour mill, the McDonalds also had a lumber trade, taking advantage of the timber cut on the Gananoque River and floated downstream. There were two important wood docks in front of Gananoque. The first was located at the foot of Main Street; a second ran along the river to the east. The Britton family supplied wood and later coal to the passing steamers. The hill above the docks from the foot of Stone Street to the foot of William Street (two long blocks) and south of John Street was a solid mass of piled-up cordwood.

Thus, the north shore resembled other Canadian villages and farmland, but most of the islands remained essentially wilderness.

9 THE PATRIOT WAR,
1837–1838

For a second time in the 1800s there was political unrest in the Thousand Islands. The so-called Patriot War, or the Rebellion of 1837–38, has been much publicized and glamorized over the years. Today's guidebooks and tour-boat commentary always include stories about the infamous pirate William (Bill) Johnston and his attack on the steamship *Sir Robert Peel*. The captains proudly point to the landmarks that are associated with Johnston's escapades.

After the War of 1812 Canada attracted hundreds of Irish, Scottish and English immigrants from the British Isles. Many crossed the ocean poor and destitute; all wanted an opportunity to prosper in the British province. Unlike the United Empire Loyalists, who settled because of their strong association with England, these immigrants had different ideas and political beliefs. Political action against the established rule soon began. Newcomers wanted a share of revenues and a say in the distribution of the land.

There was little representative government. Local inhabitants elected a lower assembly, but the British governor appointed high officials, judges and other well-established citizens, such as wealthy landowners, to the upper assembly. Thus the governor had control over the province.

Upper Canada was not the only scene of unrest. In Quebec, Louis Papineau also wanted a more republican democracy. When the Quebec government rejected his resolutions for change, he organized his followers into the Fils de la Liberté. Unfortunately he did not have the powerful support of the Catholic Church and his planned attacks failed. He and his followers escaped to Vermont, where they joined forces with American sympathizers and formed the Frères Chasseurs, or the Hunters' Lodges.

In Ontario, William Lyon Mackenzie, a Scottish journalist, led the opposition to the government and its alleged "oppressive acts." When Mackenzie failed to win over Parliament by political manoeuvres he tried to do so by force. After losing a skirmish in Toronto, he fled to Buffalo. There he found small groups of Americans who sympathized with his opposition to British rule.

In the early 1800s New Englanders whose families supported and fought for freedom in the American Revolution moved west and settled in New York along the St. Lawrence River and Lake Ontario. These Americans believed Mackenzie's claims that most Canadians wanted to overthrow British rule, so many were willing to join the secret lodges. The Ontario contingent moved to Navy Island, in the Niagara River, where they established the Provisional Government of the Republic of Upper Canada. The island was on the Canadian side of the river, so the group was not defying the American laws.

The capture of an American ship was the first official attack in the so-called war. On December 29, 1837, a small group of Canadian volunteers captured the *Caroline*, which was bringing supplies to the island. (It is interesting to note that a former British hydrographer and member of Captain Owen's crew, John Harris, was a member of this volunteer group and possibly suggested the attack.) They set the ship on fire and cut her adrift to go over the Niagara Falls. By all rights this was an act of aggression against the United States, but President Van Buren insisted on neutrality.

Soon afterwards, another plan was made, this time involving the St. Lawrence River and Kingston. Newspaper reports of the raid, recorded many years later, described the incident with gusto.

One February night in 1838 a young American girl in Gananoque warned of an impending attack by the patriots. Elizabeth Barnett was teaching school there at the time and was betrothed to a Canadian. She had been visiting friends and relatives in Lafargeville when she overheard that patriots were assembling nearby, at French Creek (now Clayton), presumably readying to cross the river and attack Gananoque and Kingston.

The story of Elizabeth's warning and the attack has been recorded many times over the years, but one of the most lively tales comes from an article printed in the June 16, 1888 *Gananoque Reporter*.

"Immediately," said Robert Colton, then a young man, "the gentler sex was moved inland to Charleston Lake and Mr. Rogers took a group to Marble Rock. Gananoque was full of reports of various kinds, full of volunteers and full of whisky!" Scouts from Grindstone Island said that sleighs, horses and men with rifles were making their way across the ice to Hickory Island, located west of Grindstone Island in Canadian waters. By noon everyone knew the reports were true: Hickory Island was the base for a massive military operation, and as a result "another load of ladies was sent to the rear."

Under the direction of Joshua Legge, the Gananoque militia made a timber wall with a dozen logs piled by the water's edge at the foot of Main Street. These logs were destined for the timber rafts built each summer and sent downriver.

At four o'clock in the afternoon Colton was sent on a round of Gananoque homes, knocking on all the doors and requesting that "every able-bodied man report to the Gananoque Blockhouse."

Excitement grew: "Hoot, Molly, so you think I'm going to allow the Yankees to raid Gananoque and I never get a shot at them. Get down my rifle while I clean it!" Yes, the town residents were ready for the great attack. About a mile out of town to the west, Colton met the Kingston Militia coming to Gananoque's aid. The day was sunny but so bitterly cold that frost formed a blanket over the men and their horses.

At five o'clock the next morning the commander instructed Colton to venture as close as possible to Hickory Island. He and another soldier crossed the ice to Forsyth Island, off Gananoque. It was still dark, and they judged the current incorrectly, so that Colton's mount broke through the ice on the south side of MacDonald Island, but neither horse nor rider suffered any harm. After making their way past Mudlunta Island, they met a local resident who reported that the so-called patriots' army had retreated, having left Hickory Island the night before. Colton continued on his mission, and arriving at Hickory Island, he estimated that more than two thousand men had assembled the day before. He found a Mrs. Livingston alone in her house, but 8 or 10 acres of trampled snow gave evidence of men, horses, and sleighs. There was also the remains of a large piece of artillery. The threat of an attack was over. The military operation had been abandoned because there was little discipline among the young and untrained troops. The weather was such that only a well-organized army would have been able to mount an attack.

Then in May 1838 pirate Bill Johnston, self-proclaimed commander-in-chief of the patriots' naval forces, led another attack. Born 50 miles below Montreal on the St. Lawrence River, Johnston had settled in Kingston as a grocer. Accused of insubordination during the War of 1812, he had been imprisoned but eventually escaped and fled to the States, vowing to be an enemy of his homeland forever. He served the Americans as a spy for the remainder of the war, even acting as a river pilot to Col. James Wilkinson. Johnston is credited with leading the Wilkinson vessels and gunboats through the maze of the Thousand Islands in their abortive attempt to capture Montreal.

His strong dislike of Canadian officials made him a perfect candidate to join Mackenzie in his fight for Canadian independence from British rule. Johnston and his dozen men devised a plan to capture two British steamboats to use for transporting his "troops and provisions" in the Islands.

House of Johnston.
— William Denny, Artist, National Archives of Canada C139366

The steamship *Sir Robert Peel*, owned by a group of Brockville businessmen, was travelling between Prescott and Toronto on the night of May 29, 1938. Her captain took no notice of rumours of an impending attack and continued his passage. It was dark and raining when the ship pulled into the wood station on Wellesley Island, with nineteen passengers on board. While her crew loaded on wood, a group of men disguised as natives attacked with bayonets and muskets, all the time shouting, "Remember the *Caroline*!" There was a lot of confusion, and passengers later described the number of men and the details of the attack in different ways, but all agreed that Johnston and his men did force the passengers onto shore, some in their nightclothes. Intending to confiscate the ship for their navy, the attackers tried to light the boilers, but not knowing the procedures, they

Bill Johnston's island.
— William Denny, Artist, National Archives of Canada C139368

were unsuccessful and the boat drifted, eventually running aground on a shoal. Johnston set the *Sir Robert Peel* on fire, and it burned to the waterline.

This flagrant attack was angrily criticized on both sides of the border, and Lord Durham, then governor-general of Upper Canada, offered a $1,000 reward "to any person who shall identify any person engaged in or directly abiding and abetting this outrage." A month later Johnston issued a "manifesto" in the local newspapers, openly admitting the attack on the steamboat and claiming he fought for the independence of Canada.

Luckily for both nations, the U.S. government also expressed dismay over the burning of the *Sir Robert Peel*. They, too, offered a reward of $500 for the apprehension of Bill Johnston and $250 for each of his accomplices. But Johnston's so-called wanted poster added fuel to the fire. Soon after, he was seen on Amherst Island in Lake Ontario, walking the main street of Clayton "armed with knife and pistol." He proclaimed that he held a commission in the patriot service of Upper Canada as commander-in-chief of the naval expedition that captured and destroyed the steamer. He also said his headquarters were on an island near the boundary line. He called his island Fort Wallace (Lake Fleet Islands). It is close to the international border and its cliffs make an ideal lookout station.

Finally, in November 1838, more action took place in the region. The Hunters' Lodges were a strong and active group, and gathered to start an offensive on Canada. Their leaders told them that the Canadians across the river were waiting for the opportunity to join in the fight for independence. The eventual battle at Windmill Point, below

Prescott, saw the defeat of the invaders. Both sides fought long and hard, and the four-day battle was described as the bloodiest fighting of the rebellion. When it was over, thirteen British and Canadian troops were dead and some sixty were wounded. Twenty invaders were killed, almost as many severely wounded, and about 140 taken prisoner. The leader of the group, Nils Gustav Van Schoultz, and nine others were executed by hanging. Several prisoners were sent to the penal colony of Van Dieman's Island (Tasmania), while the youngest were returned to their homes as free men. Of the prisoners who were sent to Tasmania, only eleven were said to have returned.

Bill Johnston hid among the islands for several months. Tradition and today's tour-boat commentary say he hid in a cave on a small island near Alexandria Bay called the Devil's Oven, and that his daughter Kate rowed her skiff to bring him food and news of the day. Suffice it to say that he did hide among the islands, more likely in a safe cabin with a warm fire burning! Eventually he was apprehended and sent to an Ogdensburg jail. He tried to escape but was recaptured and sent to trial. Found guilty of breaking the United States neutrality laws, he was sentenced to one year in prison and fined $200. His daughter joined him in prison, where they were considered the "most famous" prisoners and gained great public sympathy. Upon his release he returned to Clayton, and with the continued help of his daughter, he gained a pardon. President Harrison granted it in March 1840 after receiving a petition with "many thousand signatures on it." Johnston became the lighthouse keeper on Rock Island, a few miles from the site of his attack on the *Sir Robert Peel*. The old pirate died on February 17, 1870, at the age of eighty-three.

Joseph Bonaparte, Napoleon's brother and North Country resident.

— *Wellington & Waterloo*, Major Arthur Griffiths, published by George Newnes, Limited, 1898

10 THE AMERICAN ISLANDS FOR SALE, 1822–1872

The Mississaugas surrendered the Canadian islands to the Crown; the American islands, which were originally included in the Macomb Purchase of 1792, were also sold. Alexander Macomb's title was never transferred because of the discrepency as to where the international boundary would be drawn. This line, separating the American islands from the Canadian islands, was laid down by the International Boundary Commission in 1822. Only then could the islands in the United States be patented. Elisha Camp of Sackets Harbor was the first purchaser, on February 15, 1823.

Title information, recorded by Frankin B. Hough in his Jefferson County history, gives the line of succession. Camp acquired "all the islands in the state between a line drawn at right angles to the river from the village of Morristown and a meridian drawn through the western part of Grindstone Island. The sale included islands with a total of 15,102 acres, including Grindstone Island (5,291 acres), Wellesley Island (8,068 acres), Oak Island (369 acres), and several smaller ones without names." At the time of Camp's purchase, the mainland communities of Cape Vincent, Clayton and Alexandria Bay were growing.

After the War of 1812, roads opened and these fostered settlement in Cape Vincent. Shipbuilding in the region began in 1819, and for many years the village was a shipping and lumbering centre.

As described earlier, the first south-shore settlers were French citizens brought to the region by James Le Ray and his family. Shortly after the Napoleonic Wars ended with the Battle of Waterloo and the defeat of Napoleon, more Frenchmen made their way to North America. Most of these new settlers were friends of Napoleon. By the 1820s prominent families such as those of Comte Pierre-Francois Réal, Napoleon's chief of police, and M. Louis, Napoleon's bodyguard, had settled in Cape Vincent.

Napoleon's brother, Joseph Bonaparte, the Comte de Survillers, as he wished to be called, bought more than 25,000 acres at Natural Bridge, near Carthage. He built an elaborate house and travelled extensively in the state.

Plans were made to prepare a home and a homecoming for the beloved "friend, brother, and King" by rescuing Napoleon from St. Helena Island and bringing him to Jefferson County and Cape Vincent. In fact, Comte Réal built a special house for Napoleon in the town. However, Napoleon died on St. Helena in 1821. Joseph

Bonaparte sold his New York State properties and returned to France in 1934.

By the end of 1820, Clayton was another thriving timber town. In 1820 William Angel began a lumber business and opened a small store to sell supplies to the nearby settlers. Not long after Elisha Camp purchased the islands, he subdivided Washington Island, located off the area that had been set out as a town site by the Le Ray family. Camp built a bridge to the island in 1826. At that time the Le Rays began selling their land, and it took little time before a community began to develop. At first the town was given the name Cornelia, but in 1831 the name was changed to honour the Hon. John M. Clayton, United States Senator from Delaware.

An 1835 article published in the *Watertown Eagle* described the progress of the town in a few short years: "Six years ago there were 9 buildings in this place; we now number 43 dwelling houses, 6 stores, 3 groceries, 3 taverns, 1 steam furnace, capable of melting 4 tons of iron per day, 1 machine shop, 1 ship smith's shop, 1 blacksmith's shop, 3 shoe shops, 2 tailor shops, 1 chair shop, 2 cabinet shops, 1 butcher shop, 1 baker, a schoolhouse, 5 large and momodious wharves, and within 1 mile of the village 3 saw mills."

Progress like this ensured that the area would prosper. With the shipbuilding business beginning, it was reported that the town had "7 schooners, 1 brig and 1 steam boat, making an aggregate of 1,000 tons."

The small community of Alexandria Bay, surveyed in 1804, became a regular wood station when John Fuller and Azariah Walton built their steamboat wharf in 1823. By the 1830s the village had "about a dozen frame dwellings and shops, scattered promiscuously among the granite knolls and level grades, wherever a favourable site offered."

During the next two decades the islands, either as a group or singly, were bought and sold. When Elisha Camp bought the American islands for $3,000 in 1823, he had several businesses in Sackets Harbor and was probably interested in the islands only for their timber. He sold 770 acres on Grindstone Island to William Wells, a lumberman, a Widow Fitch bought 100 acres, and Augusta Sackett bought 600 acres. Camp also sold almost 600 acres on Wellesley Island and the 20-acre Washington Island near Clayton. The next year Camp bought more islands near Clayton, which were within "100 chains of the mainland shore," between Bartlett Point and the east end of Round Island. He paid $938 for that property.

The islands changed hands several times, but there was still little interest in island real estate. Two of the buyers were land speculators Yates and McIntyre of New York City, who bought all the islands for $2,000 in 1834. Five years later, McIntyre sold his claim to Yates. Finally, in 1845, Yates sold all the islands for $3,000, excluding Hemlock (now Murray Island) and Jeffers (now Grenell Island), to Chesterfield Parsons, a resident of Alexandria Bay. Again there was speculation as Parsons sold his half interest to Azariah Walton, also of Alexandria Bay. This sale marked the beginning of island development.

Navigation improved on the St. Lawrence in 1847 when the U.S. government built lighthouses on Rock Island and Bush Island near Alexandria Bay. The existing Trippets Lighthouse at Cape Vincent and the Crossover Island light east of Alexandria Bay gave steamboats a safer course to follow through the waterway. By 1848 the whole length of the St. Lawrence River, including the sections with rapids between Kingston and Montreal, were navigable for boats and ships with as much as a 9-foot draft. The building of the locks ensured that steamboats could then ply the river all the way to the sea. Not only could cargo be transported, but so could passengers.

In 1850 Walton acquired the ownership of all the American islands. His interest was in the timber rights, but soon the river began to attract "gentlemen" from larger towns and cities, not for timber or for the excitement of a steamboat journey, but for fishing. As early as the 1830s rivers and lakes in upper New York State were gaining recognition for their fish. When fishermen told stories about the giant fish swimming in the mighty St. Lawrence, other fishermen began to arrive in greater numbers.

A well-known New York naturalist, Seth Green, came to the Thousand Islands in 1854. Realizing the potential for furthering his studies of fish, he approached Azariah Walton with a special request: could he buy an island, build a cottage and spend the summer? Walton thought this request unusual, but agreed to sell a small island lying off the village of Alexandria Bay. Green paid $40 for Meadow Island (now Manhattan Island) and received "all shoals, rocks, etc. within 30 rods unless that includes a large island." Thus, Seth Green was the first of many "summer people" to discover the Thousand Islands.

However, the islands did not sell quickly. In 1854 only two were deeded by Walton: Cedar Island in Chippewa Bay and Meadow (Manhattan) to Seth Green. Two years later the executors of Walton's estate sold only five more islands: Rabbit Island in Chippewa Bay, Steamboat Island, Deer Island, Jutts Island near Alexandria Bay and a large island that was almost connected to the mainland and known as Island Number 9. In 1864 they deeded Sweet Island to George Pullman. Cherry, Nobby and Friendly islands were sold next, in 1868. Twelve were sold in 1871, and from that year on the popularity of the islands increased.

It is true that the "fish tales" brought the first visitors to the region, but soon after the Civil War the American industrial revolution began and "gentlemen" had more free time and wealth to enjoy new sports. Resorts were developed in every part of the continent, taking advantage of the seashore, the mountains, and the inland lakes and rivers. Stories about the Thousand Islands and their hunting and fishing began to attract sportsmen to the region. Alexandria Bay was the fishing centre, with visitors staying at the Crossman House, built in 1848 for fisherman. At first the hotel accommodated ten guests, but by 1870 it had expanded to welcome about three hundred guests each summer.

Fishermen rowed from the village through the channels to the fishing grounds. These excursions fostered island ownership. Soon families with the wealth to afford the purchase price of an island and the construction of a summer home persuaded the owners of the American Thousand Islands to sell.

Andrew Cornwall and John Walton, who were the executors of the Walton estate, realized how important it was becoming to show off the large homes that were being built on the islands, so they often stipulated as part of the sale that a home had to be built within "two or three" years. This helped foster development in the region, and was possibly an incentive to build bigger and more elaborate homes. They also made

Andrew Cornwall kept a notebook that recorded the sales of islands in the Thousand Islands.
— Jno. Haddock, *A Souvenir, The Thousand Islands of the St. Lawrence River*, 1895

sure that many of the islands remained green, with tall trees left standing to increase their value.

Credit goes to George M. Pullman, of sleeping-car fame, for beginning the social era in the islands in 1872. He invited President Ulysses S. Grant, who was campaigning for a second term as president of the United States, to his Pullman Island for a vacation. Pullman approached Andrew Cornwall with a scheme. "What we want to do, Andrew," he said, "is to make much of the General's visit here, and it will advertise the islands as no other thing we can do. To have the President of the United States as our guest is quite an honour." Indeed, they obtained free publicity, as the press travelling with the President saw the opulence of this small island community and wrote articles in the papers of the leading cities in the United States.

About the same time an Editors' and Publishers' Association of the State of New York brought more favourable publicity to the region. The association, which had been formed in 1853, held a convention every year, and in June 1872 they met in Watertown. An excursion to the Thousand Islands was planned, complete with "flags, evergreens

George Pullman.
— National Archives of Canada C58803

and flowers." The train took two hundred visitors to Cape Vincent, where they boarded a steamer for a trip through the islands. They stopped at Clayton and then again on Pullman Island, where they attended a reception. A band provided music, and all in all, it was a perfect way to be introduced to this beautiful section of the country. Each reporter went home raving about the beauty of the region. They "created with many a desire to view the scenery for themselves." From that time on, interest in the area increased and hundreds of "summer people" came to the river. They pitched tents, they rented rooms in hotels, and many bought islands.

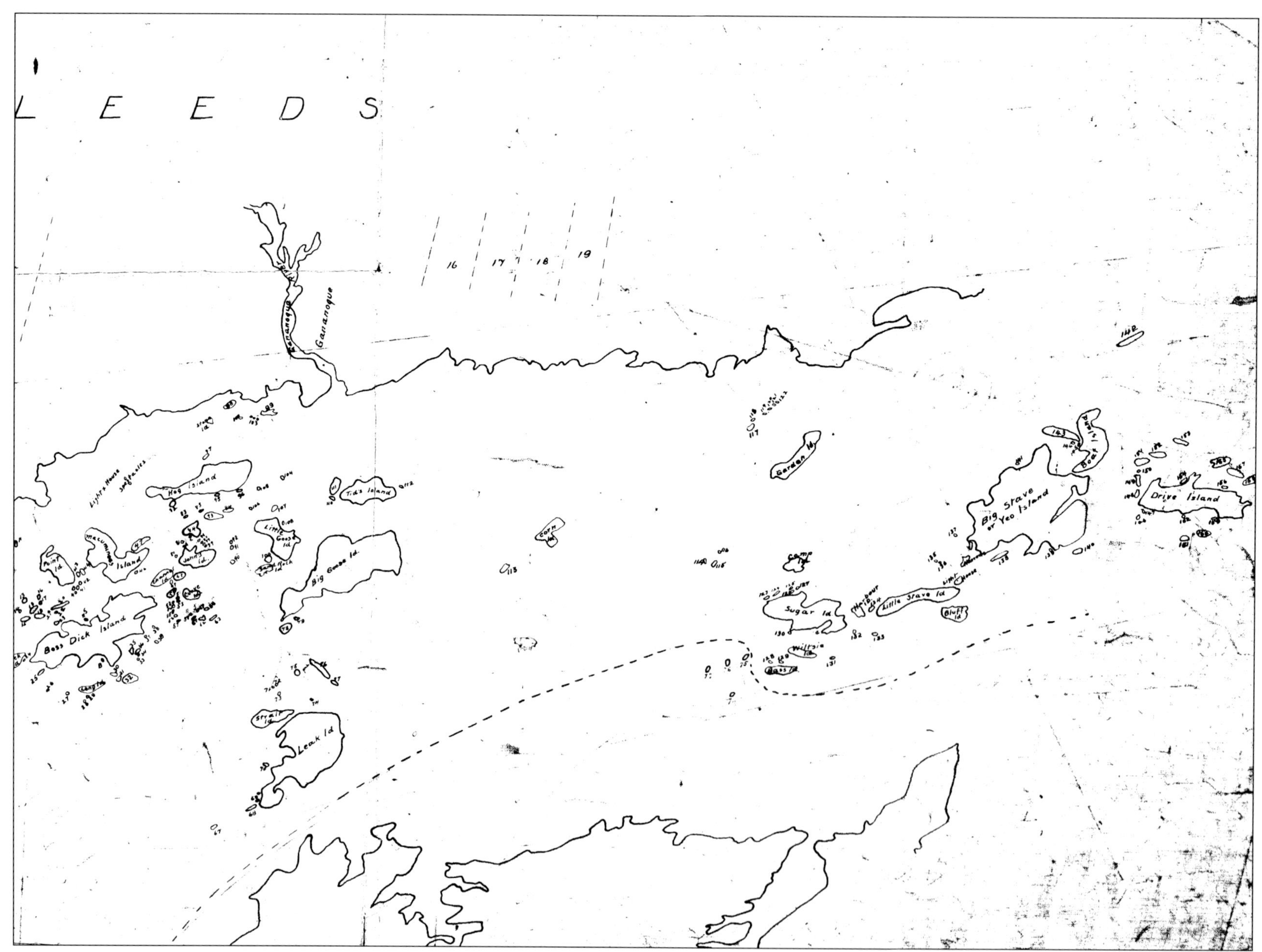

John McNaughton's survey of the Alnwick land. — John McNaughton, *Schedules and Diary Examination Survey, 1862-63*, Field book: 210A and Maps, Department of Energy, Mines and Resources

11 THE CANADIAN ISLANDS FOR SALE, 1862–1894

After the Indian Affairs Branch of the Department of Interior received the Alnwick Band's surrender in 1856, it took five years before the department began carrying out the surrender agreement to sell the islands. However, no one knew how many islands there were or what they looked like. The Alnwick Band produced a list of fourteen islands, but insisted that there were a great many more.

The Department of the Interior therefore secured the services of the Crown Lands Department, under the direction of John McNaughton, public land surveyor, to survey the surrendered lands from the Bay of Quinte to the Thousand Islands. McNaughton, who came from Glengarry County, near Lancaster, Ontario, was an experienced surveyor, having been appointed a deputy provincial surveyor in June 1821. McNaughton kept comprehensive field notes which hold valuable historical information describing the islands and their inhabitants. The survey began in the Thousand Islands during March, hardly an ideal time to inspect the islands. The survey party camped on Bear Island (now known as Aubrey Island, Admiralty Islands), and one day they got back to the island "being covered with scales of ice."

It took a month to complete the Thousand Islands section of the survey. The men covered the region from the eastern end of Howe Island to the beginning of the Navy group at Stave and Downie islands. Although the international boundary line had been set forty years before, the surveyors disregarded the official maps. In fact, their charts show that many islands in the Lake Fleet were not considered Canadian, and they did not survey the islands east of Downie in the Lake Fleet, which was probably the eastern boundary of Mississauga territory.

The surveyors met those who lived on the islands year-round, but from their notes we can see resident numbers were few. When the survey was completed, it recorded 162 numbered islands and 32 with local names, totalling over 900 acres, with an estimated value of almost $3,000.

The department never held a sale but instead kept the land for the next decade. This was probably because there was at that time hardly such a thing as free time or vacations. Leisure came, as we have learned from the sale of American islands, only after the American Civil War and the business boom that occurred in the 1870s.

By 1873, with the American islands so popular, it now seemed a prudent time to sell the Canadian ones. The government wrote to a Toronto surveyor, Charles Unwin, requesting that another survey be made, this time from the eastern end of Howe Island downriver to Brockville, more than 25 miles of islands.

Charles Unwin was also an experienced surveyor. Born in England, he came to Canada in 1843 and attended Upper Canada College, graduating in 1847. He surveyed many Ontario townships and several sections of Toronto, where he had his surveyor's office.

Like the other surveyors, Unwin also began his work in winter. He complained that the weather was foul and that his men were either blinded by snowstorms or had to walk miles along the shore looking for safe ice to cross to the islands.

Unwin's task was large. He had to traverse all the islands to determine what was saleable. His work was meticulous.

In all, Charles Unwin evaluated over three hundred islands. He was given a copy of Captain Owen's survey and instructed that if an island had been given a name by Owen and was also known by a local name, then both should be used. Thus, islands were recorded as Melville/Hay Island, Bathurst/Grenadier Island and Yorke/Bostwick Island.

Although Unwin recorded local names, he also used his own naming system or that used by the provincial land surveyors. Many were descriptive names, such as Huckleberry, Leek, Bluff and Pine.

All reasonably sized islands not already given a name were given a number. These began with Island No. 1 (northeast of Mermaid Island and east of Aubrey in the Admiralty group) and ended with Island No. 122 in the Brock group near Brockville.

After completing the survey in the spring of 1873, Unwin went back to the islands in the middle of the summer and spent time viewing each one before placing a final "upset cost" or price on the islands. This summer survey ensured that he saw how beautiful the islands were and what they looked like in the lush growing period.

The final descriptive sheets listed the islands in alphabetical order and were dated March 2, 1874. They began with a description of Astounder Island: "2.2 Acres, surveyor's evaluation $10. Description: Low rock; very few trees and brush."

After more than eighteen years of the property being in trust for the Alnwick Band of Mississaugas, the islands were ready to be sold.

∽

Charles Unwin's survey and the Canadian government's decision to sell island leases was not popular. Island residents already living on some of them considered that they already owned their land, having paid rent occasionally to the Mississaugas or having bought quit-claims dating back to the 1820s from original white settlers. Most were poor, illiterate farmers, fishermen or boatmen unable to find working land on the main shore and content to live on small rocky islands in the St. Lawrence River.

As soon as Unwin's men left the islands, letters were sent to the Department of Indian Affairs. Most were written on behalf of squatters. It was a vicious circle: a family built a house, barn and outbuilding on an island; they cleared a section of good land and planted meagre crops and orchards. The surveyors gave such an island a high evaluation because of these improvements! Poor farmers, originally driven to settle on rocky islands because of high mainland prices, found that they could no longer afford to pay for the properties they had built.

Another problem involved local townspeople. They considered the islands lying opposite their particular area as common property. Their fathers and grandfathers had cut timber from the islands, and they themselves used them during the summer months as campgrounds at no cost. Now their favourite islands might be sold to wealthy people or, worse, to American speculators!

An 1873 *Gananoque Reporter* writer was incensed: "It is stated that some American speculators have bought up all the Islands that lie on the American side of the line, and are endeavouring to secure all on the Canadian side that are yet unsold. This, if accomplished, would completely shut out Canadians from all participation in the profits arising from the summer trade, and the proposals of those speculating monopolists should not be entertained for a moment. . . ."

As the weeks wore on, the idea of selling the islands was openly contested. Letters to the editor appeared in leading newspapers. One writer wrote in 1873 that he "hoped the idea by the Canadian Government to sell the Thousands Islands was baseless." He advocated a national park system be started like "our neighbors. . .Yellowstone Reservation." The mainland communities of Prescott, Brockville and Gananoque petitioned the government to reserve the islands as parkland. The councils were not opposed to private ownership of inhabited islands, but they wanted the so-called unimproved islands to be reserved.

Probably as result of these issues, the department finally placed a moratorium on selling or leasing the islands. To settle the "squatter issue," those who could prove that they had occupied an island for "five or six years" and had made substantial improvements could purchase their island at the evaluated price. The department argued that these residents had lived rent-free for years and could afford to pay the evaluated price. They also noted that the improvement costs would be subtracted from the evaluation price. In most cases this arrangement proved to be satisfactory, and some of the large islands situated near Gananoque and others that were easily accessible to the mainland farther downriver were sold during the 1870s.

The third area of contention involved the farming families on Hill, Club and Grenadier islands. In 1876 William Hibberd, a Grenadier Island settler, wrote the department on behalf of his neighbours. He explained that the Unwin

The Massey family of Grindstone Island.

— St. Lawrence Islands National Park, Mrs. Meilahn's Collection evaluation was too high and unfair because most of the farmland was a combination of poor soil and gravel, from "small ordinary size stones to boulders." As a result, he claimed, it was necessary to "mix large amounts of manure with the earth," and then it only produced potatoes, apples, and garden vegetables. "Growing hay," he assured, was "out of the question." Island farmers had the added expense of hiring extra help to take their produce to markets. They could only go to the market on the mainland in good weather, often losing their loaded wagons in mid-stream from high winds and storms. The farmers also stressed that arranging to go to the market or local mills in good weather was one thing, but the islanders found going to church out of the question! Ministers came to the island by steamboat in the summer, but "this was at great expense . . . so as a consequence we can attend no church and the moral condition of society is very low and hardly a suitable place to bring up a family of children."

Also, a local member of Parliament wrote the department asking for a new evaluation to be made. He stated that there were three ways to evaluate the islands: first, as vacation land, which could bring as much as $10 or $15 an acre; second, at public auction which would bring an equally inflated price of $2 to $19 an acre; or based on mainland prices, as was done for Tar Island, which would bring about $1.50 an acre. He advocated the third method, and also suggested that the department give the land in grants, "which had been done on the mainland years before with the main object of settling the country."

The department again argued that these farming families had lived on the island rent-free for several generations. They cut timber "without paying for same," built homes and barns, fenced their land and used the timber as fuel.

Finally, when the government agreed to re-examine the islands, the farmers suggested that James Keeler, a highly respected town council member and reeve, do the reevaluation. The department agreed. Keeler's 1876 evaluation was considered quite fair, and as a result the farms were sold to their inhabitants.

At the beginning of the 1880s the government reviewed the situation. The moratorium on selling the islands had been in effect for six years. This meant that the Mississaugas were not benefiting from the terms of their surrender. In March 1880 the government decided to auction twenty-year leases. Toronto, Ottawa, and Montreal newspapers advertised the sales and twelve islands were leased: ". . . so far the opposition to the sale here; the people being of the opinion that, what ever may be the policy of the Government, the inevitable result will be that the Islands will get into private hands before many years."

At the same time the towns of Prescott, Brockville and Gananoque were given the opportunity to buy the undeveloped islands at the original evaluation. The only community to take advantage of this offer was Brockville, which leased the islands lying in front of the town in 1883 and bought most of them in 1933.

In 1880 the Brockville *Recorder* printed an editorial encouraging the building of a hotel that would be capable of accommodating "tourist and summer visitors." They felt that the "experience of the past five years on the American side of the River is proof that when suitable hotels are provided the guests will come to them." As they knew, Alexandria Bay and the other American resort islands were benefiting from the tourist trade, while Brockville and the other Canadian towns were not. "One visitor last year will influence two to come this year; and thousands now come who do not come to fish being satisfied with the delightful scenery of the Islands and the invigorating breezes that come over the water."

The government held more auctions. Most of these leases were only held for two or three years and then reverted to the Crown. In 1884 the Department of Marine and Fisheries bought several islands to build lighthouses.

By the 1890s there was renewed interest in island sales. Communities on the American side prospered because of the labour needed to build and maintain the elaborate homes and hotels as well as to look after the thousands of visitors who came during the summer. Because Canadians could not work on the American side of the river, the Canadian communities decided they could profit only if the Canadian islands were sold and developed.

In 1891 the Canadian government passed an order-in-council to sell the unimproved islands. It had been almost twenty years since Charles Unwin's evaluation, which had resulted in island sales representing 2,642.3 acres for a total price of $6,000, or $2.37 per acre. The government knew that the remaining eight hundred islands were worth more.

Almost from the beginning, the value of an island had depended on its aesthetic quality. Guardians had been hired during the 1870s to maintain the islands as best they could. Strict rules were enforced that prohibited cutting or destroying timber or removing soil and stone from the islands. This eventually paid off.

Not everyone was pleased with the island guardians. Several people called attention to the fact that some of the more prominent families, or "friends" of the guardians, were allowed to purchase islands, even though a moratorium had been placed on the sale of land. "How is it that these parties referred to by the *Recorder* have been allowed to go on and occupy Islands right under the eyes of the island Bailiffs?" they asked. "It cannot be supposed that the Bailiffs are ignorant in the matter — they know all about it; and consequently the general public naturally fall in to the belief that such occupation is authorized or winked at." It was true that several large islands were sold between 1873 and the 1890s, while the moratorium was in place. One was even sold to one of the guardians. Jno Ormiston purchased Little Island (Cunningham Island) beside the town of Gananoque, claiming that as customs agent he could "observe who was coming and going" and could therefore do a better job!

So finally, after forty years of administering the Indian land, the government once more made a concerted effort to sell the Canadian Thousand Islands. But again a survey was necessary, and during the summer of 1891 Walter Beatty, from Delta, Ontario, began another one. He discovered some 120 new islands. It wasn't that these islands had not existed in 1873, but in twenty years the vegetation had grown on small rocks and shoals, making them saleable as islands. In order to identify these new islands, Beatty gave them numbers and letters referring to the nearest island, which Unwin had numbered in 1873. For example, Unwin had identified Island No. 45, while tiny islets nearby were identified by Beatty as islands 45A, 45B, 45C, 45D, 45E, and 45F.

The Canadian 1000 Islands for Sale, *a Canadian government publication of 1894, listed the islands for sale, the rules for buying an island, and descriptions and prices.*
— National Archives of Canada C118601

Beatty also raised the value of acreage. Unwin's total value had been approximately $10,000, while the Beatty evaluation was over $70,000, with the average price an acre being $37.50. He also selected sixty-nine islands that he recommended should be sold, singling out several islands that he felt could be bought by their occupants. In most cases these were families who had squatted on the islands or lived on Grenadier Island and used the islands close by. He thought that the islands should sell for the price he had appraised them for, and not less. He also felt that the department should encourage settlement and that in order to do this they should ask for a building to be constructed that would not cost too much, but at the same time should not be valued at less than $500. The latter concern would keep out those who purchased an island and then built a lean-to, which would be unsightly and not add to the value of surrounding islands. After Beatty's report was received, sale lists were prepared. In one auction sale, twelve islands sold for a total of $2,420, or an average of $200 each. Many of the new owners were local residents who had expressed an interest in owning islands near their mainland properties. At that time, the conditions for buying the islands were stringent. Not taking Beatty's advice, the department created restrictions that caused problems. "A house costing $1000 shall be built on each Island sold within two years from date of purchase." Also, trees and shrubbery were not allowed to be cut, except on the building site.

There was another outcry by the press that the terms of the sale "seem to be about as absurd as could be devised, and tend to throw a doubt on the genuineness of the public sale." It was felt the terms of the sale — the expense of building the $1,000 house and the rule against cutting trees on one's own property — were not in keeping with the "right with the principle that a man has a right to do as he likes with his own."

Their arguments must have worked because the restriction on the price of the building was soon removed. People had pointed out that it cost more to build on islands. Transportation across the water was a problem: barges had to be loaded on shore and then brought to the island. Trips were always determined by the weather. In winter, contractors sometimes had to wait for safe ice to form and then used sleds and horses to transport the building materials.

In March and April 1894 reports and a formal address were given to the House of Commons containing all the reports made to the Department of the Interior, or to the superintendent general of Indian Affairs. In it were the surveyors' evaluation reports completed by Charles Unwin in 1874, James Keeler in 1876, and the valuation report made by Henry Lilly of Grenadier Island in 1873. There was also the report by Walter Beatty, with his recommendation to sell sixty-nine islands, and his full evaluation report, dated April 1893. In addition there were letters that the departments had received from individuals wanting to purchase islands.

Finally the islands were ready to be sold. Following the recommendations on both sides of the international boundary, the Canadian and United States governments reserved or purchased island property to be used as parkland. Both governments hoped to form an international park that would foster friendship on both sides of the border. Ten Canadian islands were chosen: Aubrey, Mermaid, Beau Rivage and Gordon islands near Gananoque, Camelot and Endymion islands in the Lake Fleet, Ninette Island in the Navy Islands, Georgina and Constance islands near Ivy Lea, and Adelaide Island at the east end of Grenadier Island.

Ninette Island was not kept for the park but was eventually sold. In 1904 the Mallory family in Mallorytown Landing presented a gift of land to the government for a park. With this and the reserved islands, the St. Lawrence Islands National Park began. In 1905 Stovin Island near Brockville was to be added and a portion of Grenadier Island was purchased. (More land was acquired over the years, with the park finally purchasing more than sixty small Canadian islets in 1977.)

In 1894 the Beatty sale lists were published in a booklet. A map was included, showing all the islands. Those that were reserved were clearly marked. A price list gave the lowest selling price, and if the island was sold at auction, this then would become the upset cost. Each island was described and the acreage recorded. The rules of the sale were included as was a "sales pitch," which outlined why the islands were valuable and the reasons people should summer in the Canadian Thousand Islands. Finally there was customs and sales information.

The publication of the booklet, and the advertising of future auction sales in newspapers in the vicinity, as well as in New York, Boston, Montreal, Toronto and several other cities, brought buyers. In one year, more than 170 islands were bought.

Inevitably, speculators purchased islands. One of the most prominent was William D. Morris. He lived in Ottawa and in 1901 served a term as mayor of that city. Seeing a chance to begin a real estate company in the Thousand Islands, Morris purchased a large property on Hill Island. Then he began to purchase other islands. Because the rules were quite stringent about buying only one or two if they were in close proximity, Morris had other people buy islands for him. It is said that many of those who purchased islands were his friends in Ottawa and relatives who lived as far away as Scotland and sent proxies to enable Morris to buy more islands. For some reason the department must have been unaware of the Morris plan, for no correspondence is available in the department files regarding this speculator's actions.

The rules for buying islands were well defined in the 1894 sale book *The Canadian 1000 Islands for Sale* (Ottawa, 1984).

TERMS OF SALE

The terms of sale are as follows:

- Not less than the price published in the Descriptive List will be accepted.
- In the event of there being two or more applicants for any particular island, the applicants to be asked to tender, and the island to be sold to the highest tenderer.
- The purchase money to be paid in cash, or one-quarter cash, and the balance in three equal annual installments, with interest at 6 per cent per annum on the unpaid purchase money.
- Not more than two islands to be sold to any one purchaser.
- No conditions as to settlement or improvement.
- Applications to purchase in the Gananoque district are to be made to John Ormiston, Esq., Collector of Customs, Gananoque, Ontario, and in the Rockport district to Joseph Cook, Esq., Rockport, Ontario, and to the Department of Indian Affairs, Ottawa. These districts are defined on the map in the pocket end of pamphlet.
- No sales will be made before the 2 July, 1894.

Auction sale poster.
— RG10, Vol. 2495, File 102438, C-11, 229

Memorandum dated Ottawa, January 7, 1908, changing the island names.

M E M O R A N D U M

Mr. Witcher, By Order of His Excellency in Council of the 20th of September, 1904, the following islands were transferred to the Minister of the Interior as representing the Crown, for park purposes:

Unwin's Survey	**Park Name**
Burnt, Bear, Smoke or Dark	Aubrey
Pine	Mermaid
Buck	Beau Rivage
Hog	Camelot
Johnson	Endymion
Gordon or Citron	Gordon
———	Georgina
Bowes	Constance
No. 116	Adelaide

Plans herewith

signed:
In Charge Lands & Timber Branch

He bought more than fifty islands, large and small, for a total cost of $9,552. The sales are recorded as the W.D. Morris Real Estate Company and registered in the Brockville registry at the turn of the century.

Morris formed the Thousand Islands Real Estate Company, then published a brochure that included photographs of the islands he wanted to sell. Each was given a description, often copying Walter Beatty's description and adding additional information. The brochure was expensive and, if anything, would have ensured that only the wealthy could afford a Morris property. He sold some of his islands, but not many. Most were held by the Thousand Islands Real Estate Company until the 1940s, when a group near Ivy Lea was sold.

Another speculator was the Joseph Reid family from Alexandria Bay. They were building contractors and they, too, got friends and family members to purchase Canadian islands after Beatty's evaluations. They developed several islands and were responsible for building some of the largest and most elaborate homes in the region.

In 1901 the department published another sale list. Many of the smallest islands that had not been sold in the first public sales were listed, with prices ranging from $5 to $200. Only one island, Dumfounder, was listed at $1,000. Many of the small islands were never sold and remained in the care of the department until the 1970s.

Records of the sale of the islands, and the transfer of monies to the Alnwick Band are well recorded in the department files. Now housed in the National Archives of Canada, these files contain valuable information and histories of many individual islands.

12 ISLAND LIVING, 1860–1910

Two hundred years after De Courcelle described the Thousand Islands as "a melancholy abode," another, more affable, visitor wrote his description: "There is so much that is grand, weird, sublime and exhilarating in the scenery and balmy atmosphere of the majestic river, as it passes in its onward flow from the Lake to the Gulf, that we need not for a moment wonder why it is that there is a great annual increase in the number of those intelligent people, who, from East, West and South, repair to its placid waters in summer to recuperate their wasted energies and enjoy that luxuriating season known to every American as vacation."

The author, E.F. Babbage, was a good salesman and wanted to sell his river guide, but he truly felt that the tourists of the 1880s could find all they wanted in the Thousand Islands.

The visitors needed accommodations, and accommodations they found, in the dozens of hotels and guest houses built for travelling guests. One of the largest was the Thousand Island House in Alexandria Bay. The property was given to O.G. Staples in 1872 for the chief purpose of building a hotel to attract visitors after President Grant's visit. Its popularity grew: "Everyone knew of it, and whoever came the first summer it was opened told their neighbors of the great delights of the region, and the next year other thousands were added, and as so year by year, the throng swelled."

The popularity of the Thousand Island House served to attract others to build rooms for paying guests. Soon hotels spread up and down the river, on islands and even across the river on the "Canadian" shore.

Private steamers and large steamship companies brought commercial industries to the region. Large and small communities built wood stations to supply fuel for the vessels and safe landings to welcome travellers.

Capt. E.W. Visger is credited with starting tour-boat excursions. He realized that the popularity of the islands would bring visitors — first to fish but also to enjoy the scenery. After navigation was improved on the river with the installation of lighthouses in late 1847, vessels could safely travel up and down the main channels. However, the smaller channels — hundreds of them — were unknown. One of the first tasks for a tour-boat captain was learning where his vessel could safely travel. So Captain Visger began to explore.

The Thousand Island House was a popular attraction at Alexandria Bay.

— *Guide book to the Thousand Island House,* O.G. Stapels

After the passages around the familiar islands near Alexandria Bay were sketched on a map, he headed north across the river. There were dozens of bays and channels between the islands lying north of Hill Island and the Canadian main shore. Visger had to learn about the currents that swirled through the narrow passageways, making them an exciting ride.

Visger had copies of the local county histories written in 1854 by Franklin B. Hough, and it was in one of these books that he discovered the story of the Lost Channel. If he could discover which channel was actually the one described back in 1760, when a crewman from the flotilla of British Gen. Jeffery Amherst was lost, he could publicize the Canadian side (see Part I, Discoverers and Explorers, 1650–1760). So, taking a good sounding line and his hand-drawn map, he set out to find the Lost Channel. He decided on its location (right or wrong), and also discovered that the fast current was caused not by shallow water or rapids, as expected, but rather by a drop in the river bottom from 50 to 200 feet — but invisible from the water's surface.

With the knowledge he obtained, Captain Visger could travel all around the islands without fear of going aground. At the beginning of the 1870s he acquired his first tour boat. The sixty-five-passenger *Cygnet* had been used by Sam Grennel to take supplies from the main shore of the United States to his island near the head of Wellesley Island. Visger arranged to trade some land he owned in Swan Bay for the small steamer. Thus he began his day trip around Wellesley Island. By 1879 Visger built the *Island Wanderer,* capable of taking three hundred passengers on excursions. The *Island Wanderer* made two trips a day, passing the inhabited islands near Alexandria Bay and crossing over to the Canadian shore, up through the Canadian channel and around the head of Wellesley Island. In 1888 the *New Island Wanderer* was built. It carried five hundred passengers and circled the two largest islands, Grindstone and Wellesley, stopping at what was then described as the "old fashioned town of Gananoque." By the 1890s Captain Visger's tour boats carried more than twenty thousand sight-seers each year.

Captain Visger's tour boat Islander.

— Jno. Haddock, *A Souvenir, The Thousand Islands of the St. Lawrence River,* 1985

The railroads built sidings to Clayton and Cape Vincent, and as many as twenty trains a day would come and go at the village stations in the summer. By 1886 the Rome, Watertown & Ogdensburg Railroad provided a connecting service from Ogdensburg west to Niagara Falls, with connections south to New York City. It cost $15 to buy a round-trip from New York City to the islands. Two daily trains left New York from Grand Central Station, one departing at eight o'clock in the morning and one at nine o'clock at night. It took a little over twelve hours to reach Clayton, with one transfer being made at Utica.

There was no station at Alexandria Bay, so the trains stopped at Redwood, 7 miles inland. From there, visitors hired carriages to take them to the waterfront. Some say that the Cornwall Brothers

1907 **CAPTAIN VISGER'S** 1907

WORLD-FAMOUS

50-MILE **Tour of The Islands**

(PERSONALLY CONDUCTED by Walter L. Visger, the Originator of the Yach System of Island Tours.)

We open the season of 1907 with the beautiful new

Steam Yacht **Castanet**

the swiftest, staunchest and most elegantly appointed steamer ever offered for public service (as you can see from the picture), known as

The Pullman of the St. Lawrence

and built especially to fit the narrow, tortuous waterways that the large excursion boats cannot navigate, such as **The Rift, Needle's Eye, Lost Channel, Horse Shoe, Whirlpool, Out-of-Sight,** and many others too numerous to mention.

She Has Gained a World-Wide Reputation.

The **"Castanet"** is the **swiftest steamer** making the Island Tour, and covers on every trip **10 miles** more scenery than any other yacht.

We pass close to and point out to the tourist every beautiful summer home in both the American and Canadian channels, stopping en route at all important summer resorts.

To the Stranger —

You have probably come a long distance to see the 1000 Islands. If your time is limited take this advice: **Don't buy** a ticket for the **Tour of the Islands** till you have at least seen the boat on which you are to make the trip. You will be pounced on by innumerable agents offering you all sorts of inducements to take their line. This is particularly good advice for the tourist stopping over just for the day. **All other** steamers making the Island Tour run in connection with the trains, any delay in trains might mean the cutting short of your trip, transferring passengers to other boats, etc.

You can avoid all these annoyances by purchasing tickets over the Captain Visger Line. We never wait for a train or transfer passengers. Leave it all to **Captain Visger.** 30 years' experience and not a single accident. Boats " Built to Fit," not **altered to imitate.**

Fare, Round Trip, 50c.

See other Bills for Excursions to Kingston, Canada, and Searchlight Trips.

TIME TABLE—DAILY

MORNING TOUR	Leave	Arrive	AFTERNOON TOUR	Leave	Arrive
Leave Alexandria Bay	8.15	11.00	Leave Clayton	1.00	4.30
* " Point Vivian	8.25	11.10	" Frontenac	1.10	4.40
* " St. Lawrence Park	8.30	11.15	" Thousand Island Park	1.30	5.00
* " Jolly Oaks	8.45	11.30	" Jolly Oaks	1.40	5.10
" Thousand Island Park	9.00	11.40	" St. Lawrence Park	1.50	5.25
" Frontenac	9.15	11.5[illegible]	" Point Vivian	2.00	5.30
" Clayton	9.30	12.00	" Alexandria Bay	2.20	5.45

Look here, you can save money!

Leave Alexandria Bay for Clayton and intermediate points direct.............. 8.15 and 11.00 a.m.
Leave Clayton for Alexandria Bay and intermediate points direct.............. 1.00 and 4.30 p.m.

Our fare one way is 40c. and return ticket 50c.
Thousand Island Park to Clayton or Alexandria Bay 25c. and return ticket 40c.

Time Table subject to change without notice. * Flag Port.

WALTER L. VISGER, Manager and Owner.

Hungerford-Holbrook Co., Watertown, N.Y.

Captain Visger's tour boat Castanet *made two trips a day.*

— Private collection, Kenneth Deedy, Grindstone Island

A souvenir guidebook.

Store, which held a monopoly with the steamship companies, discouraged the railroad from coming to town, while others agree that the distance kept the "poorer" visitor from stopping at this special retreat of the wealthy, and made the area more exclusive.

Not only did the railroads transport people to the region, but they also helped to promote tourist travel by advertising and publishing tour guides. In Montreal the International Railway Publishing Company conceived the idea of publishing the *All-Round Route and Panoramic Guide of the St. Lawrence*, which provided commentary for the traveller to follow while on tours to Buffalo, Niagara Falls, Toronto, the Thousand Islands, and east along the whole route of the St. Lawrence River to the Atlantic Ocean.

In 1871 the Thousand Islands Railroad was incorporated as the Gananoque & Rideau Railway. Built for the lumber trade by the Rathbun Company of Deseronto, it was a short, 6.3-mile line that connected the waterfront at Gananoque to the Grand Trunk Railway at a junction inland. The Grand Trunk Railway connected the Thousand Islands with the east and west coasts of Canada, bringing hundreds of visitors to the region each summer. There were several stops along the route of the Thousand Islands Railroad. The first stop after leaving the main line was at Cheeseboro, where local farmers brought their milk to a farmers' co-op. The second stop was at the Gananoque Cemetery. Because the road was so poor between the little town and the cemetery to the north, the railway was used to transport coffins and mourners. This became the only place where one could buy a "roundtrip" from the town to the cemetery for a quarter! The next stop was at the "Umbrella" stand in the centre of town. This was a favourite stop for young people, who could ride from the waterfront "up street" (the colloquial term for the main shopping area in Gananoque). The end of the line was at the waterfront. The station and the head office of the railway were built there in 1883. There was no roundhouse at the end of the line, so the engine could not turn around; for that reason the railway used a double-ended locomotive. The engine was uncoupled, travelled on a shore siding back to the other end of the train and was attached for the return journey.

It was said the stationmaster had an uncanny knack of identifying honeymooners. He always acknowledged them with a twinkle in his eye. How? Because unlike regular visitors, they always wore new shoes!

Ferries brought people back and forth across the river. Before the 1870s, when vacationers began to visit the Thousand Islands, the large passenger ships that plied the river between Toronto and Montreal supplied a short-haul service between Kingston, Brockville, Prescott and Ogdensburg. Most ships took the main channel through the American sector, but enough stopped at Gananoque and went along the Canadian shore to provide an adequate service. In 1872 the *D.C. West*, captained by John Roderick, began a ferry service between Clayton and Gananoque. It ran throughout the warmer seasons, but when winter came, the local residents waited for the ice to form, then an ice road was marked with Christmas trees from one shore to the other. Another popular ferry was the *Yennek*, which was the name of its captain, D.J. Kenney, spelled backwards.

Although it was the fishing and hunting that attracted the first wealthy visitors to the region, it was their families who fostered growth. Gentlemen could hire a skiff and a guide for the day, but Mother usually wanted more. Sitting on the verandah at a hotel and gazing at the vacant islands made one dream of owning an island and building a Thousand Islands cottage. It did not take long before many of the islands on the tour-boat route were purchased and houses were built.

Money seemed much in evidence. Private steamers at docks and boatyards abounded. Labour was easily found in the small communities along the shore. Launches brought the workers each

Fishing brought visitors to the islands.

— Jno. Haddock, *A Souvenir, The Thousand Islands of the St. Lawrence River*, 1895

Afternoon teas and picnics were a daily affair.
— Sagastaweka Island family papers, Helen Wright Greuter

morning; barges transported building supplies and household furnishings to the islands. In the winter these were carried across the ice by horse and wagon or sleighs. It did not seem to concern the owners how complicated the building projects were. These were large houses, and even castles, built of granite, fieldstone and wood. Most properties also included wharfs, boathouses and staff accommodations. Landscaping was another subject of great interest, and owners had unusual stone walls built; gardens to supply vegetables were planted, and trees and shrubs were pruned so that each island would look handsome and well groomed. As many as thirty or forty labourers might work on an island each summer.

Not all the dwellings were as opulent as the large homes built near Alexandria Bay. Dozens of Thousand Islands cottages were built on the rocky islands. First a clearing would be made and a canvas tent erected. Stones would be placed in a circle for a campfire and a hole dug "out back" for the privy. One of the most important concerns was a safe landing: a beach had to be cleared for pulling up the skiff or canoe, or a strong dock constructed, so that Mother and Grandmother could disembark and not worry about getting their long skirts wet. After a summer of tenting, a family often hired an architect or a construction company to design and build a summer home. Because of the inconvenience of building on the islands, construction companies often ordered the lumber pre-cut. Many island homes followed the custom of building a main dining room and summer kitchen, and two or three sleeping cabins for the family. There was usually a lean-to near the water for boating equipment and a two- or three-hole outhouse complete with a crescent-shaped moon on the door. Icehouses were constructed with stone foundations and filled during the winter. The ice was packed in sawdust, and this kept the supply in good condition throughout the summer.

It was not unusual for families to arrive at the railway station complete with a cook, nanny, several servants, and of course the children and their pets. One family even brought an iguana to the island for the summer. Accompanying the average family were a dozen trunks filled with long dresses, neatly packed undergarments, long woollen bathing suits, glove boxes. Other trunks contained the necessary linens, silver and china (taken home at the end of each season for safekeeping). There was also an ample supply of writing paper, fishing tackle, bed ticks (mattresses) and pillows. Boatmen were hired to transport the belongings to the island or the hotel. Those who lived in nearby communities often brought even more items to their summer homes, including a piano and a cow for milking!

Some summer people hired their servants when they arrived — a cook, parlour maids, a laundress, boatmen and fishing guides. One, two, or ten men were on hand to maintain the property, build a seawall, clear walking paths and weed gardens. Every large home was built with several guest rooms, and it was not unusual for the island cook to be responsible for preparing a dinner for a family with eight children, many guests and staff — sometimes a hundred a night!

Amusements were plentiful. There were games — Parcheesi, whist, hide-and-seek — and of course the making of ice cream. Preparing this frozen delight could occupy a whole day, with a journey by skiff to a local farm for the cream, then home to pack the churn with rock salt. Turning the crank led to cries of "my turn, my turn," because each time one had to dip a finger to check the consistency. The reward for all this activity was adding the wild berries gathered in the afternoon and sitting on the rocks eating the cold sweet cream dripping in the sun.

Afternoon teas and picnics were a daily affair. Invitations were written and sent by a youngster or a boatman to a neighbouring island. Cookies and cakes were prepared, cucumbers were sliced for sandwiches, and an island blanket and wicker chairs were taken off the porch and placed in the shade on the lawn. The ladies poured tea from china teapots and sat and gossiped while the men smoked their pipes near the dock and discussed the latest engines or the exciting naphtha launches that were appearing on the river. The children, after eating their "tea," explored the island. Teatime lasted late and families rowed home at dusk, enjoying a Thousand Islands sunset.

The St. Lawrence skiff was the official means of transport for island fishermen and boatmen.
— *The Thousand Islands and the River St. Lawrence*, The James Bayne Company

It did not take long before local craftsmen designed a "perfect" craft for the river. It was called the St. Lawrence skiff. It was described as being "built of perfectly knotless pine a trifle more than a quarter of an inch thick." The ribs, made of oak, were set four inches apart and the design ensured that there was a graceful line. The craft was "equally sharp at both ends."

The sailing skiff had a sail and a retractable folding centreboard. There was no rudder, which meant the boatman pulled in the sail and shifted his weight to steer "by so balancing the weight of the boat fore and aft as to drag the stern in going before the wind, and depressing the bow when coming about." But "a lazy person" or "ladies" could use an oar to swing the boat onto another tack. Most skiffs were 21 feet long and had two legless wicker chairs on board. The design of the oar was also important because it had to drop immediately when there was a fish strike. Most communities had their own boatbuilders who prided themselves on their craftsmanship. The St. Lawrence skiff often had a clear shellac finish like that of a fine piano. It cost between $60 and $125 to purchase a skiff in the late 1800s.

One of the favourite sports in the islands was paddling canoes. The American Canoe Association (ACA) fostered this sport with its constitution, which read that the association "shall unite all amateur canoeists for the purpose of pleasure, health and exploration by means of a meeting for business, camping, paddling, sailing and racing, and by keeping logs of voyages, records of waterways, routes, details, drawings and dimensions of boats, and collection of maps, charts and boats."

Originally, the ACA held regattas off Grindstone Island, on Stave Island and on Hay Island, near Gananoque. Then, in 1901, the association negotiated a purchase of Sugar Island in the Lake Fleet. From that year on, canoeing families came to the island every summer. Many who tired of the small tent sites that were the rule there decided to purchase islands for themselves. Dozens of families now living in Thousand Islands Park, and on nearby islands such as Murray and Grennell, have their ACA family members to thank for settling in the region.

Religion was another important aspect of island life. The Methodist campground established in 1874 at Thousand Islands Park, on Wellesley Island, attracted thousands of people to the area, from all parts of both Canada and the United States, to enjoy a family holiday under the direction of their religious leaders. At first the religious camps sold or rented tent lots, but before long, cottages took the place of tents. These communities thrived.

It was in the last decade of the 1800s that the millionaires established their reputation in the islands. These men brought glamour and opulence to the region. The more people saw the wealth in the homes that were built and in the steamboats and runabouts on the river, the more visitors were attracted to the region (see Part II).

The *St. Lawrence Bulletin*, a weekly tourist guide published in 1907, gives a typical review of island life:

> *FURNISHED COTTAGE FOR SALE* — the handsome Irwin place at Fine View, 1000 Islands, 11 bedrooms with running water. Up-to-date in every way. Large boathouses. Sell for cost.
>
> *HANDSOME FAMILY LAUNCH FOR SALE* at a very reasonable price. Length 40 feet x 8 ft. 18 H.P. engine. Mahogany finished, and toilet room. Great bargain for family use or charter.
>
> Dr. George M. McCombs — Resident physician, Hotel Frontenac, may be consulted in his room from 2 to 4 p.m. daily and will respond to calls at nearby resorts.
>
> Mr. and Mrs. J.S. Hood have arrived at the Park to spend their twenty-fifth summer. When Mr. Hood returns to New York the fish in the St. Lawrence will be scarce if he lives up to his past reputation.
>
> *BASEBALL:* What Gananoque did to the Park on Tuesday is a shame to tell about. The final score being 19 to 4 in favor of the visitors.

The ten months old son of Mr. and Mrs. Lee Umsey, who are occupying Bella Vista Lodge, was left near the edge of their dock in his carriage by the maid and a strong wind started the carriage rolling and the baby and it both went in the river. George B. Hartman who was close by fixing a motor boat jumped in and got the cart before it had gone down. For saving it and the baby, which fortunately was only badly frightened, Hartman received a present of a $100 bill for his quick work.

The lack of fire protection in cottages suggests the necessity of having a quick and ready protection. It is very easy to put a fire out at the start and many lives may depend upon immediate action. A good fire extinguisher is worth twenty pails of water and they all hang in one small handsome machine on the wall. Do you want one? They cost about 12 cents to load and will last forever . . .

Fire! — Les Corbin Studio, Clayton, New York

Fire was probably the first cause of change in the Thousand Islands. Until 1911 the river continued its popularity, but when a cigarette ignited a fire at the Frontenac Hotel on Round Island at nine o'clock in the evening of August 23, things began to change. The small fire soon spread, and within two hours one of the largest and most popular resorts was reduced to smouldering rubble.

In 1912 more infernos destroyed houses, boathouses and businesses. In the spring of that year a fire on Grenell Island destroyed five cottages. Several boathouses were lost at Thousand Island Park that same year, as was a whole block of houses. Then, on the afternoon of July 9, the Columbian Hotel at Thousand Island Park caught fire. The fire began innocently enough in a store near the hotel. All those close by tried to help, but short fire hoses proved useless against the intensity of the flames that exploded when a door was opened. Some burning debris caught an awning on fire on the Columbian Hotel, and from then on the flames spread from roof to roof. Burning embers landed several yards from the most concentrated areas and lay smouldering unnoticed until hours later when a house or a barn burst into flames.

The aftermath of the disaster was felt throughout the Thousand Islands. Within a single year two of the largest and most prestigious hotels were gone, never to be rebuilt.

Another indication of decline came with the deaths of some of the wealthiest islanders. George Pullman was first to die, in 1897. Another Alexandria Bay resident, William Browning, died in 1904, and in 1907 Henry Heath left the river, never to return. Heath had come to the islands for more than twenty-five years, and he had been responsible for interesting many of his guests in buying islands of their own.

Calumet Island. — Photograph from a picture book published by the Thousand Island House, Alexandria Bay, George J. Walsh, Proprietor

Boldt Castle. *The Thousand Islands and the River St. Lawrence,* The James Bayne Company

Charles G. Emery died in 1915. He built the first stone castle on his Calumet Island and invested in dozens of business enterprises to promote tourism and prosperity in the region. He purchased the Frontenac Hotel in 1890 and hired architects to renovate the building to "attract a better class" to the islands. His death was a tremendous loss to Clayton and the upper islands.

Downriver, George C. Boldt's death in 1916 was announced with dozens of inches of newsprint in the Thousand Islands and in New York City (see Part II, Heart Island). Boldt spent almost two decades building and landscaping his many island properties. He first rebuilt a wooden cottage on Hart Island (now Heart Island), designed stone walls, and in 1897 built a games room called the Alster Tower. This was followed by the stone Arch of Triumph, which was built at the opening of a lagoon on the west end of the island. A powerhouse was later erected. He also built a mammoth boathouse on Wellesley Island, which lay opposite.

In 1900 Boldt began to build a castle as a present for his wife, Louise. For the next three years workmen built the one-hundred-room granite castle. By the end of 1903 some $2 million had been spent, and deliveries of more marble, windows and wooden panelling were scheduled for the spring. Then, on January 7, 1904, Louise Boldt died. Her death brought a stop to the work on Boldt Castle, but George Boldt continued to build and develop his other properties on Wellesley Island.

A hint of another change in the Thousand Islands was given in newspaper articles. One, written in the summer of 1906 in the *Thousand Islands Sun*, read: "Mr. and Mrs. Charles Haas and daughter Lillian returned home last night in their new touring car which Mr. Haas purchased recently at Grandville. The car is a Cadilack [*sic*] touring car. There is seating capacity for four and is equipped with a 10 H.P. Cadilack engine."

Two years earlier, a Canadian, Arthur Lyman, who had a summer home on Stave Island, had the adventure of driving from Montreal to Gananoque. It took him four days, and he made over twenty-six tire changes! It was not easy to travel from the major metropolitan areas to the Thousand Islands. The roads were dirt tracks, often passing from one farmer's field to another. Visitors always came by rail or by steamer, but by the end of 1910 many were experimenting with the "horseless carriage."

These new vacationers were not interested in an extended holiday on an island but rather in exploring. After driving all day on dusty roads, they did not relish the thought of arriving at a fine hotel and having to "dress" for dinner. The "boot," or luggage compartment, had room for only a small valise. Soon cabins and a place to park a car were more popular than hotels.

Cars drove onto ferries and were taken from one side of the river to the other. Travellers could spend a day in the Thousand Islands and move on.

The First World War brought more changes. Many islands were closed when war was declared. Young men enlisted and the young women stayed home to work in factories. Hired help was scarce. Fuel for motorboats was rationed. Some islanders came back when the war ended, but the advent of income tax, high property taxes and later the Great Depression brought economic hardships to the region. It was the end of the golden era in the Thousand Islands — but not a melancholy ending.

Islands changed hands through the 1920s, '30s and '40s. The new owners, perhaps not as wealthy as the original builders, found summer retreats. Rumrunners, new boats and engines appeared, and a bridge at Ivy Lea to connect the Canadian north shore to the American south side was built in 1938.

A picnic on the American shore, possibly the fourth of July.
— Private collection, Alan Newell, Hammond

Today you can tour the Thousand Islands on a commercial tour boat, on a private yacht, in a sailboat or motorboat, even a canoe. When you find yourself in a quiet channel away from cottages and boats, you may think you have discovered the same islands that were described in the journals and diaries written over the past three centuries.

Like the French governor Rémy de Courcelle, you too will have a hard time finding your way through the labyrinth of islands. But unlike Courcelle, you will probably not describe the region as a "melancholy abode." Thanks to Capt. William FitzWilliam Owen, you will follow safe passages drawn on hydrographic charts. You will know which islands are Canadian or American. You may also have the chance to purchase an island and build a castle or a Thousand Island cottage of your own.

ENDNOTES AND FURTHER READING

References are listed in their complete form in the Bibliography. For ease of reading, there are no endnote numbers in the text, instead quoted material is cited here, using identifying passages.

CHAPTER 1 **DISCOVERERS AND EXPLORERS, 1650-1760**

P. 17 The de Courcelle voyage. . .; E.B. O'Callaghan, *The Documentary History of the State of New York* (1850), Vol. I.

P. 19 Early travel. . .; Ruth McKenzie, Leeds and Grenville (Toronto, 1967).

P. 19 Baptismal service on Tar Island. . .; Allan Westcott, *The Thousand Islands and St. Lawrence Border: Their History, Legends and Romance* (unpublished manuscript, c.1960).

P. 20 Jean Deshayes survey. . .; Don Thomson, *Men and Meridians* (Ottawa, 1966).

P. 20 Galley slaves. . .; Francis Parkman, *Count Frontenac and New France Under Louis XIV* (Boston, 1877).

P. 20 Father Millet. . .; Thwaits' *Les Rélations des Jesuits* Vol. 64.

P. 21 Frontenac's return. . .; Parkman, op. cit.

P. 22 Father Charlevoix travels. . .; Franklin B. Hough, *A History of St. Lawrence and Franklin Counties, New York* (Albany, 1853).

P.22 Account of the Lost Channel. . .; Jno. A. Haddock, *A Souvenir, The Thousand Islands of the St. Lawrence River* (Alexandria Bay, N.Y., 1895).

P.22 Bradstreet's attack on Fort Frontenac. . .; Col. John Bradstreet, *An Impartial Account of Lieut. Col. Bradstreet's Expedition to Fort Frontenac* (Toronto, 1940).

Further reading: Richard A. Preston and Leopold Lamontagne, *Royal Fort Frontenac* (Toronto, 1958); Franklin B. Hough, *A History of St. Lawrence and Franklin Counties, New York* (Albany, 1853).

CHAPTER 2 **THE FORT ON CARLETON ISLAND, 1778–1783**

The primary source for this chapter is the Haldimand Papers collection, held by the National Archives of Canada, transcribed from the originals, which are held in the British Museum.

P. 25 "This is by. . .; Richard A. Preston, *Kingston Before the War of 1812, A Collection of Documents* (Toronto, 1959).

P. 25 "I will rely. . .; Ibid.

P. 25 Site comparison. . .; Ibid.

P. 26 Military actions from Carleton Island. . .; C.C.J. Bond, "The British Base at Carleton Island," *Ontario History* (March 1960), Vol. LII, No. 11-16.

P. 27 Molly Brant. . .; Preston, op.cit.

P. 27 Description of the Fort. . .; J.H. Durham, *Carleton Island in the Revolution: The Old Fort and Its Builders* (Syracuse, 1889).

P. 28 Mississauga review. . .; Donald B. Smith, "The Dispossession of the Mississauga Indians: A Missing Chapter in the Early History of Upper Canada," *Ontario History* (June 1981), Vol. LXXIII, No. 2.

P. 29 Mississauga surrender. . .; J.L. Morris, *Indians of Ontario* (n.d.).

CHAPTER 3 **SETTLEMENT OF THE CANADIAN SHORE, 1783–1812**

Much has been written about the United Empire Loyalists' settlement in the Upper Canada, but little information is available about settlement on the islands themselves.

P. 31 "We arrived at. . ."; *Report on Canadian Archives 1884-1889*, Series B., Vol. 169, with a description given by Capt. Justice Sherwood, and again in the *Report of the Department of Public Records, and Archives of Ontario* (Ottawa, 1928), #45.

P. 32 Settlement of Gananoque. . .; H. Wm. Hawke, *Miss McCammon's Notes of the Early Days of Gananoque* (Gananoque, Ont., unpublished notes, 1967).

P. 32 Joel Stone. . .; Ronald McMurrich, "Joel Stone and the Founding of Gananoque," *Historic Kingston*, Vol. 11-12.

P. 32 Family settlement; Stone, Landon, Mallory, Sherwood, Jones (Daniel) and Jones (Charles); Thad. W.H. Leavitt. *The History of Leeds and Grenville* (Brockville, Recorder Press, 1879).

P. 35-36 Mrs. Simcoe's journey. . .; J. Ross Robertson, *The Diary of Mrs. John Graves Simcoe, Wife of the First Lieutenant-Governor of the Province of Upper Canada, 1792–96* (Toronto, 1911). The Robertson work has informative footnotes and references.

CHAPTER 4 **SETTLEMENT OF THE AMERICAN SHORE, 1790–1812**

Unlike the rich history of the United Empire Loyalist settlements on the Canadian shore, the American mainland and the islands did not receive much coverage in history books. The most information appears in the 1853 and 1854 Hough histories of St. Lawrence, Franklin and Jefferson counties.

P. 39 Macomb on Carleton Island. . .; J.H. Durham, *Carleton Island in the Revolution: The Old Fort and Its Builders* (Syracuse, 1889).

P. 39-40 Macomb purchase. . .; Hough, 1854, op. cit.

P. 40 Castorland settlement. . .; Jno. Haddock: *A Souvenir, The Thousand Islands of the St. Lawrence River* (Alexandria Bay, N.Y., 1895); T. Woods Clarke, *Émigrés in the Wilderness* (New York, 1941); Thomas F. Powell, *Penet's Square* (Lakemont, N.Y., 1976); Edith Pilcher, *Castorland, French Refugees in the Western Adirondacks 1793-1814* (Harrison, N.Y., 1985).

P. 41-42 James LeRay de Chaumont. . .; Hough, 1854, op. cit.; Haddock, op. cit.; Clarke, op. cit.; Powell, op. cit. and Pilcher, op. cit.

P. 42 Clayton, Alexandria Bay, Hammond and Morristown settlement. . .; Hough, 1854, op. cit.; Haddock, op. cit.

CHAPTER 5 THE THOUSAND ISLANDS AND THE WAR OF 1812

Finding information on the War of 1812 is not difficult. There are hundreds of books and journals devoted to that subject in both Canada and the United States. However, very little was written about the battles and events in the Thousand Islands in particular. What is available appears in the Hough and Haddock books and in the regular archival material relating to the war.

P. 45 "Some of our. . ."; Hough, 1854, op.cit.

P. 45-54 War of 1812, U.S. perspective. . .; Hough, 1854, op. cit.

P. 45-54 War of 1812, Canadian perspective. . .; Levitt, op. cit.

P. 49-50 Gunboat patrols . . .; Judith Beattie, "Gunboats on the St. Lawrence River, (1763–1839)."

P. 51-52 War of 1812. . .; G.F.G. Stanley, *Conflicts & Social Notes* (Mallorytown, Ont., 1976).

Further reading: C.P. Stacey, "The Ships of the British Squadron on Lake Ontario, 1812-14," *Canadian Historical Review*, XXXIV.

CHAPTER 6 CAPT. WILLIAM FITZWILLIAM OWEN AND THE FIRST SURVEY, 1815–1817

The most important sources of information about the survey of the Thousand Islands can be found in the National Archives of Canada, in Ottawa, where they are accessible on microfilm. More itemized references can be found in the finder's files: Admiralty 1, Secretary's Department-in-Letters, Captains' Letters "O", Numbers 1-50, 1816.

P. 55 "Wind down the. . . "; The survey instructions appear on microfilm: B-2786, Adm. 1, Vol. 2264.

P. 55, 58-60 Capt. William FitzWilliam Owen. . .; Edmund H. Burrows, *Captain William FitzWilliam Owen of the African Survey: The Hydrographic Surveys of Admiral W.F.W. Owen on the Coast of Africa and the Great Lakes of Canada* (Amsterdam, 1985). A chapter is devoted to the Thousand Islands survey and the survey of the Canadian Lakes. Other biographical information can be found in the Owen ship's logs located in the National Maritime Museum, Greenwich, England. Permission to print the portrait of Captain William FitzWilliam Owen was given by the Campobello Historical Society Museum and Library, Campobello Island, New Brunswick.

P. 56-57 The 1816 chart of the Thousand Islands appearing in Part II is housed in the British Hydrographic Archives, National Department of Defence, Taunton, England.

CHAPTER 7 CREATING THE INTERNATIONAL BOUNDARY LINE, 1818

We are fortunate to have a complete review of the International Boundary Survey recorded by Maj. Joseph Delafield in his personal diaries.

P. 61 International boundary line survey. . .; Robert McElroy and Thomas Riggs, ed., *The Unfortified Boundary: A Diary of the First Survey of the Canadian Boundary Line from St. Regis to the Lake of the Woods by Major Joseph Delafield* (privately printed, New York; 1943).

P. 61 "When the survey. . ."; James White, *Boundary Disputes and Treaties* (Toronto, 1914).

CHAPTER 8 SQUATTERS AND MISSISSAUGAS ON THE CANADIAN ISLANDS, 1820–1856

One of the best histories of Leeds and Grenville counties was written in 1879 by Thad. W.H. Leavitt. *The History of Leeds and Grenville* (Brockville, Recorder Press, 1879) describes towns, villages and crossroads in the counties. There are several sections devoted to the Thousand Islands. This book was reprinted in a facsimile edition by Mika Press in Belleville in 1972.

P. 65 "A few Indians. . ."; Leavitt, op. cit.

P. 66 Steamboat travel. . .; Richard F. Palmer, "First Steamboat on the Great Lakes," Eames papers.

P. 67-69 Mississauga Band and the Grape Island settlement. . .; Peter Jones (Kah-Ke-Wa-Quo-Na-By), *Life and Journals of Kah-Ke-Wa-Quo-Na-By* (Toronto, 1860); Donald Smith, "The Dispossession of the Mississauga Indians: A Missing Chapter in the Early History of Upper Canada," *Ontario History* (June, 1981), Vol. LXXIII, No. 2.

P. 69 Surrender No. 77. . . ; *Canada, Indian Treaties and Surrenders, From 1680-1890 in Two Volumes*; Number 77, 2 Vols. (1891, facsimile edition, 1971).

Further reading: Ina Scott, *Yesterday's News, Today's History* (Gananoque, Ont., 1982).

CHAPTER 9 THE PATRIOT WAR, 1837–1838

P. 73-77 The Patriot War. . . ; Harry F. Landon, *History of the North Country* in 3 Vols. (Indianapolis, 1932).

P. 74-75 Elizabeth Barnett. . . ; "Hickory Island Attack," *Gananoque Reporter*, June 1888.

P. 75-76 Sir Robert Peel. . . ; G.F.G. Stanley, *Conflicts & Social Notes: The War of 1812-1814, The Patriot War – 1837/8* (1976).

Further reading: Roy. F. Fleming, "St. Lawrence River Pirate," *Inland Seas* (Spring 1976), Vol. 17, No. 1.

CHAPTER 10 THE AMERICAN ISLANDS FOR SALE, 1822–1872

Good reference material on land sales of the American islands is found in Franklin B. Hough's *History of Jefferson County in the State of New York*. Also, Jno. Haddock's *A Souvenir, The Thousand Islands of the St. Lawrence River* provides valuable reference material for this chapter.

P. 79 Joseph Boneparte's presence in Jefferson County. . . ; Clarke, *Émigrés in the Wilderness*, op. cit.

P. 80-81 Land titles. . . ; Hough, 1854, op. cit.

P. 81-83 Meadow Island. . . : Andrew Cornwall's historic notebook, located in the Jefferson County Historical Society Museum under *Thousand Islands*.

P. 83 Island publicity. . . ; Haddock, op. cit.

CHAPTER 11 THE CANADIAN ISLANDS FOR SALE, 1862–1894

Much of the information concerning surveys and evaluations of the Canadian islands appears in the McNaughton, Unwin and Beatty field notes available for researchers in the Department of Mines and Resources, Ottawa, Ontario.

P. 87 "It is stated. . ."; *Gananoque Reporter*, "The Thousand Islands," 20 April 1873.

P. 87 "hoped the idea. . ."; *Gananoque Reporter*, "The Thousand Islands," 30 May 1873.

P. 90 "seem to be . . ."; *Gananoque Reporter*, "Sale of Islands," 18, July 1891.

P. 91-92 Island sales. . . ; NAC, RG10, Red Series, Vol. 2495. Islands are recorded under the heading of Alnwick Reserve but scattered in several files (see Bibliography).

P. 91-92 Island sales. . . ; NAC, RG10, Red Series C1132, Vol. 3013, File 7944.

CHAPTER 12 ISLAND LIVING, 1860–1910

Several local histories record life in the Thousand Islands

P. 93 "There is so . . ."; E.F. Babbage, *The Phat Boys Racy Description of the St. Lawrence River and Its Environs* (Rochester, N.Y., 1887).

P. 94 Island popularity. . . ; Jno. Haddock, *A Souvenir, The Thousand Islands of the St. Lawrence River* (1895).

P. 94 Capt. Visger's tours. . . ; Les and Verda Corbin, *The Visgers' World* (Clayton, N.Y., 1987).

P. 101 Fire. . . ; Helen P. Jacox and Eugene B. Kleinhans, Jr., *Thousand Island Park: One Hundred Years, and Then Some* (Thousand Island Park, N.Y., 1975).

P. 101-102 Island life. . . ; Laurie Ann Nulton, *The Golden Age of the Thousand Islands, Its People and Its Castles* (1981 as a Master of Arts thesis in History at Georgetown University). The thesis was published in a book form posthumously by her father, Thomas Nulton, and includes photographs from the Les Corbin Collection, Clayton, N.Y.

Further reading: Susan N. Manes, *Who's Up?* (Chippawa Bay, N.Y., 1981); Margaret Nulty, *Murray Isle* (Murray Island, N.Y., 1972); Elizabeth P. Stamp, *Glimpses of Grand View* (Spokane, Wash., 1988); and A.G. Ten Cate and M.B. Fryer, *Pictorial History of the Thousand Islands* (Brockville, Ont., 1982).

PART II

ISLAND DESCRIPTIONS

SECTION I **THE CANADIAN ISLANDS**

KEY TO THE CANADIAN ISLANDS

Island Name or Number

Unless otherwise identified, the island name appearing in the text was recorded in 1873 by Charles Unwin on his plan of the Thousand Islands (Plan number: 512–515). Unwin recorded names and whole numbers from Island 1 to Island 122. In 1894 Walter Beatty added numbers and letters to Unwin's plan; therefore all islands identified by numbers and letters were named by Walter Beatty.

The islands are listed in geographic order, beginning east of Howe Island, near Gananoque, Ontario, and travelling east to the islands lying off the city of Brockville, Ontario. They follow the same order as recorded in Charles Unwin's field notebook and the published records of Walter Beatty.

Historic Name

The historic name was given by Capt. William FitzWilliam Owen on the British Admiralty charts dated 1815, 1828 or 1861. Each name is identified in a group (i.e., Admiralty Islands, the Navy Group, the Brock Isles, etc.). Where possible, biographical information about the commemorated person is included.

Lists are provided that register the islands in the groups as designated by Capt. William FitzWilliam Owen. Owen did not follow the international boundary line, so some islands are recorded in groups on both sides of the border. An example is in the Lake Fleet, where all but one island, Jolly Island, falls in Canadian waters. The Lake Fleet list will appear in the Canadian section of Part II; however, the Jolly Island listing will appear in the American section. The same holds true for the Wellington Islands (those islands lying around Wellesley Island) and the Amateur Islands (near Crossover Light, east of Chippewa Bay and Grenadier Island).

Evaluations and Descriptions

The information in this section is dated and the name of the survey is included. The evaluations and descriptive paragraphs that appeared on sale lists or in government files are also included. These surveys were recorded in 1862 by John McNaughton, in 1873 by Charles Unwin, and in 1893 by Walter Beatty. The Beatty surveys were actually made in 1891 and 1893, but the work was not published until 1894.

In some cases only the Unwin evaluation is given. Many islands were leased or petitioned for ownership, and as a result Beatty was instructed not to evaluate the islands.

Island Notes

Where possible, historical information relating to the island *prior* to its purchase by "summer people" has been recorded, as well as some information about the first island purchaser. ***This is by no means a complete history, but rather an example of the information available in archive records, newspaper articles and family histories.***

Sale

Usually the name of the first island purchaser is listed. For the most part, names of those who bought islands after 1920 are excluded, as are the sale date and ownership information of islands in the St. Lawrence Islands National Park system.

The dates of island sales are approximations because the islands were sold and administered by the Department of Indian Affairs, and even though a sale took place in 1894 (the year most islands were sold), the county registry office did not record the sale until 1897, or in some cases the early 1900s. In many cases the original purchaser never went to the island, but rather sold it soon after for a profit. For that reason current island owners may repudiate the information given in the text.

Readers may be disappointed not to find more island sales recorded. Those wishing specific information will find complete records in the county registry office in Brockville, Ontario. The records are in the public domain.

More than fifty islands are recorded as sold to the W.D. Morris Real Estate Company. When possible, the date of subsequent sales of these islands is given, often demonstrating that Morris had to retain ownership for several decades before the company realized profits.

The author apologizes for possible misspellings of names and incorrect historical information. There is little primary source material, and it was necessary to rely on newspaper articles, which often contain mistakes.

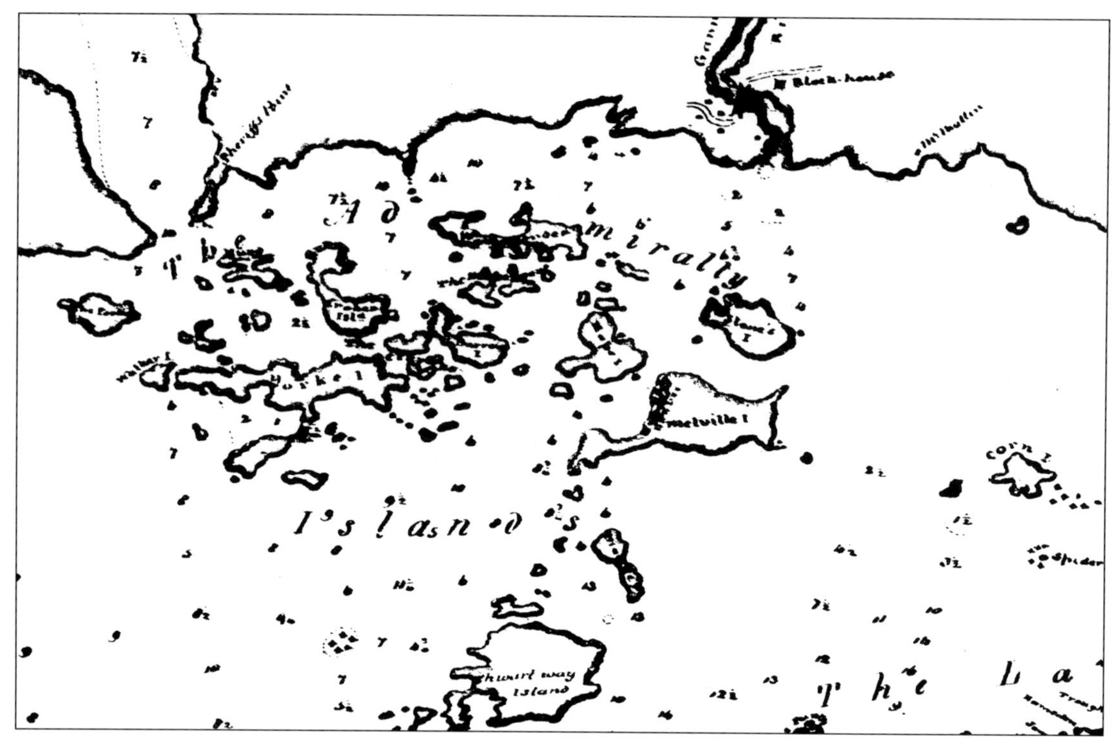

The Admiralty Islands

Capt. William FitzWilliam Owen was resourceful in setting the names on his first completed charts of the Canadian Lake Survey. He began by flattering the members of the Admiralty Office who controlled British naval affairs, by calling twelve islands the Admiralty Islands.

The Admiralty Committee consisted of a principal lord, five other lords (one being a member of Parliament), a parliamentary secretary and a permanent secretary. These were assisted by a group of civil servants, including clerks. In addition, a number of subordinate staff were employed, such as messengers, a porter, a housekeeper and even a "necessary woman."

HISTORIC NAME	PRESENT NAME	PAGE
The Porter	Aubrey Island (Canadian)	111
Walker	Mermaid Island (Canadian)	111
Hurd	Beau Rivage Island (Canadian)	113
Yorke	Bostwick Island (Canadian)	115
Croker	Lindsay Island (Canadian)	114
The Clerks	Sagastaweka Island, Island 17	121
	and Island 18 (Canadian)	122
Barrow	Mudlunta Island (Canadian)	120
Warrender	McDonald Island (Canadian)	116
The Messengers	Burnt Island, Pitch Pine Island,	119
	Island 14 (Canadian)	119
Hope	Forsyth Island (Canadian)	123
Stone's	Tremont Park (Canadian)	126
Melville	Hay Island (Canadian)	126
Moore	Huckleberry Island (Canadian)	127
Thwart Way	Thwartway Island (Canadian)	127

AUBREY ISLAND

Historic Name

1816: Owen — The Porter, the Admiralty Islands
The name *The Porter* does not appear on the engraved chart as such; rather, it is shortened to *Porter*. It honours the position, or job, of the porter in the Admiralty office. The porter during the time of the survey was James Newbegin, serving from 1808 until November 1817. The correct name did appear on the original hand-drawn chart.

This island has been known by more official names than most in the Thousand Islands. The Owen name appeared on the early (1816, 1828 and 1868) Admiralty charts. In 1862 the surveyor John McNaughton referred to the island as Bear Island. In addition, it was registered as Bird Island, Marvin Island, after a lighthouse keeper, and as Dark Island and Snake Island. When the island was reserved as a Canadian park island in the early 1900s, the name was changed to Aubrey Island. No reason for the change is given in park files. It is possible that a department employee decided on the names on his own because there is no correlation between the ten names that were used for any of the park islands.

One of the interesting mistakes that was made on Canadian hydrographic maps is the name change of Aubrey Island and that of a small island in the Wanderers Channel, Burnt Island. The names were mixed up on a chart one year and the name Burnt has remained. It is only since the 1970s that the park has made a concerted effort to use only Aubrey when referring to this park island.

Evaluations and Descriptions

1862: McNaughton 13.55 acres Value: $320
"Has light house No. 18 with house for keeper of the light house, upon it — is said to have been secured by the Board of Works, under the name of Bird Island."
1873: Unwin 14.3 acres Value: $150
"Has light house on east end and light house keepers house near the centre of Island, around the house there are one and one half acres cleared, which are very good for garden purposes, the uncleared portion is covered with scrubby timber and very little of it is tillable."

Island Notes

John McNaughton used the island as the base camp when he made his survey of Mississauga land in 1862. In the 1870s Joseph Merwin lived on the island and built his house and outbuildings, but he sold them to the government when they built a lighthouse on the island. He was lighthouse keeper for several years. Merwin cleared one acre of the island for his crops and also planted an orchard with four apple, plum and cherry trees. Some of his perennial day lily plants still bloom on the island every summer.

Sale

This island was never sold or leased but was placed on a reserve list to be used as a park island. It is now part of the National Park Service, St. Lawrence Islands National Park.

MERMAID ISLAND

Historic Name

1816: Owen — Walker, the Admiralty Islands
Probably after Michael Walker (d. 1864), supernumerary clerk, appointed in 1811. Walker was a member of the famous family who served as hydrographers, draftsmen and engravers to the British Admiralty. Michael and his brother Thomas were employed at the Admiralty as chart draftsmen. Michael Walker served for thirty years, retiring in 1864. Between 1811 and 1816 there were six supernumerary clerks hired by the Admiralty.

The island was called Pine Island by early local residents, named for the large pine trees that grew on the west end of the island. Many of these beautiful trees were destroyed by hurricane-force winds in the 1950s.

In 1904 by a government order-in-council the name was changed to Mermaid Island. No reason is given for the name change. The park erroneously says that "Mermaid" was the name of a gunboat used in the War of 1812 and named by Captain Owen. This is not so, since Owen called the island Walker.

Evaluations and Descriptions

1862: McNaughton 4.0 acres Value $10
"There are some young pines on it, which if undisturbed will, in a few years be of value."
1873: Unwin 3.8 acres Value $50
"Covered with thick brush, no large timber and no arable land."

Sale

This island was never sold or leased but was placed on a reserve list to be used as a park island. It is now part of the National Park Service, St. Lawrence Islands National Park.

WINDWARD ISLAND

Names

Unwin identified the island as Island 1.

Evaluations and Descriptions

1873: Unwin 0.8 acre Value: $20
"High rocky island pretty well covered with trees."

Sale

1897 sold to James H. Worman

PICNIC ISLAND

Names

Unwin identified the island as Island 2.

Evaluations and Description

1873: Unwin 0.4 acres Value: $25
"Very rough, high and rocky, pretty well covered with small timber."

Sale

1897: to Susan W. Ogden for $500 with Island 3.

ISLAND 2A

Evaluations and Descriptions

1894: Beatty 1/50 Value: $25
"Reef, covered in high water."

OAKDEN ISLAND

Names

Unwin identified the island as Island 3.

Evaluations and Description

1873: Unwin 1.2 acres Value: $20

"Very rough, high and rocky covered with brush and small trees, channel between it and No. 2 is dry in low water."

Sale

1897: to Susan W. Ogden for $500 with Island 2.

INDIANA ISLAND

Names

Unwin identified the island as Island 4. The Drummonds, who purchased the island, were from Indiana.

Evaluations and Descriptions

1873: Unwin 0.5 acre Value: $15

"High and rocky with a few trees on it."

Sale

1897: to Charles P. Drummond with Island 5.

BUTTON ISLAND

Names

Unwin identified the island as Island 5. The Button family gave the new name as Button Island.

Evaluations and Descriptions

1873: Unwin 0.4 acre Value: $10

"Low and rocky, a little brush on it."

Sale

1897: to Charles P. Drummond with Island 4.

ISLAND 6

Evaluations and Descriptions

1873: Unwin 2.5 acres Value: $40

"Low, some soil, chiefly covered with second growth timber, and large trees."

Sale

1891: to Dr. W.L. Atkinson for $300.

Island #4, Indiana. — Marshall Bros, 1912

THE BINNACLE

Names

Unwin identified the island as Island 7. One of the more recent owners (1960s) gave the nautical name, believing that it was more in keeping with the Admiralty Islands.

Evaluations and Descriptions

1873: Unwin 0.2 acre Value: $5

"High smooth rock, with about half a dozen small pines on."

1894: Beatty 1/5 acre Value: $200

"High; rocky; commanding a beautiful view; approach excellent; pine trees."

Sale

1908: to Elizabeth C. Forman.

ISLAND 7B

Evaluations and Descriptions

1894: Beatty 1/20 acre Value: $30

"Rocky reef."

Sale

1906: to W. John Hastings.

ISLAND 7C

Evaluations and Descriptions

1894: Beatty 1/20 acre Value: $30

"Rocky reef."

ISLAND 7D

Evaluations and Descriptions

1894: Beatty 1/10 acre Value: $80

"Long; low; well situated; some scrub."

Sale

1904: to David H. Rogers for $130.

ISLAND 7E

Evaluations and Descriptions

1894: Beatty 1/10 acre Value: $30

"Rocky reef."

Sale

1933: to Drifters Club of Gananoque Ltd. for $60.

ISLAND 7F

Evaluations and Descriptions

1894: Beatty 1/50 acre Value: $30

"Rock, 3 feet above water."

Sale

1904: to Drifters Club of Gananoque Ltd.

ISLAND 7G

Evaluations and Descriptions

1894: Beatty 1/20 acre Value: $40

"Rough; rocky; some scrub."

Sale

1904: to Drifters Club of Gananoque Ltd.

ISLAND 7H

Evaluations and Descriptions

1894: Beatty 1/80 acre Value: $10

"Rock, 3 feet above water."

Sale

1933: to Drifters Club of Gananoque Ltd.

ISLAND 7I

Evaluations and Descriptions

1894: Beatty 1/30 acre Value: $25

"Rocky reef."

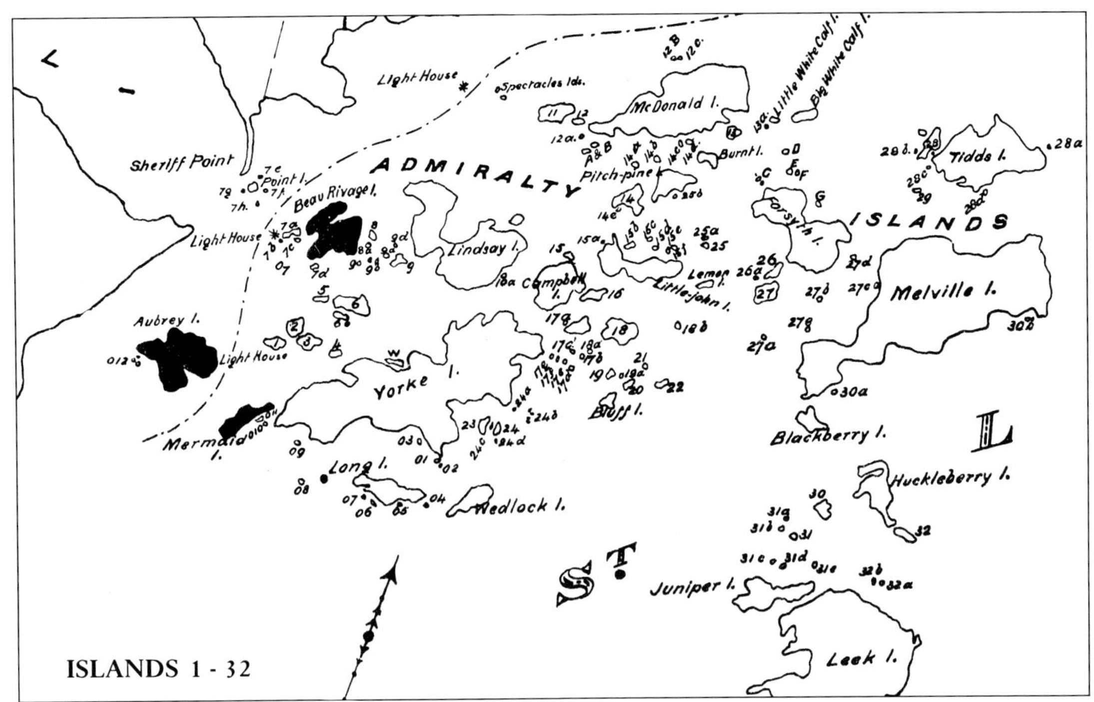

ISLANDS 1 - 32

BEAU RIVAGE ISLAND

Historic Name

1816: Owen — Hurd, the Admiralty Islands Named after Thomas Hurd (c. 1757–1823), hydrographer for the British Admiralty. Hurd first served in the British Navy in Newfoundland and on the North American Station. In the 1790s he was sent to the West Indies and made the first survey of Bermuda. In 1808 he was appointed the hydrographer to the Admiralty, an office he held for fifteen years. During this period he persuaded the Admiralty to publish their charts, and these enabled merchant ships to navigate in charted waters. Hurd died while in office.

The island was locally known as Buck Island because John Buck was the lighthouse keeper.

As in the case of the other St. Lawrence Islands National Park islands, there is no reason given for the official name change to Beau Rivage Island, which occurred by an order-in-council.

Evaluations and Descriptions

1862: McNaughton 14.25 acres Value $100

"Light house No. 17 is connected with this island by bridge. The residence of the overseer of light house in this vicinity is built upon it."

1873: Unwin 10.3 acres Value $250

"Very fine Island, with shade trees, it is occupied by John Buck who has charge of the Light Houses at west of this Id. and on the Spectacles. There is a small island between it and the light house which is used as a means of connection. There is about one acre cleared used as a garden."

Island Notes

Several lighthouse keepers occupied this island. John Buck was the keeper in the 1870s. There was a house and orchard as well as a cleared acre for crops. More than 150 cords of oak were cut off the island at one time. A government evaluation once considered the house and orchard worth $75.

Sale

This island was never sold or leased but was placed on a reserve list to be used as a Park Island. It is now part of the National Park Service, St. Lawrence Island National Park.

JACKSTRAW LODGE

Names

Charles Unwin identified the island as Island 8.

Evaluations and Descriptions

1873: Unwin 0.2 acre Value: $15

"Rocky bluff with a few trees."

Island Notes

Leased by John L. Upham for twenty years in 1893.

ISLAND 8A

Evaluations and Descriptions

1894: Beatty 1/12 acre Value: $30

"Rocky reef, valuable on account of its situation."

Sale

1911: to George H. Bowen.

ISLAND 8B

Evaluations and Descriptions

1894: Beatty 1/30 acre Value: $35

"Bluff, rocky islet."

ISLAND 8C

Evaluations and Descriptions

1894: Beatty 1/150 acre Value: $10

"High rocky islet in deep water."

BIRCHHOLME ISLAND

Names

Charles Unwin identified this as Island 9.

Evaluations and Descriptions

1873: Unwin 0.6 acre Value: $20

"Low and rocky."

Sale

1894: to Rev. James Allan for $200.

ISLAND 9A

Evaluations and Descriptions

1894: Beatty 1/10 acre Value: $75

"Wooded with pine; well located; high and suitable for building."

Sale

1898: to Rev. James Allan for $75.

ISLAND 9B & ISLAND 9C

Evaluations and Descriptions

1894: Beatty 1/10 acre Value: $50

"Two reefs, which together would form a good foundation for an island; bare, large boulders."

Sale

1898: to Rev. James Allan for $75.

ISLAND 9D

Evaluations and Descriptions

1894: Beatty 1/50 acre Value: $10

"Exposed rocks on a shoal that might be improved."

Sale

1898: to Rev. James Allan.

ISLAND 10

Evaluations and Descriptions

1894: Beatty 5/10 acre Value: $15

"Low and covered with small brush."

Sale

1897: to Elena M. Mercer.

ISLAND 10A

Evaluations and Descriptions

1894: Beatty 1/8 acre Value: $100

"Low; rocky; with a few trees and good harbour; excellent location."

Sale

1904: to G. Belfie.

Some islands were identified with letters only.

ISLAND C

Evaluations and Descriptions

1894: Beatty 1/3 acre Value: $100

"Well situated; good soil; some scrub; approach and view excellent; including shoal to north."

ISLAND D

Evaluations and Descriptions

1894: Beatty 1/5 acre Value: $100

"Well situated; good soil; scrub; approach and view excellent; a shoal on east side included."

ISLAND G

Evaluations and Descriptions

1894: Beatty 1/10 acre Value: $100

"Small island artificially joined to Parmenter or Forsyth Island by stone filling."

ISLAND G1

Evaluations and Descriptions

1894: Beatty 1/5 acre Value: $250

"High reef; well situated."

ISLAND G2 AND ISLAND G3

Evaluations and Descriptions

1894: Beatty 1/20 acre Value: $50

"Very low; rocky reefs lying together; in front of Gananoque."

LINDSAY ISLAND

Historic Name

1816: Owen — Croker, the Admiralty Islands

Named after John William Croker, a member of the British Admiralty, a politician and an essayist.

As first secretary of the Admiralty during the Owen survey, Croker wrote the dispatches between the Admiralty Office in England and Captain Owen's headquarters in Kingston.

The island was locally known in the 1860s by two names: Joel and Lindsay. The Lindsay farm was located on the mainland opposite the island, and the Lindsay family used the island as pastureland for their cattle every summer.

Evaluations and Descriptions

1873: Unwin 32 acres Value: $320

"Has about 1/4 acres cleared, it is rather rough, there was a small house on it but has fallen down. Covered with a small second growth. Was sold a good many years ago by Turcott who then occupied it to Bryant, at that time light House keeper on Bucks Island. Bryant's widow sold it to Lindsay about ten years since, Lindsay has recently sold it to J.S. Dennis of Ottawa."

Sunday evening Vesper services were held in Half Moon Bay at Bostwick Island.
— Author's collection

Island Notes

According to a government report written in 1872, "There have been 4 acres cleared. Thomas Lindsay claims as having bought from Widow Bryant, not known by whom improved. It is not at present cultivated. The clearance is worth about $20. A great quantity of timber has been removed. Coles [*sic*] Turcott (from Bostwick Island) admitted to me that he had purchased from Mr. Lindsay, who being absent from home was unable to arrive of facts. Lindsay is a well to do farmer and able to pay. There is still a great deal of young timber, maple, hemlock, birch and oak and ash, which if protected will in a few years be valuable. The island is prettily situated and has Red Granite of rich quality on it. There is also good fishing grounds. Mr. Thos. Lindsay, to whose farm it is opposite, is an applicant for the island and the light House keeper at Spectacle Shoal and the Red Horse dock wishes to have it purchased by the Marine and Fisheries Department as an adjunct to his present place of abode for pasture, garden, etc."

Sale

Originally sold by C. Turcott to Bryant, who was the lighthouse keeper on Bucks Island. Bryant's widow sold it to Thomas Lindsay about 1860, and Lindsay eventually sold it to J.S. Dennis of Ottawa for a summer home.

BOSTWICK ISLAND

Historic Name

1816: Owen — Yorke, the Admiralty Islands
Named after Sir Joseph Sydney Yorke, who was a commissioner in the British Admiralty Office. His name appears in the November 1813 *Gentlemen's Magazine* in an appointment list from Whitehall, as a commissioner for the office of lord high admiral. He is listed as being a rear admiral.

James White's *Place-Names in the Thousand Islands*, 1910, lists the island as being named in honour of Rt. Hon. Chas. Philip Yorke, but this is probably a mistake since the other islands commemorate the other commissioners appointed at the same time.

The island was locally known as Bostwick Island. The origin of this name is debatable because it is recorded on maps printed in the late 1800s as Boss Dick Island. Boss Dick is said to be the name of the foreman of the granite quarry on the island. However, one of the descendants of the Turcott family, disputes this meaning and says the island name was Bostwick, named after one of the first paying guests who stayed at the Bostwick Island Guest House, run by the Turcott family, in the late 1800s.

Evaluations and Descriptions

1873: Unwin 89.3 acres Value: $800
"About 15 acres cleared, the remainder is covered with small timber and is rocky, the cleared portion is of fair quality. Collies Turcott is the occupant, he bought the 'Right' from Mrs. Julia McDonald, widow of the late Hon. Jno McDonald of Gananoque, all papers concerning possession are in the hands of J. Parmenter J.P. of Gananoque. Improvements worth $350."

BLACKDUCK ISLAND

Names

Locally known as Long Island and Blackduck Island.

Evaluations and Descriptions

1873: Unwin 5.5 acres Value: $50
"Partially cleared — no timber scrubby brush, it is claimed by Collies Turcott who bought it from J. Turcott, but has no record of sale, about half is arable but of poor quality."
1894: Beatty 5 5/10 acres Value: $400
"Well raised, flat island, level surface plenty of scrub and some timber. Good soil, fronts on well protected channel on north and has good harbour on west for small boats — good fishing ground, can be reached by steamer from main channel."

Island Notes

After purchasing the island in the 1890s, Irving Rouse and his brother Beckman Rouse stayed in the Bostwick Island Guest House while they designed and had two cottages built. Transportation to and from an island dwelling could be complicated. Often the father of the household had to return to the city to work and leave his wife and children on the island. It was a long way to row to Clayton, where the New York trains came to the river, and those who had to catch the train on Sunday had difficulty hiring boatmen to come to an island and pick up a passenger. The solution found at Blackduck was to have the Rouse children row the skiff out into the river, with their father, dressed for the train ride, sitting in the bow. They would hail the passing ferryboat, and the boat would stop to let the passenger come aboard. Shouts including "Be a good girl and row right home" could be heard as the steamer began to move across the river.

Sale

1894: To Irving and Beckman Rouse.

HEMLOCK ISLAND

Evaluations and Descriptions

1873: Unwin 3.2 acres Value: $25

"High and rocky, no arable land, some small trees, no claimant."

1894: Beatty 3 2/10 acres Value: $350

"Beautiful view; good fishing ground; close to Bostwick and other valuable islands; good building sites, harbourage and soil; scrub and fine growth of evergreen, hemlock, pine and cedar."

Island Notes

In 1894 this island was purchased sight unseen by an American who left for Europe that same spring. On his return he planned to spend his summer holiday on the island, but was informed that it had been completely burned over by a fire. He wrote to the Department of Indian Affairs complaining that the island was worthless "barren rock" and said he did not want to buy it. The department pointed out that he had legally bought the island and would be held responsible for paying for it. He must have done some fast talking because he soon wrote to the department asking for the patent to be put in the name of Emilie L. Boas. Boas was also an American and had purchased other islands farther downriver.

Sale

1894: to Emile L. Boas.

ROCKLAND ISLAND

Names

Named Island 11 by Charles Unwin.

Evaluations and Descriptions

1873: Unwin 2.9 acres Value: $30

"Rocky with a few small trees."

Sale

1894: to W.B. Fullerton for $687.

ISLAND 12

Evaluations and Descriptions

1873: Unwin 0.2 acre Value: $10

"Low land connected with Hog Id. and No 11. Id in low water, Nos. 11 & 12 have been considered as part of Hog Id."

Sale

1894: to H.S. McDonald for $75.

NIAMA ISLAND

Names

Named island 12A, identified in 1894 by Walter Beatty.

Evaluations and Descriptions

1894: Beatty 1/12 acre Value: $50

"Low reef; soil and brush; good situation and approach; surrounding islands built on."

Sale

1903: to Thomas D. O'Conner for $50.

ISLAND 12B

Evaluations and Descriptions

1894: Beatty 1/50 acre Value: $25

"Rocky reef; 5 feet above high water; connected with 12C in low water." (See 12C.)

Sale

1894: to E. Landon for $75. Purchased with Island 12C.

ISLAND 12C

Evaluations and Descriptions

1894: Beatty 1/30 acre Value: $55

"Well wooded, evergreen and oak; splendid location; good harbour; on channel." (Islands 12B and 12C valued together at $75.)

Sale

1894: to E. Landon for $75. Purchased with island 12B.

ISLAND 13

Evaluations and Descriptions

1873: Unwin 0.5 acre Value: $10

"Rocky, covered with brush marsh between it and Hog Is. very likely to be dry in low water."

Sale

1893: to Jno. McDonald for $150.

ISLAND 13A

Evaluations and Descriptions

1894: Beatty 1/20 acre Value: $40

"Rocky reef off head of Little Calf Island; valued for location."

Sale

1900: to Wm. Henry Pennock.

SPECTACLES ISLAND

Evaluations and Descriptions

1862: McNaughton 0.10 acre Value: 25 cents

"Near lighthouse No. 16, Spectacles shoal."

McDONALD ISLAND

Historic Name

1816: Owen — Warrender, the Admiralty Islands Named after Sir George Warrender, commissioner for the Admiralty from 1812 to 1822. There were seven commissioners in the Admiralty at the time of the Owen survey. Others included Viscount Melville, Sir J.S. Yorke, W. Johnstone Hope, J. Osborn, Lorne H. Paulet and B.P. Blachford.

The island was locally known as McDonald Island and Hog Island, after the McDonald family, who started a hog farm on the isolated island after purchasing it. The McDonald family called the island Georgina, after a daughter, but that name only appears in correspondence.

The island has several other names, including Rotary Island, because the Gananoque Rotary Club sponsored a military training camp there during the Second World War.

Evaluations and Descriptions

1873: Unwin 36.2 acres Value: $600

"Near all arable 18.6 acres on Eastern end cleared and cultivated, said to be patented to H.S. McDonald of Brockville."

Island Notes

The following description sent to the Department of Indian Affairs in 1872 helped persuade the department to hire Charles Unwin to survey all the islands beginning in 1873: "Gilbert Bellefeuille of Gananoque says he is prepared to pay $500 for this island. The soil is very good. There are two log houses occupied respectively by John Macdonald [not related to the McDonalds of Gananoque] and John Cook, and a small log stable to each house. There are about 20 acres cleared and cultivated. The houses and stable belong to the heirs of the late Honorable John Macdonald, and the other stable was built by the two present occupants of the island. The land was cleared by Wm. Tunniclife. The present condition of the improvements is indifferent. The houses are worth about $40. for the two. The stables about $10. for both. The land cleared and under cultivation about $100. There is very little timber left on it by whom removed not known. The soil is of the best quality. The island might be turned to profitable use as a market garden, being near Gananoqui [*sic*]. Good fishing in vicinity."

Frank Eames, a local historian of the mid-1930s, drew this picture of the house on Pike Island. "The log house was the home of Abraham Stone, son of Raselas Stone of Howe Island. Abe married Christiana Barker, a native of Yorkshire, England. Their first log house was an Indian camp — long walls, flat roof. This *house was erected 1874, torn down 1900. The Indian camp stood on the east side at the mark X. 'Billy' Stone, son of Abe, winning pilot of the famous sailing skiff* St. Lawrence, *built by Gilberts of Brockville, was born in the first house. Also, this race (1891) proved and decided the Championship against all comers. Her sail spread was so great she would not stand alone with no crew aboard. Mrs. F. Eames was born in the first house also, at Gananoque."* — Frank Eames Collection, Susan W. Smith

Sale

The government recognized the right of ownership by the McDonald family, so the island was never placed on the open market. There were several families who squatted or lived on the island in the early years.

PIKE ISLAND

Names

During the time of Charles Unwin's survey the island was locally known as Stones Island after Abraham Stone, who was the first island resident.

Evaluations and Descriptions

1862: McNaughton Value: $3

"Has a dwelling place on it occupied by a person of the name of Stone."

1873: Unwin 0.6 acre Value: $30

"Rocky with some nice Pine on it, there is a small log house which was occupied last winter but vacated in the summer."

Island Notes

A letter, sent to the department in recognition of Abraham Stone who wanted to buy the island, says in part: "Abraham Stone and his parents before him who built the log house and planted several fruit trees which are on it now. Years ago the islet, most of which is rock and with cut timber is about one acre over all, and is of little use to any but a man of Stones position. He, being without education desired me to seek from you a clear title, or deed that his family may retain it. Should he be deprived of his support. He says the place was valued two years ago, by some government delegation surveying

Near the town of Gananoque. — Marshall Bros, 1912

the river. . . is not sure [why] they call the island Pike or Stones Island as it has long been named by the people here.

"Stone is going on a summer schooner trip. He is a chopper, and also a sailor, that he is now living, for this season on Messrs. Dempster Bros. property on the main shore opposite his island for whom he is now labouring as a chopper and that almost every season he makes one or two trips on a vessel on the lakes, when he leaves his family on Pike island. I hope my description though not very business like will be understood. There are many such men along the river that work at anything that pays the best. Signed, S. Adams, 1875."

Sale

To Abraham Stone.

CHERRY ISLAND

Evaluations and Descriptions

1873: Unwin 0.5 acre Value: $15

"High and rocky, covered with small brush."

1894: Beatty 5/10 acre Value: $200

"Fairly level; plenty of shade trees; fishing and c . . . very good."

CUNNINGHAM ISLAND

Names

This island has been known by two names: Little Island and Ormiston Island. Customs agent Jno. Ormiston purchased the island in the 1800s.

Today the island is known as Cunningham Island.

Evaluations and Descriptions

1873: Unwin 1.8 acres Value: $50

"High at West end and low at East end, there is a boat house on it claimed by S. McGammon of Gananoque who wishes to purchase."

Island Notes

Ormiston, who was well known in Gananoque, rented Little Island in the summer. When the Department of Indian Affairs began to sell islands, Ormiston petitioned to buy the one he had been renting. At that time there was a moratorium on selling or leasing the islands, but Ormiston explained that as customs agent he could use the island as a lookout for boating traffic on the river. The department agreed and the island was sold. Interestingly, Ormiston was also the island agent in the region and was instrumental in persuading the department to sell several islands to his friends and acquaintances.

Sale

To Jno. Ormiston.

LITTLE WHITE CALF ISLAND

Evaluations and Descriptions

1873: Unwin 0.3 acre Value: $20

"Cleared — arable — a small shanty on it occupied by a Frenchman."

Sale

1894: to M.P. Douglas for $351.

BIG WHITE CALF ISLAND

Evaluations and Descriptions

1873: Unwin 0.9 acre Value: $40

"Low and flat — all cleared, part arable there are two small shanties on it, this island is occupied by a Frenchman, who like the occupant of Little White Calf subsists by fishing, the consequence of these islands being owned by that class of people, would be the deterioration in value of the vicinity."

1894: Beatty 9/10 acre Value: $250

"Low, level, soil good, scrub, well situated with [?] up stream."

HERITAGE ISLAND

Names

Named Island E by Charles Unwin.

Evaluations and Descriptions

1894: Beatty 1/2 acre Value: $125

"Well wooded, scrub and evergreen; level; sheltered; beautiful situation; good harbourage and fishing."

ISLAND F

Evaluations and Descriptions

1894: Beatty 1/5 acre Value: $75

"Covered with scrub; level; 8 feet above water; situation good; shoal to eastward included."

BURNT ISLAND

Names

This small island had its named exchanged with Aubrey Island on a government chart in the 1950s. The error, which was not corrected for several years, resulted in confusion. In the case of this small island, which never had a residence built on it, there is no problem, but the mix-up has caused confusion with Aubrey Island.

Evaluations and Descriptions

1873: Unwin 0.7 acre Value: $20

"Low and flat, it is rocky, and covered with a few scrubby brush."

1894: Beatty 7/10 acre Value: $150

"Level; scrubby; high in places; divided in high water; well situated good fishing."

PITCH PINE ISLAND

Evaluations and Descriptions

1873: Unwin 3.2 acre Value: $50

"Low and flat, covered with brush, very little arable land."

Island Notes

Arthur P. Coleman, one of Canada's pioneer geologists and a professor of geology at the University of Toronto, purchased this island. In 1910 he explored the Canadian Rockies and Mount Coleman, altitude 11,000 feet, at the headwaters of the Northern Saskatchewan River in the Banff National Park, is named in his honour.

Professor Coleman's sister, Miss Helena Coleman, was also a celebrated person. She wrote numerous volumes of poetry and prose and invited some of Canada's leading poets and writers to visit her on the island each summer.

Both brother and sister were artists, and their paintings and drawings are in public and private collections in Canada. Many were drawn in and of the Thousand Islands.

Sale

1884: to Arthur P. Coleman.

Island 14.

— Photograph appearing in Jno. A. Haddock, *Island and River Pictorial, 1896*

THE MESSENGERS

A group of islands named by Captain Owen as the Messengers. They consist of the Towers (Island 14), Pitch Pine Island, Burnt Island and La Vignette (Island).

Historic Name

1816: Owen — the Messengers, the Admiralty Islands.

There were at least four messengers at the Admiralty office. This group's name, like the Clerks, was not printed on the engraved charts, but the work of the messengers was appreciated by the Admiralty Office, and the men received salary raises in every decade.

TOWERS ISLAND

Names

Named Island 14 by Charles Unwin.

Evaluations and Descriptions

1873: Unwin 2.5 acre Value: $30

"Low and flat, a little brush on it, about half arable."

Island Notes

It took Professor E. Haanel several years to have the large summer cottage known as The Towers built. Every summer Professor Haanel brought a group of students to the island for a holiday. In return, they helped construct the house, adding rooms and verandahs.

Sale

1883: to Eugene Haanel for $220.

STONESTHROW ISLAND

Names

Named Island 14A by Walter Beatty.

Evaluations and Descriptions

1894: Beatty 1/3 acre Value: $100

"High islet; well located, and with shoal on north; good soil, approach and view; a little scrub."

Sale

1901: to Frances Beall for $100.

ISLAND 14B

Evaluations and Descriptions

1894: Beatty 1/3 acre Value: $75

"High islet; good soil; good approach; well situated; rocky shore; light scrub."

Sale

1901: to H.W. Metzler.

LA VIGNETTE ISLANDS

Names

Identified by Unwin as Islands 14C and 14D.

Evaluations and Descriptions

1894: Beatty 1/5 acre Value: $30

"Rocky islet; evergreen scrub; with reef lying up stream, and between it and Hog Island."

Sale

1901: to Frank T. Lent for $60.

ISLAND 14E

Evaluations and Descriptions

1894: Beatty 1/10 acre Value: $50

"Evergreen scrub and some pine close to, but cut off from, shore of Island No. 14."

MUDLUNTA ISLAND

Historic Name

1816: Owen — Barrow, the Admiralty Islands Named after Sir John Barrow (1764–1848), second secretary. Barrow's love for adventure won him a ride in a balloon and a voyage to Greenland while taking part in a whale chase! In 1804 he was appointed second secretary to the first lord of the Admiralty, Lord Melville, a position he held for forty years. In 1817 Barrow published an account of the movement of icebergs in the Atlantic Ocean and proposed a plan for two voyages to search for the Northwest Passage. Point Barrow, Cape Barrow and the Barrow Straits in the polar seas are tributes to this industrious administrator.

In 1874 the island was locally known as Little John, after John LeShae, the island resident. He lived on the island, having paid rent to the Mississaugas. They called the island Mudlunta, meaning "half moon."

Evaluations and Descriptions

1873: Unwin 7.8 acres Value: $75

"Low, with about 1/2 acres cleared, claimed by Collies Turcott, who lives on Bostwick Id, he has an Indian lease, the rock formation is similar to Parmenter Id. on which R. Forsyth's Marble merchant of Montreal has a quarry which yields granite acceptable of a high polish, the rock on Little John Id. appears to be so full of seams that the blocks of large size could be taken out."

INDIAN LEASE

Article of agreement made this Second day of June in Thousand eight hundred and forty seven . . . Jacob Storms John Storms and John Simson of the tribe of indians called the Chipaway tribe being Council for said tribe of the first part doth Lease Mudlunta Island to Frances Kerky, of the second part as long as grass grows and water runs for the sum of five shillings, per year, HCY [?] yearly which the said Francis Kerky his heirs executors and assigns for ever are holders to pay to the said first part signed sealed and delivered,

Jacob Storms His Mark -
John Storms His Mark -
John Simson His Mark -
Francis Kerkey His Mark -

(Registered Department of Interior, Ottawa, May 6, 1874)

Island Notes

Francis Kerky (probably originally Cartier) leased Mudlunta Island from the Mississaugas. He signed a lease in 1847 that gave him occupancy of the island "for as long as the grass grows and the water runs." The lease was signed by three Mississaugas, Jacob Storms, John Storms and John Simpson. All three men were important members of the island natives. (See Part I, Squatters and Mississaugas on the Canadian Islands, 1820–56.)

Kerky lived to be 107 years of age. The year before he died he was interviewed by John McNaughton, the government surveyor hired to do a survey of aboriginal land in 1862. McNaughton recorded that Kerky and his wife, who was twelve years younger, or ninety-five years old, looked after a "cow, some pigs and two or three dozen of fowl." They had a workshop, and everything "about the place appeared neat and comfortable. At a distance he had the appearance of a youth of 12 or 14 years." Kerky complained that all the white ash in the region was gone. As his livelihood he used this strong and light wood to make oars, which he sold to passing boatmen.

LITTLE SAGASTAWEKA ISLAND

Names

Named Island 15 by Charles Unwin. It is attached to Sagastaweka Island by a small bridge.

Evaluations and Descriptions

1873: Unwin 0.2 acre Value: $10

"Low and covered with thick brush."

1894: Beatty 1/5 acre Value: $75

"Well wooded with cedar, spruce and hemlock; harbour; good view and approach; level and well located."

Sale

1894: to Samuel Finley for $75.

ISLAND 15A

Evaluations and Descriptions

1894: Beatty 1/20 acre Value: $40

"High; view and approach good; in good neighbourhood."

Sale

1901: to C.E. Britton.

ISLAND 15C

Evaluations and Descriptions

1894: Beatty 1/2 acre Value: $50

"An islet with shoals around which afford room for building."

Sale

1901: to C.E. Britton.

ISLAND 15D

Evaluations and Descriptions

1894: Beatty 1/140 acre Value: $30

"Small rock; shoal around it; some scrub."

Sale

1901: to C.E. Britton.

ISLAND 15E

Evaluations and Descriptions

1894: Beatty 1/2 acre Value: $30

"Small rock; shoal around it; some scrub."

Sale

1901: to C.E. Britton.

ISLAND 15F

Evaluations and Descriptions

1894: Beatty 1/2 acre Value: $100

"Three rocky knolls with marsh between, which can be filled and made a most desirable island."

Sale

1901: to C.E. Britton.

THE CLERKS

Historic Name

1816: Owen — The Clerks, now Sagastaweka Island, Island 16, Island 17 and Island 18. The Admiralty Islands. These islands paid tribute to the Admiralty clerks who looked after the books of this important office. This name was never transferred to the final charts and thus does not appear on the engraved sheets.

SAGASTAWEKA ISLAND

Historic Name

(See The Clerks) The island was known as Campbell Island, after Henry Campbell, who was the first owner. After arranging to purchase the island and paying a down payment, he sold his right of purchase to Agnes Penn, the wife of a Gananoque businessman. From then on, the island was registered as Penn's Island in the local registry office.

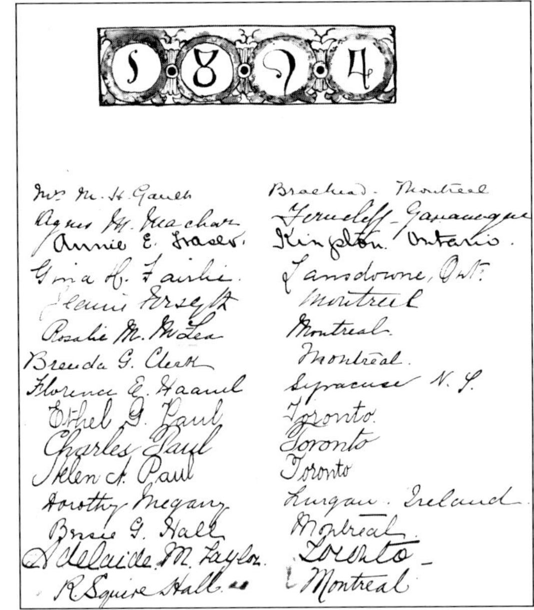

Guest books were designed to record the visitors who came to the islands for a few days or for tea.

— Sagastaweka Island collection, Helen Wright Greuter

The island was also locally known as Channel Island and Trillium Island.

The name Sagastaweka Island was given by the first house guest in 1886. He claimed the name meant "house full of sunshine."

Evaluations and Descriptions

1873: Unwin 8.7 acres Value: $100

"Rough and covered with second growth — part arable, this Id. is claimed by H. Campbell of Gananoque."

Island Notes

In 1829 Henry Campbell, a butcher from Gananoque, purchased a claim for Channel Island, then the name of Sagastaweka Island, from Benjamin Taylor for $15. Taylor had bought a native lease from the Mississaugas in the 1820s. Campbell never lived on the island, but he continued to use 3 or 4 acres of cleared land for pasture and paid the Mississauga chiefs a yearly rent. One year Campbell rented the island to Christopher Bushaw, from Kingston, who built a small shanty there.

When the Department of Indian Affairs began to sell the islands, Campbell applied for a patent. He asked that a reasonable price be given because there was only brush growing "with the tallest tree being only 20ft. high."

Campbell was an elderly man when he applied to the department to purchase the island. He agreed to pay $100 for this 8-acre island and subsequently deposited $20 to buy it. When Agnes Cowan Penn acquired the patent, she paid the balance of $80 and remained the owner until 1885, when she sold the island to Samuel Finley.

Finley, a prominent businessman from Montreal built a large summer home for his family.

Sale

1874: to Henry Campbell for $100. Later sold to Agnes Cowan Penn and then sold in 1885 to Samuel Finley.

KITSYMENIE ISLAND

Names

Named Island 16 by Charles Unwin.

Evaluations and Descriptions

1873: Unwin 1.0 acre Value: $15

"High and rocky — a little brush."

1894: Beatty 1 acre Value: $150

"High; level; covered with scrub; good approach; fine view and excellent harbourage."

Sale

1894: to J.B. McMurchy for $150.

GRANDVIEW ISLAND

Names

Named Island 17 by Charles Unwin.

Evaluations and Descriptions

1873: Unwin 1.6 acres Value $25

"Low, level and rocky, thickly covered with brush."

Sale

1907: to George H. Bowen for $395, soon after the island was sold to Oliver Adams.

ISLAND 17A

Evaluations and Descriptions

1894: Beatty 1/30 acres Value: $20

"Rocky reef; 5 feet above water; good foundation; good location."

Sale

1907: to G. H. Bowen for $395.

ISLAND 17B

Evaluations and Descriptions

1894: Beatty 1/10 acre Value: $60

"Good location, approaches and view; covered with scrub. Should be bought with 17C."

Sale

1900: to James Adams for $100.

ISLAND 17C

Evaluations and Descriptions

1894: Beatty 1/15 acre Value: $60

"Almost connected with above, and should be bought with it."

Sale

1901: to James Adams for $100, with Islands 17B and 17C.

ISLAND 17D

Evaluations and Descriptions

1894: Beatty 1/8 acre Value: $60

"Nice location; scrub and evergreen; good view; pleasant building spot."

Sale

1894: to O.V. Goulette for $60.

ISLAND 17E

Evaluations and Descriptions

1894: Beatty 1/20 acre Value: $30

"Well located rocky reef, suitable for building upon."

Sale

1912: to F. C. Bell.

ISLAND 17F

Evaluations and Descriptions

1894: Beatty 1/15 acre Value: $40

"Flat and well raised rocky shoal, which may easily be made suitable for a house; very well located."

Sale

1908: to John R. Reid.

ISLAND 17G

Evaluations and Descriptions

1894: Beatty 1/20 acre Value: $40

"Rocky reef; well located; flat and well above water; good approach."

Sale

1908: to John R. Reid.

MANITONANA ISLAND

Names

Named Island 18 by Charles Unwin.

Manitonana is a native name, often referred to as the name of the Thousand Islands, and meaning "the garden of the Great Spirit."

Evaluations and Descriptions

1873: Unwin 3.0 acres Value: $50

"Low — part arable, some of it was formerly cleared but the brush has grown up again."

Sale

1899: to Ida D. Mace and Cora D. Graham (the Gowing family) for $850.

ISLAND 18A

Evaluations and Descriptions

1894: Beatty 1/15 acre Value: $60

"Good building spot; most desirable location; good soil and earth; view pretty."

Sale

1901: to Catherine E. Campbell for $60.

ISLAND 18B

Evaluations and Descriptions

1894: Beatty 1/100 acre Value: $25

"Rocky reef, nearly covered in high water."

ISLAND 19

Evaluations and Descriptions

1873: Unwin 0.3 acre Value: $20

"Low rock covered with brush."

Sale

1902: to Jeanette Matthew for $250.

ISLAND 19A

Evaluations and Descriptions

1894: Beatty 1/20 acre Value: $30

"Rocky islet; first-rate position."

Sale

1902: to William G. Matthew for $30.

BLUFF ISLAND

Evaluations and Descriptions

1873: Unwin 0.8 acre Value: $30

"High and rocky, very little soil, scarcely any timber, has recently been burnt over."

1894: Beatty 8/10 acre Value: $200

"Bare, bald island, 40 feet above the water; with a fringe of pine and cedar; first class location."

Sale

1894: to K. McDonald for $210.

MINOTA ISLAND

Names

Named Island 20 by Charles Unwin.

Evaluations and Descriptions

1873: Unwin 0.3 acre Value: $35

"Low, rocky and thickly covered with brush."

1894: Beatty 3/10 acre Value: $150

"A very pretty little island; good approaches; in every way most desirable; well wooded."

Sale

1894: to W.G. Matthew for $160.

ISLAND 21

Evaluations and Descriptions

1873: Unwin 0.2 acre Value: $15

"Low, rocky and thickly covered with brush."

1894: Beatty 1/5 acre Value: $100

"Very prettily wooded and well located; view and approaches first-rate."

Sale

1896: to Tom P. Richardson for $150.

ISLAND 22

Evaluations and Descriptions

1873: Unwin 0.5 acre Value: $35

"Low, rocky, and thickly covered with brush."

1894: Beatty 1/2 acre Value: $175

"Good level land; mixed hardwood and cedar; beautifully placed; view and approaches excellent."

Sale

1894: to Wm. Byers for $180.

SAN SOUCI ISLAND

Names

Named Island 23 by Charles Unwin.

Evaluations and Descriptions

1873: Unwin 0.5 acre Value: $5

"Low, rocky covered with brush."

1894: Beatty 1/2 acre Value: $150

"Rugged shore; level; good soil, scrub and timber; fine harbour and easy approach; most desirable location."

Sale

1898: to Joseph Boucher.

HALE ISLAND

Names

Named Island 24 by Charles Unwin.

Evaluations and Descriptions

1873: Unwin 0.4 acre Value: $5

"Low, rocky covered with brush."

1894: Beatty 2/5 acre Value: $150

"A very pretty island; bold, level, well wooded; good approach; birch and evergreen. (See 24C, which should be bought with it.)"

Sale

1894: to William Hale.

ISLAND 24A

Evaluations and Descriptions

1894: Beatty 1/30 acre Value: $25

"A rocky knob cut off from Bostwick by narrow channel; bears a couple of trees."

Sale

1901: to Mary and William Hale.

ISLAND 24B

Evaluations and Descriptions

1894: Beatty 1/4 acre Value: $75

"Large bare reef; good duck shooting; rough and rocky; well located."

Sale

1901: to William Hale.

ISLAND 24C

Evaluations and Descriptions

1894: Beatty 1/12 acre Value: $40

"Level; well wooded; good harbour; well located; almost connected with 24."

Sale

1894: to William Hale for $45.

ISLAND 24D

Evaluations and Descriptions

1894: Beatty 1/10 acre Value: $40

"Rocky shoal off head of 24; good as a foundation on which to build; good locality."

Sale

1901: to William Hale.

LEMON ISLAND

Evaluations and Descriptions

1873: Unwin 0.4 acre Value: $20

"Low rock with a few bushes on it."

1894: Beatty 4/10 acre Value: $150

"Level; rocky; well located; no timber; approaches and view of the best."

Sale

1894: to Julia E. Cowan.

YNYSCRAG ISLAND

Names

Named Island 25 by Charles Unwin and Island 25A by Walter Beatty.

Evaluations and Descriptions (Two islands)

Island 25

1873: Unwin 0.2 acre Value: $10

"Low level rock, a few trees on it."

Island 25A

1894: Beatty 1/5 acre Value: $100

"Level; low; covered with scrub; good locality."

Sale

Sold to E. L. Nichols.

ISLAND 25B

Evaluations and Descriptions

1894: Beatty 1/10 acre Value: $50

"Rocky; low; bare; good position."

Sale

1918: to Lucetta C. Ormiston.

FORSYTH ISLAND

Historic Name

1816: Owen — Hope, the Admiralty Islands

Named after W. Johnstone Hope (1766–1831), commissioner. Sir William Hope entered the British Navy in 1777. By 1782 he had served on the home front, in Lisbon and in Newfoundland on the North American Station. In the following years he served on numerous vessels, including one

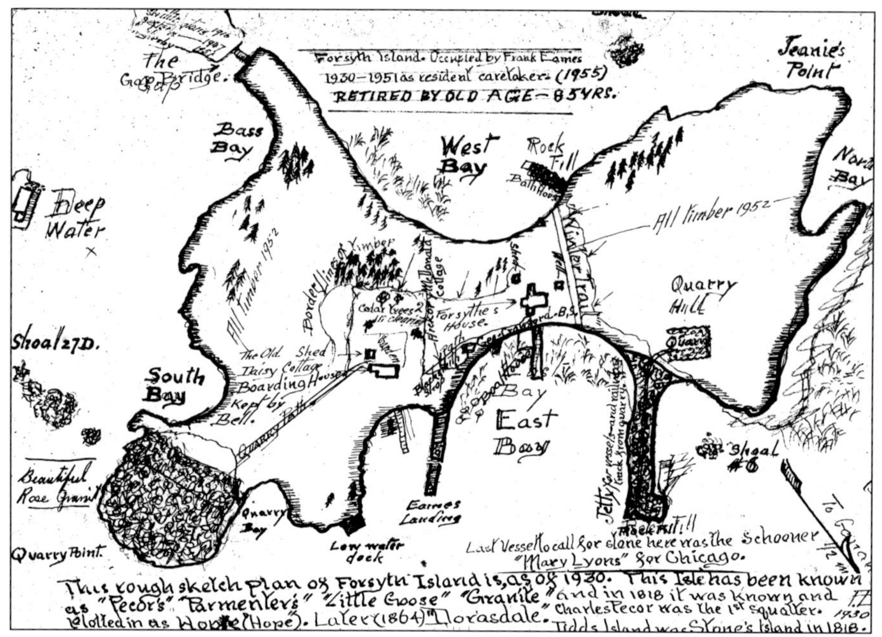

A hand-drawn map of Forsyth Island.
— Frank Eames collection, Susan W. Smith

under Lord Nelson's command. Hope was made a member of Parliament and became a lord of the Admiralty in 1808. Eventually was made a member of the Council of the Lord High Admirals.

The island was locally first known as Parmenter's Island after the first island resident, J. Parmenter. It was also called Goose Island by the Mississaugas. After Robert Forsyth bought the island it was known by his name.

Evaluations and Descriptions

1862: McNaughton Value: $60

"Greater part of this island partially cleared at one time but now growing up with bush."

1873: Unwin 20.3 acres Value: $600

"Very fine timber on northerly portion, the southerly portion is cleared and now owned by R. Forsyth of Montreal, marble merchant, who has a quarry on it."

Island Notes

Robert Forsyth, a marble works merchant, bought the island in 1874. He manufactured and sold cemetery monuments in Montreal and Toronto. Forsyth developed quarries, first on Forsyth Island and later on Juniper, Huckleberry, Thwartway and Grindstone islands. Originally, large pieces of stone were quarried and probably used for building blocks and monument works. Later, paving stones were cut from the remaining rubble.

In time Forsyth Island was completely developed. Boarding-houses housed the men who came from Scotland and Montreal to work the quarries; as well, there were three large residences, an icehouse and tool and storage sheds. Derricks were set up over the quarries and stone landings were laid for ships and barges. At one time, more than seventy people worked the island; not only derrickmen, teamsters, drivers and cutters but also cooks, housemaids and gardeners were employed. The majority came from Gananoque, but a few Americans came over from Grindstone Island.

In 1883 Forsyth opened a quarry on Grindstone Island. By then all stone sent to the United States was subject to an import duty. The stone cut on Forsyth Island was taken by ship to Montreal and Toronto for the Canadian market, while the Grindstone quarries supplied the United States. During the 1880s hundreds of thousands of paving stones were cut.

In 1890 the Forsyth Island quarry was closed. By then, large and more productive granite quarries were established in Beebe, Quebec, and in Barre, Vermont. The island became the Forsyth summer home. After Robert Forsyth died, his daughter Jeanie continued to enjoy the island for many years.

In 1930 Frank Eames became the island caretaker. One day while cleaning out an old desk he found a time book dated November 1885–1887, listing the names of quarry employees. At that time quarry men were paid $2.25 for cutting one hundred paving stones, and a good worker could average $3 to $4 a day.

Sale

1874: to Robert Forsyth.

EAGLE CRAG ISLAND

Names

Named Island 26 by Charles Unwin.

Evaluations and Descriptions

1873: Unwin 0.75 acre Value: $20

"Rocky with a little brush on it, in low water it is connected with Parmenter Id., Mr. Forsyth supposed that this Id. belonged to Parmenter as the water was low when he purchased."

Sale

1883: to Robert Forsyth.

ISLAND 26A

Evaluations and Descriptions

1894: Beatty 1/10 acre Value: $40

"Rocky reef; in good location; 3 feet above water."

Sale

1907: to Walter Nordhoff.

MONEYSUNK ISLAND

Names

Named Island 27 by Charles Unwin.

Evaluations and Descriptions

1873: Unwin 2.0 acres Value: $50

"High rocky bluff, most of the south side is arable, nearly all the timber has been recently destroyed by fire."

1894: Beatty 2 acres Value: $350

"Well wooded; a bold cliff shore on south-west; good harbour and lovely building spot on east end."

Island Notes

The island was first used by the Victoria College Science Association, whose members included Professor Haanel from The Towers and Professor Arthur P. Coleman from Pitch Pine Island. The college leased the island for five years, and as a result many of the members who visited it purchased islands of their own.

In 1907 Walter Nordhoff bought the island. Nordhoff was the son of Charles Nordhoff, a New York journalist, and the father of Charles Nordhoff, co-author of *Mutiny on the Bounty*. In time the Nordhoffs began to excavate and build an elaborate foundation for a large summer home. But when the First World War broke out, local residents became suspicious of the German Nordhoff and his deep holes on the island. They started rumours implicating him in the spying and intrigue associated with the war. "Perhaps the holes were for mounting guns?" In fact, the Nordhoffs had moved to California before the war and had abandoned their plans to build on the island. The island was soon referred to as Moneysunk Island.

In 1935 Gerald W. Birks, from Montreal, bought the island. He visited the island several summers on board his 42-foot motor yacht, and needed a convenient place to moor. He built several sleeping cabins on the island. No one has ever built on the original Nordhoff foundations.

Sale

1886: to the Victoria Science Association and leased 1886 to 1904, five years at $20 annually. Sold in 1907 to Walter Nordhoff for $1,500.

ISLAND 27A

Evaluations and Descriptions

1894: Beatty 1/10 acre Value: $30

"Rocky reef."

Sale

1907: to Walter Nordhoff.

POLARIS ISLAND

Names

Named Island 27B by Charles Unwin. This island was named, as was the Binnacle, by the owner, who considered that the islands in the Admiralty Islands should have descriptive naval names.

Evaluations and Descriptions

1894: Beatty 1/5 acre Value: $75

"Well located; small birch and oak trees; very nice view and approach."

Sale

1898: to Charles H. Hubbell for $75.

ISLAND 27C

Evaluations and Descriptions

1894: Beatty 1/10 acre Value: $30

"Barren; rocky."

Sale

1894: to Jacob Duetta for $30.

ISLAND 27D

Evaluations and Descriptions

1894: Beatty 1/10 acre Value: $40

"Rocky reef, 4 feet above water; well situated."

ISLAND 27E

Evaluations and Descriptions

1894: Beatty 1/50 acre Value: $20

"Small rocky reef, 4 feet above water."

Sale

1908: to Frank T. Lent for $30.

APOHAQUI ISLAND

Names

Named Island 28 by Charles Unwin.

Evaluations and Descriptions

1873: Unwin 1.9 acres Value: $30

"Low, thickly covered with brush in low water, is connected with Tidds Id, Mr. Hiram Wellbanks who purchased Tidds Id., March 14th, 1873, informed me that he thought this island was included."

Sale

1888: to Margaret A. Taylor.

ISLAND 28A

Evaluations and Descriptions

1894: Beatty 1/10 acre Value: $50

"Rocky island, 8 feet above water."

Sale

1898: to Alexander C. Campbell.

ISLAND 28B

Names

This island was also known as Oriole's Nest.

Evaluations and Descriptions

1894: Beatty 1/30 acre Value: $25

"Rocky reef, tied to 28 by a wooden pier."

Sale

1894: to Elizabeth Hall for $25.

ISLAND 28C

Evaluations and Descriptions

1894: Beatty 1/20 acre Value: $50

"Low islet; small cedar scrub."

Sale

1894: to Rev. William Hall.

ISLAND 28D

Evaluations and Descriptions

1894: Beatty 1/50 acre Value: $10

"A few rocks tied to shore of Tidd's Island by a wooden pier."

Sale

1902: to B. O. Britton.

Tremont Park Hotel. — Tremont Park Hotel, on Tremont Island

TREMONT ISLAND

Historic Name

1816: Owen — Stone's, the Admiralty Islands

There is no direct reference to a Stone in the available Admiralty archive records, but the name could refer to Joel Stone, the founder of Gananoque. This is the only island name written in the possessive form, "Stone's I." Stone was a United Empire Loyalist who settled on the west bank of the Gananoque River facing Tremont Island in 1792. Because he was a prominent member of the tiny community, it is understable that he would be known to Captain Owen and his men.

The island was locally known as Tidds Island after an early resident. The summer community that was built on the island was called Tremont Park. This name has been used more often than Tidds, although both have appeared on hydrographic and topographic maps and charts.

Evaluations and Descriptions

1862: McNaughton Value: $100

"Well timbered with second growth of hardwood."

1873: Unwin 24.3 acres Value: $500

"Low and pretty level, covered with thick brush, owned by Hiram Wellbanks who asks $800."

Island Notes

In 1878 Capt. Sanford Davis bought the island from Hiram Wellbanks and subdivided the east end into building lots known as Tremont Park. He advertised the lots in local newspapers and promoted the area by inviting hundreds of guests to the island each summer. The only condition to the sale of lots was that "the purchasers shall not allow any intoxicating liquors, or drinks of any kind, to be trafficked on the lots."

Captain Davis and his wife built a boarding-house called The Tremont Island House on the western part of the island. Probably because of its close proximity to Gananoque, the island attracted numerous local visitors. The house was destroyed by fire in the 1920s.

In the early years the lot owners pitched tents or built cottages called camps. Today, Tremont Park, with more than thirty cottages is still the summer home of Gananoque families, and several properties have remained in the possession of original Tremont Island families.

Sale

1873: claimed by Hiram Wellbanks. Sold in 1873 to Capt. Sanford Davis, who subdivided the island and sold cottage lots.

ISLAND 29

Evaluations and Descriptions

1873: Unwin 0.2 acre Value: $5

"Low and rocky, almost bare."

1894: Beatty 1/5 acre Value: $150

"Low; level; some soil and a few small trees."

Sale

1894: to William Melville Hall.

HAY ISLAND

Historic Name

1816: Owen — Melville, the Admiralty Islands

Named after Robert Saunders Dundas, 2nd Viscount Melville, (1771–1851). Melville was the only son of Henry Dundas, 1st Viscount Melville. He was educated in Scotland and entered Parliament in 1794. When his father died he became the 2nd Lord Melville. He was appointed first lord of the Admiralty in 1812, an office he held for fifteen years. As well, he was governor of the Bank of Scotland and chancellor of the University of St. Andrew. When he retired from political life he lived at Melville Castle near Edinburgh.

This island was originally known as Nut Island by the first residents in the region. (See Part I, Settlement of the Canadian Shore, 1789–1812.) In later years it became known as Hay Island, a descriptive name for the hay or tall grass that grew there.

Evaluations and Descriptions

1873: Unwin 96.0 acres Value: $2800

"This is the finest Island, in the vicinity of Gananoque, taking its agricultural . . . into consideration, it is nearly all arable, with 83 acres cleared, the owner is George Taylor of Gananoque. . . Mr. Taylor values it at $3000."

Island Notes

Hay island was given as a land grant to Sir John Johnson soon after the American Revolution. Johnson never used the island but his executors sold it for $2000 years later, with a guarantee that a deed could be received.

When John McNaughton surveyed the island in 1862, he found that it had "good land well cultivated with a neat frame house with large frame barn and sheds upon it."

Several interesting houses are situated on Hay Island. One of the most unusual is Napoleon's Hat, which was built in 1913 for E.K. Stabler and his business partner. It was the home of Stabler and Baker, now Graphic Controls Inc., one of Gananoque's largest business concerns. Later the company was moved to the mainland and the cottage was used as a summer residence. It was dubbed Napoleon's Hat because it resembles the chapeau worn by the famous Frenchman. Interestingly, it was necessary to build the roof first and then jack it up and build the walls underneath.

Another unusual building on the island is the large boathouse on the west end, which is known as the Head of Hay. It was constructed in 1916 for Frederick Lewis of Norfolk, Virginia. The upper floor of the boathouse was used as a games room and was an ideal place to entertain guests.

In 1882 Jacob Duetta settled on Hay Island. He, too, farmed the island and began renting some of his farmhouse rooms to guests. In 1895 he built a new house on his property. This two-storey building was one of the popular summer resorts that attracted visitors to the Thousand Islands.

Sale

1789: land grant to Sir Johnson. The island was considered part of the Johnson estate that was purchased by the McDonald family of Gananoque.

KALARIA ISLAND

Names

Named Blackberry Island by Charles Unwin. The first island residents were the Castles from Rochester, New York. The senior Castle was a Greek scholar and he was responsible for name Kalaria, which means "fair winds."

Evaluations and Descriptions

1873: Unwin 2.2 acres Value: $40

"Low and rocky, covered with small brush."

Island Notes

This island was originally included in the land grant of Hay Island to Sir John Johnson in 1789. Later it was claimed that the island was separated from Hay Island by high water and the action of the waves.

Sale

1789: land grant of Hay Island to Sir John Johnson. This small island was considered part of that original land grant. (See Hay Island.)

HUCKLEBERRY ISLAND

Historic Name

1816: Owen — Moore, the Admiralty Islands

Named after Sir Graham Moore, appointed commissioner from 1816 to 1820. His signature appears on dispatches between Owen and the Admiralty Office during the survey.

Evaluations and Descriptions

1873: Unwin 7.1 acres Value: $60

"Low, level and rocky, a few small trees on it, a kind of Sandstone was taken from this island for some years for glass making purposes."

Sale

Sold to Robert Forsyth. This was one of the islands he bought to use as a granite quarry.

JUNIPER ISLAND

Names

Named Juniper Island by Charles Unwin. The island was originally known as Straight Island and recorded by that name by John McNaughton in 1862.

Evaluations and Descriptions

1873: Unwin 7.0 acres Value: $90

"Low and flat, some arable land, covered with second growth."

Island Notes

This island was purchased by Robert Forsyth for his quarry operations. He closed his quarries in 1900, and soon afterwards George Sargent, an American industrialist, bought the island. The Sargents asked Tiffany of New York City to design a boathouse. The stone foundations of the building bridged an opening to a protected lagoon. Over the years this area has been filled in, and today it is grassed over. The boathouse is still used as a skiff house. There are several other buildings on the property including the large main house and guest or "sleep" cabins.

Sale

1883: to Robert Forsyth.

THWARTWAY ISLAND

Historic Name

1816: Owen — Thwart Way (note that the name is spelled as two words), the Admiralty Islands. Owen gave the name Thwart Way to this large island, which connects the Admiralty Islands and the Lake Fleet group. Possibly it is named after the thwart that connected the two sides of a ship. Another meaning of "thwart" is to impede or contravene, and in this case could mean to prevent a clear passage between the islands.

Named Leek Island by Charles Unwin. It is only in recent years that the St. Lawrence Islands National Park reinstated the original Owen name, but spelled it as one word.

Leek Island boathouse. — SLINP, Photographic Inventory

Evaluations and Descriptions

1873: Unwin 90.7 acres Value: $1000

"About 19 acres cleared, the soil is naturally good, but having been badly farmed for many years it is now in a very poor condition. There is a very nice grove of Norway Pines on the east side of the Island. The remainder is covered with a thick growth of small timber. There is an old gate house and barn on it, both much dilapidated. The owner is James Parmenter, J.P. of Gananoque, it is unoccupied, except as pasture."

Island Notes

In 1904 Jeanne Forsyth sold Leek Island, which her father had quarried in the late 1800s, as he had done on several other Admiralty Islands. The purchaser was Ira Kipp, from New York City. Mrs. Kipp's family came from Watertown, and she had spent many summers on Carleton Island near Cape Vincent. In 1913 the Kipps built a summer house and a two-storey boathouse on Thwartway. They also cleared 30 acres for farming. They later built a separate cottage for each of their children.

In 1917 the Kipps lent the island to the Canadian government as a convalescent hospital for forty to fifty First World War soldiers. They also provided all the necessary equipment and hired doctors, nurses and physiotherapists to look after the patients. As well, they brought in cooks and housekeepers to maintain the houses. Mrs. Kipp remained on the island throughout the summer and supervised the services. When members of the New York Stock Exchange heard of the Kipps' generosity, they offered to pay for the cost of constructing a recreation room, complete with every popular game and sports equipment available.

In 1971 the island was expropriated by the Canadian government to be conserved as a bird sanctuary by the St. Lawrence Islands National Park. The family fought the expropriation in the courts but finally accepted $108,000 for the island.

Sale

1883: first sale to Robert Forsyth as part of his quarry operations.

The Hickory Islands are located in Frontenac County, Ontario, Canada, but are close to the international boundary line and to the west end of Grindstone Island, which is in U.S. waters (see Gore's Isles, page 199).

HICKORY ISLAND

Historic Name

1816: Owen — Francis Island, Gore's Islands

The name refers to Sir Francis Gore, lieutenant-governor of Upper Canada (see Grindstone Island, the American Islands).

The island was locally known as Hickory Island.

Evaluations and Descriptions

1862: McNaughton 80 acres

"It appears for the most part to be good land well cultivated with two dwelling houses, a large frame barn, and good orchard on it. It is said to have been occupied by Mr. Livingston, the present holder, or his father, for more than 40 years . . ."

Island Notes

Patrick Henry Livingston's father was one of the first residents to live in the islands, probably coming to the river soon after the War of 1812. The island served as a landing site for soldiers coming from the U.S. during the Patriot War (see Patriot War, 1837–1838).

When Charles Unwin began his survey in 1873, Livingston began a series of letters to the Department of Indian Affairs laying claim to the island. He described how he and his family had purchased the island under a lease with the Alnwick tribe. It took more than five years before he was granted permission to purchase the island. During that time he never knew if they would be able to remain residents of the farm that had been in the family for more than 60 years.

Sale

Sold to P.H. Livingston for $320, paying $4 per acre.

GOOSE ISLAND

Historic Name

1818: Owen — Arabella Island, Gore's Islands

The name appeared only on the published Admiralty charts, dated 1818 and not on the original 1816 hand-drawn charts.

Arabella was the wife of Sir Francis Gore.

Locally the island was known as Goose Island.

Evaluations and Descriptions

1862: McNaughton

"(Islands south of Hickory) South of Hickory Island, said to have formed part of it at the early settling of the country, but were detached by action of the waves in stormy weather — a few years more and the west end of the island will be separated from the same cause."

Island Notes

Patrick Livingston, whose family laid claim to the island reported that the infamous Bill Johnston (see Patriot War, 1837–1838), claimed the island was in U.S. territory and had taken possession of it. The Livingston family had to prove that the international boundary line ran east of the island and that the island was Canadian. They wrote several letters to the boundary commissioners before being assured that the island was in Canada.

THE LAKE FLEET

This part of the hydrographic chart shows the British Survey Fleet on parade. The Fleet is led by the flagship, the *Prince Regent*, which served as the navy headquaters at Kingston.

We can assume that each of the vessels was considered part of the Royal Navy fleet and not part of the Provincial Marine fleet that also served in the War of 1812. The *Prince Regent* and the *Princess Charlotte* were the first two ships that Sir James Yeo built for the British Naval operations on Lake Ontario (see Part I, The Thousand Islands and the War of 1812–1814).

Owen had a hard time outfitting his survey team with reliable boats. He was originally given bateaux, which proved to be too cumbersome to row, were slow sailers and unsuitable. A search of the dockyards resulted in several small ships and gunboats chosen for the survey. Many had served during the War of 1812.

The gunboats were used by the survey crew. Particular names appear on Admiralty lists of gunboats that served on Lake Champlain. They were probably transported to the St. Lawrence River after the War for the survey teams, but the names never appear in Admiralty documents. In 1831 the Admiralty office asked the Navy Board to have several ships and some fifteen gunboats "broken up and their names erased from the list of the Royal Navy." This list included the names *Axeman*, *Belabourer* and *Bloodletter*.

Two months later it was suggested that the work to dismantle and break up these boats was costly and a better solution would be to sell the ships and gunboats at auction. This was not done immediately because no one was interested in the sale. However, in 1837 a sale did take place in Kingston, and several ships, including the *Niagara* and the *Netley*, as well as several unnamed gunboats, were sold.

The last group of islands commemorated in the Lake Fleet were the those named after the utility boats used during the survey: Barge, Gig, Jolly and the Punts.

HISTORIC NAME	PRESENT NAME	PAGE
Prince Regent	Prince Regent Island (Canadian)	140
Princess Charlotte	Princess Charlotte Island (Canadian)	140
St. Lawrence	Sugar Island (Canadian)	139
Brock	Squaw Island (Canadian)	139
Scorpion	Scorpion Islands (Canadian)	134
Axeman	Axeman Island (Canadian)	134
Belaborer	Belaborer Island (Canadian)	138
Bloodletter	Bloodletter Island (Canadian)	135
Deathdealer	Deathdealer Island (Canadian)	130
Charwell	Endymion Island (Canadian)	136
Johnson	Camelot Island (Canadian)	136
Jones	Wyoming Island (Canadian)	133
Ramsden	Ramsden Island (Canadian)	134
Jolly	Jolly Island (American)	200
Gig	Gig Island (Canadian)	130
The Punts	The Punts (Canadian)	130
Barge	Barge Island (Canadian)	130

The Lake Fleet begins with the islands known as the utility boats and goes eastward through the Lake Fleet, with islands and numbers following in a consecutive order. In reality the islands were named on the charts going from east to west, beginning with Prince Regent, which was the name of the ship that was used by the British Navy stationed in Kingston as their headquarters in 1816.

THE PUNTS

Historic Name

1816: Owen — Punts, the Lake Fleet
Utility boats that would have been used by the crew in shallow water and for rowing between ships.

Evaluations and Descriptions

1873: Unwin 0.8 acre Value: $10
"Rough rock, a few trees and brush."

Sale

1894: to F.A. Stephens; later sold in 1904 to F.B. Bourne for $220.

GIG ISLAND

Historic Name

1816: Owen — Jolley Island, the Lake Fleet (see Jolly Island, The American Islands)
1818: Owen — Gig Island, the Lake Fleet
The gigs were utility boats and were identified by colours during the survey: black, green and yellow. They were normally 25 feet long and clinker-built (i.e., the external planks overlapped like clapboards on a house). They were powered by five sets of oars and had a rudder.

Evaluations and Descriptions

1873: Unwin 4.8 acres Value: $20
"Rough and rocky covered with brush."

Sale

1897: to James H. Wormen; later sold in 1908 to W.T. Samson for $1,400.

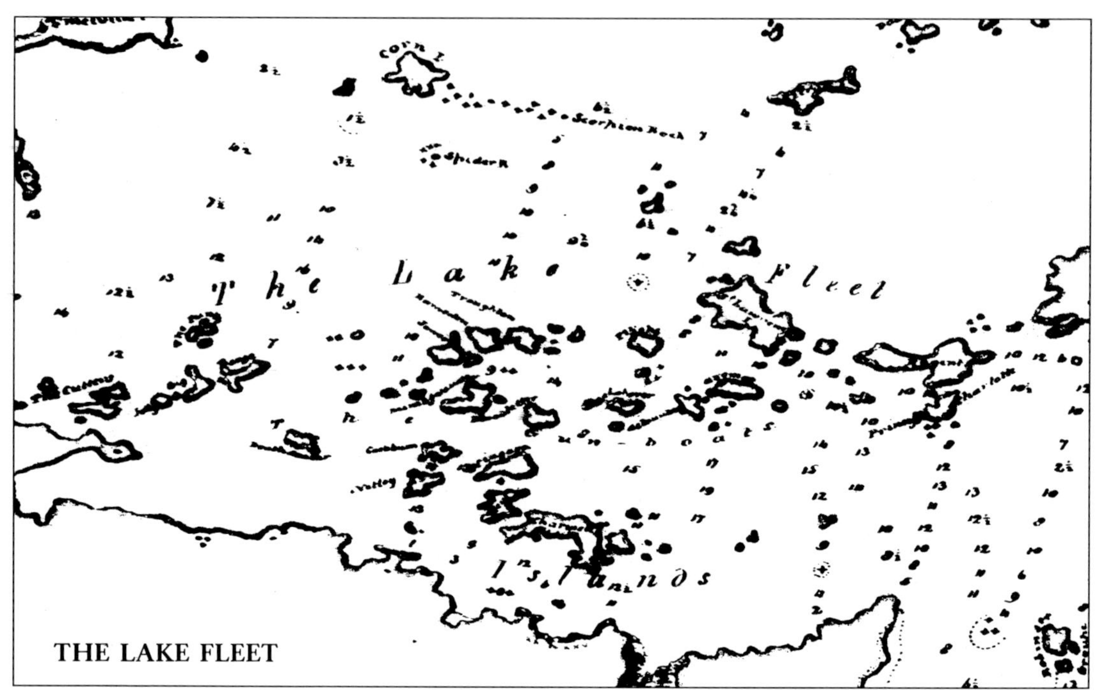

THE LAKE FLEET

BARGE ISLAND

Historic Name

1816: Owen — Barge, the Lake Fleet
Barges were used as utility boats for the survey.

Evaluations and Descriptions

1873: Unwin 2.5 acres Value: $15
"Rough and rocky, covered with brush and a few small trees."
1894: Beatty 2 1/5 acres Value: $300
"High; rocky; with evergreen wood and scrub, on south; good shelter and harbourage."

Sale

1907: William E. Miller for $300.

DEATHDEALER ISLAND

Historic Name

1816: Owen — Deathdealer, the Lake Fleet
The name of a gunboat that was used by Captain Owen during his survey.

Evaluations and Descriptions

1873: Unwin 3.3 acres Value: $20
"High smooth rock, no soil, covered with short brush."
1894: Beatty 3 3/10 acres Value: $450
"Good harbour; prettily wooded; level; very picturesque and desirable for building."

Sale

1894: to Reginald H. Sayre for $400.

ISLAND 30

Evaluations and Descriptions

1873: Unwin 1.2 acres Value: $25
"Low flat rock, with a few small trees and brush."
1894: Beatty 1 1/5 acres Value: $200
"Fairly level; some soil; small sized pine; cedars; birch and willow; good harbour; good shooting from west end."

Sale

1894: to W.G. Atkinson for $200.

ISLAND 30A

Evaluations and Descriptions

1894: Beatty 1/8 acre Value: $50

"Rocky island; good building spot; scrub cedar and willow."

Sale

1895: to Sidney Adams for $50.

ISLAND 30B

Evaluations and Descriptions

1894: Beatty 1/20 acre Value: $30

"Small rocky island; bare."

ISLAND 31

Evaluations and Descriptions

1894: Beatty 1/5 acre Value: $75

"A very pretty little island; some good pine and small cedars."

Sale

1898: to Edith F. Robinson.

ISLAND 31A

Evaluations and Descriptions

1894: Beatty 1/10 acre Value: $25

"A rocky reef, 5 feet out of water in some places, in others not more than 1 foot."

Sale

1907: to Sidney Adams.

ISLAND 31B

Evaluations and Descriptions

1894: Beatty 1/5 acre Value: $40

"Round, rocky knob 10 feet high, with shoals around; one nice pine tree and a few small cedars."

Sale

1906: to Douglas V. Ashley.

ISLAND 31C

Evaluations and Descriptions

1894: Beatty 1/10 acre Value: $20

"Barren, rocky, 5 feet above water; good fishing and shooting ground."

ISLAND 31D

Evaluations and Descriptions

1894: Beatty 1/8 acre Value: $40

"Low lying rocks partly submerged in high water; good fishing and shooting."

ISLAND 31E

Evaluations and Descriptions

1894: Beatty 1/3 acre Value: $60

"Rocky, low lying, with some scrub willow and soil; in good fishing and shooting ground."

Sale

1903: to Oliver J. Shaneman.

ISLAND 31F

Evaluations and Descriptions

1894: Beatty 1/20 acre Value: $20

"Rocky reef."

Sale

1871: to Thomas G. Rudd for $100.

ISLAND 32

Evaluations and Descriptions

1873: Unwin 0.9 acre Value: $10

"Low flat rock; a few small trees."

ISLAND 32A

Evaluations and Descriptions

1894: Beatty 1/5 acre Value: $50

"Rocky island; good fishing and shooting ground."

ISLAND 32B

Evaluations and Descriptions

1894: Beatty 1/5 acre Value: $50

"Rocky island, bare, well sheltered and good maskinonge fishing."

Islands 33 to 33K are located north of Gordon Island.

COLES ISLAND

Names

Named Island 33 by Charles Unwin.

Evaluations and Descriptions

1894: Beatty 2/5 acre Value: $75

"Good duck shooting; low; level; with a little scrub."

Sale

1900: to Charles Pécor for $75 in 1900.

ISLAND 33A

Evaluations and Descriptions

1894: Beatty 1/12 acre Value: $20

"Rocky; bare; high."

Sale

1907: to Charles Gray.

ISLAND 33B

Evaluations and Descriptions

1894: Beatty 1/10 acre Value: $20

"Rocky; bare; high."

ISLAND 33C

Evaluations and Descriptions

1894: Beatty 1/4 acre Value: $40

"High, rocky, with large shoal on Jackstraw Island side."

Sale

1902: to George K. Taylor.

ISLAND 33D

Evaluations and Descriptions

1894: Beatty 1/20 acre Value: $10
"Low."

Sale

1907: to Charles H. Gray.

ISLAND 33E

Evaluations and Descriptions

1894: Beatty 1/5 acre Value: $50
"Lightly wooded; prettily situated in bay."

Sale

1922: to R.L. McAvany for $50.

ISLAND 33F

Evaluations and Descriptions

1894: Beatty 1/10 acre Value: $30
"Rocky; high; with a little scrub."

Sale

1901: to James Reid.

ISLAND 33G

Evaluations and Descriptions

1894: Beatty 1/10 acre Value: $20
"Low, flat bare reef."

Sale

1901: to Stanley Williamson for $20.

ISLAND 33H

Evaluations and Descriptions

1894: Beatty 1/10 acre Value: $20
"Low, rocky, reef; good decoy shooting."

Sale

1901: to James Reid.

ISLAND 33I

Evaluations and Descriptions

1894: Beatty 1/10 acre Value: $20
"Low, rocky, reef; good decoy shooting."

Sale

1901: to William J. Reid.

ISLAND 33J

Evaluations and Descriptions

1894: Beatty 1/30 acre Value: $10
"Very low, completely submerged in high water."

ISLAND 33K

Evaluations and Descriptions

1894: Beatty 1/100 acre Value: $15
"Rocky knob, covered with soil and pine."

ISLAND 34

Evaluations and Descriptions

1873: Unwin 0.5 acre Value: $10
"Low rock, covered with brush."
1894: Beatty 1/2 acre Value: $200
"Rocky; situated on middle steamboat channel; high and very picturesque."

Sale

1902: to Walter T. Sampson for $200.

ISLAND 34A

Evaluations and Descriptions

1894: Beatty 1/20 acre Value: $50
"Rocky reef, 4 ft. above water."

ISLAND 34B

Evaluations and Descriptions

1894: Beatty 1/3 acre Value: $100
"Low, level; rocky; birch, white pine and cedar; forms two islands at high water; includes shoal at foot."

Sale

1904: to Fannie D. Lent for $175, with Island 73B.

ISLAND 34C

Evaluations and Descriptions

1894: Beatty 1/60 acre Value: $20
"Bluff islet with a little scrub."

Sale

1904: to David B. Lent for $50.

ISLAND 34D

Evaluations and Descriptions

1894: Beatty 1/60 acre Value: $20
"Small, bare, rock islet."

Sale

1904: to Frederick B. Deane for $200.

ISLAND 34E

Evaluations and Descriptions

1894: Beatty 1/40 acre Value: $30
"Rocky, wooded with pine."

Sale

1904: to David B. Lent for $50.

ISLAND 34F

Evaluations and Descriptions

1894: Beatty 1/60 acre Value: $10
"Low, rocky reef."

Sale

1908: to Frank T. Lent for $30.

DINGHY ISLAND

Names

Named Island 34G by Walter Beatty.

Evaluations and Descriptions

1894: Beatty 1/20 acre Value: $40
"Rocky reef."

ISLAND 34H

Evaluations and Descriptions

1894: Beatty 1/50 acre Value: $20
"Almost joined to Death-dealer Island and forms a splendid harbour on the south side of that island."

ISLAND 34I

Evaluations and Descriptions

1894: Beatty 1/5 acre Value: $60
"A little scrub."

Sale

1910: to Laura A. Bidell for $60.

ISLAND 34J

Evaluations and Descriptions

1894: Beatty 1/5 acre Value: $40

"Bare; rocky; high."

ISLAND 34K

Evaluations and Descriptions

1894: Beatty 1/3 acre Value: $200

"Pretty islet; well wooded; good harbour; grassy; very desirable."

Sale

1902: to Arthur J. Chippendale for $200.

ISLAND 34L

Evaluations and Descriptions

1894: Beatty 1/40 acre Value: $30

"Rocky knob."

ISLAND 34M

Evaluations and Descriptions

1894: Beatty 1/10 acre Value: $50

"Rocky reef."

ISLAND 34N

Evaluations and Descriptions

1894: Beatty 1/5 acre Value: No value

"Rocky reef; beaten over in bad weather."

ISLAND 35

Evaluations and Descriptions

1873: Unwin 1.8 acres Value: $25

"Rocky, covered with brush and small trees."

1894: Beatty 1 4/5 acres Value: $300

"Very pretty; beautifully situated; well wooded; bold; level; good views and fine harbours."

Sale

1889: to Joseph Boucher.

No information available for Island 35A

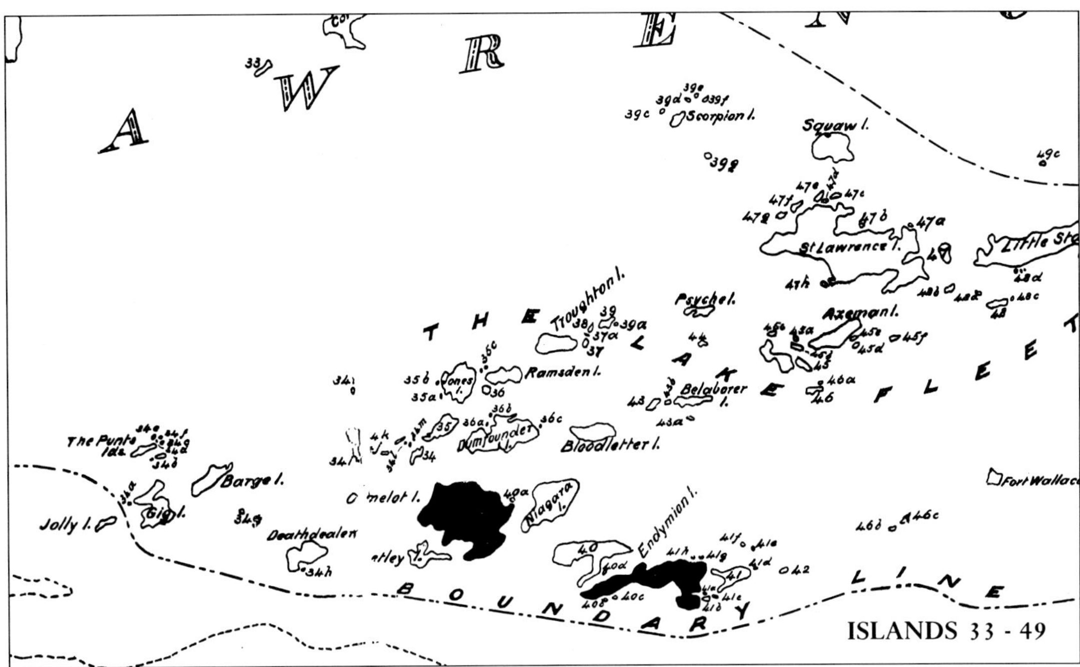

ISLAND 35B

Evaluations and Descriptions

1894: Beatty 1/20 acre Value: $20

"High rock and reef almost connected with Jones [Wyoming] Island."

ISLAND 35C

Evaluations and Descriptions

1894: Beatty 1/10 acre Value: $50

"Bare, rocky islet, embayed including reef, shown separately on plan."

WYOMING ISLAND

Historic Name

1816: Owen — Jones, the Lake Fleet

Named after the War of 1812 ship *Jones*, under the direction of Master John Harris during the Thousand Islands survey (see Part II, The Hydrographers).

Today the island is known as Wyoming Island. It was named after Wyoming College.

Evaluations and Descriptions

1873: Unwin 4.9 acres Value: $20

"Bare Rock about 20 ft high with a few brushes on it."

Sale

Sold: to Byron M. Britton for $500, sold again a few months later to E.A. Morton and J.W. Nichols.

ISLAND 36

Evaluations and Descriptions

1873: Unwin 0.4 acre Value: $5

"Low flat rock, a few bushes."

1894: Beatty 2/5 acre Value: $300

"Level; grassy; timbered with evergreen; fine harbour; well sheltered; good view and approach; in every respect a lovely spot."

Sale

1901: to Oscar F. Wood.

ISLAND 36A

Evaluations and Descriptions

1894: Beatty 1/10 acre Value: $50

"Rocky; embayed; beautifully situated."

Sale

1901: to Hernab S. and W. Rosenbaum.

ISLAND 36B

Evaluations and Descriptions

1894: Beatty 1/10 acre Value: $50

"Rocky; embayed; beautifully situated."

Sale

1901: to H.S. and W. Rosenbaum for $150 with Islands 36A, 36B and 36C.

ISLAND 36C

Evaluations and Descriptions

1894: Beatty 1/10 acre Value: $50

"Rocky islet, bare, pretty view, and good approach."

Sale

1901: to H.S. and W. Rosenbaum.

RAMSDEN ISLAND

Historic Name

1816: Owen — Ramsden, the Lake Fleet

The *Ramsden* was used by Lieut. A.E. Vidal during the Thousand Islands survey. (See Part II, The Lake Fleet, and The Hydrographers.)

Evaluations and Descriptions

1873: Unwin 2.2 acres Value: $30

"Low flat rock, a few bushes."

Sale

1906: to E. Edwin Howard for $500.

TROUGHTON ISLAND

Historic Name

1816: Owen — Troughton, the Lake Fleet

No information is available for this ship. It was probably named after the (British) Troughton family, makers of scientific equipment.

Evaluations and Descriptions

1873: Unwin 3.3 acres Value: $50

"A very high bare rock on the north and west sides, the south and east sides slop down to the water, is well wooded, there is a splendid view from the top of this Island."

Sale

1907: to W.E. Miller for $600.

ISLAND 37

Evaluations and Descriptions

1873: Unwin 0.3 acre Value: $10

"Low with small trees and brush."

1894: Beatty 3/10 acre Value: $250

"Level; well wooded; good harbour; beautifully situated."

Sale

1908: to Emma K. Reid.

ISLAND 37A

Evaluations and Descriptions

1894: Beatty 1/10 acre Value: $75

"High islet with soil; well protected; fine view; good harbourage."

Sale

1901: to Margaret Cora Brough for $225. Sold with Island 38.

ISLAND 38

Evaluations and Descriptions

1873: Unwin 0.2 acre Value: $5

"Low with small trees and brush."

1894: Beatty 1/5 acre Value: $150

"Fine view; a few trees; very level; good harbourage."

Sale

1901: to Margaret Cora Brough for $225. Sold with Island 37A.

ISLAND 39

Evaluations and Descriptions

1873: Unwin 0.6 acre Value: $15

"Low with small trees and brush."

1894: Beatty 3/5 acre Value: $200

"Pretty; level; wooded with pine and birch; good harbourage." (See 39A)

Sale

1904: to Annie Rogers. Sold with Islands 39A and 43.

ISLAND 39A

Evaluations and Descriptions

1894: Beatty 1/10 acre Value: $50

"High rocky point; makes a fine harbour on east shore of 39."

Sale

1904: to Annie Rogers for $50. Sold with Islands 39 and 43.

ISLAND 39B

Evaluations and Descriptions

1894: Beatty 1/20 acre Value: $20

"Bare reef; covered in high water."

SCORPION ISLAND

Historic Name

1816: Owen — Scorpion, the Lake Fleet

The *Scorpion* was probably a sloop or other sailing craft that was used during the survey.

Evaluations and Descriptions

1873: Unwin 0.6 acre Value: $10

"Low and rocky very little soil a few trees and brush."

1894: Beatty 3/5 acre Value: $60

"Level, rocky, fair location, some scrub."

Sale

1894: to C. Probrandt for $60.

ISLAND 39C

Evaluations and Descriptions

1894: Beatty 1/8 acre Value: $40

"Rocky, sparsely wooded."

Sale

1951: to A.F. Webster and Borden C. Miller.

ISLAND 39D

Evaluations and Descriptions

1894: Beatty 1/5 acre Value: $30

"Bare rocks, 2 feet above water."

Sale

1951: to A.F. Webster and Borden C. Miller.

ISLAND 39E

Evaluations and Descriptions

1894: Beatty 1/10 acre Value: $20

"Bare rocks, 2 feet above water."

Sale

1951: to A.F. Webster and Borden C. Miller.

ISLAND 39F

Evaluations and Descriptions

1894: Beatty 1/10 acre Value: $20

"Bare rocks, 2 feet above water."

Sale

1951: to A.F. Webster and Borden C. Miller.

ISLAND 39G

Evaluations and Descriptions

1894: Beatty 1/5 acre Value: $40

"Rocky; high; good location."

DUMBFOUNDER ISLAND

Historic Name

1816: Owen — Dumbfounder, the Lake Fleet

Named after one of the gunboats used in the survey.

Evaluations and Descriptions

1873: Unwin 8.4 acres Value: $60

Gunboats pictured in an engagement in the Thousand Islands. — Coke Smith, Artist, National Archives of Canada C1029

"High, rough and rocky, covered with brush and small trees."

1894: Beatty 8 4/10 acres Value: $1000

"A beautiful island heavily wooded, with pretty bays and sheltered waters."

Sale

1901: to Morris and Solomon G. Rosenbaum for $1,800.

BLOODLETTER ISLAND

Historic Name

1816: Owen — Bloodletter, the Lake Fleet

Named after one of the gunboats used in the survey.

Evaluations and Descriptions

1873: Unwin 3.5 acres Value: $35

"Rocky, covered with brush."

1894: Beatty 3 1/2 acres Value: $500

"Well wooded; good shore; fine view and good approaches."

Sale

1894: to C.E. Britton for $350. Bought with Netley Island.

NETLEY ISLAND

Historic Name

1816: Owen — Netley, the Lake Fleet

The *Netley* was built at York (Toronto) in 1812. Originally built as a schooner called the *Prince Regent*, it was re-rigged as a brig during the War of 1812 and the name was changed to *General Beresford*. It was in action at the Battle of Sackets Harbor in July 1812 and in May 1813. It was described as "a fine vessel for dispatch boat." Used by Captain Owen as a survey ship, the vessel was called the *Netley*.

The *Netley* was sold in Kingston in 1836, but a year later it was needed for the Rebellion of 1837–38 and was bought back. The ship's name was changed again when it was commissioned as a depot ship and called the *Niagara*.

Evaluations and Descriptions

1873: Unwin 2.5 acres Value: $20

"Low and very, well wooded."

Sale

1894: to C.E. Britton for $350. Bought with Bloodletter Island.

CAMELOT ISLAND

Historic Name

1816: Owen — Cockburn, the Lake Fleet

No information on the *Cockburn* is available. The island was locally known as Hog Island. When it was reserved as parkland the name was changed to Camelot. No reason was given for the change.

Evaluations and Descriptions

1873: Unwin 23.4 acres Value: $200

"Rough and rocky, the greater part was formerly cleared but the timber has grown again."

Sale

1880: to S.L. Cook for $35.10.

NIAGARA ISLAND

Historic Name

1816: Owen — Niagara

The Niagara was a corvette (a small frigate) built in 1809 for the Provincial Marine service and first named the *Royal George* during the War of 1812. In 1814 the vessel was taken over by the British Navy and renamed the *Niagara*. It measured over 90 feet, carried twenty-two guns and saw more action than any other ship stationed on Lake Ontario. After the war it was used by the survey crew and was eventually sold in 1837.

Evaluations and Descriptions

1873: Unwin 8.0 acres Value: $50

"Rough and rocky, covered with brush".

1894: Beatty 8 acres Value: $800

"Bold; rocky shore; pine, cedar and oak."

Island Notes

In 1929 Sherman Pratt bought Niagara Island and had an art deco house constructed in 1931. Tradition says that Pratt was going away and asked his architect friend Jack Woods, who lived on Hickory Island, to design and build a house on Niagara. Woods had designed a home for a Mediterranean island and decided to put the same house on Niagara. When Pratt returned he found "the house that Jack built." It certainly resembles a Mediterranean house with sleeping verandahs and tiled patios. Its unusual art deco architecture brings comments from passing tourists who believe the house was built in the 1960s.

Sale

1890: to Morris and Solomon G. Rosenbaum for $1,800. Sold again in 1929 to Sherman Pratt.

ISLAND 40

Evaluations and Descriptions

1873: Unwin 7.0 acres Value: $60

"Partially cleared and partly timbered, some small trees on it. Low Island."

1894: Beatty 7 acres Value: $800

"Well timbered with pine, cedar and oak; nicely situated; good harbours; has some cleared grassy patches which make it very pretty."

Sale

1903: to Margaret S. Darling.

No information about Island 40a

ISLAND 40B

Evaluations and Descriptions

1894: Beatty 1/60 acre Value: $30

"A small reef, nearly connected with Johnson or Charwell Island."

ISLAND 40C

Evaluations and Descriptions

1894: Beatty 1/50 acre Value: $30

"A small reef, nearly connected with Johnson [Endymion Island] or Charwell Island."

ISLAND 40D

Evaluations and Descriptions

1894: Beatty 1/10 acre Value: $75

"Well sheltered; pretty location; good harbourage and approach."

Sale

1905: to Margaret S. Darling.

ENDYMION ISLAND

Historic Name

1816: Owen — Charwell, the Lake Fleet

The *Charwell*, a brig, was built in 1805 at Kingston and was administered by the Provincial Marine. When it was built it was named the *Earl of Moira*. When the British Admiralty took over the naval operations on the Great Lakes in 1813, the ship was renamed the *Charwell*. It was seventy feet long and twenty feet wide and had a draft of seven feet. The *Charwell* was present at Sackets Harbor in July 1812 and in 1813. After the War of 1812 the brig served as the "powder ship" and in 1822 was used as a barracks for seamen in Kingston. It was sold for £21 in 1837 after being "hauled aground rotten to water edge."

The island was also known as Johnson before it was reserved to be used a park land.

Evaluations and Descriptions

1873: Unwin 10.9 acres Value: $100

"Low, partially cleared, a few small trees and brush."

ISLAND 41

Evaluations and Descriptions

1873: Unwin 2.6 acres Value: $20

"Low, a few small trees and brush channel between it and Johnson, shallow."

1894: Beatty 2 3/5 acres Value: $300

"Rough broken ground; wooded with scrub, pitch pine and red cedar; grassed in places."

Sale

1902: to George Bateman.

ISLAND 41A

Evaluations and Descriptions

1894: Beatty 1/10 acre Value: $30

"Rock hummock."

ISLAND 41B

Evaluations and Descriptions

1894: Beatty 1/5 acre Value: $100

"Very pretty; lightly wooded with pine and cedar."

Sale

1903: to M. Crawford.

ISLAND 41C

Evaluations and Descriptions

1894: Beatty 1/60 acre Value: $50

"Small islet, close to above."

ISLAND 41D

Evaluations and Descriptions

1894: Beatty 1/30 acre Value: $50

"Rocky knoll, bearing red cedar and scrub."

ISLAND 41E

Evaluations and Descriptions

1894: Beatty 1/10 acre Value: $50

"Bare rock; good site for a house."

ISLAND 41F

Evaluations and Descriptions

1894: Beatty 1/5 acre Value: $100

"Low; level; soil and scrub; nice location."

Sale

The island was first sold in 1960.

ISLAND 41G

Evaluations and Descriptions

1894: Beatty 1/12 acre Value: $50

"Rocky island well located."

ISLAND 41H

Evaluations and Descriptions

1894: Beatty 1/2 acre Value: $40

"Rocky island well located."

ISLAND 42

Evaluations and Descriptions

1873: Unwin 0.2 acre Value: $10

"Low rock, a few small trees on it."

1894: Beatty 1/10 acre Value: $150

"A lovely little island bearing some fine pine trees; pretty view; good approach."

Sale

1908: to James A. Latimer.

FORT WALLACE ISLAND

Names

William "Bill" Johnston is said to have named this island Fort Wallace.

Evaluations and Descriptions

1873: Unwin 0.8 acre Value: $20

"Rock, low shore, high in centre."

Island Notes

Bill Johnston (See Part I, The Patriot War, 1837–1838) published a proclamation two weeks after he burned the British steamer *Sir Robert Peel.* The statement outlined his political position:

> "I William Johnston, a native-born citizen of Upper Canada, certify that I hold a commission in the Patriot Service of Upper Canada as Commander-in-chief of the naval force and flotilla. I commanded the expedition that captured and destroyed the steamer, Sir Robert Peel. The men under my command in that expedition were nearly all natural born English subjects; the exceptions were volunteers for the expedition.
>
> "My headquarters were on an island in St. Lawrence, without the jurisdiction of the United States, at a place named by me Fort Wallace. I am well acquainted with the boundary line and know which of the islands do, and which do not, belong to the United States; and in the selection of the island I wished to be positive and not locate within the jurisdiction of the Commissioners under the sixth article of Treaty of Ghent, done at Utica, in the state of New York. 13th June, 1822. I know the number of the island, and by that decision it was British territory.
>
> "I yet hold possession of that station, and we also occupy a station some twenty or more miles from the boundary line of the United States, in what Her Majesty's dominions until it was occupied by us. I act under order. The object of my movements is the independence of the Canada. I am not at war with the commerce or property of the people of the United States.
>
> "Signed this tenth day of June, in the year of our Lord, One Thousand Eight Hundred and Thirty-Eight."

Sale

1894: to W.A. Ellie for $350. Sold with Rough or Hamilton Island.

ISLAND 43

Evaluations and Descriptions

1873: Unwin 0.4 acre Value: $10

"Low buff rock, covered with brush."

1894: Beatty 2/5 acre Value: $200

"Very pretty; a good harbour in bay on east side; wooded with pine and cedar."

Sale

1904: to Annie Rogers for $400. Sold with Islands 39 and 39A.

ISLAND 43A

Evaluations and Descriptions

1894: Beatty 1/5 acre Value: $75

"Lightly wooded; nice building site."

Sale

First sold in 1958 for $150.

ISLAND 43B

Evaluations and Descriptions

1894: Beatty 2/5 acre Value: $40

"A shoal which nearly connects 43 and Belaborer."

Sale

First sold in 1957 for $75.

BELABORER ISLAND

Historic Name

1816: Owen — Belaborer, the Lake Fleet

The gunboat *Belaborer* was used by the surveyors in Captain Owen's survey.

Evaluations and Descriptions

1873: Unwin 1 acre Value: $ 25

"Low rock, a few small trees and brush"

1894: Beatty 1.0 acre Value: $200

"Well wooded; level; good harbours."

Sale

1897: to Jessie M. Dewey.

ISLAND 44

Evaluations and Descriptions

1873: Unwin 0.2 acre Value: $5

"Low rock, a little brush on it."

1894: Beatty 1/4 acre Value: $100

"High islet and reef to eastward almost connected; might be made a very pretty site."

PSYCHE ISLAND

Historic Name

1816: Owen — Psyche, the Lake Fleet

The *Psyche*, with fifty-six guns, was launched in Kingston in 1814 as a frigate. It was 130 feet in length, 36 feet 7 inches in breadth; its depth in hold was 10 feet 3 inches, and it weighed 769 tons. The frame was built in England at the Chapman Dockyards and then brought in pieces up the St. Lawrence to Kingston at great expense to the British Navy. The ship was launched in early January 1815, but, unbeknownst to the British naval officers in Canada, the Treaty of Ghent had been signed in Europe to end the war. As a result the ship never saw active service during the War of 1812. The *Psyche* was advertised for sale in 1836 as being the ship "in frame."

Evaluations and Descriptions

1873: Unwin 1 1.2 acres Value: $25

"Low rock covered with small trees and brush, rather pretty Island."

1894: Beatty 1 1/5 acres Value: $25

"Low rock, covered with small trees and brush. Rather pretty island."

Sale

1894: to F.C. McDougall for $400. Purchased as part of the W.D. Morris Real Estate Company.

ASTOUNDER ISLAND

Historic Name

1816: Owen — Astounder, the Lake Fleet

The gunboat *Astounder* was used by the surveyor in Captain Owen's survey.

Evaluations and Descriptions

1873: Unwin 2.2 acres Value: $10

"Low rock, very few trees and brush."

1894: Beatty 2 1/5 acres Value: $250

"Level; good harbourage; fairly wooded; nice location."

Sale

1894: to Ambrose J. Norton for $600. He also purchased Axeman Island.

ISLAND 45

Evaluations and Descriptions

1873: Unwin 0.6 acre Value: $5

"Rock, a few trees and brush on it, the channel between it and 'Astounder' is very narrow and shallow."

Sale

1894: to J.A. Brophy for $160. Sold with Island 47. Purchased as part of the W.D. Morris Real Estate Company.

ISLAND 45A

Evaluations and Descriptions

1894: Beatty 1/50 acre Value: $10

"Rocky, bare."

ISLAND 45B

Evaluations and Descriptions

1894: Beatty 1/4 acre Value: $40

"Rough, rocky; good location; some timber."

Sale

1898: to Edith Fowler Robinson.

ISLAND 45C

Evaluations and Descriptions

1894: Beatty 1/10 acre Value: $20

"Round, rocky island, with a few scattered trees."

Sale

1905: to Susan C. Lancy.

ISLAND 45D

Evaluations and Descriptions

1894: Beatty 1/8 acre Value: $30

"Rocky whaleback; some timber."

Sale

1898: to W.H.F. Himes.

ISLAND 45E

Evaluations and Descriptions

1894: Beatty 1/15 acre Value: $20

"Low, barren rock."

ISLAND 45F

Evaluations and Descriptions

1894: Beatty 1/10 acre Value: $60

"Rocky; some cedar and white birch; pretty good location."

Sale

1905: to Jessie M. Taft for $60.

ISLAND 46

Evaluations and Descriptions

1873: Unwin 0.5 acre Value: $5

"Rock about 15ft. high, with a few nice Pine trees on it."

1894: Beatty 1/2 acre Value: $60

"High in centre; sloping both ways; some good pines for shade; good location."

Sale

1894: to R.A. Livingston for $60.

ISLAND 46A

Evaluations and Descriptions

1894: Beatty 1/2 acre Value: $25

"Very pretty."

Sale

1910: to Frank C. Moore for $25.

ISLAND 46B

Evaluations and Descriptions

1894: Beatty 1/5 acre Value: $30

"Low; barren; rocky."

ISLAND 46C

Evaluations and Descriptions

1894: Beatty 1/5 acre Value: $30

"Low; barren; rocky."

AXEMAN ISLAND

Historic Name

1816: Owen — Axeman, the Lake Fleet

The gunboat *Axeman* was used by the surveyors in Captain Owen's survey.

Evaluations and Descriptions

1873: Unwin 4.2 acres Value: $25

"Rough and rocky, covered with brush."

1894: Beatty 4 1/5 acres Value: $300

"High; level; well timbered; good location."

Sale

1894: to Ambrose J. Norton, with Astounder Island.

SUGAR ISLAND

Historic Name

1816: Owen — St. Lawrence, the Lake Fleet

The *St. Lawrence*, the largest ship of the line, with 104 guns, was built in four months in Kingston and launched on September 10, 1814, in Kingston. She was 191 feet in length, 52 feet in breadth and weighed in excess of 2,300 tons, over three times as heavy as the *Psyche*. Yeo was proud of this ship, and soon after it was launched he felt it had "completely gained the Naval ascendancy on this Lake, and I am happy to say, she sails very superior to anything on it."

Eventually the *St. Lawrence's* topsides rotted and the cost of removing the vast hulk from the harbour was very high, so the navy sold the ship at auction for the paltry sum of £25. Historians recall that the ship was removed to an anchorage off Mississauga Point. During gale-force winds in February 1831 the ship slipped anchor and broke up off St. Helen's Point.

Named Sugar Island by the Mississaugas. They probably made maple sugar from the trees on the island. This local name has always been used.

Evaluations and Descriptions

1873: Unwin 35.7 acres Value: $400

"About 2 acres cleared, timber nearly all cut off remainder, part arable, very prettily situated. There is a frame barn on it, erected by the Government some years ago, and formerly occupied by the late James MacDonald, lighthouse keeper, who is reported to have purchased this, Brock and Little Stave islands from some Indians about 40 years ago. And they refused to give it over to Cook when he was appointed lighthouse keeper, Cook says the Government instructed him to take possession but he never did."

1894: Beatty 35 7/10 acres Value: $1,000

"Pretty well covered with small timber on the hills and pine brush on the level. Broken, rocky."

Sale

1901: to C.E. Britton. Britton purchased the island for the American Canoe Association. The island was transferred to the association in 1906 for $1,000.

SQUAW ISLAND

Historic Name

1816: Owen — Brock, the Lake Fleet

A ship used by the survey team. No description is available except that a schooner named *Brock* was launched at Kingston in 1817 and could have been used by the survey team.

Evaluations and Descriptions

1873: Unwin 4.6 acres Value: $50

"Rather rough and rocky, thickly covered with small Norway Pine, no arable land — see Sugar Id."

1894: Beatty 4 3/5 acres Value: $300

"High; level; good timber; fine location in channel; first rate harbourage at east end."

Sale

1931: purchased as part of the W.D. Morris Real Estate Company.

PRINCESS CHARLOTTE ISLAND

Historic Name

1816: Owen — Princess Charlotte, the Lake Fleet

The *Princess Charlotte*, with forty guns, was launched as a frigate and built at Point Frederick in Kingston. While being built the ship was called the *Vittoria*, but the name was changed prior to launching. She was 121 feet long and weighed more than 756 tons. After the War of 1812 the ship's name was changed to the *Burlington*. It was "laid-up in ordinary" or reserve and was first ordered broken up and then offered for sale in 1831. The exact fate of the *Princess Charlotte* is not known. It is presumed to have sunk in a bay near Kingston.

Evaluations and Descriptions

1873: Unwin 5.0 acres Value: $40

"Some soil, thickly covered with second growth."

1894: Beatty 5 acres Value: $300

"High; rocky; fairly wooded; first rate location; perfect harbour for yachts on north side, thoroughly land-locked one of the best in the river."

Sale

1901: to Mary E. Chaffee and Arthur Lyman.

PRINCE REGENT ISLAND

Historic Name

1816: Owen — Prince Regent, the Lake Fleet

The *Prince Regent*, with sixty guns, was built as a two-decked frigate in 1814 at Point Frederick in Kingston. It was the flagship during the War of 1812 and served as headquarters for the British Navy at dockside in Kingston. After the war the *Prince Regent* was commissioned the *Kingston*. It was advertised for sale in 1832 but never sold and eventually sunk in Deadman's Bay at Kingston.

Prior to its being sold by the Department of Indian Affairs, the island was also known as Little Stave Island by local residents who lived on the islands.

Evaluations and Descriptions

1873: Unwin 27.5 acres Value: $200

"Very high bluff on north east side, slopes down to river on south east, south and west sides, timber all cut off, some soil thickly covered with second growth. For ownership, see remarks on Sugar Id."

1894: Beatty 27 1/2 acres Value: $400

"Very rough, rocky hills with scattered timber upon them and fairly wooded levels, near American Park."

CORN ISLAND

Names

This island was first named Corn Island by natives. It was called Isle Blé d'Inde by the French in their records and was granted by that name to Sir John Johnson.

Evaluations and Descriptions

Not evaluated by Unwin or Beatty since this island was originally given as a land grant to Sir John Johnson in 1789.

Island Notes

An article in the *Gananoque Reporter* written in May 1886 gave the following description of Corn Island: "A mile below Tidd's Island, and rather more than a mile from the main shore, is Corn Island, noted for its being the greatest known resort of water snakes. This island has a beautiful bay at the foot, with a smooth sandy bottom, receding gradually from the shore and making the spot a safe bathing place. This island stands pretty much alone, and has very little shade on it, for which reasons it is not much visited, and thus may account for the congregation of snakes which find there a comparatively safe abiding place."

Sale

This island was given to Sir John Johnson as part of his land grant as a United Empire Loyalist.

GORDON ISLAND

Historic Name

1816: Owen — Citron

This is one of two islands that Owen identified with their original names, given during the 1700s when the French voyageurs were plying the river. Citron is a French word meaning "lemon," probably a descriptive name referring to the shape of the island. The other island is Calumet, near Clayton, New York.

The island was named after a Mr. Gordon, an early settler. His daughter, Katie, married William Sterdivents who lived on the nearby mainland.

Evaluations and Descriptions

1873: Unwin 15.5 acres Value: $10

"Low and level, very good soil all cleared and cultivated some years ago, now over grown with brush, good building stone can be obtained from the south end. It is claimed as part of Lot 24 on the mainland — Township of Leeds."

Sale

This island was reserved for parkland and was never placed on the sale lists.

JACKSTRAW ISLAND

Evaluations and Descriptions

1873: Unwin 0.4 acre Value: $5

"Low rock, a little brush on it."

Sale

1894: to M. Gardner for $150.

SISTERS ISLAND

Evaluations and Descriptions

1873: Unwin 0.4 acre Value: $5

"Consists of 3 small islands, they are rocky, and before the trees were cut off were considered very pretty."

STERDIVENTS POINT

Evaluations and Descriptions

1873: Unwin 22.2 acres Value: $200

"This is in high water an island, in low water it is connected with the main shore, between which and the island or point, there is a stone roadway, it is all cleared. There is a fair dwelling house, and a good frame Barn and shed with stone foundations, for a great many years this Point or Island has been considered as belonging to Lot 24 1st. con. Leeds. The soil is fair and there is a young orchard on it. It is said in former years the boats passed between it and the main land."

PERCH ISLAND

Evaluations and Descriptions

1873: Unwin 1.0 acre Value: $10

"Low and rocky, some soil, takes its name from the great numbers of Perch caught near it."

Sale

1894: to G.D. Girdwood for $100.

HOG ISLAND

Evaluations and Descriptions

1873: Unwin 2.6 acres Value: $35

"Nearly all cleared, fair soil, has been 'cropped'. There is a small shanty on it, and two or three graves."

Sale

1880: to S.L. Cook for $35.

The islands in the 40s are located around Prince Regent Island in the Lake Fleet.

ISLAND 47

Evaluations and Descriptions

1873: Unwin 0.8 acre Value: $20

"Small rocky bluff, thickly covered with brush."

1894: Beatty 4/5 acre Value: $100

"High; rocky; fairly timbered."

Sale

1894: to J.A. Brophy for $160. Sold with Island 45. Purchased as part of the W.D. Morris Real Estate Company.

ISLAND 47A

Evaluations and Descriptions

1894: Beatty 1/50 acre Value: $10

"Barren rock, close to Sugar Island."

ISLAND 47B

Evaluations and Descriptions

1894: Beatty 1/10 acre Value: $30

"Low lying barren rock; fair location."

Sale

1903: to Robert J. Wilkin for the American Canoe Association.

ISLAND 47C

Evaluations and Descriptions

1894: Beatty 1/10 acre Value: $30

"Low; level; some small trees; well sheltered."

Sale

1903: to Robert J. Wilkin for the American Canoe Association.

ISLAND 47D

Evaluations and Descriptions

1894: Beatty 1/15 acre Value: $20

"Low; level; some small trees; well sheltered."

ISLAND 47E

Evaluations and Descriptions

1894: Beatty 1/5 acre Value: $40

"Low; level; some small trees; well sheltered."

Sale

1903: to Robert J. Wilkin for the American Canoe Association.

ISLAND 47F

Evaluations and Descriptions

1894: Beatty 1/3 acre Value: $50

"Low; level; some small trees; well sheltered; with some nice hemlock, cedar and small pine."

Sale

1903: to Robert J. Wilkin for the American Canoe Association.

ISLAND 47G

Evaluations and Descriptions

1894: Beatty 1/4 acre Value: $50

"Level; well timbered, connected with Island 47F in low water."

Sale

1903: to Robert J. Wilkin for the American Canoe Association.

ISLAND 47H

Evaluations and Descriptions

1894: Beatty 1/10 acre Value: $20

"Rough, rocky island; good decoy shooting."

ISLAND 48

Evaluations and Descriptions

1873: Unwin 0.5 acre Value: $12

"Low and rocky — brush on it."

1894: Beatty 1/2 acre Value: $80

"Ten feet above water; level rock; well timbered; good location."

Sale

1927: to Herbert McGregor Bowen.

ISLAND 48A

Evaluations and Descriptions

1894: Beatty 1/15 acre Value: $20

"Barren rock; good location."

ISLAND 48B

Evaluations and Descriptions

1894: Beatty 1/5 acre Value: $50

"Low; level; good timber; good location."

Sale

1898: to William H.F. Holmes.

ISLAND 48C

Evaluations and Descriptions

1894: Beatty 1/20 acre Value: $20

"Rocky; bare."

ISLAND 48D

Evaluations and Descriptions

1894: Beatty 1/20 acre Value: $30

"Bare rock, with shoal to east."

Sale

The island was first sold in 1937 for $35.

ISLAND 48E

Evaluations and Descriptions

1894: Beatty 1/15 acre Value: $25

"Rocky; some trees; good location."

ISLAND 48F

Evaluations and Descriptions

1894: Beatty 1/15 acre Value: $25

"Rocky; some trees; good location."

ISLAND 49

Evaluations and Descriptions

1873: Unwin 1.0 acre Value: $5

"Low rock with a little brush on it."

1894: Beatty 1 acre Value: $200

"High at south-west end; remainder level; wooded sparsely with good pine and cedar; good location on the steamboat channel; good harbourage on north side."

Sale

Purchased as part of the W.D. Morris Real Estate Company.

ISLAND 49A

Evaluations and Descriptions

1894: Beatty 1/20 acre Value: $25

"Barren rock; good location on channel."

ISLAND 49B

Evaluations and Descriptions

1894: Beatty 1/20 acre Value: $25

"Barren rock; good location on channel."

ISLAND 49C

Evaluations and Descriptions

1894: Beatty 1/10 acre Value: $30

"Barren rock; good location on channel."

Sale

The island was first sold in 1957.

ISLAND 49D

Evaluations and Descriptions

1894: Beatty 1/10 acre Value: $50

"High; level; grassy; a few good trees."

Sale

1919: to Norman H. Stevenson and William Cowen.

ISLAND 49E

Evaluations and Descriptions

1894: Beatty 1/10 acre Value: $30

"Barren rocks; low; level."

Sale

1919: to Norman H. Stevenson and William Cowen.

ISLAND 49F

Evaluations and Descriptions

1894: Beatty 1/50 acre Value: $20

"Low; rocky; barren."

Sale

1919: to Norman H. Stevenson and William Cowen.

ISLAND 50

Evaluations and Descriptions

1873: Unwin 0.7 acre Value: $12

"Low rock covered with brush."

1894: Beatty 7/10 acre Value: $200

"Low; level; well timbered; good shelter on north; on steamboat channel; good view of Wellesley Island and Grandview Park."

Sale

Purchased as part of the W.D. Morris Real Estate Company.

ISLAND 50A

Evaluations and Descriptions

1894: Beatty 1/10 acre Value: $80

"Very fine; level; grassy; some small cedars, white birch and pine; first class location."

Sale

1894: to Allan J. Ross.

ISLAND 50B

Evaluations and Descriptions

1894: Beatty 1/30 acre Value: $20

"Rocky; barren."

ISLAND 50C

Evaluations and Descriptions

1894: Beatty 1/20 acre Value: $30

"Rocky; barren."

BUNG ISLAND

Names

Identified as Island 51 by Charles Unwin.

Evaluations and Descriptions

1873: Unwin 0.8 acre Value: $25

"Very pretty island, rocky and thickly covered with brush and small trees."

1894: Beatty 8/10 acre Value: $150

"Low; level; well timbered; good location."

Sale

Purchased as part of the W.D. Morris Real Estate Company.

ISLAND 51A

Evaluations and Descriptions

1894: Beatty 1/10 acre Value: $40
"Rough; rocky; some stunted pine."

ISLAND 51B

Evaluations and Descriptions

1894: Beatty 1/5 acre Value: $100
"Rough; rocky; fairly timbered; with shoal extending to southwest."

Sale

The island was first sold in 1957.

ISLAND 51C

Evaluations and Descriptions

1894: Beatty 1/100 acre Value: $20
"Barren rocks."

ISLAND 51D

Evaluations and Descriptions

1894: Beatty No acreage or value available.
"Level; rocky; some scrub; good building site."

ISLAND 51E

Evaluations and Descriptions

1894: Beatty 1/10 acre Value: $30
"Barren rocks; low; separated by a 4 foot channel."

ISLAND 51F

Evaluations and Descriptions

1894: Beatty 1/10 acre Value: $60
"Flat rock; shown as two on plan; good building site."

ISLAND 51G

Evaluations and Descriptions

1894: Beatty 8/10 acre Value: $60
"Rocky; some scrub; with reef to north-east."

THE NAVY GROUP

Captain Owen and his surveyors were aware which members of the British Navy distinguished themselves in the War of 1812. He began his work in 1815, a year after the British Navy ruled supreme on the Great Lakes. Many of the heroes of that war were still on the lakes, and many would have been involved with Owen and his men. During the survey when Owen was placed in command of the whole force, he corresponded and met with these officers many times.

The British Navy arrived in Canada to assume the command of naval operations on the Great Lakes in June 1813, a year after the war began. Before that, the Provincial Marine, under the command of the British Army, was in charge. Its main purpose was to provide transportation for military supplies destined for forts along the upper St. Lawrence River and on the Great Lakes. It was administered by the quartermaster general's office of the army.

When the Royal Navy was sent to Canada they took over the Provincial Marine ships and continued its responsibility to defend the Great Lakes. The navy fought in more than twenty naval battles on the lakes between May 1813 and September 1814. The commander-in-chief was Comdr. Sir James Lucas Yeo, and under him were commanders, lieutenants, masters and midshipmen. Many of these were given the distinction of having islands named in their honour.

HISTORIC NAME	PRESENT NAME	PAGE
Sir James Yeo	Stave Island (Canadian)	144
Dobbs	Dobbs Island (Canadian)	144
Baumgart	Snake Island (Canadian)	146
Bouchier	Bouchier Island (Canadian)	147
Rowley	Rowley Island (Canadian)	148
Rich	Rich Island (Canadian)	148
Otty	Otty Island (Canadian)	147
Hickey	Hickey Island (Canadian)	145
Scott	Island 52 (Canadian)	145
Hambly	Humbly Island (Canadian)	147
Radcliffe	Turnip Island (Canadian)	149
Mulcaster	Mulcaster Island (Canadian)	150
Downie	Downie Island (Canadian)	148
Cunliffe	Cunliffe Island (Canadian)	152
Owen	Owen Island (Canadian)	152
Popham	Popham Island (Canadian)	153
O'Conner	O'Conner Island (Canadian)	154
Spilsbury	Spilsbury Island (Canadian)	151
Davis	Davis Island (Canadian)	154
Sir William	Sir William Island (Canadian)	155

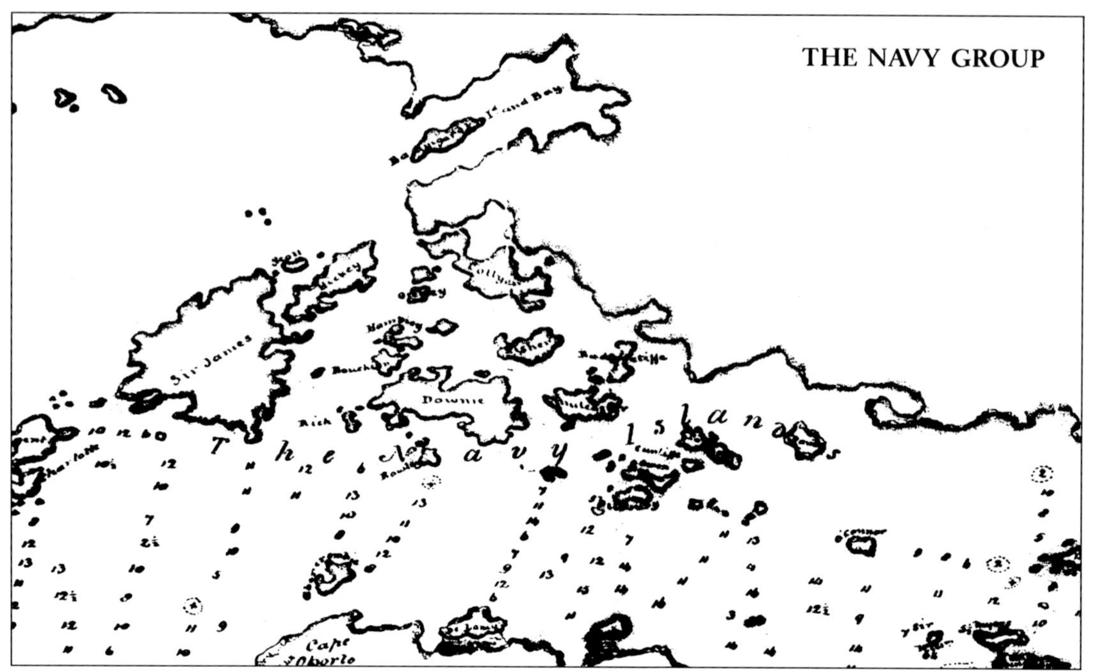

DOBBS ISLAND

Historic Name

1816: Owen — Dobbs, the Navy Islands
Named after Lieut. Alexander T. Dobbs. He served during the War of 1812 on board the *Wolfe* and the *Moira* and fought at the Battle of French Creek. He was also present at Oswego, where he commanded the *Charwell*. He served during the capture of the *Ohio* and the *Somers* on Lake Erie.

Also known locally as Hay or Hai Island.

Evaluations and Descriptions

1873: Unwin 1.4 acres Value: $10
"A narrow and irregularly sloped island, covered with brush and a few trees, water very shallow on its shores."

STAVE ISLAND

Historic Name

1816: Owen — Sir James, the Navy Islands
Named after Sir James Lucas Yeo (1782–1818). Yeo entered the Royal Navy at ten years of age. He served in the Mediterranean, the English Channel, Jamaica in the West Indies and in the North Sea.

In 1805, at twenty-three years of age, he commanded the *Confiance* and captured Cayenne in French Guiana, with four hundred troops. Yeo was left to deal with a thousand prisoners, and his biographer states that "for more than a month, till he received reinforcements, neither Yeo nor any of his officers or men slept out of their clothes."

During the War of 1812 Yeo was appointed commodore and commander-in-chief of the ships on the Great Lakes, and he arrived in Kingston in May 1813. He succeeded in making the British forces on Lake Ontario strong and is credited with providing leadership throughout the war (see Part I, The Thousand Islands and the War of 1812). Following the war he was appointed to the naval fleet on the west coast of Africa and then in Jamaica. He died while returning to England in 1818.

The island was locally known as Big Stave Island. This name would have described the large timbers that were cut as staves to be sent in timber rafts to the markets in Montreal and Quebec.

Evaluations and Descriptions

1873: Unwin 150 acres Value: $1,150
"About 60 acres cleared and 10 acres of uncleared that are arable, the soil is good clay loam, the greater part of the uncleared land is very rough, there is a beautiful Norway Pine grove at the South West end of the Island, there is also a pretty spot on the North East side. It is claimed by Cornelius Cook, light house keeper who has lived upon it for 19 years, he bought from Chas. Shipman, who inherited it from his father, who had been in possession about 30 years. There is a good frame house and barn on it. Cook values his building at $1000, he has a young orchard with about 200 apple, and 100 plum and cherry trees, which he values at $? the chief crops are spring wheat, oats, potatoes and hay. Cook would take $2000 for his claim."

Island Notes

Cornilius Cook purchased Stave Island from the Department of Indian Affairs in 1881 for $600. This was considered a reasonable charge for the 150-acre island. Cook came to Canada from the United States (no date available). He was appointed the lighthouse keeper for the Gananoque Narrows lighthouse and the Jackstraw Light. He took over from James MacDonald who lived on Sugar Island in the 1840s. Cook farmed Stave island, building a house and barn and clearing many acres of land.

In 1894 the island was purchased by A.B. Chaffee, Arthur Lyman and W.J. Wright. Lyman was a prominent businessman from Montreal. Chaffee built the cottage complex on the southeast side of the island. Instead of building a Victorian cottage he built several cottages. The kitchen and dining room were built together, and the living room and sleeping quarters were each separate cabins. This form of construction was used by several island owners and provided a relaxed and informal island life.

Sale

1881: to Cornelius Cook for $600.

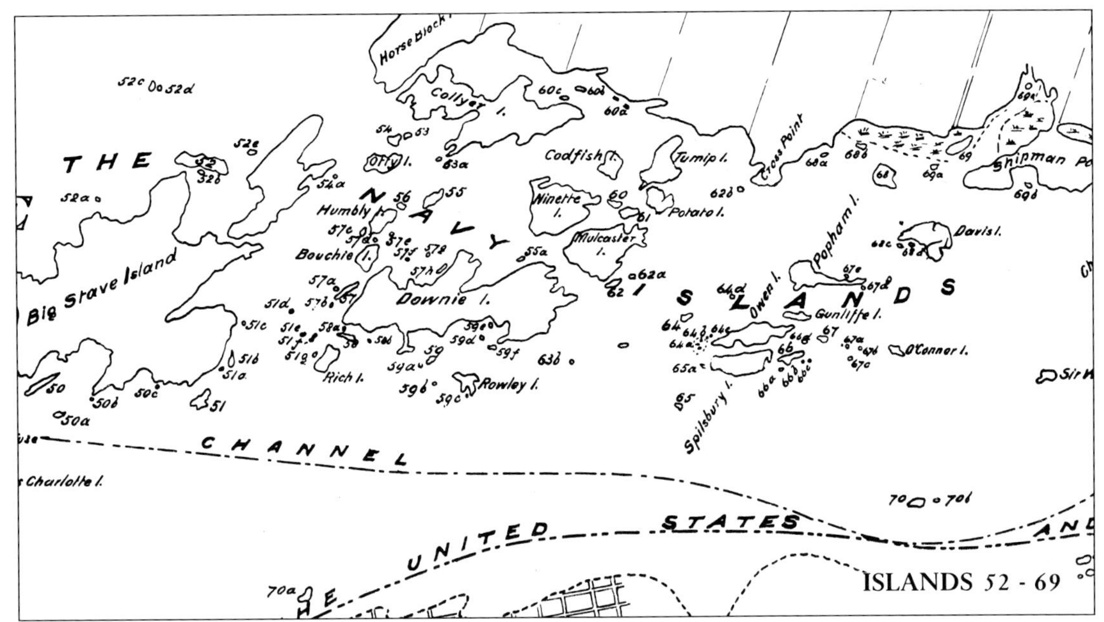

ISLANDS 52 - 69

ISLAND 52

Historic Name

1816: Owen — Scott, the Navy Islands

Probably named after Lieut. John Scott, who served Yeo as flag lieutenant. He was transferred to the lakes from Halifax. He served on the Wolfe and was present at Oswego. According to one of Yeo's dispatches, "Mr. Scott, my first Lieutenant, who was next in command, nobly led them [the seamen] on, and soon gained the ramparts."

The name Scott was only recorded on the 1816 chart and never transferred to the published 1828 charts.

Evaluations and Descriptions

1873: Unwin 3.2 acres Value: $15

Rough high and rocky timber all cut off a little brush still standing — no arable land."

1894: Beatty 3 1/5 acres Value: $150

"High, bold, rocky; covered with pitch pine and birch; level on top."

Sale

Purchased as part of the W.D. Morris Real Estate Company.

ISLAND 52A

Evaluations and Descriptions

1894: Beatty 1/10 acre Value: $30

"With reef to east; high; almost bare."

Sale

This island first sold in 1963 for $75.

ISLAND 52B

Evaluations and Descriptions

1894: Beatty 1/8 acre Value: $40

"Well protected, high, rocky; with marsh to south and south east. A few trees; ensconced in bay."

ISLAND 52C

Evaluations and Descriptions

1894: Beatty 1/4 acre Value: $50

"Rocky, high, bare; with shoal."

Sale

1904: to Adam D. Brown for $75.

ISLAND 52D

Evaluations and Descriptions

1894: Beatty 1/10 acre Value: $25

"Low, rocky."

ISLAND 52E

Evaluations and Descriptions

1894: Beatty 1/10 acre Value: $30

"Low, rocky."

HICKEY ISLAND

Historic Name

1816: Owen — Hickey, the Navy Islands

Named after Commander F. Hickey, who was the commander of the *Prince Regent*. No other biographical information is available.

Also known as Smoke Island.

Evaluations and Descriptions

1873: Unwin 23.7 acres Value: $150

"Very rough, 4.7 acres cleared which is about all the arable land on it all the timber has been cut, only brush left. It is occupied by Chauncey Fowler who has lived on it 8 years, he has a log house and stable, he purchased it from DeNoe for a cow. DeNoe made no improvements."

Island Notes

According to Chauncey Fowler's application to purchase the island, "I settled on Hickey Island in the St. Lawrence River about six miles below Gananoque in the township of Lansdowne some nine years ago. The island has about twenty five acres of rough rock and land with about eight acres of pasture and three of that eight acres is only plowable I have a small Log House and reside on the Island I have improved the few acres of plowable and pasture land and if the land is for sale, I wish to buy."

Sale

1893: to C. Fowler for $202.

BAUMGARDT ISLAND

Historic Name

1816: Owen — Baumgardt, the Navy Islands
Probably named after Capt. W.A. Baumgardt, who commanded the Lake Champlain Fleet, consisting of the flagship *Champlain* and ten gunboats with three long guns each.
Also known as Snake Island.

Evaluations and Descriptions

1873: Unwin 5.0 acres Value: $20
"High rough and rocky, Timber all cut off."
1894: Beatty 5 acres Value: $250
"Long, rounded island; covered with light timber; rocky shores; embayed, affording good harbourage."

Sale

1894: to D.R. Byers for $250.

COLLIER ISLAND

Historic Name

1816: Owen — Collier, the Navy Islands
Named after Captain Collier, who was in command of the *Magnet* (or *Majnet*), which had also been named the *Sir Sydney Smith*. Collier and the British fleet were present at the Battle of Oswego on May 5, 1814. Collier was responsible for taking "ships, boats and skiffs close to the town to see where the enemy had positioned their guns." His action was described as being performed "in a gallant manner."

In the late 1800s the island was called Nigger Island. This name probably referred to a runaway slave who used the island as a campground before and during the Civil War in the United States. Several black men and their families made their way to the Thousand Islands on their way north to escape to freedom. Beginning in the 1950s, the Canadian Names Board, which regulated the official place names of Canada, had all the names with racist overtones removed.

The Navy Group. — Marshall Bros, 1912

Evaluations and Descriptions

1873: Unwin 36.4 acres Value: $150
"Very little arable land, west end high and all rock, east lower and more level. Covered with second growth."

Sale

1885: to Jno. Dano for $150.

ISLAND 53

Evaluations and Descriptions

1873: Unwin 0.2 acre Value: $5
"Low rock with a little brush on it."
1894: Beatty 1/5 acre Value: $75
"High; rocky; slopes to south; some pitch pine; grand views; good harbours."

Sale

1901: to Noah P. McNeil.

ISLAND 53A

Evaluations and Descriptions

1894: Beatty 1/10 acre Value: $30
"High, rocky; with a few trees."

Sale

1901: to Mary S. Winant.

ISLAND 54

Evaluations and Descriptions

1873: Unwin 0.5 acre Value: $10
"High rock with a few scattered Pine trees, very narrow and shallow channel between No. 53 and this Island."
1894: Beatty 1/2 acre Value: $100
"High; rocky; fairly well timbered with pine, cedar and birch; beautiful location."

Sale

1894: to Jno. Sutherland; sold with Island 55A for $200, as part of the W.D. Morris Real Estate Company.

ISLAND 54A

Evaluations and Descriptions

1894: Beatty 1/10 acre Value: $40

"Bare, rocky; with reef to the south."

OTTY ISLAND

Historic Name

1816: Owen — Otty, the Navy Islands

Named after Lieut. Allan Otty, who commanded the *Star* on Lake Ontario during the War of 1812. (He retired as captain in 1854.) Otty served on the lakes during the survey as commander of the *Montreal* and the *Charwell*. Several times in Captain Owen's correspondence he refers to Captain Otty and his ships.

Evaluations and Descriptions

1873: Unwin 2.3 acres Value: $15

"All rock, very little brush, no timber, north end rough."

1894: Beatty 2 3/10 acres Value: $250

"Partly cleared; high; level; grassy; scattered timber."

Sale

1894: to G.S. McFarlane for $400, with O'Connor Island.

ISLAND 55

Evaluations and Descriptions

1873: Unwin 1.1 acres Value: $20

"High, some soil, covered with brush."

1894: Beatty 1 1/10 acres Value: $175

"High, grassy, nice, covered with scattered birch, pine and poplar."

Sale

1895: to A.H. Taylor for $275. Sold with Island 73B, which is in United States waters. Island 55 was part of the W.D. Morris Real Estate Company.

ISLAND 55A

Evaluations and Descriptions

1894: Beatty 2/5 acre Value: $100

"High, level; good pitch pine, poplar, birch and small oak; well located."

Sale

1894: to Jno. Sutherland with Island 54, for $200. This island was part of the W.D. Morris Real Estate Company.

ISLAND 56

Evaluations and Descriptions

1873: Unwin 0.2 acre Value: $5

"Low rock covered with brush."

1894: Beatty 1/5 acre Value: $40

"Rocky; fairly wooded; good location."

Sale

1908: to Alice Boyce.

HUMBLY ISLAND

Historic Name

1816: Owen — Hambly, the Navy Islands

Probably named after Capt. P.A. Hambly (note difference in spelling), who commanded the naval forces on Lake Huron.

Evaluations and Descriptions

1873: Unwin 2.0 acres Value: $20

"High and rough; very little soil; no trees; a little brush."

1894: Beatty 2 acres Value: $200

"High; well wooded; good location."

Sale

1894: to R.M. McLean, with Island 90, for $300. This island was part of the W.D. Morris Real Estate Company. Sold again in 1929 for $1,150.

BOUCHIER ISLAND

Historic Name

1816: Owen — Bouchier, the Navy Islands

Probably named after Capt. William Bouchier, who commanded the Lake Erie Fleet.

Evaluations and Descriptions

1873: Unwin 2.0 acres Value: $22

"High, rough covered with brush, No. 55, Otty Hambly and Bouchier have been burnt over. Fowler is said to have done it to destroy the timber and let the grass grow."

Sale

This island was part of the W.D. Morris Real Estate Company. It was not sold again until 1959 for $1,800.

ISLAND 57

Evaluations and Descriptions

1873: Unwin 0.7 acre Value: $25

"Low, thickly covered with brush, very pretty."

1894: Beatty 7/10 acre Value: $100

"High, rough, rocky; well timbered; good view."

Sale

This island was part of the W.D. Morris Real Estate Company. It was not sold again until 1962.

ISLAND 57A

Evaluations and Descriptions

1894: Beatty 1/10 acre Value: $30

"Low, rocky; some scrub; with shoal to the west end."

ISLAND 57B

Evaluations and Descriptions

1894: Beatty 1/80 acre Value: $20

"Bare rock almost adjoining west end of 57."

ISLAND 57C

Evaluations and Descriptions

1894: Beatty 1/5 acre Value: $40

"High rock; with nice pitch-pine trees."

Sale

1902: to C.M. Quinn and W.P. Moore.

ISLAND 57D

Evaluations and Descriptions

1894: Beatty 1/50 acre Value: $20

"Rocky, some small pines and cedars."

ISLAND 57E

Evaluations and Descriptions

1894: Beatty 1/15 acre Value: $30

"Level, low; some scrub; quartz rock on edge."

Sale

The island was first sold in 1957.

ISLAND 57F

Evaluations and Descriptions

1894: Beatty 1/20 acre Value: $20

"Low, treeless, rocky."

ISLAND 57G

Evaluations and Descriptions

1894: Beatty 1/20 acre Value: $20

"Low, treeless, rocky."

Sale

1905: to J. Moore.

ISLAND 57H

Evaluations and Descriptions

1894: Beatty 1/2 acre Value: $75

"Low, level; well timbered; good harbourage for boats."

Sale

1905: to J. Moore.

ISLAND 58

Evaluations and Descriptions

1873: Unwin 0.4 acre Value: $10

"Low and rocky; covered with small brush."

1894: Beatty 1/5 acre Value: $120

"Low, level, covered with small trees; good shelter."

Sale

1905: to J. Moore.

ISLAND 58A

Evaluations and Descriptions

1894: Beatty 1/20 acre Value: $30

"Barren, low, rocky."

ISLAND 58B

Evaluations and Descriptions

1894: Beatty No acreage or value recorded.

"Point of rock just showing at low water."

RICH ISLAND

Historic Name

1816: Owen — Rich, the Navy Islands

Probably named after Captain Charles Rich. He was Flag-Lieutenant to Sir Edw. W.C.R. Owen on the Canadian Lakes.

Evaluations and Descriptions

1873: Unwin 1.5 acres Value: $20

"Low and rocky, nearly bare."

ISLAND 59

Evaluations and Descriptions

1873: Unwin 0.3 acre Value: $5

"Bluff and rocky, a little brush on it."

1894: Beatty 3/10 acre Value: $100

"Level, rocky; good location; wooded with small cedars and pine."

Sale

1897: to William G. Hurdman for $105.

ISLAND 59A

Evaluations and Descriptions

1894: Beatty 1/20 acre Value: $25

"Rocky, no timber."

ISLAND 59B

Evaluations and Descriptions

1894: Beatty 1/15 acre Value: $25

"Bare rock in good location."

Sale

Island first sold in 1982.

ISLAND 59C

Evaluations and Descriptions

1894: Beatty 1/6 acre Value: $40

"Low lying, rocky, bare."

ISLAND 59D

Evaluations and Descriptions

1894: Beatty 1/20 acre Value: $30

"Bare, rocky; including reef to north-east."

ISLAND 59E

Evaluations and Descriptions

1894: Beatty 1/20 acre Value: $30

"Low, bare, rocky."

ISLAND 59F

Evaluations and Descriptions

1894: Beatty 1/5 acre Value: $100

"Low, level, some small trees."

Sale

1901: to Thomas A. Shipman.

ROWLEY ISLAND

Historic Name

1816: Owen — Rowley, the Navy Islands

Named after Lieut. Edward Rowley. He was among the naval officers who arrived in Halifax and marched from Saint John, New Brunswick, to Kingston during the winter of 1814.

This island is also known as Crow Island.

Evaluations and Descriptions

1873: Unwin 1.4 acres Value: $40

"Low, flat and rocky, very little soil, prettily covered with brush, and second growth."

Sale

This island was part of the W.D. Morris Real Estate Company. It was sold again in 1950.

DOWNIE ISLAND

Historic Name

1816: Owen — Downie, the Navy Islands

Probably named after George Downie, who was appointed lieutenant in 1802. He transferred from commanding the *Montreal* on Lake Ontario to commanding the *Confiance* on Lake Champlain. Downie was killed in action at Plattsburgh in September 1814.

The island was also known as Float Island.

The Float Island House, Downie Island.
— Susan W. Smith, SLINP, Photographic Inventory, 1985

Evaluations and Descriptions

1862: McNaughton 54 acres Value: $100

"Island is partly clear and under meadow, has well sheltered bays, said to be valuable for catching Pickerel in them at certain seasons of the year."

1873: Unwin 66.5 acres Value: $500

"20 acres cleared, fair arable sandy loam, the unclear portion is very rough, and has had a great deal of the timber taken off. There are two small dwelling houses on it, a man named Filo lives there, but it is claimed by his son-in-law Chas. Shipman."

Island Notes

National Archives of Canada notes record: "Samuel Covey was the first person whom I know as having possession of the island who transferred it to one Joseph Davis over 30 years ago. Joseph Davis transferred the same island to David Shipman, who was father to Charles Shipman, transferred the island about 12 years ago. . . When the same Charles Shipman first obtained the island from his father he built a house which was subsequently destroyed by fire and he erected a second house which now stands on it. He also planted a hundred apple trees on the island. He cultivated pasture."

In later years Downie Island was the site of the Boys' Summer Boarding School, built by the Reverend August Ullmann, rector of the Trinity College in New York City. He bought the island from Thomas Shipman in 1901. The school, built on the south side of the island, existed for only a couple of years. Although Ullmann retained ownership of the island for a decade, he rented the school buildings to Alexander MacFarlane in 1913. MacFarlane converted the building into the Float Island House, a hotel that could accommodate seventy-five guests. The lease was renewed for fifteen years. A steamer dock was built, as well as a road around the island and many walking paths. The property surrounding the hotel was landscaped, and a vegetable garden provided the hotel kitchens with produce.

Sale

1881: to L. Steward. Later the island was leased to the Shipman family for $30 a year and then sold to them. Sold to A. Ferguson for $900 (no date available).

NINETTE ISLAND

Historic Name

1816: Owen — Fisher, The Navy Islands

No biographical information is available.

Prior to 1873 it was also known as Mink Island. In 1894 when it was reserved as a park island the name was changed to Ninette Island. It was later sold as a private island, and the name used in correspondence by the Department of Indian Affairs was Ninette.

Evaluations and Descriptions

1873: Unwin 13 acres Value: $120

"Very pretty rocky island, patches of soil in the middle of it, a few good sized trees."

Sale

This island was reserved to be used for park purposes, but after several appeals had been made to the Department of Indian Affairs the island was placed on the open market and sold privately.

COD FISH ISLAND

Evaluations and Descriptions

1873: Unwin 2 acres Value: $10

"Rocky, no arable land, some brush on it."

Sale

1898: to James Adams.

RADCLIFFE ISLAND

Historic Name

1816: Owen — Radcliffe, the Navy Islands

Probably named after Charles Radcliffe (also called Coleston Radcliffe). He was present at the Battle of French Creek, serving on the *General Beresford* on Lake Ontario, and also was commander of the *Netley*. He was killed in 1814 in the "act of boarding" at the capture of the *Ohio* and the *Somers*. Sir James Lucas Yeo recorded his death: "The service lost a very zealous and valuable officer."

Named Turnip Island by Charles Unwin.

Evaluations and Descriptions

1873: Unwin 6.0 acres Value: $25

"Rocky, and rough, a little soil nearly all the grass gone, and grown up with brush."

Sale

1903: to E.J. Wohlgemuth for $400.

POTATO ISLAND

Evaluations and Descriptions

1873: Unwin 2.8 acres Value: $10

"Rocky and rough, timber and soil same as Turnip."

Sale

1894: to J.M. Craig for $300 with Island 60.

ISLAND 60

Evaluations and Descriptions

1873: Unwin 0.4 acre Value: $2

"Low and rocky, some brush."

1894: Beatty 2/5 acre Value: $100

"Pretty, well wooded, well sheltered, good building site."

Sale

1894: to J.M. Craig for $300 with Potato Island. Described as Island 60 or Huckleberry Island.

ISLAND 60A

Evaluations and Descriptions

1894: Beatty 1/20 acre Value: $30

"Low ridge; some nice pine and white birch."

Sale

1902: to Thomas J. Darling.

ISLAND 60B

Evaluations and Descriptions

1894: Beatty 1/20 acre Value: $40

"Low, fairly level; good small trees."

ISLAND 60C

Evaluations and Descriptions

1894: Beatty 1/10 acre Value: $20

"Low, level, willow scrub, marsh on south-west."

Sale

This island was first sold in 1959.

ISLAND 61

Evaluations and Descriptions

1873: Unwin 0.8 acre Value: $5

"Low and rocky, some brush."

1894: Beatty 1/6 acre Value: $100

"Levels for building; high, rocky heads; plenty of scrub; some pines; in sheltered waters; fine harbourage."

Sale

The island was purchased as part of the W.D. Morris Real Estate Company. It was not sold again until 1950.

MULCASTER ISLAND

Historic Name

1816: Owen — Mulcaster, the Navy Islands

Probably named after Sir William Howe Mulcaster (1785–1837). He was appointed lieutenant in 1800 and served as first lieutenant on the *Confiance* under Captain Yeo at the capture of Cayenne, in French Guiana. For his services, the Prince Regent of Portugal presented him with a gold sword, and he was made a commander of the Tower and Sword. He was transferred to the North American Station in 1813, served as a commander at French Creek and was made a post captain in 1813. Mulcaster was severely wounded at the Battle of Oswego and invalided out in 1814. Years later he was knighted and made aide-de-camp to King William IV.

The island was also known by the Mississaugas as Sugar Island, named for the maple sugar they made from a large stand of maple trees.

Evaluations and Descriptions

1873: Unwin 13.3 acres Value: $150

"About 2 acres in the centre arable which was cleared some years ago, but is now grown up with brush, a few nice trees still standing."

1894: Beatty 13 3/10 acres Value: $700

"Splendid island in beautiful locality; good fishing; excellent soil; land rolling and well timbered; plenty of good harbours convenient to all the channels; good approach for steamers."

Island Notes

According to the application of Benjamin Cross to purchase Sugar or Mulcaster Island in 1873: "My father Moses Cross went on to an island called Sugar Island about forty years ago and he now is a very old man and resides with me but several years ago when he came to live with me he gave up his right to the island unto me Island which is very rough and not over two or three acres tillable but lies in from my other land on the main shore and would like to buy same."

Sale

Sold to A. Ferguson for $900.

ISLAND 62

Evaluations and Descriptions

1873: Unwin 0.4 acre Value: $5

"Low flat rock with a few trees."

1894: Beatty 1/3 acre Value: $80

"Level, low; nice small trees; very well situated; good harbour."

Sale

1894: to Julia Graham for $80.

ISLAND 62A

Evaluations and Descriptions

1894: Beatty 1/30 acre Value: $25

"High, rocky head, with rock to north-east."

ISLAND 62B

Evaluations and Descriptions

1894: Beatty 1/4 acre Value: $75

"Low, level, some soil, well timbered with oak, cedar and hemlock; good location."

Sale

1894: to A.P. Holmes for $75, with St. Gabriel Point Island.

ISLAND 63

Evaluations and Descriptions

1873: Unwin 0.2 acre Value: $2

"Low flat rock a little brush."

1894: Beatty 1/5 acre Value: $75

Nice, level; grassy; some trees."

Sale

1896: to Eva H. Lahmer.

ISLAND 63A

Evaluations and Descriptions

1894: Beatty 1/15 acre Value: $30

"Bare, rocky islet."

Sale

1896: to Eva H. Lahmer.

ISLAND 63B

Evaluations and Descriptions

1894: Beatty 1/50 acre Value: $20

"Bare, rocky islet."

ISLAND 64

Evaluations and Descriptions

1873: Unwin 0.3 acre Value: $5

"High rock with a little brush."

1894: Beatty 3/10 acre Value: $70

"High rock; fine small timber; good location."

Sale

1894: to Charlotte E. Hurdman.

ISLAND 64A

Evaluations and Descriptions

1894: Beatty 1/3 acre Value: $100

"Low, rocky, submerged in places at high water; cedar and willow scrub."

Sale

The island was first sold in 1959.

ISLAND 64B

Evaluations and Descriptions

1894: Beatty 1/20 acre Value: $25

"Low, barren, rocky, good location."

ISLAND 64C

Evaluations and Descriptions

1894: Beatty 1/20 acre Value: $25

"Low, barren, rocky, good location."

ISLAND 64D

Evaluations and Descriptions

1894: Beatty 1/20 acre Value: $25

"Bare, rocky islet."

ISLAND 65

Evaluations and Descriptions

1873: Unwin 0.2 acre Value: $2

"Low flat rock with a few trees and a little brush."

1894: Beatty 1/5 acre Value: $100

"Level, grassy, some small pines and scrub, very nice for building."

Sale

1905: to Frank T. Taft for $100.

ISLAND 65A

Evaluations and Descriptions

1894: Beatty 1/10 acre Value: $75

"Low, level, some nice trees, good location."

Sale

1907: to Thomas E. Rope (spelling?) for $75.

SPILSBURY ISLAND

Historic Name

1816: Owen — Spilsbury, the Navy Islands

Probably named after Francis Brockell Spilsbury, who was a commander in the British Navy during the War of 1812. He commanded the *Melville* and the *Beresford* and was captain on the Niagara. He was present at the Battle of Oswego and was taken prisoner at Sandy Creek.

Evaluations and Descriptions

1873: Unwin 5.2 acres Value: $40

"Rough and rocky, high west end, very little soil and few small trees and brush."

1894: Beatty 5 1/5 acres Value: $300

"Second growth timber; good location, in sight of American Park; good harbourage; sheltered waters; good fishing."

Sale

1894: to A. Ferguson for $300.

ISLAND 66

Evaluations and Descriptions

1873: Unwin 0.8 acre Value: $10

"Low and rocky, some brush."

1894: Beatty 4/5 acre Value: $150

"Low, level, well timbered; good locality; a very pretty piece, which is almost separated by marsh, might be bought separately at $75."

Sale

1897: to the W.D. Morris Real Estate Company.

ISLAND 66A

Evaluations and Descriptions

1894: Beatty 1/50 acre Value: $25

"Barren rock."

ISLAND 66B

Evaluations and Descriptions

1894: Beatty 1/10 acre Value: $30

"Barren rock, contiguous to 66."

Sir Edward William Campbell Rich Owen.
— National Archives of Canada C2591

ISLAND 66C

Evaluations and Descriptions

1894: Beatty 1/10 acre Value: $30
"Barren rock, contiguous to 66."

ISLAND 66D

Evaluations and Descriptions

1894: Beatty 1/2 acre Value: $50
"Barren; rocky; including shoal to the west."

Sale

The island was first sold in 1958.

OWEN ISLAND

Historic Name

1816: Owen — Owen, the Navy Islands
Probably named after Sir Edward Campbell Rich Owen (1771–1849). (See Part I, Capt. William FitzWilliam Owen and the First Survey, 1815–17.) He was born on Campobello Island in New Brunswick, but moved to England as a small boy. He entered the navy on board the *Culloden* in 1786. He served in the Mediterranean, in North America and in the West Indies.

During the period 1802–09 he was serving on the coast of France, capturing or destroying the enemy's gunboats. In January 1815 he was sent to Canada to replace Sir James Yeo as commander-in-chief of His Majesty's Service on the Great Lakes. He served in this position at Kingston during the year that his brother, Capt. William FitzWilliam Owen, began his surveys.

After his retirement in 1816 he served as commander of the Royal Sovereign Yacht. In 1825 he was appointed to the Council of Lord High Admirals.

Evaluations and Descriptions

1873: Unwin 4.8 acres Value: $40
"About half arable, fair soil, a little brush, timber was cut a short time ago."
1894: Beatty 4 4/5 acres Value: $100
"A succession of small hills 10 to 12 ft. in height with low levels between; some good timber, and scrub; good harbourage good fishing."

Sale

1894: to E.A. Le Sueur for $150.

CUNLIFFE ISLAND

Historic Name

1816: Owen — Cunliffe, the Navy Islands
Named after Charles Cunliffe Owen, who entered the British Navy as midshipman in 1801. He was promoted to lieutenant and served as flag lieutenant. He was taken prisoner by the French at Île d'Aix, but escaped after three years. In 1813 he joined the British Lake Service, fighting in the War of 1812 as lieutenant on the *Wolfe* and as lieutenant commander on the *Sir Sidney Smith*. He was present in action at French Creek. Later he was appointed acting commander of the "gunboat establishment." Both army and navy troops were crews in the gunboat fleets and played a major role in the Lake Command. All those assigned to the gunboat flotilla were senior navy men, so the service was held in great esteem. Charles Cunliffe Owen was invalided in March 1815.

Evaluations and Descriptions

1873: Unwin 1.0 acre Value: $20
"Low and rocky, some brush."
1894: Beatty 1 acre Value: $150
"Level; well timbered; beautifully situated; good harbourage; fine fishing; a most desirable island."

Sale

1894: to Evelyn W. Wood for $150.

ISLAND 67

Evaluations and Descriptions

1873: Unwin 0.2 acre Value: $10
"Low and rocky, some brush."
1894: Beatty 1/5 acre Value: $60
"Well timbered, good location, between Thousand Island Park and Canadian fishing grounds."

Sale

1894: to G.F. Macdonald for $270, with Rattlesnake Island. The island was part of the W.D. Morris Real Estate Company.

ISLAND 67A

Evaluations and Descriptions

1894: Beatty 1/10 acre Value: $40
"Two small islands."

Sale

The island was first sold in 1859.

ISLAND 67B

Evaluations and Descriptions

1894: Beatty 1/50 acre Value: $20
"Bare, rocky islet."

ISLAND 67C

Evaluations and Descriptions

1894: Beatty 1/20 acre Value: $30
"Barren rock, good location."

ISLAND 67D

Evaluations and Descriptions

1894: Beatty 1/15 acre Value: $40
"Almost connected with Popham Island but not valued with it; good location; wooded; nice boat harbour."

Sale

The island was first sold in 1959.

ISLAND 67E

Evaluations and Descriptions

1894: Beatty 1/5 acre Value: $60
"Rocky islet, lightly wooded; with rocky points extending south and east."

POPHAM ISLAND

Historic Name

1816: Owen — Popham, the Navy Islands
Probably named after Steven Popham (1780–1842), who entered the navy as midshipman in 1795 and became a lieutenant. He fought at Copenhagen and at Wacheren as aide-de-camp to the commander-in-chief. He was sent to the North American Station as a commander and was wounded at the Battle of Oswego. He was taken prisoner at Sandy Creek in 1813. He was made a post captain in 1814 and after retirement settled in Wales.

Evaluations and Descriptions

1873: Unwin 4.6 acres Value: $30
"High at west end, low at east a little soil, a few small trees and some brush."
1894: Beatty 4 3/5 acres Value: $250
"Low; indented; well timbered; fine, level land; nicely located."

Sale

Sold, with Rowley Island, to T. Saunders for $500.

ISLAND 68

Evaluations and Descriptions

1873: Unwin 1.7 acres Value: $10
"Low, all cleared, soil very full of small boulders."
1894: Beatty 1 7/10 acres Value: $150
"Level; grassy; fairly timbered; good location."

Sale

1894: to W.G. Atkinson for $150.

ISLAND 68A

Evaluations and Descriptions

1894: Beatty 1/30 acre Value: $20
"Low, rocky, some timber."

Sale

1904: to J.D. Wetherell and W.P. Moore.

ISLAND 68B

Evaluations and Descriptions

1894: Beatty 2/5 acre Value: $50
"Covered with small oak; grassy; good view to south-west."

Sale

1901: to Fairman Cross.

ISLAND 68C

Evaluations and Descriptions

1894: Beatty 1/60 acre Value: $20
"Bare, rocky, low, level."

ISLAND 68D

Evaluations and Descriptions

1894: Beatty 1/60 acre Value: $20
"Bare, rocky, low, level."

ISLAND 69

Evaluations and Descriptions

1873: Unwin 1.2 acres Value: $5
"High, rocky, no soil a few trees and bushes."
1894: Beatty 1 2/5 acres Value: $80
"High, rough; fairly timbered; marsh to North and East."

Sale

1905: to Freeman Shipman.

ISLAND 69A

Evaluations and Descriptions

1894: Beatty 1/10 acre Value: $40
"Low, level, grassy."

Sale

The island was first sold in 1959.

ISLAND 69B

Evaluations and Descriptions

1894: Beatty 1/20 acre Value: $10
"Barren, low."

Sale

1907: to Walter L. Visger.

ISLAND 69C

Evaluations and Descriptions

1894: Beatty 1/10 acre Value: $25
"Well timbered; surrounded by marsh."

ISLAND 69D

Evaluations and Descriptions

1894: Beatty No acreage given Value: $50
"Low, rocky, some scrub."

Sale

1907: to Walter L. Visger.

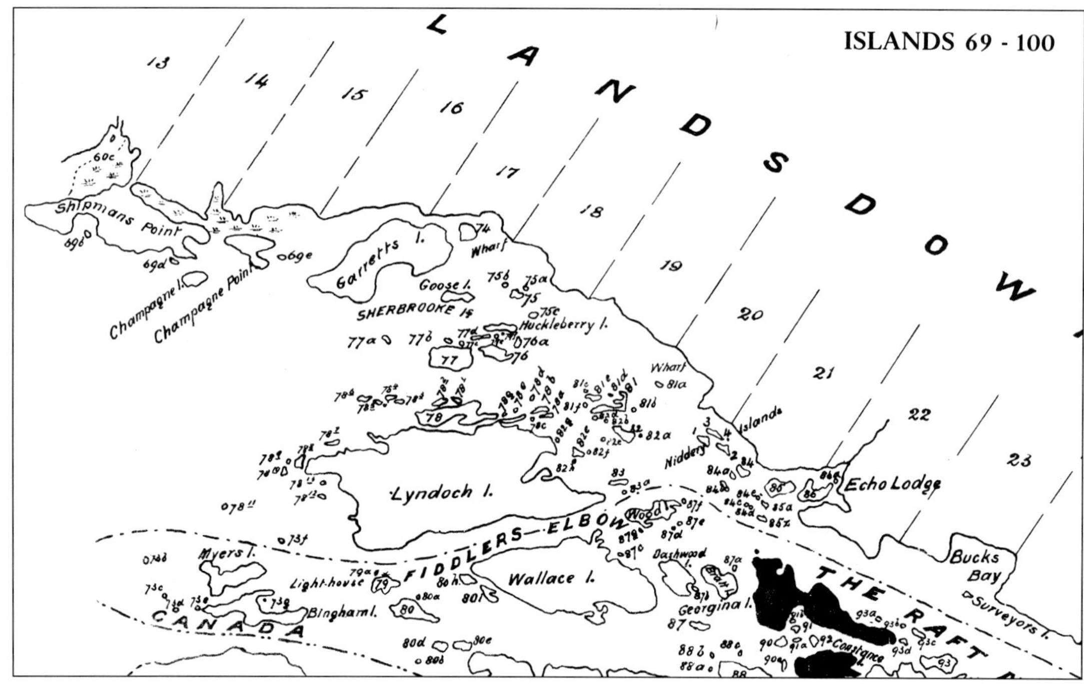

ISLAND 69E

Evaluations and Descriptions

1894: Beatty 1/10 acre Value: $25

"Low, stony; with adjunct to the south-west; marshy to Champagne Point."

DAVIS ISLAND

Historic Name

1816: Owen — Davis, the Navy Islands

Probably named after Commander Henry Thomas Davies, who entered the navy in 1794. He served under Lord Hope and was present at the surrender of the Cape of Good Hope in 1795. He served as lieutenant in Egypt in 1801. He was promoted to commander in 1806 after his distinguished conduct. In Canada he served as commander on board the *Niagara* in 1814 and also on the *Prince Regent*. He retired in 1846.

Also known as Gull Island in early days.

Evaluations and Descriptions

1873: Unwin 5.8 acres Value: $40

"Rough, rocky, some soil, two or three small trees, brush, has been cropped and pastured."

Sale

1894: to S. Bendit for $300.

O'CONNOR ISLAND

Historic Name

1816: Owen — O'Connor, the Navy Islands

Probably named after Sir Richard James Lawrence O'Connor (sometimes spelled O'Conner), who entered the navy in 1798. He served as lieutenant on the *Confiance* under Captain Yeo. He later served as flag lieutenant to Rear Adm. Sir E. Nagle and was appointed commander in 1810. By 1814 he was appointed commander of the *Duke of Kent* at Kingston and flag captain on the *Prince Regent*. He later commanded the *Princess Charlotte*. O'Connor became a post captain in 1815, was knighted in 1836 and retired from the navy in 1846.

Evaluations and Descriptions

1873: Unwin 0.5 acre Value: $15

"High in centre, some soil a few trees and bushes."

Sale

1894: to G.S. McFarlane for $400, with Otty Island.

ISLAND 70

Evaluations and Descriptions

1873: Unwin 0.5 acre Value: $5

"Rock, no soil, a few Pine trees on it."

1894: Beatty 1/2 acre Value: $80

"Level, rocky, good pine shade trees.

Sale

1897: to the W.D. Morris Real Estate Company.

ABERCROMBIE ISLAND

Historic Name

1816: Owen — Abercrombie (*sic*), the Wellington Islands

Probably named after Col. Hon. Alexander Abercromby (1784–1853), who was the fourth son of Lieut.-Gen. Sir Ralph Abercromby (1738–1801). He was educated at the Royal Military College from 1801 to 1802, and served in the quartermaster general's department attached to the 6th Division, the 2nd Division and the 7th Division.

This island was identified as Island 70A by Walter Beatty. It was not included on the Charles Unwins' plan; probably he thought it was in United States waters.

Evaluations and Descriptions

1894: Beatty 1 1/2 acres Value: $200

"Covered with scrub and fair shade trees; good soil; good view; within 200 yards of Fairview Park, United States."

ISLAND 70B

Evaluations and Descriptions

1894: Beatty 1/80 acre Value: $10

"Bare rock, partly submerged in high water."

ISLAND 71 and ISLAND 72B

Evaluations and Descriptions

1873: Unwin 0.1 acre Value: $2

"Rock, no soil, a few Pine trees on it."

> Islands 72 and 73B are in United States waters. See American Islands, Derey Island, Wellesley's Island.

ISLAND 72

Evaluations and Descriptions

1873: Unwin 0.5 acre Value: $15

"Rocky, pretty well covered with trees and brush."

Sale

1899: to Frederick A. Folger.

ISLAND 73

Evaluations and Descriptions

1873: Unwin 0.3 acre Value: $20

"Same as Island 72."

Sale

This island is in United States waters.

ISLAND 73B

Evaluations and Descriptions

1894: Beatty 1/5 acre Value: $75

"Nice shade pines; fine view; good approach; between two channels; level; nice locality."

Sale

1894: to A.H. Taylor, with Island 55, which is in Canadian waters, for $275. Island 73B is in United States waters, and details of how this sale and transfer of funds was resolved are not available.

ISLAND 73C

Evaluations and Descriptions

1894: Beatty 1/100 acre Value: $10

"Bare, rocky."

ISLAND 73D

Evaluations and Descriptions

1894: Beatty 1/10 acre Value: $25

"Bare rocks."

ISLAND 73E

Evaluations and Descriptions

1894: Beatty 1/10 acre Value: $25

"Bare, rocky."

Sale

1901: to Andrew Devine, with Island 84E, for $45.

SIR WILLIAM ISLAND

Historic Name

1816: Owen — Sir William, the Navy Islands

There are several Sir Williams who could have been commemorated with this island name, including Sir William Owen, Captain Owen's father, and Sir William Rich, Captain Owen's benefactor. (See Part II, Capt. William FitzWilliam Owen and the First Survey, 1815–1817.)

Evaluations and Descriptions

1873: Unwin 0.6 acre Value: $15

"Some soil, timber and brush near all burnt."

CHAMPAGNE ISLAND

Evaluations and Descriptions

1873: Unwin 1.1 acres Value: $20

"High rock well covered with small trees and bushes."

1894: Beatty 1 1/10 acre Value: $100

"Good shade trees; high on north side sloping to south."

Sale

1894: to David Scott for $300, with Island 113G. Both islands were part of the W.D. Morris Real Estate Company. It was not sold again until the 1940s.

CHAMPAGNE POINT

Evaluations and Descriptions

1873: Unwin 4.2 acres Value: $10

"This is an island in high water. Jno. Crae who owns land at the back of it, claims it as part of this lot, being afraid of losing it, he last winter cut down all the timber, thereby destroying one of the prettiest spots on the River."

1894: Beatty 4 1/5 acres Value: $300

"Cleared; some good scattered shade trees; good location; marsh to north."

WESTON ISLAND

Names

The island was locally known as Garretts Island at the time of the Unwin survey in 1873. The Weston family purchased the island in the 1870s.

Evaluations and Descriptions

1873: Unwin 30 acres Value: $200

"There are 3.6 Acres cleared, the soil of which is fair, the uncleared part is rocky, has some pretty trees. The occupant is Widow Garrett, whose husband died last winter at the age of 106, he lived there 40 years, at one time an acre of it was cleared, Mrs. Garrett has no family and is about 90 years of age, she values her improvements at $150, which is reasonable, there is a pretty good log house on it. [?] is partly supported by township of Lansdowne.

"In low water this island is nearly connected with the mainland. Her husband 'Squatted' there."

Island Notes

In 1875 the island was purchased by Edith Weston, a widow from Lansdowne. The present island residents, descendants of the Weston family, celebrated the island centennial in 1973.

Sale

1875: to Edith Weston.

ISLAND 74

Evaluations and Descriptions

1873: Unwin 1.0 acre Value: $5

"Rocky, a few trees on it. Is used in winter for cutting wood for shipping in summer. Is connected with mainland in low water."

1894: Beatty 1 acre Value: $100

"Some good soil, grass, fine large pine shade trees."

Sale

Purchased as part of the W.D. Morris Real Estate Company. It sold again in 1947.

GOOSE ISLAND

Historic Name

1816: Owen — Sherbrooke Islands, the Wellington Islands

Named after Sir John Coape Sherbrooke (1764–1830). Sherbrooke served many years in the British Army. In 1809 he was appointed Wellington's second in command at Talavera. He was knighted following that victory, but because of poor health, he had to return to England. During the War of 1812 Sherbrooke was appointed lieutenant-governor of Nova Scotia, and during the time of the survey of the Thousand Islands he was governor-general of Canada (1816–18).

Named Goose Island by Charles Unwin.

Evaluations and Descriptions

1873: Unwin 1.1 acres Value: $12

"Rocky with brush and small trees."

1894: Beatty 1 1/10 acres Value $100

"Some scattered trees; level; fair location."

Sale

Purchased as part of the W.D. Morris Real Estate Company.

ISLAND 75

Evaluations and Descriptions

1873: Unwin 0.5 acre Value: $5

"Low and rocky with brush and small trees."

1894: Beatty 1/2 acre Value: $50

"Fine, level, good soil and timber, good location."

Sale

1894: to John G. Wallace.

ISLAND 75A

Evaluations and Descriptions

1894: Beatty 3/10 acre Value: $30

"Rocky shoal, slightly above water; good location."

Sale

1902: to Stephen Findlay.

ISLAND 75B

Evaluations and Descriptions

1894: Beatty 3/10 acre Value: $30

"Square, rocky, two feet above water."

Sale

1902: to Stephen Findlay.

ISLAND 75C

Evaluations and Descriptions

1894: Beatty 1/5 acre Value: $50

"Good location, but in swift water."

Sale

1905: to M.R. Macdonald.

HUCKLEBERRY ISLAND

Historic Name

1816: Owen — Sherbrooke Islands, the Wellington Islands

See Goose Island for Sherbrooke's biography.

Evaluations and Descriptions

1873: Unwin 0.9 acre Value: $15

"High rock at East end low at West, small timber and brush, no soil."

Sale

Purchased as part of W.D. Morris Real Estate organization. Not resold until the 1940s.

ISLAND 76

Evaluations and Descriptions

1873: Unwin 1.2 acres Value: $20

"Low, some soil, nearly all Timber recently cut off, a few bushes left."

1894: Beatty 1 1/5 acres Value: $150

"Nice harbourage; wooded; good approach; well situated; pretty view down river."

Sale

Purchased as part of the W.D. Morris Real Estate Company. It was sold again in 1944 for $750.

ISLAND 76A

Evaluations and Descriptions

1894: Beatty 1/8 acre Value: $50

"Well timbered, good location."

Sale

1894: to Allan J. Ross for $130.

ISLAND 77

Evaluations and Descriptions

1873: Unwin 4.7 acres Value: $50

"High on South side low on North, nearly all the timber recently cut off, a few small trees and brush left, rocky."

1894: Beatty 4 7/10 acres Value: $300

"A very pretty island; wooded; commands good view to west; good harbourage and fishing."

Sale

1898: to Philip D. Ross.

ISLAND 77A

Evaluations and Descriptions

1894: Beatty 1/5 acre Value: $40

"With reef to south-east; rocky, some scrub."

Sale

1901: to J.P. Krauss.

ISLAND 77B

Evaluations and Descriptions

1894: Beatty 1/8 acre Value: $40

"Rocky, level, some small pines and cedar."

Sale

1898: to John A.D. Holbrook.

ISLAND 77C

Evaluations and Descriptions

1894: Beatty 1/10 acre Value: $40

"Low, rocky; with adjunct to south; cedar, pine and scrub."

Sale

1898: to John A.D. Holbrook.

ISLAND 77D

Evaluations and Descriptions

1894: Beatty 1/5 acre Value: $75

"Long, narrow island; rocky; some good timber."

Sale

1901: to Jean Haig.

ISLAND 77E

Evaluations and Descriptions

1894: Beatty 1/50 acre Value: $25

"Level, rocky; cedar scrub; separated from 77D by 30 ft. rapid channel."

Sale

1901: to Jean Haig.

ISLAND 77F

Evaluations and Descriptions

1894: Beatty 1/100 acre Value: $10

"Reef slightly above water; barren."

ISLAND 78

Evaluations and Descriptions

1873: Unwin 5.4 acres Value: $60

"High and rock, some soil a little timber and brush on east end."

1894: Beatty 5 2/5 acres Value: $400

"Fine, well-timbered island; good harbourage; nice view; near channel; good soil on east end; west end rocky. Might be bought in separate lots, being nearly cut in two, east lot containing about 1 2/5 acres for $104, west containing about 4 acres for $296."

Sale

Purchased as part of the W.D. Morris Real Estate Company. The island soon sold again, in 1902, to W.G. Saunders, for $1,675.

Beatty named the islands 78/1 to 78/13.

ISLAND 78/1

Evaluations and Descriptions

1894: Beatty 1/5 acre Value: $50

"High, rocky, pretty channel inshore; small shade trees; fine view."

Sale

Purchased as part of the W.D. Morris Real Estate Company. The island was sold to W.G. Saunders in 1902.

ISLAND 78/2

Evaluations and Descriptions

1894: Beatty 3/10 acre Value: $75

"Level; well wooded with pine; pretty view; fine harbourage; with adjoining shoal."

Sale

1903: to Edna Haig.

ISLAND 78/3

Evaluations and Descriptions

1894: Beatty 1/5 acre Value: $100

"Well wooded; on channel; pine and cedars; good view; connected by strip with 78/4."

Sale

Purchased as part of the W.D. Morris Real Estate Company. The island was sold again in 1961 for $1,650.

ISLAND 78/4

Evaluations and Descriptions

1894: Beatty 1/2 acre Value: $130

"Thickly wooded; very pretty; good approach; good harbourage."

Sale

Purchased as part of the W.D. Morris Real Estate Company.

ISLAND 78/5

Evaluations and Descriptions

1894: Beatty 1/4 acre Value: $130

"Round, level; well wooded; fine view; cedar and pine; with reefs to east."

Sale

Purchased as part of the W.D. Morris Real Estate Company. It sold again in 1956.

ISLAND 78/6

Evaluations and Descriptions

1894: Beatty 1/5 acre Value: $125

"Good shade trees, level, fine view."

Sale

1901: to John P. Krauss, with Island 77A.

ISLAND 78/7

Evaluations and Descriptions

1894: Beatty 3/10 acre Value: $50

"High, rocky, some scrub; rough."

Sale

1902: to Charles Murphy.

ISLAND 78/8

Evaluations and Descriptions

1894: Beatty 1/2 acre Value: $100

"High, level at east end, well timbered, good view."

Sale

Purchased as part of the W.D. Morris Real Estate Company, with Island 78/9 and sold again in 1901 to Seleh R. von Duzer for $4,000.

ISLAND 78/9

Evaluations and Descriptions

1894: Beatty 1/8 acre Value: $35

"High, rocky, some timber."

Sale

1894: to Stuart Henderson. Sold again in 1896 to the W.D. Morris Real Estate Company. Sold with Island 78/8.

ISLAND 78/10

Evaluations and Descriptions

1894: Beatty 1/10 acre Value: $20

"Low, level, partly submerged in high water; barren; with reef to south."

Sale

1901: to Seleh R. von Duzer for $20.

ISLAND 78/11

Evaluations and Descriptions

1894: Beatty 1/10 acre Value: $10

"Barren rock."

Sale

1901: to Samuel Herron for $20.

ISLAND 78/12

Evaluations and Descriptions

1894: Beatty 1/10 acre Value: $10

"Barren rock."

Sale

1901: to Samuel Herron for $20.

ISLAND 78/13

Evaluations and Descriptions

1894: Beatty 1/20 acre Value: $10

"Barren rock, in shelter."

Sale

Island first sold in 1962.

ISLAND 78A

Evaluations and Descriptions

1894: Beatty 3/10 acre Value: $150

"High, level; well wooded; good view of channel; good harbourage."

Sale

Purchased as part of the W.D. Morris Real Estate Company, and sold again in 1902 to Seleh R. von Duzer.

ISLAND 78B

Evaluations and Descriptions

1894: Beatty 1/2 acre Value: $100

"Cleared and grassy; level; affording beautiful building site; some good shade trees; well located."

Sale

1897: to Charlotte E. Herdman.

ISLAND 78C

Evaluations and Descriptions

1894: Beatty 1/10 acre Value: $30

"Round, rocky; no timber, good location."

Sale

1911: to Thomas B. Wilson for $60, with Island 78D.

ISLAND 78D

Evaluations and Descriptions

1894: Beatty 1/10 acre Value: $30

"Round, rocky; no timber, good location."

Sale

1911: to Thomas B. Wilson; sold with Island 78C.

ISLAND 78E

Evaluations and Descriptions

1894: Beatty 1/12 acre Value: $50

"Low, level, some trees on south side; shady on north side; good view."

Sale

1910: to William Kall (spelling?) for $90.

No information available for Island 78F.

ISLAND 78G

Evaluations and Descriptions

1894: Beatty 1/10 acre Value: $40

"Rough, rocky; some small white birch; adjunct to north-west."

Sale

1910: to William Kall (spelling?), with Island 78E.

Thomas Graham, Baron Lyndoch.

— *Wellington & Waterloo,* Major Arthur Griffiths, published by George Newnes, Limited 1898

LYNDOCH ISLAND

Historic Name

1816: Owen — Lyndoch, the Wellington Islands Named after Thomas Graham, Baron Lyndoch (1778–1843). Graham, a Scotsman, bought a small estate at Lyndoch in 1785 after leading a "gentleman's life." (This included playing in the first cricket match in Scotland.) He married in 1774, and he and his wife spent several years in Spain and Portugal. When she died, he volunteered to serve in the British Army without pay, as aide-de-camp to Lord Mulgrave at Toulon, on the coast of France. It is said that Lyndoch was so upset by the way the French authorities looked after his wife's corpse that he developed a fanatic hatred for the French.

He continued to serve his country, finally joining the Peninsular forces in 1811 as a lieutenant general.

He fought at the siege of Ciudad Rodrigo and at Badajoz. He also fought at the Battle of Vittoria in 1813 and commanded the left wing of the allied army.

He fought next to Wellington, but poor health forced him to return to England for a brief time in 1813. At the conclusion of the war, Graham was created Baron Lyndoch of Balgowan, but he refused the monetary compensation that accompanied the peerage. In 1815 he founded a general military club called the United Services Club, which officers could visit while in London, instead of having to rely on taverns. When he returned to Scotland he concentrated on farming and cattle breeding.

The island was called Ash Island by Charles Unwin.

Evaluations and Descriptions

1873: Unwin 110 acres Value: $800

"About 66 Acres cleared, the greater part of which is arable soil fair. Buildings, frame house 1 1/2 storeys, log house, 1 storey — frame shanty — old barn and outbuildings, value of which about $600. The island is occupied by Stephen Patterson and his sons, said S. Patterson is nearly blind, has lived there 42 years — 'Squatted' on it. Nearly all the timber has been taken off, part by Patterson, and part before he came, there is a small orchard, but not a very good one — island high and bluff on side next to Steamboat Channel."

Island Notes

When the Unwin survey and report were published and the department made plans to sell the islands, a petition was sent on behalf of Stephen Patterson, the island squatter. Written by Herbert McDonald of Gananoque, it stated that Patterson was an "old man who has been an occupant of Ash island for the last 41 years, is nearly blind, is about 70 years of age, has a very helpless family, has one son blind and is not in a position to pay for the island if sold." He urged the government to give a "free grant" to Patterson, as had been done for the mainland property to foster settlement after the American Revolution. If this was not possible, then Mcdonald suggested that the island be sold at nominal price. The department agreed.

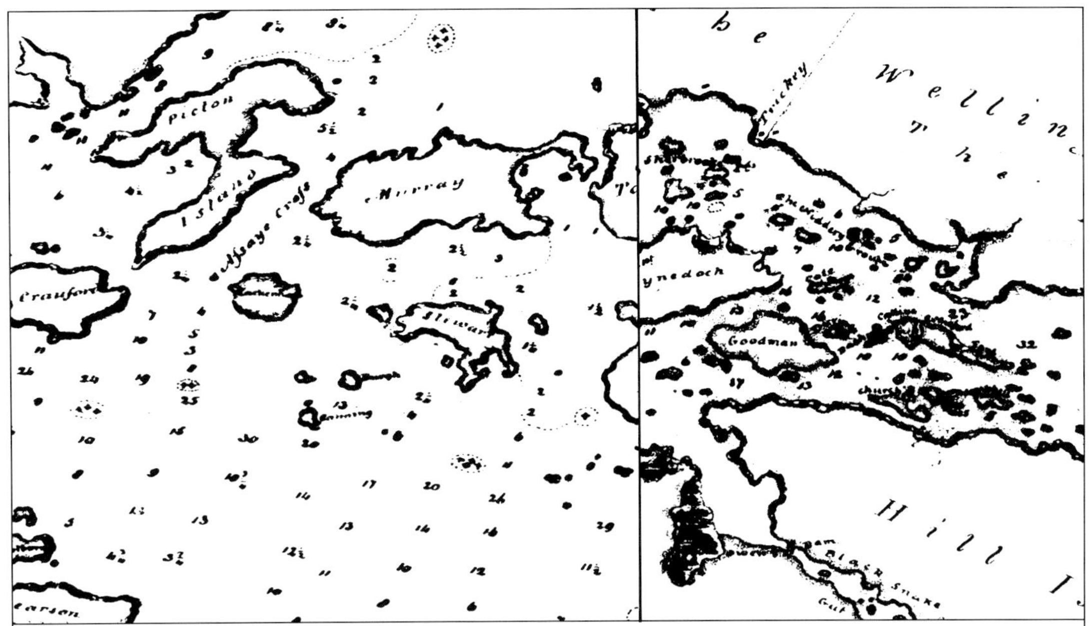

THE WELLINGTON ISLANDS

More than fifty islands surrounding Wellesley Island, near Ivy Lea in Canada, and near Alexandria Bay, in the United States, were named in honour of the officers who fought with the Duke of Wellington in the Peninsula. In fact, many times during the survey Owen referred to "The Wellington Islands" in his correspondence.

HISTORIC NAME	PRESENT NAME	PAGE
Picton	Picton Island (American)	204
Murray	Murray Island (American)	205
Craufurd	Bluff Island (American)	203
Packenham (*sic*)	Maple Island (American)	205
Stewart	Grenell Island (American)	206
Burgh	Basswood Island (American)	207
Canning	Woronoco Island (American)	207
Beckwith	Pine Island (American)	202
Perason	Round Island (American)	203
Colbourn	Little Round Island (American)	203
Barnard	Washington Island (American)	202
Power	Rock Island Light (American)	212
Brisbane	Mandolin Island (American)	211
Fitzroy Group	Rylston Island (American)	212
The Somerset Islands	Pullman Island (American)	216
Chapman	Cuba Island (American)	215
Jones	Cherry Island (Amerian)	215
Tweedall	Big Gull, Eel Bay (American)	211
Robinson Group	Robinson Islands (American)	211

HISTORIC NAME	PRESENT NAME	PAGE
Abercromby	Abercrombie Island (Canadian)	154
Myers	Myers Island (Canadian)	160
Bingham	Bingham Island (Canadian)	160
Lyndoch	Lyndoch Island (Canadian)	159
Goodman	Wallace Island (Canadian)	161
The Sherbrooke Islands	Goose Island (Canadian)	156
	Huckleberry Island (Canadian)	156
Cole	Wood Island (Candian)	162
During	Dashwood Island (Canadian)	164
Dashwood	Bratt Island (Canadian)	165
Hill	Hill Island (Canadian)	166
The Niddery Group	Fish Dam Group, Numbers 1,2,3 and 4 (Canadian)	163
Churchill	Island 88 (Canadian)	165
Bowes	Constance Island (Canadian)	168
Catline	Georgina Island (Canadian)	169
Fane	Georgina Island (Canadian)	169
Craufurd	Georgina Island (Canadian)	169
Combermere	Club Island (Canadian)	172

Chauncey Patterson was the blind son. He was hired by American tour-boat operator Captain Visger to popularize Fiddler's Elbow, which is the name of a small channel that goes by Ash Island. It was originally named by sailors travelling in the first fleet of bateaux that made their way up the St. Lawrence River during the 1700s. Patterson sat on the high cliffs and played his fiddle for the passing tour boats. For many years the channel was known as the Blind Fiddler's Elbow.

In 1890 Chauncey Patterson drowned near Alexandria Bay while returning to Canada in a rowing skiff with his son-in-law. They were swamped by a passing steamer, and Patterson, unable to swim and being blind, could not catch the life rings thrown by the steamer's crew.

Sale

This island was sold to J. Patterson.

MYERS ISLAND

Historic Name

1816: Owen — Myers, the Wellington Islands Named after Lieut. Col. Christopher Myers, 7th Regiment. In 1810 Myers served in Jamaica. He arrived in Canada in 1812 and reported to York, serving as quartermaster general to the army staff in Canada. He was the commander at Kingston, and was wounded three times at the Battle of Fort George, where he was taken a prisoner. His dispatch reads: "A zealous and meritorious officer." He was released on parole and resumed duties in 1814. Myers also fought in the Battle of Fort Erie. He died in 1817.

Evaluations and Descriptions

1873: Unwin 5.6 acres Value: $100

"Chiefly rock, a little soil — a Pretty Island well timbered."

1894: Beatty 5 6/10 acres Value: $600

"High rolling land; well timbered with pine, hemlock, birch and oak; fine harbours."

Sale

1898: to Philip T. Dodge.

BINGHAM ISLAND

Historic Name

1816: Owen — Bingham, the Wellington Islands Named after Sir George Ridout Bingham (1777–1833). Bingham entered the British Army in 1793, becoming a major in 1801 and in 1805 a lieutenant colonel in the newly raised 2nd Battalion 53rd Foot, in Ireland. In 1809 he went to Portugal as head of his battalion and remained there throughout the war.

Bingham was sent as senior officer to St. Helena Island in the Atlantic Ocean to guard Napoleon. "He is described as having been a gentleman as well as a brilliant soldier."

Evaluations and Descriptions

1873: Unwin 6.8 acres Value: $75

"Much the same as Myers."

1894: Beatty 6 2/5 acres Value: $1000

"Rough at both ends; well timbered on the end; partly cleared in centre, which is low and level; good harbour; location."

Sale

1894: to Andrew Devine for $1,000.

LINDOE ISLAND

Names

Charles Unwin identified the island as number 79.

Evaluations and Descriptions

1873: Unwin 1.4 acres Value: $60

"Rock with a few trees and brush. Light house on it, pretty location."

ISLAND 79A

Evaluations and Descriptions

1894: Beatty 1/40 acre Value: $30

"Small bare islet."

ISLAND 80

Evaluations and Descriptions

1873: Unwin 2.4 acres Value: $80

"About the same as Island 79."

Sale

1902: to George Douglas Miller.

ISLAND 80A

Evaluations and Descriptions

1894: Beatty 1/40 acre Value: $20

"Low, level reef; submerged in high water."

ISLAND 80B

Evaluations and Descriptions

1894: Beatty 1/30 acre Value: $20

"Bare rocks."

ISLAND 80C

Evaluations and Descriptions

1894: Beatty 7/10 acre Value: $150

"High, level, rocky; plenty of pitch pine; shade trees; good location."

Sale

1895: to William H. Cronk for $300. Purchased as part of the W.D. Morris Real Estate Company. The island did not sell again until 1958, for $1,950.

PALM ISLAND

Names

The island was identified by Walter Beatty as Island 80D.

Evaluations and Descriptions

1894: Beatty 7/10 acre Value: $150

"High, level, rocky; plenty of pitch pine; shade trees; good location."

Sale

1895: to W.H. Cronk for $300, with Island 80C. Purchased as part of the W.D. Morris Real Estate Company.

ISLAND 80F

Evaluations and Descriptions

1894: Beatty 1/10 acre Value: $20

"Rocky, level; some trees; good shooting."

Sale

1902: to George D. Miller.

ISLAND 80G

Evaluations and Descriptions

1894: Beatty 1/10 acre Value: $40

"Level; well timbered; in 'The Rift.' "

Sales

This island was first sold in 1958.

TRIDENT ISLAND

Names

This island was identified by Walter Beatty as Island 80H.

Evaluations and Descriptions

1894: Beatty 7/10 acre Value: $300

"Bold to west; level; well timbered with evergreens; beautiful view westward; on main steamboat channel; good harbourage and sheltered waters."

Sale

Purchased as part of the W.D. Morris Real Estate Company. It sold again in 1959 for $2,150.

ISLAND 80I

Evaluations and Descriptions

1894: Beatty 7/10 acre Value: $250

"Beautifully timbered with cedar, pine and birch; level, with rocky point; good location; fine harbourage for yachts."

Sale

Purchased as part of the W.D. Morris Real Estate Company. It sold again in 1957 for $1,500.

ISLAND 80J

Evaluations and Descriptions

1894: Beatty 3/10 acre Value: $25

"Lies near yacht channel in 'The Rift' level, covered with scrub; a few trees."

Sale

This island was first sold in 1962.

ISLAND 80K

Evaluations and Descriptions

1894: Beatty 1/5 acre Value: $50

"Pretty; well timbered; on yacht channel; good fishing."

WALLACE ISLAND

Historic Name

1816: Owen — Goodman, the Wellington Islands Sir Stephen Arthur Goodman (d. 1844) joined the British forces in 1794, fighting in Minorca and Malta. In 1810 he went with his regiment to the Peninsula and commanded a light company in Hill's division at the Battle of Talavera. In 1810 he was appointed deputy judge-advocate and served again in that capacity in 1815 with the army at Waterloo and then in the occupation of Paris.

The island was locally known as having been named for John Wallace, the lighthouse keeper.

Evaluations and Descriptions

1873: Unwin 47 acres Value: $300

"About 7 acres cleared, which is all arable, the remainder is rocky but well timbered with soft maple, Poplar, small Pine and Cedar — Good frame house, stone foundation, built by the government for James Wallace, Light House keeper who lives in it and has been in charge of Light house 13 years. There is also a small frame barn which Wallace says he built. Island low but very picturesque."

Island Notes

John Wallace first came to live on Wallace Island in 1856. He was hired to man the lighthouses in the region and to watch over the islands as a guardian before they were sold by the Department of Indian Affairs. He was responsible for seeing that "squatters" did not take up residence on the islands and that no one cut timber or removed stone. Wallace was also given the title of fisheries officer, watching to make sure that fishermen obeyed the rules set down by the Canadian government.

The Wallace family retained ownership of the farmhouse and island until the 1970s, when the island was sold to William Browning. He subdivided it and sold cottage lots.

ISLAND 81

Evaluations and Descriptions

1873: Unwin 1.3 acres Value: $25

"Little soil — few small trees and bush."

Sale

1899: to M.H. Folger. Purchased as part of the W.D. Morris Real Estate Company. The island was sold again in 1952 for $1,800.

ISLAND 81A

Evaluations and Descriptions

1894: Beatty 1/5 acre Value: $50

"Low, level, rocky; some scrub; good location."

Sale

1905: to M.R. Macdonald.

ISLAND 81B

Evaluations and Descriptions

1894: Beatty 1/20 acre Value: $30

"High, rocky; some cedar and white birch; good location; good shelter; on channel."

Sale

1902: to Henry Crofts Munro.

ISLAND 81C

Evaluations and Descriptions

1894: Beatty 1/80 acre Value: $20

"Low, level; barren."

ISLAND 81D

Evaluations and Descriptions

1894: Beatty 1/80 acre Value: $10

"Stony reef, covered in highest water."

Sale

1903: to Henry Folger for $10.

ISLAND 81E

Evaluations and Descriptions

1894: Beatty 1/2 acre Value: $80

"Rather rough; some fine shade trees; good shelter."

Sale

1894: to Francis L. Donohue.

ISLAND 81F

Evaluations and Descriptions

1894: Beatty 1/20 acre Value: $30

"Round, rocky knoll; some scrub; good location; open water the year round."

Sale

1894: to Francis L. Donohue.

ISLAND 82

Evaluations and Descriptions

1873: Unwin 0.8 acre Value: $20

"Low and rocky — little soil — a few small trees and bush."

Sale

1897: to Joseph Taylor. Purchased was part of the W.D. Morris Real Estate Company. It sold again in 1899 for $1,100.

ISLAND 82A

Evaluations and Descriptions

1894: Beatty 1/100 acre Value: $10

"Small, barren rock."

Sale

1902: Purchased as part of the W.D. Morris Real Estate Company.

ISLAND 82B

Evaluations and Descriptions

1894: Beatty 1/100 acre Value: $10

"Small, barren rock, submerged in high water."

Sale

Purchased as part of the W.D. Morris Real Estate Company.

ISLAND 82C

Evaluations and Descriptions

1894: Beatty 1/40 acre Value: $25

"Small, barren rock; good view."

Sale

Purchased as part of the W.D. Morris Real Estate Company.

ISLAND 82D

Evaluations and Descriptions

1894: Beatty 1/20 acre Value: $40

"Low, level; slightly above water; submerged in high water; beautiful view in all directions; good site can be made here."

ISLAND 82E

Evaluations and Descriptions

1894: Beatty 1/4 acre Value: $100

"Fairly timbered; grand view; level." (See 82H.)

Sale

1894: to J. Dunlop for $100. Purchased as part of the W.D. Morris Real Estate Company. The island was owned by the Field and Stream Publishing Company and by Henry Holt and Company, Inc.

ISLAND 82F

Evaluations and Descriptions

1894: Beatty 1/40 acre Value: $20

"Stony reef; covered in high water."

Sale

Purchased as part of the W.D. Morris Real Estate Company.

ISLAND 82G

Evaluations and Descriptions

1894: Beatty 1/10 acre Value: $40

"High, level; some good shade trees; good location."

Sale

1898: to Alfred F. Holmes.

ISLAND 82H

Evaluations and Descriptions

1894: Beatty 1/100 acre Value: $20

"Round rock knob; might be bought as an adjunct of 82E."

Sale

Purchased as part of the W.D. Morris Real Estate Company.

ISLAND 83

Evaluations and Descriptions

1873: Unwin 0.5 acre Value: $15

"High rock, nearly all timber and brush cut off."

Sale

1906: to Allan McRossie (spelling?).

ISLAND 83A

Evaluations and Descriptions

1894: Beatty 1/120 acre Value: $30

"Low, rocky islet; on main channel."

Sale

Purchased as part of the W.D. Morris Real Estate Company.

WOOD ISLAND

Historic Name

1816: Owen — Cole, the Wellington Islands

Named after Sir Galbraith Lowry Cole (1772–1848), leader of the 4th Division. He arrived in the Peninsula in 1808, serving in command for almost four years. He was wounded at Alberera and Salamanca.

Sir John Hope, lieutenant general, 4th Earl of Hopetoun (1765-1823), later Lord Niddry.
— National Archives of Canada C12256

Evaluations and Descriptions
1873: Unwin 3 acres Value: $100
"Low, chiefly rock, some soil — winter nearly all recently cut off — There was a wharf on this island many years ago, for 'wooding' steamers."

Sale
1893: to John David W. Darling.

FISH DAM GROUP

Historic Name
1816: Owen — Niddery (*sic*) Group, the Wellington Islands
Named after Sir John Hope, lieutenant general, 4th Earl of Hopetoun (1765–1823), later Lord Niddry.

A division commander at Corunna, Hope returned to the Peninsula in 1813, replacing the ailing Graham (Lyndoch) as the head of the army's left wing. He was made Lord Niddry and appointed Military Knight of the Grand Order in June 1815. Wellington recommended Lord Niddry as the replacement for Sir George Prevost in Canada when the latter was recalled to England. "Lord Niddry is certainly the best you can choose to succeed to Sir George Prevost," stated Wellington. For some reason he was not appointed.

Evaluations and Descriptions
1873: Unwin 1.0 acre Value: $20
"This consists of a group of four small islands, Low, rocky, a few small trees and brush on them."
1894: Beatty #1 Value: $50
"Number 1 Island, 1/3 Acre, is well timbered; nicely located; good fishing."

Sale
1898: to Henry Crofts Munro.

1894: Beatty #2 Value: $50
"Nicely timbered; well sheltered; good harbourage; good fishing."

Sale
1896: to Rev. Charles Young; sold again in 1897 by Young to Henry Crofts Munro.

1894: Beatty #3 Value: $50
"Nicely timbered; well sheltered; good harbourage; good fishing."

Sale
1898: to Henry Crofts Munro.

ISLAND 84

Evaluations and Descriptions
1873: Unwin 0.5 acre Value: $10
"Rocky — with brush and few trees."
1894: Beatty 1/2 acre Value: $100
"Fairly timbered; well sheltered; good location; level; good harbourage."

Sale
1894: to Noah P. McNeil for $180, with Island 84A.

ISLAND 84A

Evaluations and Descriptions
1894: Beatty 1/100 acre Value: $80
"Pretty, well rounded; with nice shade trees; pretty location on channel."

Sale
1894: to Noah P. McNeil, with Island 84.

ISLAND 84B

Evaluations and Descriptions
1894: Beatty 1/20 acre Value: $20
"Low, barren; good location."

Sale
1902: to Charles Murphy.

ISLAND 84C

Evaluations and Descriptions
1894: Beatty 1/100 acre Value: $20
"Small, rocky islet."

Sale
1901: to Alexander M. Tennant.

ISLAND 84D

Evaluations and Descriptions
1894: Beatty 1/5 acre Value: $50
"Level, rocky; some trees for shade."

Sale
1897: to Alexander M. Tennant.

ISLAND 84E

Evaluations and Descriptions
1894: Beatty 1/50 acre Value: $20
"Barren, rocky islet."

Sale
1901: to Andrew Devine.

The Devine Cottage, Island 84A.

— Photograph appearing in picture book published by the Thousand Island House, Alexandria Bay, George J. Walsh, Proprietor

MADAWASKA ISLAND

Names

The island was identified by Charles Unwin as Island 85.

Evaluations and Descriptions

1873: Unwin 1.8 acres Value: $15

"High rock timber all cut off."

1894: Beatty 1 4/5 acres Value: $200

"Rough, high, rocky; fairly timbered."

Island Notes

The Devine Cottage was built in 1896 by Andrew Devine. The large cottage, boathouse and tennis court were maintained by three generations of the Devine family. They also had a farm on the mainland at Ivy Lea where they kept polo horses. The property was last sold in 1974.

Sale

1901: to Andrew Devine.

ISLAND 85A

Evaluations and Descriptions

1894: Beatty 1/5 acre Value: $60

"High; level; some small pine shade trees."

Sale

1897: to John McMillan Shaw.

ISLAND 85B

Evaluations and Descriptions

1894: Beatty 1/3 acre Value: $75

"High; some shade trees; commanding view; good harbourage."

ISLAND 86

Evaluations and Descriptions

1873: Unwin 2.3 acres Value: $20

"High rock timber all cut off."

1894: Beatty 2 3/10 acres Value: $25

"Broken, rocky island; some good timber; good harbour to north-east."

Sale

Purchased as part of the W.D. Morris Real Estate Company. Sold again in 1956.

ISLAND 86A

Evaluations and Descriptions

1894: Beatty 1/10 acre Value: $25

"Low, rocky island, bearing small scrub."

Sale

Sold to Thomas James Darling.

PINE ISLAND or DASHWOOD ISLAND

Historic Name

1816: Owen — During, the Wellington Islands Named after Lieut. Gen. Georg von During (d. 1872), who served mostly in the adjutant-general's office.

The name of this island was changed after the original hand-drawn charts were completed. The island was called Dashwood on the charts that were eventually printed by the Admiralty Office in 1828.

Evaluations and Descriptions

1873: Unwin 4 acres Value: $25

"High rock a few small trees and bush."

Island Notes

The Opawaka Lodge on Pine Island was built in 1900 by M.P. Davis. It was the largest home built on a Canadian island and remains a showplace for passing tour-boat passengers. In 1923 the island was sold to Joseph H. Himes. He purchased it for $16,000 and renamed the lodge Opawaka, which is suppose to mean "swift water," describing the current in the channels that surround the island.

The tour-boat captains knew that Himes held a political position in the United States, but they mistakenly thought he was a senator. In fact, Himes served one term in the House of Representatives, from 1921 to 1923. Years later, when his health failed, he gave the island to the Wesley Theological Seminary of the Methodist Church in Washington, D.C. The seminary sold the island after only two years.

Sale

Sold to M.P. Davis, later sold to Joseph H. Himes.

BRATT ISLAND

Historic Name

1816: Owen — Dashwood, the Wellington Islands Named after Lieut. Col. Charles Dashwood (1787–1832), third son of Sir Henry Watkin Dashwood, 3rd Bart, of Kirtlington Park. Educated at Harrow, he was lieutenant, then captain, in the 3rd Guards. Dashwood was appointed assistant adjutant-general in September 1813 and served in the 1st Division. He also served in the D.A.A.G. office and to the 4th and 6th Divisions.

Note: The name of this island was switched with Pine Island on the charts published in 1828. On the original hand-drawn chart, which is used in this listing, the name Dashwood appears next to today's Bratt Island.

Evaluations and Descriptions

1873: Unwin 2.9 acres Value: $20

"High rock, a few small trees and brush."

1894: Beatty 2 9/10 acres Value: $450

"Exceedingly pretty, well wooded island; splendid view of main channel; well wooded with pine, birch and hardwood; beautiful site; fine harbourage."

Sale

1894: to Clarence Chester Cleveland, member of Parliament for Danville, Quebec, and president of the Godhue Company and the Leather Belting Company.

ISLAND 87

Evaluations and Descriptions

1873: Unwin 0.5 acre Value: $5

"Low rocky bluff, almost barren."

1894: Beatty 1/2 acre Value: $150

"Bold; nice shade trees; in beautiful locality; deep water; fine harbourage."

Sale

Purchased as part of the W.D. Morris Real Estate Company.

ISLAND 87A

Evaluations and Descriptions

1894: Beatty 1/20 acre Value: $25

"High rock head; some scrub."

Sale

1912: to T.J. Darling.

ISLAND 87B

Evaluations and Descriptions

1894: Beatty 3/10 acre Value: $50

"Nice shelter; good building site; some trees."

Sale

1902: Purchased as part of the W.D. Morris Real Estate Company.

ISLAND 87C

Evaluations and Descriptions

1894: Beatty 1/100 acre Value: $30

"Low, rocky reef."

Sale

Purchased as part of the W.D. Morris Real Estate Company.

ISLAND 87D

Evaluations and Descriptions

1894: Beatty 1/50 acre Value: $25

"Islet; shrubby; with shoal to east."

Sale

1901: to John D.W. Darling.

ISLAND 87E

Evaluations and Descriptions

1894: Beatty 1/15 acre Value: $40

"High; shrubby; on channel."

Sale

1901: to John D.W. Darling.

ISLAND 87F

Evaluations and Descriptions

1894: Beatty 1/5 acre Value: $60

"High; shrubby."

Sale

1894: to John D.W. Darling for $60.

ISLAND 87G

Evaluations and Descriptions

1894: Beatty 1/10 acre Value: $80

"Pretty; well sheltered; nice small trees and shrub."

Sale

1901: to John D.W. Darling. This island was expropriated (no date available) to improve the middle channel. The government paid $300 at the time of expropriation.

ISLAND 88

Historic Name

1816: Owen — Churchill, the Wellington Islands Probably named after Col. Chatham H. Churchill (1791–1843), who was attached to the 2nd Division as Hill's military secretary. The name Churchill was never transferred to the printed charts; therefore, it was not recorded by Charles Unwin.

Locally known as Benson's Island.

Evaluations and Descriptions

1873: Unwin 5 acres Value: $20

"High rock, small timber and brush on it."

Sale

1894: to George F. Benson for $300.

Benson's cottage on Island 88. — Photograph appearing in *The Thousand Islands and the River St. Lawrence*, The James Bayne Company

ISLAND 88A

Evaluations and Descriptions

1894: Beatty 1/100 acre Value: $10
"A rocky reef just above water."

Sale

1894: to George F. Benson.

ISLAND 88B

Evaluations and Descriptions

1894: Beatty 1/100 acre Value: $10
"A rocky reef just above water."

Sale

1900: to George F. Benson.

ISLAND 88C

Evaluations and Descriptions

1894: Beatty 1/100 acre Value: $30
"Rock head in mid-channel; high, resting on shoal; can be made a building site."

Sale

1901: to W.E. Miller; sold again to George F. Benson.

ISLAND 88D

Evaluations and Descriptions

1894: Beatty (no acreage recorded) Value: $75
"Long, narrow islet; with pine and cedar scrub; well sheltered."

Sale

1900: to George F. Benson.

HILL ISLAND

Historic Name

1816: Owen — Hill, the Wellington Islands
Named after Sir Rowland Hill (1772–1842), whom Wellington liked because he "always did as he was told"! He was also respected by his men, who referred to him as "Daddy Hill," "Father Hill," and "Farmer Hill." One of his biographers said he had "rosy cheeks that reminded his men of home." He was the commander of the 2nd Division in the Peninsular War and corps commander at Waterloo. After that he was appointed second in command in the Army of Occupation in France until November 1818. He was made a general in 1825 and served as commander-in-chief of the British forces. He was made a viscount in 1842. As commander of the 2nd Division he supervised many officers who are commemorated on Captain Owen's chart.

The island was locally called Leroux Island. The name also appears as Le Roux and La Rue.

Evaluations and Decriptions

1873: Unwin
"Parcel No.1 Sale 29 [punctuation as written in survey journal] John Landon has about 295 acres of which about 109 are cleared, nearly all the arable land is cleared, most of the cleared land is of fair quality, soil clay loam He has a log house one storey high, a frame barn, there is also an unfinished squared log house.

"John Landon inherited from his father Dan J Landon who bought a squatters claim from J and Dan Wright about 30 or 32 years ago, was informed so, by the widow of D.J. Landon."

"Parcel No.2 Sale 13 [punctuation as written in survey journal] Sold to Charles Cornwall Augustus Landon has 20.6 acres all cleared and cultivated and is nearly all arable There are a few rocky ledges There is a small log house 1 storey, worth probably $50 A. Landon bought from his Brother John who inherited from his father D.J. Landon, he has occupied this portion about 9 years."

Sir Rowland Hill, commander of the 2nd Division.
— *Wellington & Waterloo*, Major Arthur Griffiths, published by George Newnes, Limited, 1898

"Parcel No. 3 Sale 16 [punctuation as written in survey journal] Robert Carnegie has 198.2 acres of which 113.4 are cleared, there is very little of the uncleared portion arable. Most of the cleared land is very good clay loam Carnegie is a very good farmer, and has improved his farm since purchasing The valuable timber was all cut off before he purchased, there is now nothing but Brush and "second growth" He has recently built a new frame house lined with Brick well built and finished one and a half storeys high worth $1200 also a large frame Barn with a stone foundation worth $200 and some other small out-buildings Carnegie has lived on this farm for nineteen years up to last April, he purchased from Thos Darling who lives on the main land just opposite."

"Parcel No. 4 Sale 21 [punctuation as written in survey journal] Owned by Thos McGrath — has 104.3 acres, of which 50 are cleared, The most of the cleared portion is arable, all the uncleared portion is rocky — no timber of any value — The arable land is of fair quality — Has a frame barn worth probably $300 — A log house say $100 he has lived on the Farm seven years, he purchased from Wm Porter, who bought from J Dery and Jan who bought from his father who 'squatted' on it many years ago — McGrath paid $600 United States currency, for Porters claim."

"Parcel No. 5 Sale 22 [punctuation as written in survey journal] Owned by J Bayley contains 217.4 acres of which 51.8 are cleared, the cleared portion is all arable, very good soil, There is very little of the uncleared portion arable — No timber of any value — Bayley came to live on this farm in March 1852, he purchased from Joseph Buck, he has a small orchard on it which yields fair fruit, There is a good frame house with a stone foundation, one and a half storeys high 24'x30' built 8 years ago — A Frame Barn 32x42 with a stone foundation, in a good state of preservation, There were only 4 or 5 acres cleared when Bayley purchased This is a tolerably good farm."

"Parcel No. 6 Sale 10 [punctuation as written in survey journal] Owned by Henry Hunt There are 247 acres of which 75 acres are cleared, nearly all the arable land is cleared, the uncleared portion is very rough and rocky, There is no timber of any value The soil is clay loam and the greater part of it very good quality, he has a small frame house 20'x26' one storey high and a good frame barn and shed with stone foundations Barn 30'x?? shed 30x30 There is also a young orchard of about 200 apple trees yeilding a good quality of fruit just beginning to bear He is a tolerably good farmer, he purchased portions from three different claimants he had a house burnt about 9 years ago and lost all his papers, had a quit claim deed from J Deryan of 100 acres which he purchased some 27 years ago, and gave Deryan $100 for his claim. There was only an old log house and about ten acres cleared when he purchased About eighteen years ago he purchased 50 acres more or less lying South of the Marsh and East of the portion he bought from Deryan, from Thos Rosenbourgh, This Rosenbourgh purchased from A. Elliott, When Hunt purchased, there was a small shanty on it, and three acres cleared, he gave $50 for it Hunt also purchased a piece North of the Marsh, and East of the portion he purchased from Deryan, from Fred Edgely, for which he paid $100, There are about 20 acres improved, with a few apple trees upon it, of this he sold about 25 acres to Jm Hoadley. The areas given, like those in Hoadley and HW Hunts portion do not include the Marsh, which is flooded in high water, some years a great deal of coarse Hay could be procured from it."

"Parcel No. 7 Sale 25 [punctuation as written in survey journal] Owned by Jm Hoadley contains 32 acres of which 13.8 are cleared, the uncleared portion is all rock The soil is of fair quality Purchased from Henry Hunt about eight years ago, for $75— Has a house 13x18 worth $50 — Frame barn with underground stable worth about $300. A log workshop worth about $100 Hoadley makes his living by building boats and rowing, during the fishing season."

"Parcel No. 8 Sale 18 [punctuation as written in survey journal] Owned by Thos Hunt contains 179.7 acres, of which 62.3 are cleared, the uncleared portion is chiefly rock. The soil on the cleared portion is of very good quality and is in a good state of cultivation — Has a frame house 18x24 one and a half storeys high, lined with brick, with an addition 16x24 one and a half storeys high, the latter was built in 1873 The other part in 1858, the house is in good condition, he has also a good high frame barn 30x44 and a shed in course of erection Thos Hunt has lived where he now does for twenty two years, he bought quit claims from former occupants, part from Jacob Rosenborough and part from his brother H Hunt, Thos Hunt says that the timber was all taken off before he came to live on it, and he had to buy the timber for his buildings."

Island Notes

Lot 7 on Hill Island was patented to John Hoadley, a farmer, in 1877 by the Crown. The property, consisting of 32 4/10 acres, was sold to William H. Hunt in 1889 and then to J.G. Fairchild, who came from Leavenworth, Kansas. Fairchild hired the Mitchell and Wilson Construction Company from Gananoque to build a large summer home, which was designed by Gananoque architect Frank T. Lent. The house, with its impressive architecture, was always pointed out from passing tour boats. It was one of the few large homes built on the Canadian islands.

In 1901 Sara E. Batterman of Brooklyn, New York, brought the property for $12,000, an expensive property in those days. A steam launch, three skiffs and a billiard table were listed in the deed as property sold with the house. At that time the point became known as Batterman's Point.

Other owners in the early 1900s included A.B. Nichols and H. Hinck. In 1921 Wallis C. Bird, a Standard Oil heir, purchased the property. He made extensive renovations to the house. Bird was considered one of the modern millionaires in the islands. He also owned a fifty-room mansion on Long Island, where he kept seventeen sports cars in a twenty-seven-car garage. Bird remained a summer resident for twenty-one years, losing his life in a small sea-plane accident in 1941. After that his wife lost interest in the estate and left the river. It is interesting to note that after her departure Marjorie Bird went to Switzerland, where she assumed the lifestyle of the aristocracy. She dreamed of being a princess and began a relationship with a Romanian boyfriend, Nicholas Sturd. In 1961 she was murdered by Sturd and her Swiss doctor, Gerard Savoy. News accounts of the murder and trial were described in newspapers in North America and Europe. *Life* magazine described Mrs. Bird as a rich widow, "a pathetic person with the mind of a little girl — [she] was dominated, drugged and used by a pair of adventurers who catered to her wistful hope of becoming a member of the European aristocracy."

ISLAND 89

Evaluations and Descriptions

1873: Unwin 1.1 acres Value: $5

"Rocky, small timber and brush on it."

1894: Beatty 3/4 acres Value: $150

"Beautiful building site; wooded with birch, pine and cedar; good harbourage; pretty views." (See Island 89B.)

Sale

1897: to George F. Carter.

ISLAND 89A

Evaluations and Descriptions

1894: Beatty 1/4 acre Value: $75

"Separated part of Island 89; birch and willows; good harbourage and views." (See Island 89B.)

Sale

1897: to George F. Carter.

ISLAND 89B

Evaluations and Descriptions

1894: Beatty 1/10 acre Value: $20

"Sandy shoal lying between 89A and 89B, separated slightly from both; should be bought with one of them as boat house site."

Sale

1897: to George F. Carter.

ISLAND 89C

Evaluations and Descriptions

1894: Beatty 1/2 acre Value: $200

"Thick cedar and white birch; bold, but with nice levels for building, &c; fine harbourage; a lovely spot; fine channel inshore."

Sale

Purchased as part of the W.D. Morris Real Estate Company. The island sold again in 1951 for $850.

ISLAND 89D

Evaluations and Descriptions

1894: Beatty 2/5 acre Value: $125

"A few nice shade trees; pretty view; good building site."

Sale

1904: to Eva G. Horton.

CONSTANCE ISLAND

Historic Name

1816: Owen — Bowes, the Wellington Islands

Named after Gen. B.F. Bowes, commander of four hundred light infantry at the Battle at San Cayetano. Bowes was killed along with 120 others.

Evaluations and Descriptions

1873: Unwin 7.8 acres Value: $30

"High at East, low at west end, a little soil at west end covered with 'second growth.' "

Sale

This island was never offered for sale or lease but was reserved as a park island.

ISLAND 90

Evaluations and Descriptions

1873: Unwin 0.5 acre Value: $5

"High rock — timber cut off."

1894: Beatty 1/2acre Value: $100

"High and very bold; a little scrub; good harbourage and approach; north side low and level, and well covered with soil."

Sale

1894: to R.M. McLean for $300. Bought with Humbly Island. Purchased as part of the W.D. Morris Real Estate Company.

ISLAND 90A

Evaluations and Descriptions

1894: Beatty 3/10 acre Value: $70

"Round; bold; wooded with pine; lovely view; in deep water; good harbourage."

Sale

Sold to J.A. McDougal, with Pilot Island. Purchased as part of the W.D. Morris Real Estate Company. The island did not sell again until 1960.

ISLAND 91

Evaluations and Descriptions

1873: Unwin 0.2 acre Value: $5

"Low rock — a few trees and bushes."

1894: Beatty 1/5 acre Value: $200

"Level; a few nice pines; beautifully situated; good harbourage; deep water."

Sale

Purchased as part of the W.D. Morris Real Estate Company. The island did not sell again until 1960.

ISLAND 91A

Evaluations and Descriptions

1894: Beatty 1/10acre Value: $75

"With shoal to north; a few scrub pine; good harbourage; suitable for building site."

Sale

1902: to William K. Rose.

ISLAND 91B

Evaluations and Descriptions

1894: Beatty 1/50 acre Value: $30

"Small reef."

ISLAND 92

Evaluations and Descriptions

1873: Unwin 0.5 acre Value: $5

"Low and rocky, a few trees and bushes."

1894: Beatty 1/2 acre Value: $100

"Beautifully situated; good harbourage; sheltered waters; nice shade trees; approach good."

Sale

Purchased as part of the W.D. Morris Real Estate Company. The island sold again in 1958.

GEORGINA ISLAND

Historic Name

1816: Owen — This island was drawn as three on the 1816 map. The three names are as follows: Fane, the Wellington Islands, named after Gen. Sir Harry Fane, head of a calvary brigade at the Battle of Talavera. Further biographical information is unavailable.

Catline, the Wellington Islands, no biographical information is available, but it can be assumed that Catline served with Hill and the other men listed on the charts.

Craufurd, the Wellington Islands, probably named after Sir Robert Craufurd who was killed at the Battle of Ciudad Rodrigo. (See Bluff Island, Part II, The American Islands, Clayton.) He was in charge of the battalion that fought beside Fane and Bowes.

Charles Unwin identified the island as Deer Island on his 1873 chart. He also recorded the name Catline.

Evaluations and Descriptions

1873: Unwin 23.3 acres Value: $120

"High rough and rocky. Very little arable soil Timber nearly all cut off."

Sale

This island was never offered for sale or lease but was reserved for use as a park.

SURVEYORS ISLAND

Evaluations and Descriptions

1873: Unwin .02 acre Value: $10

"Low and rocky, a few trees and, bushes on it."

1894: Beatty 2/10 acre Value: $150

"Beautiful view; good harbourage; a few nice pines; situated on channel."

Island Notes

The island name came from the fact that during the 1880s Mr. Rubidge, dominion surveyor, camped there when he made a survey of native lands in 1885.

Sale

1897: to M.D. Horton.

ALNWICK ISLAND

Names

Charles Unwin identified the island as Island 93. It has also been known as Sunset Island. Today it is known as Alnwick Island, probably named after the Mississauga band that originally owned the islands.

Evaluations and Descriptions

1873: Unwin 2.0 acres Value: $20

"High and rocky, a few trees and bushes."

Sale

1898: to Ben Webster Folger for $150.

ISLAND 93A

Evaluations and Descriptions

1894: Beatty 1/100 acre Value: $25

"Rocky reef."

ISLAND 93B

Evaluations and Descriptions

1894: Beatty 1/100 acre Value: $25

"Rocky reef."

ISLAND 93C

Evaluations and Descriptions

1894: Beatty 1/10acre Value: $50

"Round; well wooded; fine view; on channel."

Sale

1894: to Catherine Lynch for $200, with Island 114.

ISLAND 93D

Evaluations and Descriptions

1894: Beatty 1/4 acre Value: $70

"Low; surrounded by shoal water; a little pine scrub."

Sale

1904: to Eva G. Horton.

ISLAND 94

Evaluations and Descriptions

1873: Unwin 0.6 acre Value: $5

"Rocky, a few trees and bushes."

1894: Beatty 1/2 acre Value: $200

A lovely little island; large shade trees; as dense as possible; perfect view and location."

Sale

1894: to C.W. Windsor for $240, with Island 94A.

ISLAND 94A

Evaluations and Descriptions

1894: Beatty 1/40 acre Value: $40

"Low islet with a few scrub pine."

Sale

1894: to C.W. Windsor for $240, with Island 94.

HUCKLEBERRY ISLAND

Historic Name

1816: Owen — Campbell, the Wellington Islands Probably named after Maj. Gen. William Campbell (1783–1852), who was the second son of William Campbell, commissioner of the Navy Board. Campbell was attached to the 3rd Division and the Light Division. For a short time he acted as adjutant quartermaster general to the cavalry and remained attached to the cavalry to the end of the war.

Evaluations and Descriptions

1873: Unwin 6.1 acres Value: $50

"Low and rocky covered with 'second growth'".

RECIPROCITY ISLAND

Names

Charles Unwin identified this island as Island 95. It was also identified as one of a group of islands called Carnegies Islands.

Evaluations and Descriptions

1873: Unwin 0.6 acre Value: $10

"Low and rocky, and covered with second growth timber."

Sale

1895: to W.W. Stearne; sold in 1903 to J. Morris for $500. Morris was a member of the W.D. Morris family. The island sold again in 1913 to Isaac P. Wiser.

GANAWAGA ISLAND

Names

Charles Unwin indentified the island as Island 96. The island was also identified as one of a group called Carnegies Islands.

Evaluations and Descriptions

1873: Unwin 1.4 acres Value: $12

"Same as Island 95."

1894: Beatty 1 2/5 acres Value: $200

"High heads and nice levels for building; a little soil; fine views; good harbourage."

Sale

1897: to J.A. McDonald.

ISLAND 96A

Evaluations and Descriptions

1894: Beatty 1/60 acre Value: $20

"Low; rocky; five feet above water; in shoal water."

Sale

1894: to J.A. McDonald for $201.

ISLAND 96B

Evaluations and Descriptions

1894: Beatty 1/80 acre Value: $15

"Rocky islet."

Sale

1901: to Hannah M. Herron for $15.

ISLAND 97

Names

The island was also identified as one of a group known as Carnegies Islands.

1873: Unwin 1.2 acres Value: $11

"Same as Island 95."

Sale

1895: to Robert A. Campbell. In 1906 the island was purchased as part of the W.D. Morris Real Estate Company for $425. It was sold in 1959 for $3,600.

ISLAND 97A

Evaluations and Descriptions

1894: Beatty 1/100 acre Value: $5

"Low, rocky shoal."

Sale

1908: to J.W. Wilson.

ISLAND 98

Names

The island was also identified as one of a group known as Carnegies Islands.

Evaluations and Descriptions

1873: Unwin 0.4 acre Value: $5

"Same as Island 95."

1894: Beatty 2/5 acre Value: $100

"Smooth, rocky; good shade pine; nice location on channel."

Sale

1894: to F.C. Chittick for $100. Purchased as part of the W.D. Morris Real Estate Company. This island was sold again in 1966, for $1,100.

ISLAND 98A

Evaluations and Descriptions

1894: Beatty 1/10 acre Value: $40

"Rocky, some scrub, good location.

Sale

1901: to Jessie Darling.

ISLAND 98B

Evaluations and Descriptions

1894: Beatty 1/10 acre Value: $50

"With adjunct to east; rocky; good shade trees; well located."

Sale

Purchased as part of the W.D. Morris Real Estate Company. This island did not sell again until 1967, for $1,100.

ISLAND 98C

Evaluations and Descriptions

1894: Beatty 1/10 acre Value: $35

"Bare, low lying rock, with shoal to north-east, and adjoining."

Sale

1894: to F.F. Morris for $200.

ISLAND 98D

Evaluations and Descriptions

1894: Beatty 1/10 acre Value: $40

"Level, rocky, some scrub."

ISLAND 98F

Evaluations and Descriptions

1894: Beatty 1/5 acre Value: $75

"Low, level; good small trees; with adjunct at west coast."

ISLAND 98G

(Now considered Island 89G.)

Evaluations and Descriptions

1894: Beatty 1/10 acre Value: $40

"Level rock; some scrub."

Sale

1894: to Charles Donohue.

ISLAND 98H

Evaluations and Descriptions

1894: Beatty 1/80 acre Value: $30

"Rocky, barren."

Sale

1894: to F.L. King for $30.

ISLAND 98I

Evaluations and Descriptions

1894: Beatty 1/20 acre Value: $60

"Rocky, some scrub."

ISLAND 98J

Evaluations and Descriptions

1894: Beatty 1/10 acre Value: $50

"Level, stony, some good shade; in open waters."

Sale

1901: to Joseph Peno.

No information is available for Island 98K.

ISLAND 98L

Evaluations and Descriptions

1894: Beatty 1/10 acre Value: $30

"Low, level; some scrub; including adjoining shoal."

Sale

1903: to Clayton E.B. Horton.

ISLAND 98M-N

Evaluations and Descriptions

1894: Beatty 1/5 acre Value: $100

"Rocky, some good trees, good shelter, well located."

Sale

1895: to Edwin A. Coater.

ISLAND 98O

Evaluations and Descriptions

1894: Beatty 1/10 acre Value: $20

"Low, level."

Sale

1901: to Freland Jewett.

ISLAND 98P

Evaluations and Descriptions

1894: Beatty 1/20 acre Value: $20

"Bare, rocky."

PINES ISLAND

Names

The island was also identified as one of a group known as Carnegies Islands.

Evaluations and Descriptions

1873: Unwin 1.4 acre Value: $10

"Same as Island 95."

HOG ISLAND

Names

The island was also identified as one of a group known as Carnegies Islands.

Evaluations and Descriptions

1873: Unwin 1.5 acres Value: $15

"Same as Island 95."

WATCH ISLAND

Historic Name

This was the name first recorded on Unwin's map. It is a descriptive name because the island was used as a "watch station" for horse thieves.

Evaluations and Descriptions

1873: Unwin 0.1 acre Value: $3

"Low rock with 2 or 3 trees."

1894: Beatty 1/10 acre Value: $80

"Low; level; some good trees; in mid channel."

Island Notes

Watch Island was described in the early 1910s by J.D.W. Darling, in *Sketch of the Early History of the Front Concessions of Lansdowne and the Thousand Islands*: "Among the noted places of the 1000 Islands group on the north and the north shore was Sherwood Bay, a point used to transfer hundreds of horses stolen and brought from long distances to Hill Island and thence to the United States. The rocky hills surrounding this bay made an excellent cover for concealment. This was about the year 1800. Watch Island was used as a lookout for soldiers and guards stationed there to spy on all traffic passing, and it was from this island that the horse stealers were finally rounded up."

Sale

1894: to de Forrest Fairchild.

Sir Stapleton Cotton, 1st Viscount Combermere.

— *Wellington & Waterloo*, Major Arthur Griffiths, published by George Newnes, Liited, 1989

CHUB or CLUB ISLAND

Historic Name

1816: Owen — Combermere, the Wellington Islands Named after Sir Stapleton Cotton, 1st Viscount Combermere (1773–1865). He was born into a wealthy family; his father owned large estates and had a reputation for "high living." As a youngster he was known as "Young Rapid" by his family and "Little Cotton" by his friends. After attending various schools he joined the army and served in France, Britain, India and Cape Town. Combermere's career covered seventy years of service to the British government. He joined the Peninsular War in 1808, serving in various brigades. He gained a reputation as a calvary officer and inspector of the troops. Later Combermere was appointed governor in Barbados and commander-in-chief in the Leeward Islands, in Ireland and in India. During the last year of his life, he was a member of Parliament.

Named Chub Island by Charles Unwin.

Evaluations and Descriptions

1873: Unwin 146.3 acres identified as separate parcels of land.

(Punctuation as in original.)

"This is a high rough and rocky Island, occupied by Frank and Vere Hunt, the line between them was new to agree very nearly with their existing line fence. All the timber of any value has been cut off, the timber now standing is second growth soft Maple Pine Oak & c"

"Parcel No. 1 Sale 19 Sold to Francis Hunt Owned by Frank Hunt contains 67.5 acres, of which 31.2 are cleared All the arable land is cleared — soil sandy and of fair quality There is a log dwelling house, one story high on it, worth about $150 Also a frame barn with a stable underneath, worth about $100 There is also an orchard of about fifty trees Frank Hunt has lived on it about twenty one years, he claims under his brother Fitz Maurice Hunt of Belleville who bought from Edw.d Lee"

"Parcel No.2 Sale 31 Sold to Robt Vere Hunt Owned by Robt. Vere Hunt contains 75.8 acres of which 19 are cleared All the arable land is cleared soil sandy and of fair quality There is a log House worth about $100 also a log barn worth about the same R.V. Hunt has lived on this portion about twelve years, he purchased from his brother Fitz Maurice Hunt."

ISLAND 99

Evaluations and Descriptions

1873: Unwin 1.1 acres Value: $10

"High rock thickly covered with scrubby bushes."

1894: Beatty 1 acre Value: $150

"High, rocky; good small pines."

Sale

1894: to Emile L. Boas, with Hemlock Island in the Admiralty Islands.

ISLAND 99A

Evaluations and Descriptions

1894: Beatty 1/10 acre Value: $30

"Rocky, bears small cedar, scrub."

Sale

1895: to Herbert A. Boas.

ISLAND 100

Evaluations and Descriptions

1873: Unwin 3.4 acres Value: $40

"Low, well covered with soil and timber."

ISLAND 101

Evaluations and Descriptions

1873: Unwin 3 acres Value: $30

"Same as Island 100."

Sale

1883: to T. Hunt for $130.

No information is available for Islands 101A, 101B, and 101C; they do not appear on island charts. Islands in the 101 series are located in the International Rift and could have originally been recorded but excluded if they fell in the United States.

ISLAND 101C

Evaluations and Descriptions

1894: Beatty 1/5 acre Value: $75

"Level; nice shade trees; on yacht channel."

Sale

1903: to Willard Davis for $75.

ISLAND 101D

Evaluations and Descriptions

1894: Beatty 1/4 acre Value: $80

"Good pine and white birch shade trees; level, well sheltered; on yacht channel."

Sale

1917: to Henry Crofts Munro for $80.

ISLAND 101E

Evaluations and Descriptions

1894: Beatty 1/10 acre Value: $40

"In marsh; pine trees and scrub."

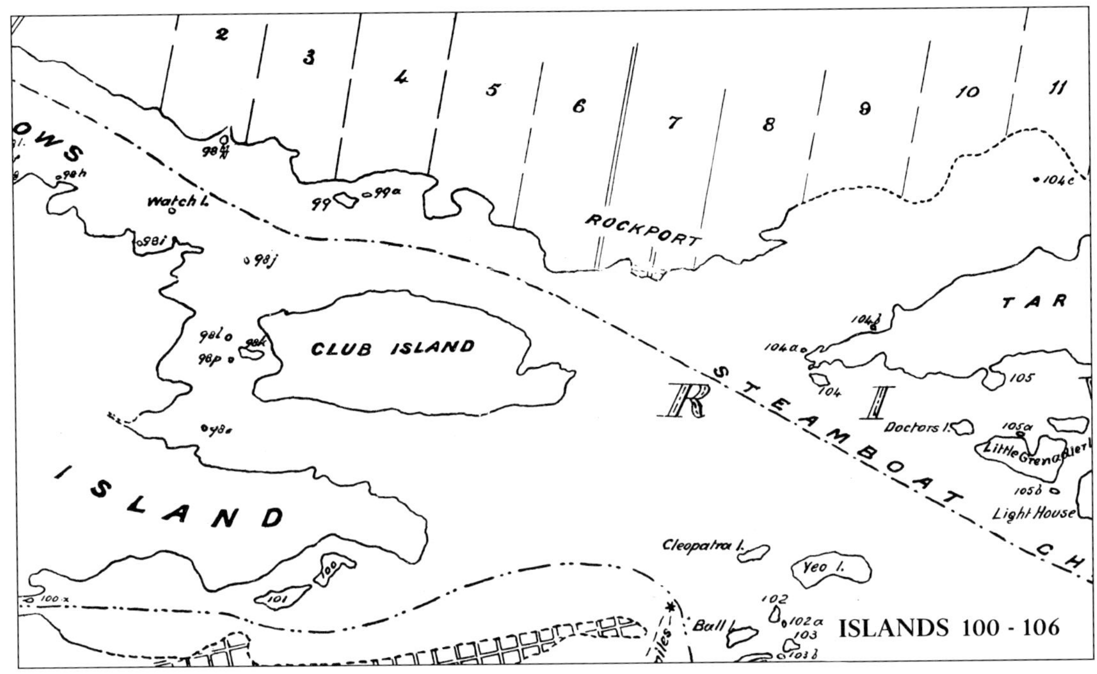

ISLAND 101F

Evaluations and Descriptions

1894: Beatty 1/15 acre Value: $40

"Low; in deep water."

Sale

1907: to Mary Weeks for $40.

ISLAND 101G

Evaluations and Descriptions

1894: Beatty 1/10 acre Value: $75

"Pretty; nice shade trees; level; good views; sheltered waters; on yacht channel."

Sale

1909: to Henry C. Munro.

ISLAND 101H

Evaluations and Descriptions

1894: Beatty 1/8 acre Value: $125

"Pretty; nice shade trees; between two channels; includes small shoal at head, and islet at foot standing out into channel."

Sale

The island was first sold in 1958.

ISLAND 101I

Evaluations and Descriptions

1894: Beatty 1/6 acre Value: $100

"Cut in two at high water; nice shade on upper half; level; on channel."

ISLAND 101J

Evaluations and Descriptions

1894: Beatty 1 acre Value: $150

"Level, well timbered; point to south almost severed; on yacht channel; good fishing."

CLEOPATRA ISLAND

Historic Name

1816: Owen — Cleopatra, the Hydrographers
No biographical information is available. The name Cleopatra probably refers to a sloop or boat used by the surveyors.

Evaluations and Descriptions

1873: Unwin 1.4 acres Value: $50

"High rock, a few trees on it."

1894: Beatty 1 2/5 acres Value: $150

"Rocky, well located; some good scattered pine; between United States boundary and Steamboat Channel."

BALL ISLAND

Evaluations and Descriptions

1873: Unwin 1.6 acres Value: $500

"Well timbered, occupied by Gifford Benson and Henry Campbell, they have an unfinished frame house which cost $500, Campbell has lived on the Island two summers."

Sale

1894: to W.B. Abbott for $350.

ZAVIKON ISLAND

Historic Name

1816: Owen — Aspasia Island, the Hydrographers
No biographical information is available. Aspasia was possibly the name of a sloop or boat used by the surveyors.

Evaluations and Descriptions

1873: Unwin 1.4 acres Value: $100

"Low at West end rough at East, poorly wooded, small shanty 8'x10' built this summer occupied."

1894: Beatty 1 2/5 acres Value: $200

"Nice shade trees; adjacent to improved islands in United States waters."

Zavikon Island, with its International Bridge.
— Photograph appearing in picture book published by the Thousand Island House, Alexandria Bay, George J. Walsh, Proprietor

Island Notes

For many years this island and the one adjacent were considered to be in separate countries, Aspasia or Zavikon Island being in Canada and Island 103A in the United States. The owners of the island built a bridge to connect the two and claimed was the smallest international bridge in the world. In reality, both islands are in Canadian waters, but the tradition of flying two national flags from the flag poles continues — much to the delight of the passing tourists!

Sale

1894: to C. Berkley Powell.

ISLAND 103A

(Considered part of Zavikon Island)

Evaluations and Descriptions

1894: Beatty 3/10 acre Value: $100
"Level, rocky; some timber; good location on channel."

ISLAND 102

Evaluations and Descriptions

1873: Unwin 0.6 acre Value: $25
"Rough and rock, small timber on it."
1894: Beatty 3/5 acre Value: $100
"Rough, rocky; some timber; good location."

Sale

Sold to Florence S. Livingston for $100.

ISLAND 102A

Evaluations and Descriptions

1894: Beatty 1/10 acre Value: $30
"Rocky, four feet above water; barren."

Sale

1910: to Agnes Riley for $30.

ISLAND 103

Evaluations and Descriptions

1873: Unwin 0.6 acre Value: $100
"Rocky, tolerably level, very pretty, frame house 12'x24' on it."
1894: Beatty 3/5 acre Value: $150
"Well timbered; high; rocky; first-class location on channel."

Sale

1894: to Douglas Merritt.

(See Zavikon Island for a description of Island 103A.)

ISLAND 103B

Evaluations and Descriptions

1894: Beatty 1/20 acre Value: $30
"Bare rock, four feet above water, with shoal between it and Aspasia Island."

Sale

Sold to E.D. Robb.

YEO ISLAND or OLD BLUFF ISLAND

Historic Name

1816: Owen — Yeo, the Hydrographers
Probably named after the gunboat *Yeo*, named for Sir James Yeo.

Evaluations and Descriptions

1873: Unwin 9.4 acres Value: $400
"High rough rock, a few trees, a small shanty built by [?] of Ogdensburg N.Y. who wishes to buy it."

Island Notes

A newspaper article written in 1921 in the *Gananoque Reporter* carried this headline: "Tells History of the Cross on Bluff Island Erected in Memory of a Mr. Stout who Died at the Bay in 1874."

J. Herbert Carpenter, of Ossining and New York City who was a guest yesterday at the Thousand Islands House, related an interesting bit of history in regard to the cross on Bluff Island.

"It was put up," said Mr. Carpenter, "in memory of a Mr. Stout who died in Thousand Island House in 1874.

Mr. Carpenter was an executor of Mr. Stout's will. The cross is one that interests all tourists and if the boatmen on the tours do not tell what the cross was placed there for, there is always a chorus of inquiries from the sight seers in the boats. The cross here to fore has been known as "the Cross of the Good Women." and so denoted by the boatmen of the St. Lawrence River."

ISLAND 104

Evaluations and Descriptions

1873: Unwin 0.8 acre Value: $15

"High and rocky, some small timber and brush."

1894: Beatty 4/5 acre Value: $150

"High, rocky; well timbered; fine location on steamboat channel."

Sale

1894: to F.P. Bronson.

ISLAND 104A

Evaluations and Descriptions

1894: Beatty 1/10 acre Value: $40

"Rocky; small scrub; with bare rocky adjunct to east, which is just above water level."

Sale

1902: to Emile S. Eaton.

ISLAND 104B

Evaluations and Descriptions

1894: Beatty 1/30 acre Value: $25

"Rocky knob; some good cedars."

ISLAND 104C

Evaluations and Descriptions

1894: Beatty 1/80 acre Value: $5

"Bare rock, just showing."

Sale

First sold in 1957. The island was not drawn on either Unwin or Beatty's map.

BRITISH STATESMEN

Twenty-six islands were named after British statesmen and others who served in the Treasury Office in London.

The latter group is not well known today, but during the time of the survey the Treasury Office members' names appeared on correspondence from the survey team to the Admiralty Office. It must have seemed prudent to commemorate those who were responsible for Admiralty budgets and in fact for the navy's payroll.

OWEN	PRESENT NAME	PAGE
Tar	Tar Island (Canadian)	175
Palmerston	Doctor Island (Canadian)	177
Sidmouth	Little Grenadier Island (Canadian)	177
Bathurst	Grenadier Island (Canadian)	177
Sydenham	Van Buren Island (Canadian)	181
O'Neille	O'Neill Island (Canadian)	181
Rolleston	Jeroy Island (Canadian)	181
The Treasury Chambers	Indian Island, Car Island Shoe Island (Canadian)	182
McMahon	Shanty Island (Canadian)	182
Bloomfield	Snake Island (Canadian)	183
Liverpool	Ironside Island (American)	227
Castlereath	Little Ironside Island (American)	227
Vansittart	Long Island (Canadian)	186
Goulbourn	St. Helena Island (Canadian)	187
Cook	Cook Island (Canadian)	187
Hamilton	Rough Island (Canadian)	187
Bagot	Rattlesnake Island (Canadian)	187
Robert	Cherry Island (Canadian)	188
Peel	Prince Edward Island (Canadian)	188
Broughton	Corn Island (Canadian)	191
Chatham	Dark Island (American)	232

TAR ISLAND

Evaluations and Descriptions

1873: Unwin 248.9 acres (identified as separate parcels of land)

(Original punctuation)

"This is a high sandy island, nearly all cleared, it derives its name from the fact of Tar being manufactured on it, a great many years ago from the Pitch Pine, with which it was thickly covered. There are only two occupants on this island, and the line was run, agreeing as nearly as possible with their line fence.

"*Parcel No.1* Owned by Harvey Andres contains 181.9 acres, of 153.4 are cleared There is a very nice Pine grove on the West end of the island, also one on the South side of the island. The soil is very light sand good for Potatoes and other root crops, a great deal of Buckwheat is grown. The centre of the island is pretty, high and slopes down to the water on both sides; There is very little of this parcel so rocky that it can not be cultivated There is a frame house 18'x24' width about $70 also a frame barn 26'x52' worth, say, $100 Harvey Andres has a quit claim deed from his brother Richard Andres, the latter purchased from Thos Lean, who inherited from his father Jm Lean. This parcel is now leased to Messrs Ira and John Wood, four years of their lease yet to come."

"*Parcel No.2* Owned by David Andres containing 67 acres, all cleared at one time, but the timber on the rocky portion has been allowed to grow up again.

"About one half of this parcel is covered with this 'second growth,' near the East end there are three or four acres on which the sand is drifted about by the wind so that nothing grows on it.

"There is a board house 16'x 18' — cost $75 when built (18 years ago) There is also a log barn 14'x 20' The arable soil is similar to that on parcel No.1

"David Andres has a 'Quit Claim' from his brother R.T Andres who purchased it from Thos Lean, who inherited from his father Jm. Lean."

The Eaton Cottage on Tar Island.
— Private Collection: Mrs. Robert Hewett, Tar Island

Island Notes

The west end of Tar Island was purchased in 1899 by Dr. Eaton, a Universalist minister from New York City. The Eatons built a large summer home that was admired by many tourists. Their daughter, Anne Thaxter Eaton, was a professor of children's literature at St. John's University in New York City. She was also the children's book reviewer for the Sunday edition of the *New York Times*. Every week she received a supply of new books. After reading them and writing her reviews, she would send the books to the Rockport Public School, thus providing a valuable library for the summer community she loved so much. As a tribute to her memory, the new Escott Township library, dedicated in 1985 in Springfield House, was named in her honour.

The Eaton house was sold several times in the 1900s. In 1920 G.E. Thing bought the property. The Things collected totem poles and native artifacts for the island. They remained the owners until in 1956.

(See also Chapter 1.)

Sale

Originally sold to Harvey E. Andress and Ira Mallory, and later sold to Dr. Eaton.

ISLAND 105

Evaluations and Descriptions

1873: Unwin 1.6 acres Value: $30

"High and rocky, some small timber brush, connected with Tar Island in low water and marshy, between the high water."

1894: Beatty 1 2/5 acres Value: $100

"High, rocky; some good shade trees; with low points to east; attached in very low water to Tar Island."

Sale

1897: Purchased by the W.D. Morris Real Estate Company. It was not sold again until 1920, for $1,000.

ISLAND 105A

Evaluations and Descriptions

1894: Beatty 1/20 acre Value: $40

"Rocky, round; some nice small timber."

Sale

1920: to Leonard Williams.

ISLAND 105B

Evaluations and Descriptions

1894: Beatty 1/8 acre Value: $75

"Rocky, well wooded, good view of American islands and channel."

Sale

1907: to Elizabeth W. Miller.

ISLAND 105C

Evaluations and Descriptions

1894: Beatty 1/20 acre Value: $40

"With shoal to west; bare; good location, in sight of channel."

Sale

1909: to Richard H. Hibberd.

ISLAND 105D

Evaluations and Descriptions

1894: Beatty 1/3 acre Value: $100

"Low, level; nice pines; good building spot, well located."

Sale

1897: to William G. Hurdman.

ISLAND 105E

Evaluations and Descriptions

1894: Beatty 1/5 acre Value: $100

"Level; good harbour; good timber."

Sale

1902: to Milo L. Cleveland, with Island 105G.

ISLAND 105F

Evaluations and Descriptions

1894: Beatty 1/5 acre Value: $100

"Level; good timber; good harbour."

Sale

1897: Purchased as part of the W.D. Morris Real Estate Company. It was not sold again until 1967, for $1,250.

ISLAND 105G

Evaluations and Descriptions

1894: Beatty 1/10 acre Value: $40

"Barren rock; good locality."

Sale

1902: to Milo L. Cleveland, with Island 105E.

DOCTOR ISLAND

Evaluations and Descriptions

1873: Unwin 1.1 acres Value: $30

"Rocky, very little soil, a few small trees and bushes."

BUCK ISLAND

Evaluations and Descriptions

1873: Unwin 2.4 acres Value: $40

"Rocky at both ends some soil in the centre. Thickly covered with small trees. F.R. Dunkirk of Binghamton, N.Y. has built a shanty 7'x12', it is said that if he can buy the Island he will put up a house costing $2000."

Sale

1900: to John D. Reid.

LITTLE GRENADIER ISLAND

Evaluations and Descriptions

1873: Unwin 3.4 acres Value: $200

"Rough — some soil — timber nearly all cut off. Pastured for about ten years by Albert Root, Light House Keeper on Grenadier Id. who wants to purchase this, Doctor and Buck Islands."

GRENADIER ISLAND

Historic Name

1816: Owen — Bathurst, the British Statesmen Named after Henry Bathurst (1762–1834). Earl Bathurst was a statesmen first, a member of Parliament from 1793 to 1794, and teller of the Exchequer from 1790 until his death. It is most likely that his role with the Treasury warranted his commemoration on the Owen charts.

Among the offices he held was lord of the Admiralty from 1789 to 1791, and commissioner of the Board of Control, 1793–1802. He also assumed the mastership of the Mint and president of the Board of Trade from 1807 to 1812. In 1809 he was appointed foreign secretary and in Lord Liverpool's ministry he was secretary of War and

Henry Bathurst.

— *Wellington & Waterloo*, Major Arthur Griffiths, published by George Newnes, Limited, 1898

The Colonies. He completed his political career under the Duke of Wellington from 1828 to 1830.

Evaluations and Descriptions

1873: Unwin 1198.1 acres (identified as separate parcels of land)

(Original punctuation)

"This island is more than four miles in length The greatest part of it low — Soil light sand, in some places thickly covered with small round stones from three to eight inches in diameter.

"It has been settled for more than 60 years. There is very little timber left on it.

"Several years ago a road was laid out in the Island, by the municipality of the Township of Escott, it commenced on the North side of the island, between parcels 11 & 12 and followed the road as shown on the map, to the line between parcels 1 & 2 which it followed to the South side of the island, it has not been opened along the line between parcels 1 & 2 for several years as the water on the South side of the island at this place, is so shallow that it is impossible to land with a large boat, there are several land places on the North shore where the road touches. I laid out a road through the centre of parcel No 1 up to the property reserved for Light house purposes, so as to give the occupant of those premises communication with other points of The Island, the road is in good condition, for travel, from one end of the Island to the other, except through parcel No 1 and it could be made good very easily through it, as it follows the top of the ridge of the Island If laid out on the shore it could not be made nearly so cheaply, and as laid out it will be more convenient for the owner of No 1, giving him access to every field on his property, the road is laid out follows as nearly as possible the present travelled road, it being straightened in a few places, the road has been laid out sixty one links (40ft) in width, which is sufficient for all the travel on it, There is a public School on the Island, and an acre of ground has been reserved for school purposes There is also a public burying ground in the Island.

"In the subdivision, the division lines have been run conforming as nearly as possible to their present line fences. In the line between Poole and Massey, the line was run about on the course of their present boundary line, to the westward of it south of the road, and as the eastward of it north of the road, carrying it straight through and leaving each with about the same quantity they formerly held.

"The Reserve for Light house purposes contains 9.8 acres, of which 3.7 are cleared the uncleared portion is rocky and thickly covered with Pitch Pine trees which makes a very fine grove — the cleared portion has a fair soil — there is a very good frame house erected by the Government for the Light House keeper, a good board fence separates this reserve from A. Root portion (parcel No. 1)"

"Light House Reserve . . . average value per acre $10. Sale 476 Dominion Park Reserve"

"Parcel No.1 Sale 24 Sold to Albert Root Owned by Albert Root contains 80.6 acres, of which 49.8 are cleared About two thirds of the uncleared portion is rocky, the soil sandy, of fair quality There is a small young orchard which seems to be thriving, planted two or three years ago There is a small frame barn Root is Lighthouse Keeper, and has lived there about fourteen years — claims from Jos H Austin the former Lighthouse Keeper — Has a 'quit claim' from him, received it for taking care of him and his wife for five years, after Mrs. Austins death, Root gave her husband (Austin) $200 Root sold the portion reserved for Lighthouse purposes to the Government, for $50, some years ago — Average value per acre $10."

"Parcel No.2 Sale 20. Sold to Jas P. Hooper Owned by Jas Parker Hooper contains 32 acres, all cleared, about one and a half acres of it, rock, The soil is sandy, and not very good There are about fifty apple trees, of which only one is grafted, some of the trees are so old that they do not bear well There is a frame house one and a half storeys high 30'x18' built about ten years ago, with a stone cellar under it, value $500 A log barn 30'x18' with a frame 'Lean-to' 9'x30' value $200 Also landing piers in front of house worth $50 Hooper purchased from Jm Birch about 6 years ago, and paid him $609 — Birch bought from a Frenchman named Goslow — Average value per acre $10."

"Parcel No.3 Sale 28. Sold to Wm L. Hibbard Owned by Wm LeRoy Hibbard. Contains 67.6 acres, of which 56 are cleared, on the uncleared portion there is a very nice grove of Maple from which Hibbard makes sugar, the soil is principally sandy and of fair quality There is an orchard of about 100 trees most of them large, they bear well and the fruit is of fair quality. There is a frame house 15'x18' a storey and a half high, with a good stone cellar — value $300 — a Frame shop 14'x14' with stone storeroom underneath — value $60 An old frame barn 26x36 worth probably $70 An old log house, used as a barn, worth say $50 — a well 80 feet deep near dwelling house, stoned up — An ice house 12'6"x12'6" not quite finished — will cost about $50 — Granary 11x12 in course of erection — will cost about $40 — Wm LeRoy Hibbard bought "Quit Claim" from Chas Cornwall of Rockport, about seven years ago, and says he paid $1000 United States currency. Hibbard says Cornwall bought from Michael Goslui (Goslow?), who got it from his father, who purchased it from A. Root, The Root family at one time owned the four Westerly farms on this Island, Hibbard says that Shanty and Snake islands lying to the Southward, and Duck on the Northward, belong to this place, and that he purchased with that understanding. Average value per acre, $15."

"Parcel No.4 Sale 30. Sold to Chauncey Root Owned by Chauncey Root — contains 132.7 acres, of which 70.5 are cleared. All the soil is arable, except the uncleared portion lying to the Eastward of the marsh This parcel has a fair sandy soil. There is a beautiful grove of small Pitch Pine as on the South side, and a belt of marsh running across the island, through this parcel, over which boats have passed, in high water, from one side of the island to the other The marsh is not included in the area of this parcel, a good deal of hay and pasturage is obtained from it by C. Root There is an old orchard, containing sixty or seventy trees, said to have been planted sixty four years ago, by Roots father and Uncle, there is also a young orchard of about forty trees, which are now in good bearing condition, Root says that his father and Uncle settled on this Id. seventy years ago There is a frame house 26x30 one and a half storeys high worth $600 A Frame Barn 20x35 with a stone wall underneath, value $100 An old log barn 26x36 worth say $70 C. Root purchased part from his mother and part from his brother A. Root."

"Parcel No.5 Sale 12 Sold to Joseph Senecal Owned by Joseph Senecal — contains 204.1 acres of which 166.8 are cleared — nearly the whole of this parcel is arable and the soil of fair quality. This is the best farm on the island, and the proprietor displays by far the most enterprise in improving his property he has at several different times planted a good many apple trees, but has been unfortunate in having them killed by mice. There is a good cherry orchard, also a small apple orchard. There is a very nice piece of bush on this parcel which Senecal has preserved, he paid $3000 for this parcel, and has since spent more than $1000 in buildings and improvements — he has new frame barn 38'x48' worth $400 An old barn and piggery $75 A new granary worth $180 A good frame house worth $1000 Senecal also claims — Indiana, Squaw, Car and Shoe islands, as belonging to this parcel, he purchased from Wm Thompson in 1863."

"Parcel No.6 Sale 14 Sold to Hiram T. Buell Owned by Hiram Buell Contains 102.8 acres of which 93.1 are cleared There is a small piece of very nice bush on the North side of this parcel. There is very little rock on Buells property, it is intersected by Marsh in several places In season when the River is low a great deal of Hay and pasturage is obtained from the marsh St. Gabriels Point is connected with this parcel in low water, and Buell says that it has always been claimed as belonging to it — See report on St. Gabriels Point — The soil is sandy There is a good orchard of about 150 apple trees, now bearing, and about 50 more not yet bearing There is a frame house and Barn, which together are worth, say $1000 Buell and Reuben Williams purchased from Hiram Mallory, in March 1871, since that time Buell has bought out Williams' claim."

"School Lot 1 Acre Value $40"

"Parcel No.7 Sale 23 Sold to Chr Cornwall Owned by Charles Wright — contains 41.3 acres, of which 22.6 are cleared. The whole of the soil is arable light sand, the portion north of marsh has some nice small timber on it, there is communication between it and the portion south of the marsh only during the winter season, except by going through Buells property The River washes away a considerable portion of the land on the South side of this parcel each year The buildings on this parcel are

worth about $400 C. Wright has lived on this, about four years, he purchased from his father, and gave him $1500 for it, he says his father lived on it for more than twenty years. Average value per acre $12."

"Parcel No.8 Sale 13 Sold to C. Brooker Owned by Chas Brooker[?] — contains 35 acres, all partially cleared — soil light sand The only communication with this parcel, except through the marsh, is by going over other property It would cost a great deal to make a passable road across the marsh, to it. Brooker subsists chiefly by fishing, and does not require a road There is an old board house one story and a half high 18'x18' worth say $150 There are also a few fruit trees."

"Parcel No.9 Sale 21, Sold to Wm Poole Owned by Wm Poole contains 90 acres of which 54.2 are cleared, the uncleared portion consists of 'second growth' no timber of any value This lot is thickly covered with small round stones — soil sandy loam — a frame house 26'x36' and an addition 14x26 worth in all $300 A log barn 30x20 $30 A frame house one and a half storeys high, with a stone cellar underneath, worth say $200 A log house adjoining frame house 18x18, value $50 Orchard containing 50 apple trees, now bearing Poole purchased from Spicer — Spicer purchased from Senecal."

"Parcel No.10 Sale 17. Sold to Wm Massey Owned by Wm Massey contains 77.5 acres of which 22 are cleared No timber of any value on uncleared portion — not well cultivated — Massey appears to be a very poor farmer Soil fair but somewhat stoney There is an old log house one and a half storeys high worth $75 An old stable value $30 A few apple trees worth say $50 — Massey has a 'Quit Claim' from Jas Carter, had it about four or five years — paid $850 American currency has been in possession about eight years. Average value per acre $11."

"Parcel No.11 Sale 27. Sold to Nancy Comstock. Owned by Eliza Ann Comstock wife of Merrick Comstock — contains 48 acres, of which 42.5 are cleared The uncleared portion is fairly timbered — soil rather poor and stoney A small frame house and barn together worth $250 A small orchard. Average value per acre $9 See No.3,678."

"Parcel No.12 Sale 34. Owned by Sam Mitchell contains 65.9 acres of which 37.4 are cleared The uncleared portion lying on South Easterly side of this parcel is rocky. The remainder is arable There is a very fine grove of Black Oaks at the East end of the Island A frame house 20x24, value $300 A frame barn 30x40 worth say $100 An orchard of about 200 trees, of which upwards of 100 are now bearing Mitchell has a 'Quit Claim' from Annison Malory dated Jan 7 1873 consideration $900 Malory came into possession about fifteen years ago Average value per acre $12.00."

"No distinction is made between the land under cultivation and bush land, as I consider them of equal value. C.U." (Charles Unwin)

No additional island history has been included because there are several histories written about Grenadier Island life. *The Story of Grenadier Island*, written by Jane Allan in 1971, gives a good historical perspective. Members of the St. Lawrence Islands National Park have also completed a research paper on Grenadier Island.

ISLAND 106

Evaluations and Descriptions

1873: Unwin 1.4 acres Value: $50

"High and rocky, covered with trees and small bush, connected with Tar Id. in low water and marsh between them in high water."

1894: Beatty 1 2/5 acres Value: $200

"High in centre, with a number of low points affording good landings and building sites."

Sale

1894: to Reginald H. Jones.

ISLAND 106A

Evaluations and Descriptions

1894: Beatty 1/80 acre Value: $20

"Barren, rocky; 4 ft. above water."

Sale

1908: to Charles A. Duke.

ISLAND 106B

Evaluations and Descriptions

1894: Beatty 1/10 acre Value: $40

"Low, level; some poor scrub."

ISLAND 106C

Evaluations and Descriptions

1894: Beatty 1/80 acre Value: $10

"Bare rock; low."

ISLAND 106D

Evaluations and Descriptions

1894: Beatty 1/10 acre Value: $60

"Low, level; some good timber."

Sale

1908: to James Cline.

ISLAND 106E

Evaluations and Descriptions

1894: Beatty 1/25 acre Value: $20

"Round, rocky."

Sale

This island was first sold in 1941.

ISLAND 106F

Evaluations and Descriptions

1894: Beatty 1/30 acre Value: $25

"Bare rock."

DUCK ROCK BEACON LIGHT

Names

Named Island 106G by Walter Beatty.

Evaluations and Descriptions

1894: Beatty 3/10 acre Value: $60

"Rocky; light scrub; including rocks to east."

Sale

1910: to George Riles. This island was expropriated for a light beacon in 1921.

ISLAND 107

Evaluations and Descriptions

1873: Unwin 0.8 acre Value: $5

"Low rock, a few bushes on it."

1894: Beatty 4/5 acre Value: $80

"Level, well-sheltered, lightly wooded."

Sale

1907: to James M. Grier.

ISLAND 107A

Evaluations and Descriptions

1894: Beatty 1/20 acre Value: $5

"Low, rocky reef."

ISLAND 108

Evaluations and Descriptions

1873: Unwin 0.5 acre Value: $5

"Low rock, a few bushes on it."

1894: Beatty 1/2 acre Value: $80

"Round, level."

Sale

The island was first sold in 1982.

ISLAND 108A

Evaluations and Descriptions

1894: Beatty 1/10 acre Value: $10

"Round bare rock."

ISLAND 108B

Evaluations and Descriptions

1894: Beatty 1/10 acre Value: $10

"Low bare reef."

ISLAND 108C

Evaluations and Descriptions

1894: Beatty 1/20 acre Value: $20

"High islet in shoal water."

Sale

The island was first sold in 1960.

ISLAND 108D

Evaluations and Descriptions

1894: Beatty 2 acres Value: $300

"Well wooded, nicely situated; deep water; level, medium height."

Sale

1894: to J.B. Lynch for $500 with Blackberry Island (Island 112). Purchased as part of the W.D. Morris Real Estate Company. The island was sold again in 1947 to J.A. Dunn.

ISLAND 108E

Evaluations and Descriptions

1894: Beatty 1/10 acre Value: $30

"Bare level granite rock."

Sale

1905: to Alfred M. Scott.

ISLAND 108F

Evaluations and Descriptions

1894: Beatty 1/80 acre Value: $20

"Low bare rock."

Sale

1909: to Nicholas Toerge, with Islands 108G, 108H and 112G.

ISLAND 108G

Evaluations and Descriptions

1894: Beatty 1/80 acre Value: $20

"Low bare rock."

Sale

1909: to Nicholas Toerge.

ISLAND 108H

Evaluations and Descriptions

1894: Beatty 1/20 acre Value: $30

"Low bare rock."

Sale

1909: to Nicholas Toerge.

Charles Poulett Thomson, Baron Sydenham.
— Metropolitan Toronto Reference Library, T15463

ISLAND 108I

Evaluations and Descriptions

1894: Beatty 1/10 acre Value: $50

"Barren rock; good location."

Sale

1894: to F.T. Bronson for $50.

DUCK ISLAND

Evaluations and Descriptions

1873: Unwin 2.4 acres Value: $30

"Low and rocky, a little soil, some brush — Pastured and cleared by Hibbard who lives on Grenadier Island he says he bought this, Shanty and Snake as belonging to his Farm."

VAN BUREN ISLAND or SYDENHAM ISLAND

Historic Name

1816: Owen — Sydenham, the British Statesmen Named after Charles Poulett Thomson, Baron Sydenham (1799–1841). Thomson was a British economic expert, and was most likely a member of the British Treasury at the time of the survey. He became a member of Parliament in 1826 and was made vice-president of the Board of Trade in 1830. His name is well known in Canada because he served as governor-general from 1839 to 1841.

Evaluations and Descriptions

1873: Unwin 4.2 acres Value: $60

"High and rocky, some pretty trees on it."

BLUFF ISLAND or O'NEILL ISLAND

Historic Name

1816: Owen — O'Neill, the British Statesmen No biographical information is available. Probably O'Neill worked in the Treasury Office with Rolleston in 1816.

Evaluations and Descriptions

1873: Unwin 6.3 acres Value: $40

"Rocky — High in centre, a little soil, small trees and bushes."

1894: Beatty 6 3/10 acres Value: $500

"Low; level; with rocky knolls; partly cleared; some good timber left on west end; reeds on north and west; front good."

Sale

1905: to Alfred M. Scott.

BERRY ISLAND

Evaluations and Descriptions

1873: Unwin 2.0 acres Value: $15

"Rocky small trees and bushes."

1894: Beatty 2 acres Value: $150

"High; rough; rocky."

Sale

1905: to Alfred M. Scott.

Bronson's cottage on Poole Island. — National Archives of Canada PA9284

GOOSE ISLAND

Evaluations and Descriptions

1873: Unwin 0.6 acre Value: $15

"High rock — a few trees."

1894: Beatty 6/10 acre Value: $200

"Sloping; level; fairly timbered; well placed; good fishing."

GRASSY-POINT

Evaluations and Descriptions

1873: Unwin 4.0 acres Value: $15

"Low bare rock, marsh between it and main land."

Sale

1901: to Frederick A. Berham (?) for $250.

POOLE ISLAND

Name

The island was known locally as Poole Island when Charles Unwin made his survey in 1873.

Evaluations and Descriptions

1873: Unwin 2.7 acres Value: $25

"High — some soil, nicely wooded."

Sale

1874: to Robert Poole for $25.

JEROY ISLAND or ROLLESTON ISLAND

Historic Name

1816: Owen — Rolleston, the British Statesmen Probably the island was named after Stephen Rolleston, writer of the Treasury Department's *Gazette*. He held this position in the Home Office until 1828.

Evaluations and Descriptions

1873: Unwin 2.2 acres Value: $40

"High and rocky, a little timber and brush. This and Poole Island have been pastured for a great many years by Poole, who owns Lot 21, Con. 1 Escott."

Sale

1905: to George Kinkel.

INDIAN ISLAND

Historic Name

(Also applies to Squaw, Shoe and Car islands)

1816: Owen — The Treasury Chambers, the British Statesmen

The members of the Treasury Chambers who signed documents sent to Kingston during the survey included N. Vansittart, Wm. O'Dell and C. Grant.

Evaluations and Descriptions

1873: Unwin 1.1 acres Value: $10

"Almost bare rock, these islands, See Indian, Squaw, Car and Shoe are occupied by Joseph Senecal who lives on Grenadier Island, he gets a good deal of March hay from around them. He cut the timber off them to prevent people from camping and destroying his Hay."

1894: Beatty 1 1/10 acres Value: $150

"Level; some good trees."

SQUAW ISLAND

Historic Name

1816: Owen — the Treasury Chambers, the British Statesmen

Evaluations and Descriptions

1873: Unwin 4.2 acres Value: $30

"See Indian Island."

Sale

1894: to E.A. Olver (?) for $500.

CAR ISLAND

Historic Name

1816: Owen — the Treasury Chambers, the British Statesmen

Evaluations and Descriptions

1873: Unwin 1.4 acres Value: $10

"See Indian Island."

1894: Beatty 1 2/5 acres Value: $150

"Level; well timbered; good location."

Island Notes

Registered in the deed as being rented at one time to A. Senecal to run sheep and cut hay.

SHOE ISLAND

Evaluations and Descriptions

1873: Unwin 0.7 acre Value: $10

"See Indian Island."

1894: Beatty 7/10 acre Value: $40

"Low; level; surrounded by reeds; a few trees."

Sale

The island was first sold in 1957.

ISLAND 109

Evaluations and Descriptions

1873: Unwin 0.7 acre Value: $10

"See Indian Island."

1894: Beatty 7/10 acre Value: $50

"Low, level, grassy, surrounded by rocks."

ISLAND 109A

Evaluations and Descriptions

1894: Beatty 1/8 acre Value: $25

"Low, level; nice shade trees."

ISLAND 109B

Evaluations and Descriptions

1894: Beatty 1/10 acre Value: $30

"Two barren reefs."

ISLAND 109C

Evaluations and Descriptions

1894: Beatty 1/8 acre Value: $25

"Barren reef."

ISLAND 109D

Evaluations and Descriptions

1894: Beatty 2/5 acre Value: $50

"Low level island at edge of reeds, near Grenadier Island."

ISLAND 109E

Evaluations and Descriptions

1894: Beatty 2/5 acre Value: $50

"Low level island at edge of reeds, near Grenadier Island."

HOOPERS ISLAND

Evaluations and Descriptions

1873: Unwin 1.2 acres Value: $15

"High and rocky — no soil a few small trees and brush."

1894: Beatty 1 1/5 acres Value: $200

"High; well timbered; good location."

Sale

Purchased as part of the W.D. Morris Real Estate Company. The island was sold again in 1949.

SHANTY ISLAND or McMAHON ISLAND

Historic Name

1816: Owen — McMahon, the British Statesmen

Named after Sir John McMahon, private secretary to the Prince of Wales.

Evaluations and Descriptions

1873: Unwin 4 acres Value: $60

"Rocky, with some soil and brush on it. See Duck Island."

1894: Beatty 4 acres Value: $200

"High well timbered; good location."

Sale

1893: to W.L. Hibberd for $9.

SNAKE ISLAND or BLOOMFIELD ISLAND

Historic Name

1816: Owen — Bloomfield, the British Statesmen The island was probably after Benjamin Bloomfield (1768–1846). After studying at the Royal Military Academy, he became a second lieutenant in the royal artillery at the age of thirteen. He served in Newfoundland and later in Gibraltar and saw action in the Irish Rebellion.

Although he was a poor man, his social and musical abilities attracted the notice of the Prince of Wales (George IV). He was made a gentleman-in-waiting, and was appointed aide-de-camp in 1811. He served as a member of Parliament for Plymouth from 1812 to 1818. In 1817 he succeeded Sir John McMahon as private secretary to the Prince of Wales and was recognized as his confidant in 1822.

Evaluations and Descriptions

1873: Unwin 2.4 acres Value: $35

"Rocky with some soil and brush on it. See Duck Island."

1894: Beatty 2 2/5 acres Value: $400

"Fine; level; partly cleared; nearly cut in two. Can be bought in east and west lots for $200 each or both for $400."

Sale

1907: to A.P. Nichols.

SLIM ISLAND

Names

Named Island 110 by Charles Unwin.

Evaluations and Descriptions

1873: Unwin 1.3 acres Value: $25

"Low and rocky, covered with small brush and trees."

1894: Beatty 1 3/10 acres Value: $300

"Level, rocky; some good shade trees. Might be bought in separate lots, east and west of Narrows, at $150 each."

Sale

1901: to Nellie Darling.

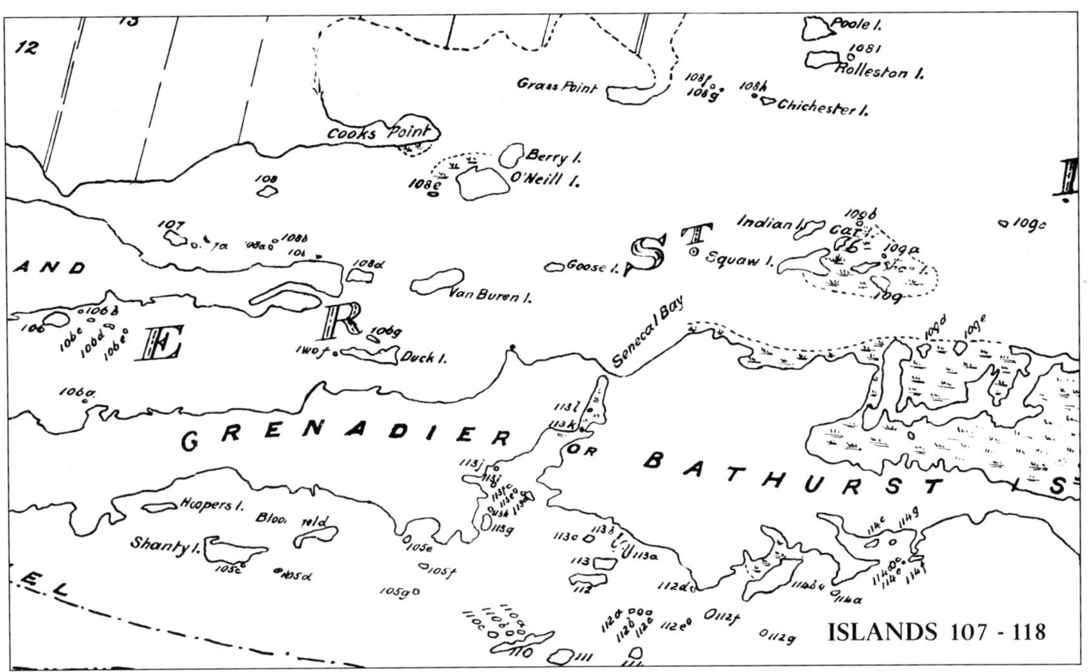

ISLAND 110A

Evaluations and Descriptions

1894: Beatty 1/12 acre Value: $50

"Low, rocky; well timbered."

Sale

1901: to George H. Darling.

ISLAND 110B

Evaluations and Descriptions

1894: Beatty 1/12 acre Value: $50

"Well timbered; low and rocky."

Sale

1901: to George H. Darling.

ISLAND 110C

Evaluations and Descriptions

1894: Beatty 1/3 acre Value: $150

"High, rocky; well timbered with pitch pine."

Sale

1901: to Nellie Darling.

ROUND ISLAND

Names

Named Island 111 by Charles Unwin.

Evaluations and Descriptions

1873: Unwin 1.0 acre Value: $25

"Same as 110."

1894: Beatty 1 acre Value: $300

"High; beautifully timbered with pine; views superb; on channel; perfect in every respect."

Sale

1898: to S. Miller.

BLUEBERRY ISLAND

Names

Named Island 112 by Charles Unwin.

Evaluations and Descriptions

1873: Unwin 1.4 acres Value: $15

"High and rocky covered with small brush and trees."

1894: Beatty 1 2/5 acres Value: $200

A fishing party at ease. — *The Thousand Islands and the River St. Lawrence*, The James Bayne Company

"A very prettily situated island; fine views; good harbourage; some small timber; good fishing."

Sale

1894: to J.B. Lynch; sold with Island 108D for $500.

Purchased as part of the W.D. Morris Real Estate Company. The island was not sold again until 1956.

ISLAND 112A

Evaluations and Descriptions

1894: Beatty 1/10 acre Value: $50

"Rocky; with some scrub; well placed; on channel."

Sale

1907: to Nellie M. Tomkins.

ISLAND 112B

Evaluations and Descriptions

1894: Beatty 1/10 acre Value: $50

"Rocky; with some scrub; well placed; on channel."

Sale

1907: to Nellie M. Tomkins.

ISLAND 112C

Evaluations and Descriptions

1894: Beatty 1/20 acre Value: $30

"Rocky; with some scrub; well placed; on channel."

Sale

1907: to Herbert B. Tomkins.

ISLAND 112D

Evaluations and Descriptions

1894: Beatty 1/20 acre Value: $30

"Bare, rocky."

ISLAND 112E

Evaluations and Descriptions

1894: Beatty 1/40 acre Value: $20

"Bare, rocky."

BAGGAGE ISLAND

Names

Named Island 112F by Walter Beatty.

Evaluations and Descriptions

1894: Beatty 1/5 acre Value: $75

"Low, level, rocky, some good pine."

Sale

1907: to F.E. Taft.

MANOMIN ISLAND

Names

Named Island 112G by Walter Beatty.

Evaluations and Descriptions

1894: Beatty 1/10 acre Value: $75

"Level, rocky, fine view."

Sale

1909: to Nicholas Toerge with Islands 108F, 108G and 108H.

HEATHER ISLAND

Names

Named Island 113 by Charles Unwin.

Evaluations and Descriptions

1873: Unwin 1.1 acres Value: $10

"Low and rocky covered with small bushes and trees."

1894: Beatty 1 1/10 acres Value: $200

"Rocky; high; fairly timbered."

Sale

1910: to Mary E. Sherwood and Jessie M. Tait.

ISLAND 113A

Evaluations and Descriptions

1894: Beatty 1/2 acre Value: $30

"Low, marshy in places; some timber."

ISLAND 113B

Evaluations and Descriptions

1894: Beatty 1/4 acre Value: $10

"Low, marshy in places; some timber."

ISLAND 113C

Evaluations and Descriptions

1894: Beatty 1/4 acre Value: $50

"Level, rocky; some good oak trees."

Sale

1910: to Marie Helena Pierce.

ISLAND 113D

Evaluations and Descriptions

1894: Beatty 3/5 acre Value: $50

"Level, rocky; some good oak trees."

Sale

1910: to Gerald Richard, with Island 113E.

ISLAND 113E

Evaluations and Descriptions

1894: Beatty 1/20 acre Value: $20

"Rocky; some good trees; good duck shooting ground in adjacent marsh."

Sale

1910: to Gerald Richard, with Island 113D.

ISLAND 113F

Evaluations and Descriptions

1894: Beatty 1/20 acre Value: $5

"Island in marsh; good duck shooting spot."

Sale

1904: to Gerald Richard.

RHINOCEROS ISLAND

Names

Named Island 113G by Walter Beatty.

Evaluations and Descriptions

1894: Beatty 3/4 acre Value: $200

"High; beautifully timbered with pitch and white pine, oak and poplar; good shelter."

Sale

1894: to David Scott. Sold with Champagne Island, the Navy Islands. Purchased as part of the W.D. Morris Real Estate Company. It was sold again in 1962 for $1,800.

ISLAND 113H

Evaluations and Descriptions

1894: Beatty 1/10 acre Value: $30

"Low, level; good timber."

Sale

1907: to M.E. Rickard.

ISLAND 113I

Evaluations and Descriptions

1894: Beatty 1/50 acre Value: $20

"Low, level; a few good trees."

Sale

1907: to William H.C. Brown.

ISLAND 113J

Evaluations and Descriptions

1894: Beatty 1/20 acre Value: $5

"Lying in marsh."

ISLAND 113K

Evaluations and Descriptions

1894: Beatty 1/20 acre Value: $10

"Very low, covered with willow scrub."

ISLAND 113L

Evaluations and Descriptions

1894: Beatty 1/20 acre Value: $10

"Very low, covered with willow scrub."

POVERTY ISLAND

Names

Named Island 114 by Charles Unwin.

Evaluations and Descriptions

1873: Unwin 0.4 acre Value: $5

"Same as 113."

1894: Beatty 2/5 acre Value: $150

"Fine granite; some good trees; good location."

Sale

1894: to Catherine Lynch; sold with Island 93C. Purchased as part of the W.D. Morris Real Estate Company and not sold again until 1967.

ISLAND 114A

Evaluations and Descriptions

1894: Beatty 1/10 acre Value: $75

"Low, level rock, lightly timbered."

Sale

1901: to Charles Cornwall.

ISLAND 114B

Evaluations and Descriptions

1894: Beatty 1/100 acre Value: $5

"Small, low shoal."

Sale

1901: to Charles Cornwall.

ISLAND 114C

Evaluations and Descriptions

1894: Beatty 3/4 acre Value: $150

"Nicely wooded; lying in clear water; good harbourage; fine view."

Sale

1902: to Harold Cleveland.

ISLAND 114D

Evaluations and Descriptions

1894: Beatty 1/10 acre Value: $60

"Level; a few trees; can be made a nice site; good timber; fine view."

Sale

The island was first sold in 1960.

ISLAND 114E

Evaluations and Descriptions

1894: Beatty 1/50 acre Value: $30

"Good view; fit for building site."

ISLAND 114F

Evaluations and Descriptions

1894: Beatty 3/4 acre Value: $150

"Fine view; good harbourage; a few nice trees."

ST. GABRIEL POINT

Evaluations and Descriptions

1893: Unwin 4.2 acres Value: $40

"Rocky, some nice trees on it. Connected with Grenadier Island in low water, and marshy between them in high water; it is claimed by H. Buell who owns farm opposite, on Grenadier Island."

Sale

1894: to A.E. Holmes for $300, with Island 62B.

ISLAND 115

Evaluations and Descriptions

1873: Unwin 0.1 acre Value: $10

"Low and rocky — some brush and timber."

1894: Beatty 7/10 acre Value: $100

"Level; rocky; well timbered."

ISLAND 115A

Evaluations and Descriptions

1894: Beatty 1/10 acre Value: $40

"Cleared, some scrub, marshy to north; good location."

ISLAND 115B

Evaluations and Descriptions

1894: Beatty 1/80 acre Value: $20

"Rocky knoll covered with scrub."

ISLAND 115C

Evaluations and Descriptions

1894: Beatty 1/3 acre Value: $50

"Low level land; timbered with white birch and oak."

ISLAND 115D

Evaluations and Descriptions

1894: Beatty 1/5 acre Value: $25

"Level land; good fishing."

Sale

The island was first sold in 1960.

ISLAND 115E

Evaluations and Descriptions

1894: Beatty 2 1/2 acres Value: $250

"Partly cleared; good location; scattered oak and pitch pine shade trees; southern frontage good, reedy water to north."

Sale

The island was first sold in 1964.

ISLAND 115F

Evaluations and Descriptions

1894: Beatty 1/80 acre Value: $25

"Small rocky island; some small scrub; sheltered waters; pretty view."

ISLAND 115G

Evaluations and Descriptions

1894: Beatty 1/10 acre Value: $20

"Bare rocks, a few feet above water; fine bass ground."

ISLAND 115H

Evaluations and Descriptions

1894: Beatty 1/10 acre Value: $50

"Smooth rocks; some scrub; fine bass ground."

Sale

The island was first sold in 1959.

ISLAND 115I

Evaluations and Descriptions

1894: Beatty 1/30 acre Value: $20

"Low, bare rocks."

WILLOUGHBY ISLAND

Evaluations and Descriptions

1873: Unwin 0.8 acre Value: $15

"Rough and rocky — some brush and timber on it."

1894: Beatty 8/10 acre Value: $200

"Rocky; good timber; harbour and location."

Sale

Purchased as part of the W.D. Morris Real Estate Company.

PILOT ISLAND

Evaluations and Descriptions

1873: Unwin 0.1 acre Value: $15

"Very pretty low rock, covered with trees."

1894: Beatty 1/10 acre Value: $100

"Very pretty, well timbered; good shelter."

Sale

Sold to J.A. McDougal and sold with Island 90A. Purchased as part of the W.D. Morris Real Estate Company.

VANSITTART POINT

Historic Name

1816: Owen — Vansittart, the British Statesmen Named after Nicholas Vansittart, the 1st Baron Bexley, (1766–1851). He held the position of joint secretary of the Treasury until 1804, and he was appointed chancellor of the Exchequer in May 1812. Although he possessed no special qualifications for this position, he held it during "perhaps the most difficult financial period in English history." Vansittart was considered "a mild-mannered man" and his moderate views allowed him to make and keep friends easily. His biographer felt that this was one of the reasons he was able to hold his office for more than twenty-five years.

The island was also known as Long or Schooner Point, and was recorded by Charles Unwin by all three names: Long, Schooner Point or Vansittart.

Evaluations and Descriptions

1873: Unwin 12.2 acres Value: $100

"Rough — some soil. Timber all cut off, a little brush left, it is claimed by Wm. Wright an old man who has lived on it for a short time and has a small house and stable, he has a quit claim deed from Wm. Reynolds, dated March 7th 1872 of Pilot, Willoughby and this island and marsh north of it — consideration $125."

COOK ISLAND

Names

Sometimes said to be named after James Cook, the famous British explorer, but it is more likely to be named after the Cook family who lived on the mainland opposite Tar Island.

Evaluations and Descriptions

1873: Unwin 0.1 acre Value: $5
"Low and rocky — a few trees standing — Lately burnt over."
1894: Beatty 1/10 acre Value: $60
"Level grassy; good shade."

DROMEDARY ISLAND

Evaluations and Descriptions

1873: Unwin 0.9 acre Value: $15
"High rocky and covered with bushes."
1894: Beatty 9/10 acre Value: $200
"Level, rock; good shade trees."

Sale

First sold to G.P. Brophy for $350. Purchased as part of the W.D. Morris Real Estate Company.

ST. HELENA ISLAND

Historic Name

1816: Owen — Goulbourn, the British Statemen
Named after Henry Goulbourn, under-secretary to Sherbrooke in the Colonial Office during the time of the survey. He was also listed in the *Gentlemen's Magazine* in September 1814 as being appointed a "Commissioner for negotiating and concluding a treaty of Peace with Commissioners from the United States of America."

Evaluations and Descriptions

1873: Unwin 0.9 acre Value: $20
"Same as Dromedary Island."
1894: Beatty 9/10 acre Value: $200
"Some shade trees, mostly pine smooth rock with shoal to north-east."

Sale

1903: to Ralph L. Reid.

ROUGH ISLAND or HAMILTON ISLAND

Historic Name

1816: Owen — Hamilton, the British Statesmen
Probably named after William Richard Hamilton (1777–1859), who studied at Harrow, Oxford and Cambridge and in 1799 began public life as secretary to Lord Elgin, when Elgin was ambassador to Constantinople. He is credited with saving many valuable pieces of art, including the entire cargo of a vessel containing Grecian marbles that sank in 1802. In 1809 Hamilton was appointed under-secretary of state for Foreign Affairs, a position he held during the Owen survey. He became a well-known antiquarian and was appointed a trustee of the British Museum in 1838.

Evaluations and Descriptions

1873: Unwin 1.5 acres Value: $15
"Rocky and covered with bushes."
1894: Beatty 1 1/2 acres Value: $200
"Rocky; some timber; good location in a lovely group; splendid fishing."

Sale

1894: to W.A. Ellis, with Fort Wallace Island in the Lake Fleet.

RATTLESNAKE ISLAND or BAGOT ISLAND

Historic Name

1816: Owen — Bagot, the British Statesmen
Named after Sir Charles Bagot (1781–1843). Bagot served as parliamentary under-secretary for Foreign Affairs in 1807 and was appointed minister plenipotentiary to France in 1814 and to the United States from 1815 to 1820. He became governor-general of Canada in 1841.

He is best known for the agreement he negotiated between London and Washington after the end of the War of 1812. This agreement was written not as a treaty at first but as an exchange of notes between Richard Rush, acting secretary of state for the United States, and Charles Bagot.

Sir Charles Bagot. — Metropolitan Toronto Reference Library, T14942

The agreement provided that "each side should maintain on Lake Ontario only one vessel of not more than 100 tons and armed with one eighteen-pound gun; on the upper lakes each might have two vessels of the same size and armament and on Lake Champlain one." All other vessels were to be dismantled and no more warships were to be "built or armed." This agreement, submitted to the U.S. Senate and approved, was proclaimed in effect in April 1818.

Evaluations and Descriptions

1873: Unwin 1.3 acres Value: $15
"Same as Rough or Hamilton Island."
1894: Beatty 1 3/10 acres Value: $200
"Nice shade and scrub; good harbour at east end; fine fishing; beautiful views; lies in pretty group."

Sale

1894: to G.F. MacDonald. Purchased as part of the W.D. Morris Real Estate Company. It sold again in 1919 for $600.

Sir Robert Peel.

— *Wellington & Waterloo*, Major Arthur Griffiths, published by George Newnes, Limited, 1898

CHERRY ISLAND or ROBERT ISLAND

Historic Name

1816: Owen — Robert, the British Statesmen
See Peel Island or Prince Edward Island. Named after Sir Robert Peel (1788–1850). He was educated at Harrow and Christ Church, Oxford, and became a member of Parliament in 1801 at the age of twenty. He gave his first House speech in 1810, "judged to be the best first speech since that of Mr. Pitt." Soon afterwards, Peel became under-secretary for war in the colonies. In 1812, when Lord Liverpool became prime minister, Peel was made chief secretary of Ireland. Throughout his career he was a prominent statesman, writing much legislation, such as the Peel Act. Long after the Owen survey, which honoured Peel by giving two islands his name (Robert and Peel), he continued his political career, serving as prime minister from 1834 to 1935 and again from 1841 to 1846.

Evaluations and Descriptions

1873: Unwin 1.5 acres Value: $20
"Same as Rough or Hamilton."
1894: Beatty 1 1/2 acres Value: $200
"Fairly level; plenty of shade trees; fishing, & C, very good."

Sale

1901: to Joseph B. Reid, with Prince Edward Island.

PRINCE EDWARD ISLAND

Historic Name

1816: Owen — Peel, the British Statesmen
Named after Sir Robert Peel (1788–1850).

Evaluations and Descriptions

1873: Unwin 3.5 acres Value: $25
"Same as Rough or Hamilton."
1894: Beatty 3 1/2 acres Value: $400
"Small wood and clear spaces; good soil."

Sale

1901: to Joseph B. Reid, with Cherry or Robert Island.

ADELAIDE ISLAND

Name

Identified as Island 116 by Charles Unwin. There is no reason for the name Adelaide, given by the Department of Indian Affairs when the island was reserved to be used for park purposes.

Evaluations and Descriptions

1873: Unwin 13.1 acres Value: $20
"Flat bushy rock; marsh between it and Grenadier Island."

Sale

This island was never sold or leased but was placed on a reserve list to be used as a park island. It is now part of the National Park Service, St. Lawrence Islands National Park.

No information is available for islands 116A or 116B.

ISLAND 116C

Evaluations and Descriptions

1894: Beatty 1/80 acre Value: $20
"Rocky, a few trees."

ISLAND 116D

Evaluations and Descriptions

1894: Beatty 1/50 acre Value: $20
"Bare rock, low."

Sale

1901: to J.B. Reid, with Islands 116E and 116F.

ISLAND 116E

Evaluations and Descriptions

1894: Beatty 1/100 acre Value: $5
"Low, bare rock."

Sale

1901: to J.B. Reid, with Islands 116D and 116F.

ISLAND 116F

Evaluations and Descriptions

1894: Beatty 1/3 acre Value: $50
"Flat rock, some scrub, together with small rock immediately north."

Sale

1901: to J.B. Reid, with islands 116D and 116E.

ISLAND 116G

Evaluations and Descriptions

1894: Beatty 1/5 acre Value: $30
"Low, level, bare rock."

Sale

1908: to Robert A. Brown, with Island 116I.

ISLAND 116H

Evaluations and Descriptions

1894: Beatty 1/2 acre Value: $50
"Low, level; land in edge of marsh; some good timber; good shooting ground."

ISLAND 116I

Evaluations and Descriptions

1894: Beatty 1/5 acre Value: $10

"Low, with willow scrub."

Sale

1908: to Robert A. Brown, with Island 116G.

ISLAND 116J

Evaluations and Descriptions

1894: Beatty 1/2 acre Value: $50

"Long, low, level, connected with Grenadier Island by marsh; rocky; some scrub."

Sale

1923: to T.O. Patterson.

ISLAND 116K

Evaluations and Descriptions

1894: Beatty 1/3 acre Value: $30

"Low; rocky; some scrub."

Sale

1924: to Joseph Gladd (?).

ISLAND 116L

Evaluations and Descriptions

1894: Beatty 1/5 acre Value: $30

"Low; rocky; barren."

Sale

1922: to Charles A. Duke.

ISLAND 116M

Evaluations and Descriptions

1894: Beatty 1/5 acre Value: $50

"Low, level; with adjunct; some scrub."

Sale

1909: to Harry Willard Senecal.

ISLAND 116N

Evaluations and Descriptions

1894: Beatty 1/80 acre Value: $10

"Low, bare rock."

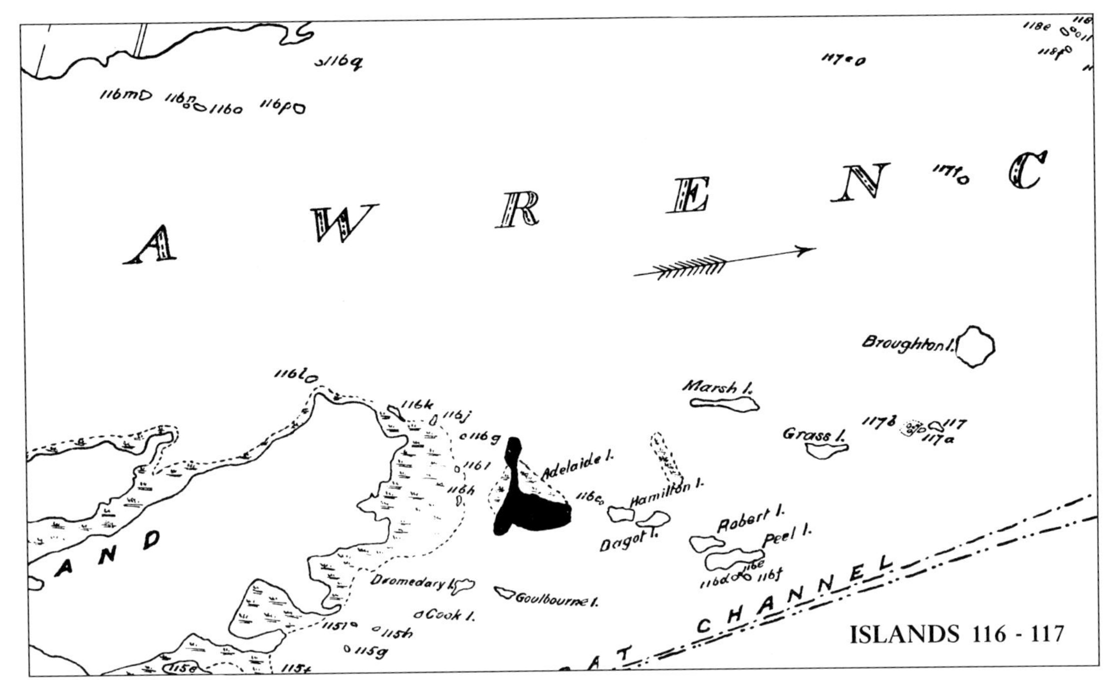

ISLAND 116O

Evaluations and Descriptions

1894: Beatty 1/5 acre Value: $50

"Barren rock about 6 feet above water."

Sale

The island was first sold in 1950.

ISLAND 116P

Evaluations and Descriptions

1894: Beatty 1/5 acre Value: $50

"Flat rock; with adjunct to north."

Sale

1901: to Gilbert T. Rafferty.

ISLAND 116Q

Evaluations and Descriptions

1894: Beatty 1/5 acre Value: $50

"Bare rock."

Sale

The island was first sold in 1940.

ISLAND 116R

Evaluations and Descriptions

1894: Beatty 1/80 acre Value: $10

"Small, bare rock."

Sale

1901: to John Mallory.

ISLAND 117

Evaluations and Descriptions

1873: Unwin 0.3 acre Value: $10

"Rock with a few trees."

1894: Beatty 3/10 acre Value: $75

"High, bare islet in channel; fine duck shooting and fishing."

Sale

1903: to Joseph A. Auerbach. In 1905 it was purchased by the Ice Island Shooting Company and held until 1961.

ISLAND 117A

Evaluations and Descriptions

1894: Beatty 1/4 acre Value: $40

"Low; rocky reef; good shooting and fishing."

Sale

1903: to Joseph A. Auerbach. In 1905 it was purchased by the Ice Island Shooting Company and held until 1961.

ISLAND 117B

Evaluations and Descriptions

1894: Beatty 1/5 acre Value; $50

"Low; rocky reef; good shooting; includes four islands."

Sale

1902: to Harold Cleveland.

ISLAND 117E

Evaluations and Descriptions

1894: Beatty 1/100 acre Value: $10

"Smooth; bare; rocky."

Sale

1901: to John R. Gibson.

ICE ISLAND

Names

Named Island 117F by Walter Beatty.

Evaluations and Descriptions

1894: Beatty 1/5 acre Value: $80

"Smooth; bare; rocky."

Island Notes

An article appearing in the October 31, 1894, edition of the Brockville *Recorder* described the sale of Ice Island:

It is reported here that Ice Island, for many years an objective point for local duck hunters, was bought at the recent government sale by a syndicate of Gananoque sportsmen who are taking extra precautions to guard their property from encroachment. A party is said to have been secured to exercise a jealous watch over the premises when the owners are not on hand, and anyone landing at once ordered to move on. This is all right, however and will give those who were anxious to see the island disposed of, a beautiful chance to see what is in the site for the average seeker after rest and pleasure up the river with in a few years. Keep off the grass signs are likely to be so plentiful that the camper will have to anchor his boat out on the broad river and camp in it. No one can blame the Gananoque men, however, for exempting what has long been considered one of the most desirable shooting spots on the river. Ice Island is nothing more or less than a small bare rock. So small and so rocky in fact the owners are understood to have been obliged to drill holes in which iron pins are inserted for supporting the tent guy ropes. . . .

The *Gananoque Reporter* printed another article a week later, stating that the island had been purchased by Messrs. J.B. McMurchy, David Bain, W.S. Robinson, C.K. Wright, Myles Wright and Percy Wright of Gananoque. It went on to say that the island was not bought to keep people off, but rather only for the duck-hunting season and that rather than only camping on the island they had planned to plant trees, "hoping in some time to have a shady grove."

Sale

1894: to W.M. Wright. The island was sold, or registered as sold, in 1905 to the Ice Island Shooting Company and held for seventy years until 1975.

ISLAND 117G

Names

Also called Lower Corn Island Shoal.

Evaluations and Descriptions

1894: Beatty 1/5 acre Value: $40

"Smooth; bare; rocky."

Sale

1902: to Frederick G. Bourne with Island 117. Both were sold in 1905 to the Ice Island Shooting Company and held until 1960.

ISLAND 117H

Names

Also called Lower Corn Island Shoal

Evaluations and Descriptions

1894: Beatty 1/5 acre Value: $40

"Bare; rocky."

Sale

1902: to Frederick G. Bourne with Island 117G. Both were sold in 1905 to the Ice Island Shooting Company and held until 1960.

ISLAND 117I

Evaluations and Descriptions

1894: Beatty 1/80 acre Value: $10

"Bare; smooth; rocky."

Sale

1902: to Charles M. Engles; sold again in 1905 to the Ice Island Shooting Company and held until 1960.

ISLAND 117J

Evaluations and Descriptions

1894: Beatty 1/10 acre Value: $30

"Bare; smooth; rocky."

Sale

1902: to Charles M. Engles; sold again in 1905 to the Ice Island Shooting Company and held until 1960.

GULL ISLAND

Names

Named Island 117K by Walter Beatty.

Evaluations and Descriptions

1894: Beatty 1/2 acre Value: $15

"Bare; smooth; rocky."

Sale

1907: to William E. Miller.

MARSH ISLAND

Evaluations and Descriptions

1873: Unwin 2.3 acres Value: $5

"Flat rock covered with bushes."

Sale

1895: to C. Probandt for $25.

GRASS ISLAND

Evaluations and Descriptions

1873: Unwin 2.1 acres Value: $40

"Flat — good arable land, a little brush on it."

Sale

1901: to Frederick A. Buharm (?) for $250.

CORN ISLAND or BROUGHTON ISLAND

Historic Name

1816: Owen — Broughton, the British Statesmen Named after John Cam Hobhouse, Baron Broughton (1786–1869). This statesman was educated at Trinity College, Cambridge. He became a close friend of Lord Byron, the poet, and they travelled together across Europe. Broughton was best man at Byron's wedding.

Evaluations and Descriptions

1873: Unwin 5.2 acres Value: $100

"High — good arable land no timber."

Sale

1894: to A.W. Mallory for $400.

CORDWOOD ISLAND

Names

Named Island 118 by Charles Unwin.

Evaluations and Descriptions

1873: Unwin 0.6 acre Value: $5

"Rocky — a little brush."

1894: Beatty 3/4 acre Value: $100

"With low rocks to the west; some timber; good shelter."

Sale

1903: to Joseph Shane (?) and John C. Raphael.

ISLAND 118A

Evaluations and Descriptions

1894: Beatty 1/5 acre Value: $20

"Scattered; broken rocks."

Sale

1901: to Frederick K. Burham for $30, with Island 118B.

ISLAND 118B

Evaluations and Descriptions

1894: Beatty 1/80 acre Value: $10

"Low; bare rock; partly submerged in high water."

Sale

1901: to Frederick K. Burham for $30, with Island 118A.

ISLAND 118C

Evaluations and Descriptions

1894: Beatty 1/20 acre Value: $25

"Bare; rocky."

Sale

1903: to Julian T. Davis.

ISLAND 118D

Evaluations and Descriptions

1894: Beatty 1/80 acre Value: $5

"Low; bare."

Sale

1903: to Julian T. Davis. This island was sold to the Ice Island Shooting Company in 1905 and held until 1960.

ISLAND 118E

Evaluations and Descriptions

1894: Beatty 1/80 acre Value: $20

"Bare; rocky."

Sale

1903: to Julian T. Davis. This island was sold to the Ice Island Shooting Company in 1905 and held until 1960.

ISLAND 118F

Evaluations and Descriptions

1894: Beatty 3/10 acre Value: $20

"Barren; rocky."

Sale

1903: to Julian T. Davis. This island was sold to the Ice Island Shooting Company in 1905 and held until 1960.

ISLAND 118G

Evaluations and Descriptions

1894: Beatty 1/8 acre Value: $50

"High; rocky; forming harbour at east end of Green Island."

Sale

The island was first sold in 1957 for $50.

ISLAND 118H

Evaluations and Descriptions

1894: Beatty 1/180 acre Value: $5

"Low; rocky reef."

ISLAND 118I

Evaluations and Descriptions

1894: Beatty 1/4 acre Value: $75

"High; rocky; with level for building; fair harbourage."

Sale

The island was first sold in 1950.

ISLAND 118J

Evaluations and Descriptions

1894: Beatty 1/100 acre Value: $5

"Rocks 2 feet above water; bare."

ISLAND 118K

Evaluations and Descriptions

1894: Beatty 1/5 acre Value: $50

"Rocky islet; might be made into a good building place."

ISLAND 118L

Evaluations and Descriptions

1894: Beatty 1/50 acre Value: $20

"Rock head." (Together with Island 118M completes the harbour of Princess Island.)

Sale

1905: to Thomas L. Willson.

ISLAND 118M

Evaluations and Descriptions

1894: Beatty 1/10 acre Value: $40

"High rock head." (Together with Island 118L completes the harbour of Princess Island.)

Sale

1905: to Thomas L. Willson.

ISLAND 118/1

Evaluations and Descriptions

1894: Beatty 1/80 acre Value: $5

"Known locally as 'Sugar Loaf'; rock; 4 feet high."

ISLAND 118/2

Evaluations and Descriptions

1894: Beatty 1/10 acre Value: $40

"Bare of vegetation; 4 feet above water; nicely sheltered."

CHIMNEY ISLAND

Historic Name

1816: Owen — Bridge, the Amateur Islands

During the War of 1812 a blockhouse was constructed on the island, and it was used to overlook the transport of naval operations on the Upper St. Lawrence River. It was during a low-water period that a land bridge was constructed to connect the island to the mainland.

Evaluations and Descriptions

1873: Unwin 2.4 acres Value: $10

"Rock about one quarter of an acre, arable, a little brush on it."

THE AMATEUR ISLANDS

One group known as the Amateur Islands was probably named in jest since it commemorates many who served in the Royal Engineers and not in the Royal Navy — thus "amateurs" in the Navy's opinion. So it would seem that Captain Owen and the draftsmen enjoyed the banter that was exchanged between the regiments serving in Kingston.

It is interesting to note that some of those listed in the "Amateurs" were members of the 70th Foot Regiment, which arrived in Kingston in 1814, near the end of the War of 1812. Several of these men were discharged at the same time as Lieutenant Cranfield, Owen's draftsman, and they could have travelled back to England on the same transport ship, the *Vittoria*, with him. It is also conceivable that Cranfield worked on the charts during the voyage and named the islands after his shipmates.

OWEN	PRESENT NAME	PAGE
Robinson	Partridge Island (Canadian)	193
Ingall	Jarvis Island (Canadian)	193
Brown	Princess Island (Canadian)	193
Spong	Raleigh Island (Canadian)	193
Green	Green Island (Canadian)	193
Savage	Savage Island (Canadian)	193
Buchanan	Snakeoil Island (American)	233
Shacklock	Snakeoil Island (American)	233
Jebb	Bluff Island (American)	233
Herbert	Lone Tree Island (American)	233
Stephenson	Elm Tree Island (American)	233
Goldfarp	Chippewa Point Island (American)	233
Redigar	Indian Chief Island (American)	233
Smeachman	Middle Island (American)	233
Ross	Big Island (American)	233
Wood	Bilberry Island (American)	233
McKay	Crossover Island (American)	233

Island Notes

The present chimney is the third built on the island. The first dates back to 1799, when the French were travelling back and forth to Montreal and Quebec from the Great Lakes. The story of this chimney is a romantic one that has been told in several early histories.

In 1799 a French Canadian lived on the island with a "beautiful Indian girl and two halfbreeds." The man built the house first, and "as soon as the river was navigable" he went to Kingston for limestone to build his chimney. The following autumn the house burned to the ground. Two local farmers, seeing the fire, rowed over to a little cove on the south side of the island. They were horrified to find a "half burned canoe containing the body of the young French Canadian with a new Indian tomahawk buried in his skull. Of the women or anyone else there was no trace." It was assumed his death had been the "revenge of some tribe from whom the Frenchman had taken his bride."

The next chimney on the island was built during the War of 1812, when the British constructed a blockhouse on Chimney Island. The chimney and accommodations were described as "the worst I have ever witnessed. I stayed one night in the place and between the smoke and the cold it was intolerable. The party is badly in need of rugs and pallasses to make them comfortable at least at night." Although the blockhouse disappeared or was dismantled, the chimney remained for one hundred years. In 1913, its mortar crumbling, it was toppled by a violent wind storm.

Local residents were sorry to see the chimney disappear, so William Gilbert, a summer resident from Tar Island, built a new one. Frederick Curry, author of several historical reviews of the chimney, sketched the old chimney, but Gilbert did not follow Curry's drawings and today's structure is "absolutely modern and efficient and guaranteed not to smoke."

PARTRIDGE ISLAND or ROBINSON ISLAND

Historic Name

1816: Owen — Robinson, the Amateur Islands
No biographical information is available. Robinson was probably a member of the 70th Foot Regiment or a Royal Engineer.

Evaluations and Descriptions

1873: Unwin 4.6 acres Value: $40
"Rocky, covered with bushes a little soil."
1894: Beatty 4 2/5 acres Value: $500
"Level and high; splendid views; well timbered with pine, white birch and cedar; good shooting and fishing; on daily steamer route; deep water approach."

JARVIS ISLAND or INGALL ISLAND

Historic Name

Named after a Lieutenant Ingall, a member of the 70th Foot, who was discharged on the same day as the other members of the regiment.

Evaluations and Descriptions

1873: Unwin 2.1 acres Value: $30
"Rocky, a little soil and brush."
1894: Beatty 2.1 acres Value: $250
"Bare rock on each end; low in centre; some scrub and trees; good shooting ground."

PRINCESS ISLAND or BROWN ISLAND

Historic Name

Named after an Ensign Brown, member of the 70th Foot, who was discharged at the same time as the other members of the regiment.

Evaluations and Descriptions

1873: Unwin 6.0 acres Value: $20
"Flat and rocky, a few bushes on it."
1894: Beatty 6 acres Value: $800
"Half level, with soil on a third; fine views; a few shade trees; good landing harbourage, fishing and shooting."

Sale

1901: to Henry Mathen (?), with Raleigh or Spong Island.

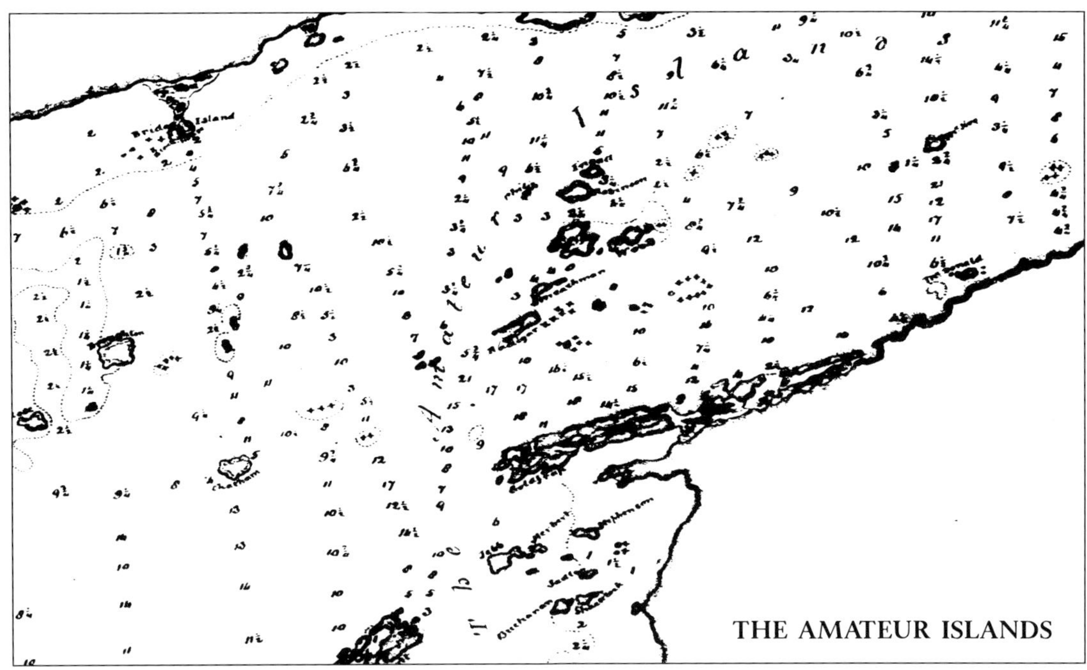

THE AMATEUR ISLANDS

RALEIGH ISLAND or SPONG ISLAND

Historic Name

1816: Owen — Spong, the Amateur Islands
No biographical information is available. Spong was probably a member of the 70th Foot.

Evaluations and Descriptions

1873: Unwin 2.3 acres Value: $10
"Rough and rocky — a few bushes on it."
1894: Beatty 2 3/10 acres Value: $300
"Level; rocky; good shade trees; harbourage fine; lovely building site."

Sale

1901: to H. Mathen (?), with Princess or Brown Island.

GREEN ISLAND

Historic Name

1816: Owen — Green, the Amateur Islands
Named after Deputy Quarter Master General Green, a member of the 70th Foot.

Evaluations and Descriptions

1873: Unwin 0.6 acre Value: $5
"Low flat rock, very little brush on it."

SAVAGE ISLAND

Historic Name

1816: Owen — Savage, the Amateur Islands
Named after an Ensign Savage, a member of the 70th Foot; his name appears on records listing those member of the regiment who were discharged at the time same time as Captain Owen's draftsman, Cranfield. Most of this regiment travelled on the same ship back to England.

Evaluations and Descriptions

1873: Unwin 2.3 acres Value: $10
"Low flat rock with a few small trees and bushes on it."
1894: Beatty 2 3/10 acres Value: $450
"Level; grassy; plenty of nice shade trees pine and birch; good harbourage; lovely views."

Island Notes

This island was not sold in 1894 when the majority of islands were purchased. In the 1920s an application was received but at a price well below the evaluation of $450 set by Walter Beatty in 1894.

The Department of Indian Affairs inspected the island and reported: "Mr. O'Conner, who is well acquainted with the islands reports that since the valuation, the island has been burned over and only a small growth of pines remains. This coupled with the fact that it is not as desirable, owing to a number of cheap buildings having been erected along the shore not too distant." The selling price was reduced to $250 and sold to Kalmas Foldeck, Sr., in 1925.

Sale

1925: to Kalmes Foldeck, Sr., for $250.

GREEN ISLAND

Evaluations and Descriptions

1873: Unwin 0.6 acre Value: $5

"Low flat rock, with a few small trees and bushes on it."

THE BROCK ISLES

Many of the officers who fought in the British campaigns during the War of 1812 are commemorated in the Brock Islands. When the war began, on June 18, the British regular forces numbered four thousand. They were stationed along an almost undefendable border, over 1,600 kilometres (1,000 miles) long. The British forces were under the command of Gen. Isaac Brock, who also served as civil administrator of Upper Canada. The first British victory was at Detroit in August 1812, almost a month after war was declared. With the help of the Indian Allies, under the leadership of Tecumseh, Brock and his officers began their two-year campaign. Within the year, both Brock and Tecumseh were killed, but eight campaigns and a series of isolated raids are recorded. The end result was the signing of the Treaty of Ghent, which restored original territories to both Canada and United States.

OWEN NAME	PRESENT NAME	PAGE
De Wattville	De Wattville Island (Canadian)	194
Sheaffe	Brush Island (Canadian)	194
Brock	American Island (American)	235
Rottenberg	Bluff Island (Canadian)	195
Battersby	Barnstone Island (Canadian)	195
Sparrow	Huckleberry Island (Canadian)	195
Stovin	Refugee Island (Canadian)	195
Everest	Sumach Island (Canadian)	195
Cockburn	Picnic Island (Canadian)	195

OWEN	PRESENT NAME	PAGE
Harvey	Gilbraltar Island (Canadian)	195
Montgomery	Montgomery Island (Canadian)	196
Conran	Smith Island (Canadian)	196
Riall	Miller Island (Canadian)	196
Skelton	Big Round Island (Canadian)	197
Brock	Old Man Island (American)	235
McNair	The Brothers (Canadian)	197
Murray	The Brothers (Canadian)	197
Glegg	Bogardus Island (American)	235

DE WATTVILLE ISLAND

Historic Name

1816: Owen — De Wattville, the Brock Isles Named after Maj.-Gen. Abraham Louis Charles de Wattville, who became a colonel in the British Army in 1812 and a major-general in 1813.

Charles Unwin recorded the island by its two names, Guide and De Wattville.

Evaluations and Descriptions

1873: Unwin 6.1 acres Value: $60

"Rocky with a few small trees and bushes on it."

Sale

1933: to the City of Brockville.

ISLAND 119

Evaluations and Descriptions

1873: Unwin 1.0 acre Value: $20

"Rocky, with a few small tees and buses on it."

MYERS ISLAND

Evaluations and Descriptions

1873: Unwin 1.9 acres Value: $20

"Rocky, with a few trees on it."

TWIN SISTERS ISLAND

Evaluations and Descriptions

1873: Unwin 0.8 acre Value: $30

"Two islands with small trees and brush on them."

BRUSH ISLAND or SHEAFFE ISLAND

Historic Name

1816: Owen — Sheaffe, the Brock Isles Named after Maj.-Gen. Sir Roger H. Sheaffe (1763–1851). Sheaffe was born in Boston in 1763, the third son of William Sheaffe, who had served as deputy comptroller of Customs. He married Margaret Coffin in Quebec and served in Canada in 1797 as a captain in the 5th Foot. When Sir Isaac Brock was killed at Queenstown, Sheaffe took over his command and defeated the Americans. He was made a baronet for his services in 1812.

Charles Unwin recorded the island by its two names, Brush and Sheaffe.

Evaluations and Descriptions

1873: Unwin 6.4 acres Value: $60

"Low rock covered with brush — a little soil. There is a small island of 0.8 acre to the north of this with a very narrow channel between them, this is similar to Brush Island and would be sold with it."

Sale

1933: to the City of Brockville.

BLUFF ISLAND or ROTTENBURG ISLAND

Historic Name

1816: Owen — Rottenburg, the Brock Isles

Named after Maj.-Gen. Francis Baron de Rottenburg (d. 1832). De Rottenburg joined the Hussars in 1795. His "exercises for riflemen and the light infantry" were adopted by the British Army. He came to Canada in 1812 and as major-general took command of the Montreal District and a year later he was sent to Upper Canada. He was commander of a light division in 1814–15.

Charles Unwin recorded the island by its two names, Bluff and Rottenburg.

Evaluations and Description

1873: Unwin 5.3 acres Value: $100

"Low at west end the rest high. Bluff on north side. It is well covered with small trees and brush."

Sale

1933: to the City of Brockville.

BARNSTONE ISLAND or BATTERSBY ISLAND

Historic Name

1816: Owen — Battersby, the Brock Isles

Probably named after Lieut.-Col. F. Battersby, who was in command of the Glengarry Light Infantry.

Charles Unwin recorded the island by its two names, Barnstone and Battersby.

Evaluations and Descriptions

1873: Unwin 0.5 acre Value: $20

"Low and rocky, a few trees and bush on it."

SNAKE ISLAND

Evaluations and Descriptions

1873: Unwin 0.2 acre Value: $15

"Low and rocky, a few trees and bushes on it."

HUCKLEBERRY ISLAND or SPARROW ISLAND

Historic Name

1816: Owen — Sparrow, the Brock Isles

Named after Maj. E.P. Sparrow, who was member of the 61st Regiment and a member of the army staff and assistant adjutant-general.

Charles Unwin recorded the island by its two names, Huckleberry and Sparrow.

Evaluations and Descriptions

1873: Unwin 3.2 acres Value: $50

"Low and rocky a few trees and bushes on it."

Sale

1933: to the City of Brockville.

NEEDLES EYE ISLAND

Evaluations and Descriptions

1873: Unwin 0.7 acre Value: $10

"High and rocky a few trees and bushes on it."

Sale

1933: to the City of Brockville.

REFUGEE ISLAND or STOVIN ISLAND

Historic Name

1816: Owen — Stovin, the Brock Isles

Names after Maj.-Gen. Richard Stovin. He joined the British Army as an ensign in 1780, became a captain in 1788 and a lieutenant-colonel in 1798. As major-general he commanded the Montreal District in 1811.

Charles Unwin recorded the island by its two names, Refugee and Stovin.

Evaluations and Descriptions

1873: Unwin 10.2 acres Value: $100

"High and rocky, a few trees and bushes on it."

Sale

1905: to the St. Lawrence Islands National Park.

SUMACH ISLAND or EVEREST ISLAND

Historic Name

1818: Owen — Everest Island

No biographical information is available.

Evaluations and Descriptions

1873: Unwin 1.2 acres Value: $40

"High and rocky, a few trees and bushes on it."

PICNIC ISLAND or COCKBURN ISLAND

Historic Name

1816: Owen — Cockburn, the Brock Isles

Named after Maj. Francis Cockburn, son of Sir James Cockburn, Bart. He served in South America and in the Peninsula from 1809 until 1810. In 1811 he was sent to Canada and then to the Bahamas as the governor in 1819. He was knighted in 1841. Cockburn died in Dover, England, in 1868.

Charles Unwin recorded the island by its two names, Picnic and Cockburn.

Evaluations and Descriptions

1873: Unwin 5.2 acres Value: $70

"Low and rocky, a few trees and bushes on it."

Sale

1933: to the City of Brockville.

GIBRALTAR ISLAND or HARVEY ISLAND

Historic Name

1816: Owen, Harvey, the Brock Isles

Probably named after Maj. John Harvey. He enlisted in the British Army as ensign in 1794 and served on the Continent, at the Cape of Good Hope and in Egypt. He was deputy adjutant-general of the forces, and is mentioned in war dispatches of the War of 1812, at the battles of Stoney Creek, Crysler's Farm, Fort Niagara, Black Rock, Oswego, Lundy's Lane and Fort Erie. He was made a companion of the Order of Bath in 1815.

Major John Harvey.

— Metropolitan Toronto Reference Library, J. Ross Robertson Collection, T14964

(This is an example of Captain Owen's naming an island after a person who later became prominent.)

Harvey returned to North America in 1837 as lieutenant-governor of New Brunswick and was governor of Newfoundland from 1841 to 1846. He became lieutenant-governor of Nova Scotia in 1846 and remained in that post until he died in 1852.

Charles Unwin recorded the island by its two names, Gibraltar and Harvey.

Evaluations and Descriptions

1873: Unwin 2.7 acres Value: $40

"High and rocky, a few trees and bushes on it."

Sale

1933: to the City of Brockville.

ROYAL ISLAND

Evaluations and Descriptions

1873: Unwin 1.1 acres Value: $20

"Low and rocky, a few trees and bushes on it."

Sale

Sold to C.J. Hope for $325.

MONTGOMERY ISLAND

Historic Name

1816: Owen — Montgomery, the Brock Isles

Named after Brevet Maj. H. Montgomery, assistant quartermaster general. No other information is available.

Evaluations and Descriptions

1873: Unwin 3.1 acres Value: $40

"Flat rocks — a few trees and bushes on it."

SMITH ISLAND or CONRAN ISLAND

Historic Name

1816: Owen — Conran, the Brock Isles

Possibly named after Maj.-Gen. Henry Conran, ensign in the 49th Regiment. Conran was appointed to command a brigade in Upper Canada, beginning in June 1814. He was appointed lieutenant-governor of Jamaica in 1816 and died in 1829 at the age of sixty-two.

Charles Unwin recorded the island by its two names, Smith and Conran.

Evaluations and Descriptions

1873: Unwin 10.7 acres Value: $100

"Flat rocks, a few trees and bushes on it."

Sale

1933: to the City of Brockville.

MILLER ISLAND and RIALL ISLAND

Historic Name

1816: Owen — Riall, the Brock Isles

Named after Sir Phineas Riall (1775–1850), who entered the army as ensign in 1794. He served in the West Indies and fought under Gen. George Beckwith in Martinique and Guadeloupe. In 1813 he was promoted to major-general and sent to Upper Canada. He is credited with attacks on Buffalo during the War of 1812. He was severely wounded, losing an arm, and was taken prisoner. It was written of him: "His bravery, zeal, and activity have always been conspicuous." After the war he was appointed governor of Grenada and remained there for several years. He was knighted in 1833.

Charles Unwin recorded the island by its two names, Miller and Riall.

Evaluations and Descriptions

1873: Unwin 13.6 acres Value: $100

"Flat rock, a few trees and bushes on it. A low marshy strip cuts this island nearly in two."

Sale

1880: to Herbert C. Jones; sold again in 1881 to William Sherwood.

ISLAND 120

Evaluations and Descriptions

1873: Unwin 0.5 acre Value: $10

"Low rock with a little brush on it."

Sale

1933: to the City of Brockville.

ISLAND 121

Evaluations and Descriptions

1873: Unwin 0.5 acre Value: $10

"Low rock with a little brush on it."

Sale

1933: to the City of Brockville.

ISLAND 122

Evaluations and Descriptions

1873: Unwin 0.6 acre Value: $15

"Low at East end, high at west, with brush on it."

Sale

1885: to Wilmot E. Cole, who leased the island in 1882 for ten years but purchased it for $250 three years later.

The Brockville Islands.
— Metropolitan Toronto Reference Library, J. Ross Robertson Collection, T15330

VICTORIA ISLAND

Evaluations and Descriptions

1873: Unwin 0.5 acre Value: $25

"High rock with brush and a few trees on it."

Sale

1902: to Anna Bertha Schofield.

MILE ISLAND

Evaluations and Descriptions

1873: Unwin 1.1 acres Value: $30

"Low rock, with brush and a few trees on it."

Sale

1933: to the City of Brockville.

BIG ROUND ISLAND or SKELTON ISLAND

Historic Name

1816: Owen — Skelton, the Brock Isles

Probably named after Brevet Maj. Henry Skelton, 19th Light Division, who was appointed major of the brigade in Canada in August 1813.

Charles Unwin recorded the island by its two names, Round and Skelton. Today it is called Big Round Island.

Evaluations and Descriptions

1873: Unwin 4.5 acres Value: $100

"High rock with brush and a few trees on it."

Sale

1933: to the City of Brockville.

THE BROTHERS ISLAND or McNAIR ISLAND

Historic Name

1816: Owen — McNair, the Brock Isles

Probably named after Colonel McNair, commander of the 90th Regiment during the War of 1812. No other information is available.

Charles Unwin recorded the island by its two names, the Brothers and McNair.

Evaluations and Descriptions

1873: Unwin 3.3 acres Value: $30

"Low rock a few trees."

Sale

1893: to the Brockville and St. Lawrence Bridge Company.

THE BROTHERS ISLAND or MURRAY ISLAND

Historic Name

1816: Owen — Murray, the Brock Isles

Named after Lieut. Col. John Murray, 100th Regiment, who was appointed inspector of the field officers in Lower Canada in 1811. He commanded attacks at Fort George and Fort Niagara, where he was wounded. He was later made a lieutenant-general and died in 1832.

Charles Unwin recorded the island by its two names, the Brothers and Murray.

Evaluations and Descriptions

1873: Unwin (no acreage available) Value: $10

"High rock, a few trees."

Sale

1933: to the City of Brockville.

SECTION II **THE AMERICAN ISLANDS**

KEY TO THE AMERICAN ISLANDS

Names

The islands are listed in geographic order, beginning with Grindstone Island, near Clayton, New York, and going eastward to the islands lying in front of the town of Morristown, New York.

The recorded names appear on present-day county tax maps or hydrographic charts. If an island was recorded by other names in newspaper articles, on charts or was locally known by other names, those names have often been included.

Unlike the Canadian islands, where descriptive information can be found in government surveys, in the American listing several small islands and shoals are excluded because little or no information is available in written form. This applies especially to islands in Goose Bay.

Historic Name

Like the Canadian listing, the historic name that was given by Capt. William FitzWilliam Owen on the British Admiralty charts dated 1816, 1828 or 1861 is listed. Each name is identified in a group (i.e., the Old Friends, the Hydrographers, the Indian Allies and so on). For convenience cross-reference page numbers are given for the boxed text information about these groups. (The boxed text for the Lake Fleet, the Wellington Islands, the British Statesmen and the Amateur Islands will be found among the Canadian Islands in Part II, Section 1.) Where possible, biographic information and the probable reason for individual commemoration is included.

Sale

Those islands that were sold by Cornwall and Walton and described in Andrew Cornwall's notebook (see Introduction) are recorded. This information appears as written in the notebook, with the same misspellings and incorrect punctuation. In some cases Cornwall's handwriting is difficult to decipher.

Some additional sale information is provided for several islands, but this information is not complete. More can be found in the county registry offices in Canton and Watertown, New York.

Island Notes

Island notes include information often recorded in newspapers, guidebooks or published community histories. Unfortunately there are mistakes in this section because too often facts have been mistakenly printed once and passed on in subsequent publications. Several descriptions of cottage construction and island living have been quoted from these sources.

Description

Where possible, an approximation of the acreage is given. This information was found on present-day county maps. This is provided only to help identify islands and should not be confused with real estate evaluations.

The author apologizes for possible misspelling of names and incorrect historical information.

GORE'S ISLES

Captain Owen named a small number of islands surrounding Grindstone Island for Sir Francis Gore, Lieutenant-Governor of Upper Canada. Captain Owen's first map, the one that is reproduced in this book, did not record Arabella Island. This name was added in 1828 when the charts were engraved and published.

OWEN NAME	PRESENT NAME	PAGE
Gore	Grindstone Island (American)	191
Francis	Hickory Island (Canadian)	128
Arabella Island	Goose Island (Canadian)	129
Calumet Island	Calumet Island (American)	201

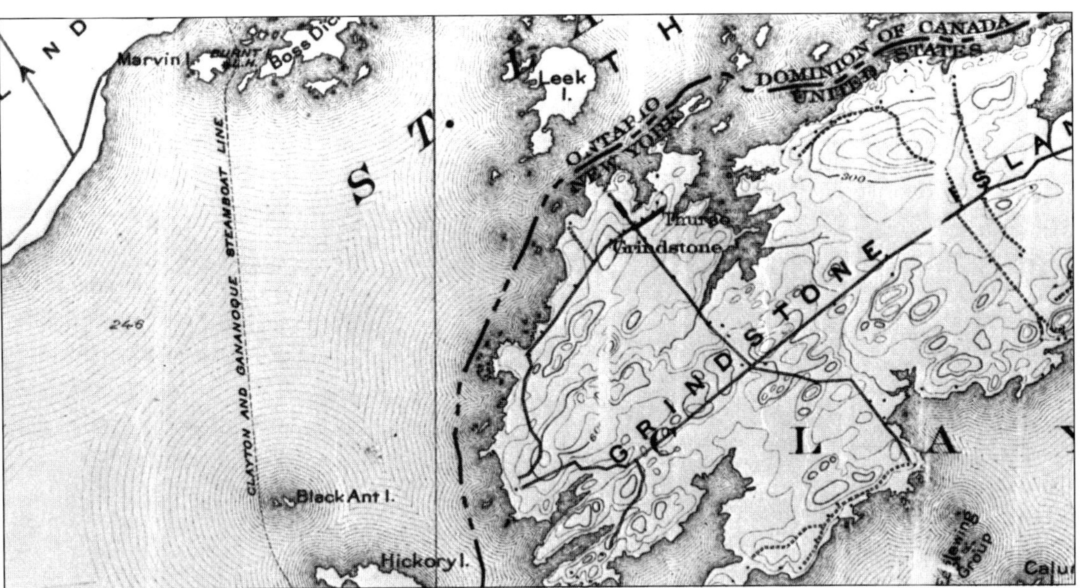

— U.S. Geological Survey, 1903

Sir Francis Gore, lieutenant-governor of Upper Canada.

— Metropolitan Toronto Reference Library, J. Ross Robertson Collection T15491

GRINDSTONE ISLAND

Historic Name

1816: Owen — Gore, formerly Grindstone Island, Gore's Islands

Named after Sir Francis Gore (1759–1852). Gore first served in the British Army and obtained a commission in an infantry regiment. He retired a major. In 1804 he was appointed lieutenant-governor of Bermuda; in 1806 he became lieutenant-governor of Upper Canada. He was serving in this position when the War of 1812 was declared. During the war he left Canada on leave and did not return until 1815. He was not a popular governor, and he is said to have carried on his official duties "in a high-handed behaviour." After leaving Canada he was appointed a deputy teller of the Exchequer and held this position for twenty years.

The island was traditionally known as Grindstone Island before Captain Owen made his survey in 1816 and has always been known locally by that name.

Island Notes

Grindstone Island was first settled in 1802. The first island residents were lumbermen who cut the timber from the island and lashed the logs into rafts to be sent downriver and sold in Montreal or Quebec City. Among the first settlers were Amariah Howe, Daniel Gross, Lewis Jones, Anthony Lince, Samuel Johnson and William Wells. The international boundary line was drawn through the islands in 1822, allowing the first patent of sale of the United States islands in 1823 to Elisha Camp of Sackets Harbor. The island then became private land and those living there had to purchase their properties. One of the problems of ownership was described in early county histories as the "War of Grindstone Island" and was depicted in this way:

> A quantity of pine timber had been cut and prepared for rafting, which was claimed by the patentee, but was refused to be given up by the parties in whose possession it was. Finding it probable that any attempt to serve legal papers

One of these ladies is Aunt Jane Johnson, who was commemorated with the naming of Aunt Jane's Bay on the south side of Grindstone Island. — Les Corbin Studio, Clayton, N.Y.

upon those alleged to be trespassers would be resisted, a detachment of militia from Lyme, under Captain S. Green, was called out. The timber had mostly been passed over into British waters, and after some firing, the party in charge of the timber dispersed. One of the militia-men was accidentally killed by the discharge of his own gun. The questions subsequently became a subject of litigation, and was finally settled by arbitration.

In the late 1870s Robert Forsyth, who had come from Thurso, Scotland, and had settled in Montreal, began to quarry the granite from Grindstone Island to use in his cemetery monument works in Montreal. He brought Scottish stonecutters to the island and developed several quarries. (See Part II, The Canadian Islands, Forsyth Island, the Admiralty Islands).

These new residents gave the name Thurso to the post office. David Black, nephew of Robert Forsyth's wife, was in charge of the quarry. James Kelley was the foreman. Derricks were erected and docks built to take the granite to cities along the St. Lawrence and the Great Lakes. About 250 quarry men were employed, and at one time there for four quarry operations on the island; most of them closed about 1900.

See boxed text The Lake Fleet for a full description of islands listed in the Lake Fleet.

JOLLY ISLAND

Historic Name

1816: Owen — Gig Island, the Lake Fleet (see Gig Island, The Canadian Islands)

1816: Owen — Jolly, the Lake Fleet

Named after the "jolly" boats that served as utility boats during Captain Owen's survey (see Part II, The Lake Fleet). These, as well as punts and gigs, were used by the surveyors to move among the islands and take soundings. The international boundary line that was laid down in 1818 put Jolly Island on the United States side. It is the only American island named in the Lake Fleet by Captain Owen.

Description

8.1 acres

WHISKEY ISLAND

Names

Known as Silkirk or Whiskey or Coral Island

Island Notes

An article that appeared in the Clayton *Independent* (c. 1890s) reported:

Our correspondent had the pleasure of visiting Mr. C. Wolfe of New York, who has purchased Coral Island — formerly known as Whiskey Island — at the head of Grindstone Island, near the boundary line between the United States and Canada. He is very pleasantly situated, has three tents, one occupied by himself which is nicely furnished, and has just built a splendid boat house, which he uses for his cooking and dining hall for the present and has also erected a flag staff some seventy feet long and the stars and stripes float to the breeze. It is his intention next spring to build a fine residence of a Swiss design such as seen in the Alps, which will be one of the nicest on the river. The island is a beauty of itself. Walks are to be laid out around the island and the view from his point is splendid; Clayton, Governor's Island, Gananoque, and all the passing boats of both channels, are in sight. And the fishing grounds around Coral Island is one of the best in the river. We should not forget to mention Mr. Wolfe's right hand man, Mr. Robert Bulloch, who acts the caterer in good style. Fishing parties in that vicinity must beware of the dogs.

Description

3.0 acres

PAPOOSE ISLAND

Names

Registered in the deed is the statement "formerly known as Hen Island."

Description

0.6 acre

CLUB ISLAND

Island Notes

The former home of May Irwin, a well-known actress in the late 1800s. May Irwin first came to the Thousand Islands to recuperate from exhaustion. She found the peace and tranquillity of island life to her liking and returned to buy Club Island. She later moved to the mainland and purchased a farm near Clayton. Her performances were lauded by the press, and she became a celebrity in the North Country.

Description

0.6 acre

GOVERNOR'S ISLAND

Names

Known as Shot Bag Island and located with two other islands, Powderhorn (Calumet) and Cap Box (also called Cat Box on the Clayton town tax maps).

When former Lieut.-Gov. of New York Thomas G. Alvord purchased the island, the name of Shot Bag was dropped, and the newly acquired summer home was rechristened Governor's Island. He indicated that he had nothing to do with this decision but that his family had made the change.

Island Notes

According to Thomas Alvord, "I became acquainted with the owner, a gentleman by the name of Lawrence, a successful hat, cap and fur dealer in the city of New York. By the way, it might as well be noted right here, that he was an accomplished fly-catcher, his daily catch of beauties being seldom second in number in the friendly struggle of the jovial anglers for preeminence.

"For a number of years I was advised that it was not for sale, and other spots were urged upon my attention, but I still hoped for my first choice, and finally declining health induced my friend to make me a proposition to part with it at the price of $400. At length, confirmed in his own belief by the judgement of others whom he considered experts, that the island would measure at least four acres, he closed the deal with myself and son-in-law, James A. Cheney, at $100 per acre; and then the survey demonstrated that $170 paid for 1 70-100 of an acre (the area of the island), with great disappointment, somewhat forcibly expressed but with unhesitating adherence to his pledged word, the owner executed the deed of transfer."

Description

1.7 acres

Calumet Castle.
— Les Corbin Studio, Clayton, N.Y.

CALUMET ISLAND

Historic Name

1816: Owen — Calumet, Gore's Islands

Calumet is the word for an ornamental ceremonial pipe used by aboriginals. Owen named only two islands that were originally named by the passing French voyageurs who used the island as "pipe stops" on their journey through the Thousand Islands. Calumet Island was one; Citron Island (Gordon) near Gananoque was the other.

In 1881 the island was known as Powderhorn Island, and when Charles Emery purchased the island, he must have seen a deed or a map and decided to revert to the original 1816 name Calumet.

Island Notes

In 1881 tobacco millionaire Charles Goodwin Emery bought Calumet and Governor's islands. He had visited the Thousand Islands and was intrigued by the beauty of the region. He was born in 1835 in the state of Maine. He founded the Goodwin and Company Tobacco, which eventually merged with J.B. Duke of W. Duke, Sons and Company, from Durham, North Carolina, and several others to form the American Tobacco Company. Emery was appointed the company treasurer.

He bought his islands from Thomas G. Alvord. Emery first arranged to have a large wooden house built on the island, incorporating some of the finest and most beautiful woods from around the world. He also began landscaping, including smoothing out the hills by grading. In 1893–94 Emery began to built a new house on Calumet Island. It was a stone "castle," with more than thirty family rooms. Much of the granite used for the foundations of the house and the seawall was quarried from Picton Island. He later added a famous mahogany-panelled ballroom and a cellar completely equipped with provisions — in case there was a cyclone! Many of the rooms in the castle were photographed, and those photographs and other material on Emery's

Islands and business enterprises helped to publicize the Thousand Islands.

He also entered into several business ventures in the region, many of which were a success because of his interest and personal involvement. In 1887 he became a partner in A. Bain and Company, which built the famous St. Lawrence skiffs. He also bought the large Round Island Hotel and proceeded to renovate and change the hotel in order to attract more wealthy visitors.

After Emery's death in 1915, Calumet Castle became the property of his sons. Although he had established a trust fund to maintain the island, it was hardly enough to cover the upkeep and taxes. Over the years many attempts were made to sell the property, and finally in 1950 the courts ruled in favour of breaking the will and allowed Calumet Island to be sold for the sum of $11,500. The property became a tourist attraction for a few years, but on a warm summer night in July 1957 the castle caught fire and fell in ruins.

At the same time that the castle was sold, some twenty other island properties were disposed of, including many small islands surrounding Grindstone Island that the Emerys had acquired. The 600-acre farm on Grindstone Island was sold for $6,000 and more than four hundred cottage lots were sold in 1940 for a total $3,000.

In 1901 Emery wrote a letter that he placed in the cornerstone when he built the west wing of his castle. It read: "My faith in the future of this grand old river as a summer resort is so great that I firmly believe that it will be the watering place of America before many years have passed. I have travelled the world over, but have failed to find the anything like it elsewhere, Signed. . .Charles Goodwin Emery, Calumet Island, Clayton, New York. August 15th, 1901."

Description

6.0 acres

CAP BOX ISLAND

Names

Originally known as Cat Box Island, because it was close to Powderhorn Island (Calumet) and Shot Bag Island (Governor's Island).

See boxed text on p.159, the Wellington Islands, for a full description of islands listed in the Wellington Islands.

WASHINGTON ISLAND

Historic Name

1816: Owen — Barnard, the Wellington Islands Probably named after Sir Andrew Francis Barnard (1773–1855), who was born in Ireland and entered the army in 1794. He was a good soldier, and, as will be apparent below, well respected.

He became first a lieutenant and then a captain and served in Santo Domingo with Sir Ralph Abercromby in an expedition to the West Indies. In 1808 he was appointed lieutenant colonel and went to Canada as inspector of the field officers of the militia. He returned to England and was sent to the Peninsula in 1813, with the rank of colonel. A year later he was commander of the 2nd Light Brigade. After the renewal of war with Napoleon in 1816, Barnard commanded six companies and fought at the Battle of Quatre Bras and was slightly wounded at Waterloo. He became commander of the British division during the occupation of Paris.

Barnard must have been an unusual officer. As leader of a light brigade, he needed to be stern and command respect from his foot soldiers. When Barnard died in 1855 the pensioners, or ordinary soldiers, who had served under him in the Peninsular Wars went to his home and asked to see his coffin. Although this was considered an unusual request at the time, the family agreed and left the room. When the men left and the family returned they discovered that the coffin was covered in laurel leaves. Each man brought in a leaf "unobserved" — a tribute to their former commander.

Sale

Washington Island was one of the first sold by Elisha Camp soon after he purchased the Thousand Islands.

Description

Boyd's Illustrated Guide 1882 says, "lies to the right of Clayton, and but a few yards from its shore. It is a low, barren stretch of ground. 'Years ago the busy whirr of a saw-mill made this island seem alive;' but the old mill is among the 'things that were,' and the island seems to have returned to its primitive state."

PINE ISLAND

Historic Name

1816: Owen — Beckwith, the Wellington Islands Named after John Charles Beckwith (1789–1862). Beckwith became a lieutenant in 1805 and a captain in 1808. His regiment was sent to Portugal and was a member a member of Brig.-Gen. Andrew Barnard's celebrated light division and was present at the battles of Salamanca, Vittoria, the Pyrenees and Nivelle, the Nive and Orthez. He was honoured by Wellington and appointed deputy assistant quartermaster general to the division.

In 1816 he was sent to the Netherlands and fought in the Battle of Waterloo, where he was wounded and lost his leg. He was only twenty-six years old when he retired from active service. He devoted the rest of his life to missionary work in Italy. When Beckwith died, "his funeral was attended by thousands of peasants, whose lives he made happy and cheerful."

Today the island is known as Pine Island.

Description

7.7 acres

Hotel Frontenac, Round Island.

— *The Thousand Islands and the River St. Lawrence,* The James Bayne Company

LITTLE ROUND ISLAND

Historic Name

1816: Owen — Colborne, the Wellington Islands
Probably named after Sir John Colborne who was first Baron Seaton (1778–1863). He served in Egypt and Sicily and fought at Waterloo during the Peninsular War. He was given the honour of having an island named after him because he was a member of Wellington's army.

He was later promoted to major-general and became the lieutenant-governor of Upper Canada in 1830. He held that position during the time of the Patriot War of 1837–38. He founded Upper Canada College in Toronto and was lieutenant-governor of Upper Canada from 1828 to 1835. After he returned to England, he was made Lord Seaton.

ROUND ISLAND

Historic Name

1816: Owen — Pearson, the Wellington Islands
No biographical information is available.

Island Notes

The Round Island Park began as a Baptist Church resort in the 1880s. Described in *Boyd's Illustrated Guide* of 1882, it "comprises some one hundred acres, with pretty cottages nestled here and there along its shores; also a comfortable farm house and barns belonging to a well cultivated portion of the island. Now owned by the Round Island Park Association."

The Round Island House was a fashionable hotel on the island, but Charles Goodwin Emery decided it could be better managed and improved. He purchased it in 1890 and hired one of the best New York architects, J.W. Davidson, to remodel the New Frontenac Hotel. On the top of the seven-storey building was a tower that rose a further two storeys. There were rooms for five hundred guests; each room had its own bath and electric lights. Attention was paid to every detail to make the hotel up to date and luxurious; even the furnishings were brought from places as far away as Europe. No expense was spared to make the New Frontenac a world-class establishment.

The hotel brochure advertised that it was a place of "perfect freedom from malaria, black flies and mosquitoes. It offers boating, fishing, tennis, bowling, billiards and ping pong." Photography was popular, so Emery also included dark-room facilities for the amateur photographer. The hotel attracted the very wealthy and, to prove the point, the tour boats would pass close by the island hotel so that the "passengers might have a glimpse of a life of luxury." In 1911 the hotel caught fire and burned to the ground.

BLUFF ISLAND

Historic Name

1816: Owen — Craufurd, the Wellington Islands
Named After Maj.-Gen. Robert Craufurd (1764–1812). He entered the British Army in 1799 and received various promotions. He was sent to South America to serve on the staff of General Whitelock, and took command of a light brigade. His conduct on the expedition established him as a leader. Craufurd was known as "Black Bob" and was "loved by his men despite his reputation as a strict disciplinarian."

Craufurd was on his way to join Wellington when he was told that the general was dead. He decided to force-march to the front and arrived on the day after the Battle of Talavera. He had his troops march 62 miles in twenty-two hours, a feat unparalleled in modern warfare.

Craufaud was shot and killed in 1812 after storming Ciudad Rodrigo. A monument was erected to him and another soldier in St. Paul's Cathedral. He was considered the finest commander of the light brigade in the Peninsula.

Today the island is called Bluff Island.

Description

61 acres

Sir Thomas Picton, commander of the 1st Division.
— *Wellington & Waterloo*, Major Arthur Griffiths, published by George Newnes, Limited, 1898

Picton Island Quarry.
— Les Corbin Studio, Clayton, N.Y.

PICTON ISLAND

Historic Name

1816: Owen — Picton Island, the Wellington Islands

Named after Sir Thomas Picton (1758–1815). Picton was promoted to lieutenant in 1777 after serving as ensign and attending a military academy. He joined a regiment at Gibraltar and learned Spanish. In 1778 he was made captain and for the next five years served in various garrisons. When Britain began to reduce its army, Picton was placed on half pay, and for twelve years he remained "in obscurity, enjoying field sports, studying the classics and reading professional books."

In 1794 he travelled to the West Indies and volunteered to fight for Sir John Vaughn. He was appointed to a regiment and became an extra aide-de-camp to Vaughn. He remained in the West Indies Station for two years and accompanied Sir Ralph Abercromby to Martinique. When the Spaniards surrendered Trinidad in 1797, Picton performed translation services; as well, he established trade with neighbouring countries, organized a police system and helped foster building. He was governor of Trinidad from 1797 to 1803, when he was charged with cruelty and became embroiled in lengthy court proceedings. The charges were never proven, but his biographer states the experience saddened him for the rest of his life.

In 1810 Picton went to Portugal, where he was placed in command of the 3rd Division. It is said he fought with "vigour, fearlessness and courage, though not as able as Hill or Graham [Lyndoch]." He was wounded at Badajoz in 1812 and invalided to England later that year. At the end of the war he expected to be honoured with a peerage, as the others were, but he was not.

He remained in England until 1815, when Napoleon escaped from Elba, at which time Picton joined Wellington at Waterloo. He was severely wounded on the day before the final battle but is said never to have mentioned the wound to his troops. The next morning Picton began his attack while in great pain and received a fatal shot. As a tribute to this remarkable soldier, the British House of Commons erected a public monument to his memory at St. Paul's Cathedral.

When the islands were first sold to summer people, Picton Island was also called Robbins Island. Today it is identified with the original Owen name of Picton.

Island Notes

When Charles Emery built his castle on Calumet, he had his old wooden cottage taken apart and moved to Picton Island. It was said that the new cottage was exactly like the old one but smaller. Emery also tried to develop Picton Island by subdividing it into building lots. He farmed the island, growing vegetables for the New Frontenac Hotel located on Round Island. In addition, he planted hundreds of fruit trees.

On the northeast end of the island, Emery established a stone quarry. Most of the stone was taken to Calumet Island and used as the foundation for his castle and for the surrounding seawalls.

Description

207 acres

MAPLE ISLAND

Historic Name

1816: Owen — Packenham (*sic*), the Wellington Islands

Probably named after Sir Edward Michael Pakenham (1778–1815). He and his brother both served in the Peninsular War and had illustrious careers in the army. Their sister married Sir Arthur Wellesley, the Duke of Wellington, in 1806. Edward was sent to the Peninsula after the battle of Talavera. He was the vice-commander of the 3rd Division. After the Peninsular Campaign, Pakenham was sent to the North American Station during the War of 1812. He was killed in the Battle of New Orleans after the Treaty of Ghent had been signed to end the war.

Island Notes

Perhaps one of the most fascinating mysteries in the Thousand Islands region relates to Maple Island. Evidence of the mystery first appeared in newspaper articles describing a bizarre murder that took place in the fall of 1865. A "southern gentleman" was found dead on Maple Island. His throat had been slashed from ear to ear and three "bloody crosses" had been carved on his chest to form a triangle. The story was pieced together, and it was believed that the man was Kentucky-born John C. Payne. He was described as a "broad-shouldered, dark-haired man, moustache and goatee, genteelly dressed, evidently not more than twenty-five years of age, probably less; of very agreeable manners, but very reticent, and with the characteristics of a Southerner."

Thirty years later another man, Robert McAdam of Binghamton, New York, confessed on his deathbed to the crime and identity of the murdered man. John Payne had sworn an oath to the Knights of the Blue Gauntlet, a secret society that had plotted to kill President Lincoln and his cabinet.

Payne, McAdam, John Wilkes Booth and several others met in Toronto to plan the assassination of Lincoln. Donations of gold were raised in Britain. Then on April 14, 1865, the assassination took place in Washington, D.C., in Ford's Theatre. During the second scene of the third act, John Wilkes Booth shot and killed the president.

Payne, one of the conspirators, had made his way, presumably with the gold, to Clayton in early June. After spending several days in the region, he decided to build a cabin on Maple Island, within view of Clayton. He placed the cabin deep in the woods against a stone-faced cliff that provided shelter and concealment from the shore. Payne remained on the island throughout the summer, only going to Clayton for supplies.

In late August three men arrived in Clayton and Fishers Landing and started making inquiries about a missing "friend." Somehow they found Payne of Maple Island and after a struggle slit his throat and left the symbols on his chest. The men escaped the region and no more evidence was ever discovered until Robert McAdam made his deathbed confession.

MURRAY ISLAND

Historic Name

1816: Owen — Murray, the Wellington Islands

Named after Sir George Murray (1772–1846). Murray was educated in Scotland and commissioned in the 71st Regiment in 1789. He fought with Maj.-Gen. Alexander Campbell and under Sir Ralph Abercromby. In 1808 he was sent to the Peninsula as quartermaster general. In 1809 he was appointed quartermaster general under Wellington and fought in all the major battles.

In 1812 he was promoted to major-general, and at the end of 1814 he was sent to govern the forces in Canada as lieutenant-general. Shortly after the war he was made governor of the Royal Military College at Sandhurst.

When the island was first purchased it was locally known as Hemlock Island. After the island was developed as a settlement, its name reverted to the original Owen name of Murray. Very few of the residents who now reside on Murray Island know of George Murray and his illustrious career.

Sir George Murray.

— *Wellington & Waterloo*, Major Arthur Griffiths, published by George Newnes, Limited, 1898

Island Notes

The island was included in the original island purchase by Elisha Camp. It was not sold to the Walton and Parsons partnership in Alexandria Bay (see Part I, The American Islands for Sale, 1822–72), but it did pass among several owners until 1865, when it was sold for $60 to William Walton. He soon sold the island to Alonzo and Sarah Church, who kept a small section of it and sold the remainder to James A. Taylor for $150. Taylor used the island as pasture land for several years until 1890, when he sold the remainder of the island to the Thousand Islands Investment Company. From then on the island was developed and enjoyed by many summer residents.

Murray Hill Hotel, Murray Island.

— Photograph appearing in picture book published by the Thousand Island House, Alexandria Bay, George J. Walsh, Proprietor

The Murray Hill Hotel was built in 1895 and opened for the 1896 season in June. The main floor contained the lobby, offices, a wide stairway, a dining room, lounge, a ladies' billiards parlour and a ballroom complete with wicker chairs "in conversation groupings."

Unlike most of the other hotels in the region, the Murray Hill Hotel did not succumb to flames. Instead, it experienced a "slow decay." Amasa Corbin, proprietor of the Murray Hill Hotel, is credited with saving as much of the hotel as possible. He acquired all the shares in 1908, when there was a threat of it not opening. He negotiated a sale in 1912 to the Republic Trust Company of Dallas, Texas. The hotel remained open until 1915, when it closed in mid-season. In 1920 it reopened under new ownership and remained on the verge of bankruptcy for four seasons. Finally, in 1925, after unsuccessful attempts to sell, the building was partially torn down. It took two more decades of uncertainty before the remains of the once-famous Murray Hill Hotel were cleared and this section of the island reverted to nature.

WINTERGREEN ISLAND

Names

Also known as Whippoorwill Island.

Island Notes

A small camp was first cleared on the island when Murray Island was being settled. In 1895 General Johnston built a large house on the island.

GRENELL ISLAND

Historic Name

1816: Owen — Stewart, the Wellington Islands Probably named after Sir William Stewart (1774–1827), who received his commission in the army in 1786. After an illustrious career he was appointed lieutenant-general to the army in the Peninsula. He was popular with his men, among whom he was known as "auld grog Willie" because of the extra allowance of rum that he authorized — and for which Wellington made him pay.

In the 1840s the island was known as Jeffers Island, named after a man who lived on the island. Jeffers lived in a log cabin that was a landmark to early settlers. The island received its present name after its developer, Samuel Grinnell.

Island Notes

In the later 1840s a man named Jeffers built a small shanty on Grenell (also spelled Grennell) Island, where he fished, hunted and grew a few vegetables. When more men came to the islands and began fishing and hunting, Jeffers left his island home and moved to Gananoque. Another man, by the name of Pécor, also lived on the island until it was sold to Samuel Grinnell in 1868.

The Grinnells did not do much with their property until the late 1870s. In 1878, with the Thousand Islands gaining great popularity, Grinnell began his development by building a tavern and rooming house. Grinnell sold one lot on his island in 1879 and four more in 1880. Three years later there were more than twenty families living on the island.

Grenell Island was laid out into 177 lots, and fifty cottages were built. According to one source, "Captain Grinnell has devoted considerable time and attention to the development of this island and in contributing to the comfort of the cottagers." In 1892 he opened a store that also served as the post office.

PULLMAN ISLAND

Connected to Grenell Island. In 1890 Sam Grinnell built the Pullman House. It was a "most celebrated hotel," with thirty rooms for guests. The hotel was destroyed by fire in 1904.

Description

0.9 acres

HUB ISLAND

Names

Also known as Calf and Hog Island.

Island Notes

The Hub House was built in 1877 to accommodate two hundred guests. An article appearing in the

The Pullman Hotel. — Les Corbin Studio, Clayton, N.Y.

Gananoque Reporter in 1879 gives an example of social life on the river and at the Hub House: "Mr. Geo. H. Best proprietor of the new and elegant popular summer hotel known as the Hub House having extended an invitation to a few gentleman of this place to visit him, same evening, and "bring their friends," on Tuesday evening last the favourite steamer *Geneva* was chartered for the occasion and left Brough's wharf [Gananoque] a little after eight o'clock with over a hundred ladies and gentlemen aboard. Additions were made to the party at Tidd's and Coral Islands, and also at Clayton, which must have swelled the party aboard to over 200. Arriving at the Hub, which was brilliantly illuminated, Mr. Best placed all the public rooms at their disposal, including the spacious dining hall where dancing was indulged in for a couple of hours to the strains of Montgomery's band, which accompanied the excursion. The *Geneva* arrived home again shortly after two A.M. . . .

Description

0.6 acres

HUCKLEBERRY ISLAND

Names

Locally known as Little Basswood.

Description

0.2 acres

WORONOCO ISLAND

Historic Name

1816: Owen — Canning, the Wellington Islands No biographical information is available about this particular soldier, but it is certain the Canning fought in the Peninsular War and probably beside Sir Ulysses Burgh (see Basswood Island).

Description

1.3 acres

BASSWOOD ISLAND

Historic Name

1816: Owen — Burgh, the Wellington Islands Named after Sir Ulysses Bagenal Burgh, 2nd Baron Downes (1788–1863). The fact that Burgh was from an illustrious Irish family ensured his rapid promotion in the army; he joined as an ensign in March 1804 and was promoted to lieutenant by November and captain two years later. He served in the West Indies and Gibraltar and went to Portugal in 1808. Burgh's father was a good friend of Wellington's, and this probably accounted for Burgh's being chosen as Wellington's aide-de-camp.

Burgh fought in most of Wellington's winning battles, and although slightly wounded in the Battle of Talavera, he remained close to Wellington. He was wounded again at the Battle of Toulouse. At the end of the war, he was made Knight Commander of the Order of Bath. He was remembered by Wellington after the war and received several important postings. He became surveyor general of the ordnance in 1829, and he also served as a member of Parliament for Carlow County in Ireland.

Today the island is known as Basswood Island.

TWIN ISLAND

Description

0.6 acres

Sale

Twin island was sold in 1877 to Mrs. Huntington of Watertown. Andrew Cornwall recorded the sale in his notebook as: "1877, Augt. . . to Mrs. Huntington, Watertown." "Two Islands called 'Twin' Islands near together about South west from One Tree Island and about South from Dock on Thousand Island Park ground and near One Tree Island. $75.00."

WELLESLEY ISLAND

Seven prominent points of land on Wellesley Island, as well as the so-called lake separating Hill Island in Canada and Wellesley Island in the United States, were named after battles the Duke of Wellington fought during the Peninsular War in Portugal and Spain against Napoleon.

HISTORIC NAME	PRESENT NAME	PAGE
Wellesley Island	Wellesley Island (American)	208
Oporto Head	Grand View Park	208
Toulouse Point	Near the entrance to the International Rift	209
Badajoz Head	The International Rift	209
Salamanca Point	At the far end of Lake of the Isles	209
Busacoe Point	North part of Thousand Island Park	210
Talavera Point	Near Thousand Island Park	210
Point Vittoria	Mary's Island	210
Lake Waterloo	Lake Isles	209

Individual family homes are not described in the review for Wellesley Island. Rather, information about various communities is included. A more complete study of Thousand Island Park, its history, its people and its unique personality can be found in *Thousand Island Park: One Hundred Years and Then Some*, by Helen P. Jacox and Eugene B. Kleinhans, Jr.

WELLESLEY ISLAND

Historic Name

1816: Owen — Wellesley Island, the Wellington Islands

Named after Sir Arthur Wellesley, the Duke of Wellington. Wellington was born in Dublin and lived at the family seat near Trim, County Meath, Ireland. He was educated at Eton and entered the army in 1787. He was sent to India in 1796 and began his career as one of the greatest officers in British history.

Napoleon.

— *Wellington & Waterloo*, Major Arthur Griffiths, published by George Newnes, Limited, 1898

Wellington entered the Peninsular War in 1808 with the belief that training would make a difference to the survival of his men. He was also convinced that food, clothing, tents, blankets, boots and even "pay" were vital aspects to a battle won or lost.

Instead of relying on regiments, he established "divisions." Each division was made up of officers and soldiers as well as supplies. These units could remain together and be self-sufficient no matter where they were on the battlefield.

In the Peninsular Wars, the French outnumbered Wellington's troops. He began with twenty-one thousand troops and soon raised that number to eighty thousand. However, the French had more than two hundred and fifty thousand soldiers. To better the odds, Wellington relied on the Peninsular troops of the Spanish and the Portuguese.

When the two great battles of Salamanca and Vittoria were fought in 1813, the Peninsular War was over.

Napoleon was sent to the small island of Elba off the west coast of Italy in May 1814. He was permitted a bodyguard of four hundred troops, but he evidently had over six hundred volunteers from his "old Guard" with him. His mother and sister visited him, as did former ministers and servants. Napoleon was kept informed of all the activities in France and later, in February 1815, he escaped with about one thousand men to begin the "Hundred Days."

As soon as word was out that Napoleon had escaped, the campaign of 1815 began. The Bourbon court fled Paris, and Wellington again mounted an attack on his arch-rival, which culminated in the four-day campaign in Belgium and the final triumph of Waterloo.

The Battle of Waterloo signalled the end of Wellington's active military career and the beginning of a political career that ended almost four decades later.

GRAND VIEW PARK, Wellesley Island

Historic Name

1816: Owen — Oporto Head

This part of Wellesley Island bears the name of Oporto, to commemorate the second battle of Oporto, which was fought between the newly armed Wellington and the French commander, Soult, who had captured the town in March 1815.

This particular battle is interesting because the British had to devise a method of crossing the Douro River, which was deep and had a swift current. The French commander had removed all available boats from the south side of the river.

Grand View House, Wellesley Island.
— Jno. Haddock, *A Souvenir, The Thousand Islands of the St. Lawrence River, 1895*

With the help of a Portuguese barber, Wellington found a small abandoned rowboat, which some of his troops used for crossing the river. There, they found three wine barges, which they then used to carry almost a full battalion across the river, making four trips When the battle was lost by the French, they retreated by ferry a few miles upstream before there were discovered.

Grand View Park, Island Notes

In a recently published community history of Grand View written by Elizabeth P. Stamp, *Glimpses of Grand View*, we learn that the park was established by Hamilton Child, the publisher of gazetters and business directories in Syracuse. In 1885 he purchased 25 acres and laid out a summer community with the Grand View Hotel at its centre. When the financial burden of maintaining the hotel became too great, Charles Emery stepped in and purchased 20 acres. The Hotel was turned into a summer camp for girls from New York City. About 1910 Emery had the hotel "cut into two sections" and moved across the river on the ice to Picton Island.

It was described in Jno. Haddock's *Picturesque St. Lawrence River* as follows: "The post-office, established three years go, receives and dispatches mails twice daily, and at the dock Uncle Sam's customs officer will attend to the imposts and other dusties of his office. The docks are ample for the landing of any of the Folger boats. . . ."

INTERNATIONAL RIFT, Wellesley Island

Historic Name

1816: Owen, Toulouse Point, near the entrance to the International Rift

Named after the last battle of the Peninsular War. The Battle of Toulouse Point was fought on Easter Sunday, April 10, 1814. It was a costly battle with the allied army recording more than four thousand allies killed or wounded. When the day ended, the news arrived that Napoleon had abdicated some days earlier.

1818: Owen, Badajoz Head, the International Rift

This site is named after the battle of Badajoz, which was really a combination of three battles. The first was fought from January 26 to March 10, 1811, the second from April 20 to June 10, 1811, and the third from March 16 to April 7, 1812. The first battle was between the Spanish and the French. The French fought to capture Badajoz, one of the strong fortresses of the Portuguese. After a month and a half the Spanish surrendered to the French commander, Maréchal Soult.

The second battle was fought between the allied army and the French. Wellington's plan was to recover the fortress and secure the defence of southern Portugal. After a two-month siege, Wellington abandoned his plans.

The third and final battle was fought almost a year later. This time Wellington captured the fort to prepare the way for an offence into Spain. It is this battle that is commemorated in Owen's survey.

The battle was a severe one, with the British, Portuguese and Spanish troops suffering many casualties. When the French finally surrendered, the British and their allies went on a rampage. The battle was documented as having a record number of rapes, thefts and murders — a disgrace to the British Army.

LAKE OF THE ISLES, Wellesley Island

Historic Name

1816: Owen — Salamanca Point,

The Battle of Salamanca, fought on July 22, 1812, gave this point its name. Wellington wanted to defeat the French before they could be reinforced. The French hoped Wellington would make a mistake so they could push him back into Portugal. The battle began when the Portuguese army challenged the French. This was swiftly followed by a thrust of British troops, which broke up the French division. A second attack caused the French "defence to buckle." After this battle Wellington was made a marquess. "Salamanca was undoubtly one of his tactical masterpieces and showed the French that he was more than a defensive general."

1816: Owen — Lake Waterloo, Wellesley Island and Hill Island

The Battle of Waterloo was fought on June 15, 1815. The battlefield was considered small, stretching only 4 miles from east to west and a little over 2 miles from north to south. Much has been written about the battle, which was divided into six phases. The fighting began before noon and ended in the evening, close to nine o'clock. The allies lost more than twenty thousand men, but Napoleon lost twice that number. Many of them had fought with Napoleon as trusted soldier and veterans. With the loss of his troops and his reputation as a winner, Napoleon knew his political career was over. He abdicated and was sent in exile to St. Helena Island, off the coast of Africa.

Battle of Waterloo.
— *Wellington & Waterloo*, Major Arthur Griffiths, published by George Newnes, Limited, 1898

WESTMINISTER PARK, Wellesley Island

Westminister Park, Island Notes

Westminster Park Association was established in 1878. The association owned 500 acres. The religious "privileges" are described in *Boyd's Illustrated Guide*: "This enterprise has received the endorsement of the Presbytery of St. Lawrence. . . The religious privileges will include preaching as often in the week as those who become purchasers of lots may desire. The Park will be conducted under the general away of morality and religion, but with no view to large public gatherings or exercises, affording protection and quiet, under just restraints, to all persons who desire to be free from the vexatious annoyances and the corrupting influences, habits and practices which prevail at many places of public resort. Camp-meetings, so called, are not embraced in the plan or management of the Association."

Battle of Vittoria.
— *Wellington & Waterloo*, Major Arthur Griffiths, published by George Newnes, Limited, 1898

THOUSAND ISLAND PARK, Wellesley Island

Historic Name

1816: Owen, Talavera Point

This battle, which gave the point its name, was fought on July 28, 1809. The French, in order to foil the attempt of the British to join forces with the Spanish, attacked Wellington's forces at Talavera. The British held out against several attacks, and the French were finally forced to withdraw. Wellington never received food and supplies from the Spanish and eventually had to fall back into Portugal.

1818: Owen — Busacoe Point

The battle of Busaco (or Bussaco) was fought on September 27, 1810. The French lost five generals and suffered more than four thousand casualties. The allies, including the British and Portuguese army, had twelve hundred killed or wounded. Although the French were not turned back completely, the defensive battle was considered a moral victory for the allies.

Thousand Island Park cottages, Wellesley Island.
— Photograph appearing in Jno. A Haddock, *Island and River Pictorial, 1896*

Thousand Island Park, Island Notes

The popular *All-Round Route and Panoramic Guide*, published in 1911 by the International Railway Publishing Company, describes the park: "Thousand Island Park began as a religious summer encampment under the charge of the Methodist organization, which purchased a large territory at the head of Wellesley Island. Since 1875 near 400 cottages and several hotels have been built there, also an immense tabernacle for worship on Sunday, and for lectures, concerts and the instruction of classes during week days; but the enjoyment of yachting, boating, fishing and flirting takes up much more time among all the visitors and residents than does attention to the season's instructive exercises."

SARGENT ISLAND

Sale

The island is recorded in Andrew Cornwall's notebook as being sold in "1872 . . . to E.S. Sargent Watertown . . .Two Small islands on the North Side of Eel Bay near the Mass which extends the Island and on the South Side of the North point of Wells Island, about 10 to 15, Rods apart the last one Containing about one acre & the Smaller one half an acre. Consideration $75."

FLATIRON ISLAND

Sale

One of two islands sold to E.S. Sargent in 1872. The island is shaped like a flat iron.

THE ROBINSON GROUP

Historic Name

1816: Owen — Robinson Group, the Wellington Islands

Named after Sir Frederick Phillip Robinson (1763–1652), who first fought with the British Army in the American Revolution. When the war ended, the Robinson family were among the United Empire Loyalists who petitioned the Crown for loss of property. Sir Frederick returned to England and served in the West Indies. He was present at the capture of Martinique, St. Lucia and Guadeloupe.

In 1812 Robinson was sent to Spain to fight with Wellington. He came under heavy attacks and was later severely wounded in the face. During the War of 1812, he was sent to America and fought in the Battle at Plattsburg, New York. After the war he served as provisional lieutenant-governor of Upper Canada. He served in this important postion during the summer of 1815, the time of Captain Owen's survey.

Robinson received the Knight Grand Cross of the Bath in 1852, "being at that time the soldier of the longest service to the British Army."

BIG GULL ISLAND

Historic Name

1816: Owen — Tweedall (*sic*), the Wellington Islands

Probably named after George Tweeddale (1787–1876), the 7th Marquess. He served with Wellington in the cavalry under Rowland Hill. He was wounded at Vittoria and was sent home. He never returned to the army.

MANDOLIN ISLAND

Historic Name

1816: Owen — Brisbane, the Wellington Islands

Probably named after Thomas M. Brisbane, who was born in Scotland and went to the University of Edinburgh to study astronomy and mathematics. In 1790 he was sent to Ireland, where he met Wellington. They remained friends for the rest of their lives. He was promoted to lieutenant and then captain. After an illustrious career, including serving in Sir Ralph Abercromby's expedition to the West Indies, Brisbane joined Wellington in 1812 as brigadier general. He fought under Picton at Vittoria, the Pyrenees, the Nive, Orthez and Toulouse. Wellington recommended him for command in America during the War of 1812, where he commanded the troops at Plattsburg, New York. When he returned to England, he went back to war with Wellington and fought in the Battle of Waterloo. He was rewarded in 1814 as a Knight Commander of the Order of Bath.

He was later appointed governor of New South Wales, Australia, where he introduced sugar cane and tobacco and encouraged horse breeding. Brisbane's interest in astronomy led him to write several books on navigation while he was in the West Indies. During the Peninsular War he "kept the time of the Army." He was admitted to the Royal Society of Edinburgh in 1811. After returning from Australia, he received a number of degrees and honours. He was also noted for endowing the Brisbane Academy in Scotland. He died at eighty-seven in 1860.

This island has also been called Picnic Island, Madeline, or Madelin Island in deeds.

Description

0.9 acres

WEE ISLAND

Names

Described in deed as "Originally designated as 'No Name Island' and here forth known in the 1950s as Wee Island."

Description

0.3 acres

ROCK ISLAND LIGHT

Island Notes

The decision to build a lighthouse on Rock Island was made in 1853. The first light keeper was the infamous Bill Johnston, who is known in the Thousand Islands as the pirate who burned the steamer *Sir Robert Peel* on May 29, 1838, during the Patriot War (see Part I, The Patriot War, 1837–38).

ISLE OF PINES

Names

This island was originally called Nigger Island, but in the 1950s the Names Board of both the United States and Canada decreed that names like "Nigger" were racist; thus, places bearing this name were changed.

Sale

The island is recorded in Andrew Cornwall's notebook as being sold in "1872, Sept 5th . . . to Eugene N. Robinson . . . [who] Bargained with Edward Robbins to Sell him Nigger Island near the upper or Rock Island Light House for $90. Paid us $75. and we gave him deed when he paid $15 . . . ."

Island Notes

Several years before the Civil War, the island was occupied by an escaped slave from Virginia. He provided temporary shelter and protection to many other runaways en route to Canada and to freedom. These passages, known as the Underground Railroad, were responsible for bringing hundreds of former slaves across New York State. Old histories say that a half a mile inland from Mullet Creek a log house was built that originally housed the slaves as they made their way north across the islands to Canada. Other slaves are recorded as living on islands in Chippewa Bay and also in the Navy Islands near the Canadian shore.

Description

Boyd's Illustrated Guide, 1882, mentions that the island "is owned by Mrs. Eugene N. Robinson, of New York, who has rendered what was at first a very unattractive island into a 'thing of beauty,' by the generous use of abundant means. She has erected a magnificent summer residence, and improved its natural advantages until it bears little resemblance to its primitive state."

RYLSTONE ISLE

Historic Name

1816: Owen — Fitzroy Group, the Wellington Islands

Named after Lieut.-Col. Lord Charles Fitzroy (1791–1865), who was the second son of the 4th Duke of Grafton. Educated at Harrow, he was appointed acting adjutant-general of the 2nd Division in 1813.

Description

0.8 acres

OCCIDENT ISLAND AND ORIENT ISLAND

Sale

According to Andrew Cornwall's notebook records, the sale of these islands was "1873, Sept 11th . . . to Eugene Washburn of City of New York." He described them as follows: "Two Islands in a Block of 7 Islands at High Water and at Low Water are connected by land or marsh and lying in the town of Orleans and north from Mullett Creek and are separated from the other Islands by a narrow channell nearly East & West, and about 25 Chains from the point at Mullett Creek and nearly East by North and about Half a Mile from Rock Island Light House and between Said Light House & Grassey Point so called and together Supposed to contain together about 3 to 4 Acres The West one is named 'Occident' & the East one is named 'Orient'. Consideration $200, To build within 2 years from this date."

Description

Occident Island, 1.7 acres; Orient Island, 2.0 acres.

ISLE HELENA

Names

Helena was a family name of a "Cuban born wife Helena" who was described as being "the lovliest dispositioned woman that ever came from New York to the River." The tour-boat captains told the tale that the name was given by one of the owners who was a great admirer of Napoleon. Although the new owner could have been infatuated, it is not the reason for the name.

Sale

Andrew Cornwall's notebook records the sale of this island in 1873 to "Helen S. Taylor. New York City." Cornwall wrote: "An Island in the town of Orleans Jeff Co. N.Y. Called 'Isle Helena' next North from Orient & near to it. [A small island] about North from Fishers Landing and Westerly from Grassey Point. Paid $100."

Description

0.4 acres

CENTER ISLAND

Sale

Described in the deed as "it being the center island of a group of seven small islands near Fisher's Landing conveyed to Helen Staylen, 28 August, 1874."

Description

1.2 acres

FREDERICK ISLAND

Sale

Purchased by Carlos L. Frederick, attached to Susan, also called Sophia, Island. Frederick came from nearby Carthage, New York.

Description

Boyd's Illustrated Guide, 1882, says the island "is owned by C.L. Fredericks [*sic*], of Carthage, N.Y., who has erected a charming cottage, where he ertertains with his accustomed liberality. These are near Fisher's Landing."

1.7 acres

SUSAN ISLAND

Names

Also known as Sophia Island.

Sale

Purchased with Frederick Island by Carlos L. Frederick.

ISLAND NO. 3

Sale

Described in Andrew Cornwall's notebook as being sold in "1875 to Carlos S. Frederick, Carthage." He referred to it as "An Island called 'Island No. 3' situated in Orleans, Jefferson Co. N.Y. and is the third Island South from the Steam Boat Channel and in a Group of Seven Islands and the next Island South of Fredrick Island and nearest to it and the next Island North of Center Island conveyed to E.R. Washburn, Apr 24th/75. $75."

Description

1.25 acres

Rosette Island.

Comfort Island.

— Photograph appearing in picture book published by the Thousand Island House, Alexandria Bay, George J. Walsh, Proprietor

VANDERBILT ISLAND

Sale

Described in Andrew Cornwall's notebook as "Vanderbilt Island, 1875 . . . to J.B Hamilton . . . An Island just below Grasse Point near Mullet Creek called 'Vanderbilt' Island, was not entered at time deeded, $150."

Description

1.1 acres

LONG VUE ISLAND

Names

Also known as Rosette Island and today referred to as Artificial Isle.

Island Notes

This island was originally sold as four small rock shoals. The owner, H.P. Rose, from Cleveland, Ohio, built a retaining wall and brought rock fill from the mainland. The result was an artificial island.

COMFORT ISLAND

Names

Originally the island was known as Pratts Island. In 1882 when the Clark family purchased the island they changed the name to Comfort.

Sale

The island was recorded in Andrew Cornwall's notebook as sold in 1871 "to Humphry Sisson." "An Island called Pratts Island on the South East Side of Steam Channel and is directly North from White Fish Bay and East and across the Channel from Knapps Islands and South Westerly from Surveyors Island and what shoals or rocks there is within one Rod of said Island that are out of water at low water mark. To build house in two years. [written with another pen] $100."

Island Notes

The two properties on this island were separated by a small artificial channel. The original purchaser, H. Sisson, held the island until 1882, when Alson E. Clark, who visited the region from Chicago, purchased the island and built a large Victorian cottage. The family called the island Comfort.

To take advantage of summer activities, the house was built with a large living room and two dining rooms, one inside and one in the screened porch. There were family bedrooms and a dormitory space in the tower. Clark travelled back and forth between the island and Chicago, sometimes with his neighbour George Pullman, who had his own private rail car to transport him to the Thousand Islands.

There was a second home on the island called Neh Mahbin. In 1893 James H. Oliphant built a new home on this property. It was beautifully constructed with a wide piazza, or balcony. All the rooms had magnificent views, and they were lined with finished oak panelling. One of the most outstanding architectural features in this house was a circular room. Even the window-panes were specially fired so that they, too, curved to fit the window frames. Oliphant was a New York City stockbroker; he met his death at the hands of a client who lost many thousands of dollars in a misguided stock venture. The man went to Oliphant's office for revenge and killed him on Boxing Day, December 26, 1907.

Sale

Registered as being sold to H. Sisson in 1882 for $150.

Description

Boyd's Illustrated Guide, 1882, notes that the island "is located about one mile above Alexandria Bay; has an area of two acres, and is owned by Mr. H. Sisson, of Alexandria Bay, who has erected a elegant residence on his island which enhances the beauty greatly. This was formerly known as Pratt's Island."

4 acres

Jewel Island. — *The Thousand Islands and the River St. Lawrence*, The James Bayne Company

STONEY CREST ISLAND

Names

Originally called Warners Island and later renamed Jewel Isle, about 1918. The island name was changed again in 1941, when new owners called it Stoney Crest.

Sale

The island was registered in Andrew Cornwall's notebook as being sold in 1872 to Herbert H. Warner of Rochester, "An Island called formerly 'Surveyors' Island now named Warner Island, South West from Cherry Island and nearest to the Steam Boat Channel and West from Chub, now 'Cuba' Island. [written with another pencil] To build within one year."

Island Notes

H.H. Warner was known for selling his patent medicine "Warner's Safe cures." He built a large home on the island and installed a special lighting system that allowed light standards to be lit at night to give a spectacular diplay for the passing tour boats. A *Gananoque Reporter* article reports that the "the current in the river at H.H. Warner's summer home is sufficient to turn a water wheel, which supplies the power for pumping water and running an electric dynamo, by which the castle and grounds are illuminated."

In 1895 the island was sold to S.R. Van Duzer, and about 1918 Julie Burke purchased the island. The twenty-six-room mansion was razed in 1956. Part of the island was blasted away in the 1950s to make way for the St. Lawrence Seaway.

Description

0.8 acre

Wauwinet.
— Photograph appearing in picture book published by the Thousand Island House, Alexandria Bay, George J. Walsh, Proprietor

CUBA ISLAND

Historic Name

1816: Owen — Chapman, the Wellington Islands Named after Sir Stephen R. Chapman (1776–1851). Chapman received his professional training at Woolwich and joined the Royal Engineers in 1793. He went to Portugal in 1809 and served in the environs of Lisbon, preparing for its defence during the campaign of Talavera; he suggested the formation of the famous Lines of Torres Vedras. In 1810 he was commander of the Royal Engineers at the Battle of Bussaco. By 1813 he was a lieutenant-colonel in the Royal Engineers and secretary to the master general of ordnance. He later served as governor of Bermuda and the Somers Islands.

Sale

The island was first sold in 1872 to "Mr. E. Story of Buffalo." It is described in Andrew Cornwall's notebook as "Those two Islands described herein, first the Island called Chub Island now named 'Cuba' and is SouthWesterly from Oven Island and is on the South East side of the Steam Boat Channel and East from Surveyors Island. The second Island is in shore about East, from the Island and described, and opposite the House of Thos. Elliot on the main shore and is named 'Story' Island. [See Wauwinet] to build on one within a year and the other two years."

Description

1.1 acres

WAUWINET ISLAND

Sale

The island was sold with Cuba Island to W.E. Story. He purchased both islands for a total of $200.

Island Notes

In 1902 the island home of Comdr. Thomas H. Wheeler of New York City was built on Wauwinet. The large house and boathouse were built to provide a beautiful view of the passing steamers using the American Channel. Wheeler gained the title of commodore when he assumed that position at the Thousand Islands Yacht Club. The house was destroyed by fire in the 1960s.

Description

0.8 acre

DEVIL'S OVEN ISLAND

Island Notes

Tour-boat captains identified this island as being the hiding place for the infamous pirate Bill Johnston (see Part I, Patriot War, 1837–38) who hid among the Thousand Islands during the Patriot War. It is true that in times of low water there is a cave in which a small boat could fit, but it is much more probable Johnston, being a resourceful man, would have much preferred a wooden hut or tent hidden on an island to the dark, musty and tiny cave.

In the later 1800s a gazebo that was built on the island made a picturesque setting for photographers to view the islands.

Description

0.2 acre

CHERRY ISLAND

Historic Name

1816: Owen — Jones, the Wellington Islands Probably named after Sir Harry Jones, who was an officer of the engineers in Spain. He saw service throughout the Peninsula.

The island was locally known as Cherry Island, a name that has remained.

Sale

Registered by Andrew Cornwall in his notebook as "Deeded by A. Walton some years ago to Geo Rockwell. The Island called Cherry Island next to Steam Boat Channel and the first Island up the River from the Saw Mill."

Island Notes

Local residents were kept informed about island development through newspaper articles. The following gives an account of the "Twin" houses that were built on Cherry Island:

Nathan Strauss, of New York City, proprietor of Macy's Store, and Abraham Abraham, of Abraham & Strauss of Brooklyn, have purchased the lower end of Cherry Island, at Alexandria Bay, adjoining the property of Louis Marks of Cuba, a brother-in-law of Mr Strauss, and will erect thereon two handsome summer cottages. Designs have been made by Williams & Johnson . . . and contract for construction awarded to J. Dall, New York City. The building will be complete in every detail and will form a valuable addition to the large elegant summer residences for which the islands are noted.

. . . The cottages will be set upon the highest point of the island at an elevation of about thirty-five feet above the water, and will stand side by side. They are of picturesque and beautiful design. Each has a central tower, and is four stories high, with a series of wings on either side gradually decreasing in height. Four large rustic stone outside chimneys, starting from the stone walls at first story, form conspicuous features.

The houses are entirely surrounded by piazzas averaging twenty feet in width, the roofs being supported by clusters of columns standing upon a rustic stone wall in some places twenty feet about the ground.

PULLMAN ISLAND

Names

The island was first known as Sweet Island, but was soon renamed after its owner, George M. Pullman.

Sale

Recorded by Andrew Cornwall in his notebook as being sold "About 1864. . . to Geo M. Pullman (Chicago). . . An Island opposite Cherry Island and next to Steamboat Channel, called Sweet Island. The deed was not recorded and Mr. Pullman writes that it is lost. Supposed to be lost in Chicago, and gave him another deed 19th September, 1872. Reciting fact of lost deed."

Island Notes

George Pullman is credited with bringing President Ulysses S. Grant to the Thousand Islands in 1872 and thus also bringing popularity to the region. Pullman was born in Chautaqua County, New York. In 1848 he joined his brother as a cabinet-maker in Albion, New York. A few years later he moved to Chicago, Illinois, where he was given the contract to convert two day coaches into sleeping cars. He built a third car in 1859. Although his cars were successful, the railroads were reluctant to expand the service, so Pullman left Chicago for a Colorado mining town, where he ran a general store for four years. It was there that he began to design the real Pullman Car. He returned to Chicago and formed a partnership with B. Field, and in April 1864 they patented their "folding upper berth." After the initial success of their new design in 1867 they formed the Pullman Palace Car Company, which "grew to the greatest car building organization in the world."

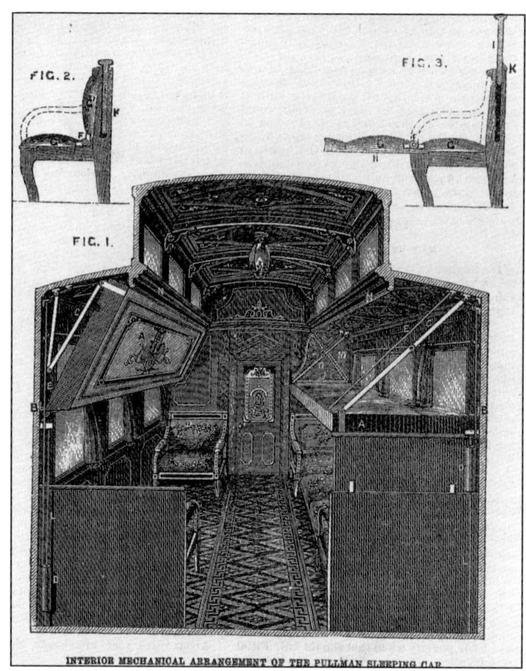

"Interior mechanical arrangement of the Pullman sleeping car." — *Canadian Illustrated News*, Vol. VI, Sept. 21, 1872, p. 189

Pullman first constructed a wooden cottage on the island soon after he bought it in 1864. Then in 1888 he built a new house — a stone structure that was called Pullman Rest. By then he was a powerful businessman, and his visits to the Thousand Islands were brief. In August 1888 he gave the new home as a gift to his mother on her eightieth birthday. The house had more than fifty rooms and the added luxury of indoor plumbing facilities.

It could be said that George Pullman not only began the influx of tourism in the Thousand Islands by inviting President Grant, but he also helped usher in the "Golden Era," with the construction of one of the first palatial residences in the islands. The building, with its tall tower, which many said depicted one of the Pullman rail cars standing on end, remained a landmark in the region until the 1950s when Pullman descendants had a major part of the edifice razed. The taxes were exorbitant and the upkeep on such a home was cost prohibitive. In addition, it was becoming increasingly difficult to find local residents as servants and caretakers.

Description

1.6 acres

NOBBY ISLAND

Names

The spelling of this island name also appears as Knobby Island.

Sale

Recorded by Andrew Cornwall in his notebook as being sold in "1868" to J.M. Pullman and J.W. Clow, "Sold by them to Goodwin and Heath, New York, 'An Island called Nobby Island between Friendly and Pullman Island,' $40."

Island Notes

E.A. Heath of New York City built his home on Nobby Island. It became a social centre for Alexandria Bay families. Heath brought many prominent businessmen to the Thousand Islands, and many returned as guests at hotels or purchased islands for themselves. The family is remembered in the town of Alexandria Bay by the beautiful stained-glass window in the Alexandria Bay Reform Church.

Description

1.7 acres

WELCOME ISLAND

Island Notes

The island was originally purchased by Charles Myers and S.G. Pope. In 1894 the island became the headquarters for the Thousand Islands Yacht Club. The club members wanted a place that would resemble their clubhouse at home. The clubhouse was described as "few club houses on the continent that have interior decoration and convenience for their members as the Thousand Islands Yacht Club. It is truly one of the most delightful places within a few minutes of Alexandria Bay."

The members of the Thousand Islands Yacht Club were considered the most affluent in the region. They were all "millionaires" and were able to purchase and race the newest "motor" boats that appeared on the river. When these members died or left the river, the club fell on hard times. In 1944 the island was sold for property taxes. Subsequent owners razed the building.

Description

2.1 acres

FRIENDLY ISLAND

Names

This island was originally known as Tallman Island after its purchase by Julia Tallman, who came from Wilmington, Delaware, about 1868. It was recorded as Friendly Island when sold to A.B. Parker and Abner Miller, Jr., New York, for $40.

Island Notes

In 1883 Edward Dewey purchased the island. He was a business partner of William Browning and one of the many influential men who attracted attention to the Thousand Islands.

In June 1907 an article about the island appeared in the *Thousand Islands Sun*:

June 6, 1907. Dewey Island. The summer home of late heirs of E.W. Dewey "the Philippine of the St. Lawrence" is the ideal dream realised. The wooden section is blended in harmoniously with the rolling river and it is to this we attribute the comment "oft in the stilly night. The home is beautifully situated. The island possesses fertile soil and vegetables of all kinds can be grown. The house is roomy and large and contains enough room to entertain a party of 50. A fine wharf permits the docking of many craft and is the busy scene during the fashionable season. . . .

Description

2.1 acres

ST. ELMO ISLAND

Sale

Sold to J.H. Hunt, New York.

Island Notes

A simple yet decisive statement printed in the "River Items" of the *Gananoque Reporter* describes the opulence of the Hunt Family: ". . .it is an established fact that the millionaires come here early and stay late. Mr. Hunt, of New York, is already at his beautiful summer house, 'St. Elmo' near Alexandria Bay."

Description

2.4 acres

FLORENCE ISLAND

Names

Named after the original owner, Florence Proctor. It was also called Proctor Island.

Sale

Sold to E.R. Proctor, Cincinnati, Ohio, and H.S. Chandler.

Description

1.0 acre

BELLE ISLAND

Names

Known as Maud Island in the 1870s. Also known as Lillithgow Island, which was a family name.

Sale

The island was recorded in Andrew Cornwall's notebook as: "1871. . .to F.B.A. Lewis of Watertown, H. Grennell, Adam, Steamer of Albany. . .An Island Called Maud Island on the North West side of the Steam Boat Channel and about North from Titusville Island and the nearest to Lotus Island. . .$50."

Island Notes

The house on Belle Island, which was built by Alex E. Peacock, was described in the *Thousand Islands Sun* in 1906:

Ideal in every respect with all the convenience which modern skill in plumbing, sanitation and ventilation can accomplish is here demonstrated. The building is a three storey structure with a deep basement and contains upwards of forty suites and sleeping rooms. . .the large and commodious verandah is a retreat. . .a fine view can be had. There is also a large entertainment room with a seating capacity of about one hundred and fifty. Here are held amateur theatricals and some of the most noted artists and opera etc, entertain the numerous guests of Mr. Peacock during the summer. . . .

Peacock built a large yacht house on Wellesley Island in 1906 that was also described as of "mammoth proportions." Peacock reportedly once had a serious quarrel while staying at the Waldorf Astoria Hotel. Apparently while having breakfast with his wife, he was found arguing over his wealth, she saying he was worth $3 million more than he thought!

Peacock began his business career in New York as a poorly paid clerk in a drygoods shop. A lady customer once wanted a certain piece of silk that could not be found. Peacock, the floor manager, was asked what could be done, and without knowing who the lady was, he offered to send to Europe and have the goods made, "which he did." The lady turned out to be Mrs. Andrew Carnegie, who spoke to her husband about the polite and

Imperial Isle. — Photograph appearing in *The Thousand Islands and the River St. Lawrence*, The James Bayne Company

helpful employee. Mr. Carnegie soon hired Peacock, and he went to Pittsburgh to work for the Carnegie Steel Company and to become a millionaire!

The island eventually became the property of George Boldt and passed to E.J. Nobel and his Thousand Islands estate.

IMPERIAL ISLE

Names

Also known as Prince Island.

Sale

Recorded by Andrew Cornwall in his notebook as "1871. . . to Joseph McNaughton, Ogd. and Jos N. Hale of Boston. . . An Island called Prince Island, now called Isle. Imperial and is on the North West side of the channel and near Frontenac Shoal. . .West from the Westerly door of Cornwall and Walton Stores and together with the Rocks and projections above the Water adjacent there to and lying in a circle of twenty Rods and radius from Center of Said Island, [written with another pencil] $25."

Island Notes

When Gilbert T. Rafferty became the owner of the island, he built his grand home. He was from Pittsburgh, Pennsylvania, and made his fortune in coal and coke manufacturing. It is probable that the design of the house was made to fit the name, its architecture like that of a European castle.

HUB ISLAND

Names

Named after Hub Clark, youngest son of H.R. Clark.

Sale

The sale of the island was recorded in Andrew Cornwall's notebook as "1873, Aug. 18th. . . to Will. Clark, Jersey City. . . An Island on the North West Side of the Steam Boat Channel named 'Hub Clark' and is north East from Isle Imperial and North west from Harts Island and Northwesterly from Cornwall & Waltons Store at Alexandria Bay and is the only Island between Isle Imperial & Harts Island near the channel."

OLD FRIENDS

Five vessels were considered the "Old Friends" of Capt. William FitzWilliam Owen, for he considered them "home" for at least two decades before making his survey on the Great Lakes. His handwritten ships' journals are on file in the National Maritime Museum in Greenwich, England. These notes describe his life aboard these ships and the various battles he fought.

HISTORIC NAME	PRESENT NAME	PAGE
Nancy	Heart Island (American)	218
Flamer	Steamboat Island (American)	221
Seaflower	Manhattan Island (American)	221
Barracouta	Harbor Island (American)	220
Corneilia	Fairyland Island (American)	222

(see map on page 224)

Island Notes

The island was given as a birthday present from Cornwall and Walton to H.R. Clark's son, Hub. Today the island has the distinction of being called "Just Room Enough." Tour boat hawkers say that Boldt built the castle for his wife and the house on Hub Island for his mother-in-law.

HEART ISLAND

Historic Name

1816: Owen — Nancy, Old Friends

Capt. William FitzWilliam served on the *Nancy* when he was selected by Lord Nelson to burn the French flotilla at Boulogne, but the action was not taken because England signed the Peace of Armines. Owen was then placed on half pay.

Originally the island was known as Hemlock Island.

Sale

According to Andrew Cornwall's notebook the sale was in "1871. . . to E. Kirk Hart (Albion). . . An Island called Harts Island (formerly Hemlock

Island) next to the Steam Boat Channel and North Easterly from Frontenac Shoal [written with another pencil] $100."

Island Notes

E. Kirke Hart, from Albion, New York, purchased the island the summer before President Grant visited the islands. The next summer he built his summer home and began a twenty-year association with the river that only ended with his death in 1893.

In 1895 a new visitor to the region inquired about purchasing the 5-acre island lying opposite the small village of Alexandria Bay. George Boldt and his wife, Louise, and their two children, George, Jr., and Clover, came to the river for a holiday at the Thousand Islands House. George Boldt, Sr., fascinated by the beauty of the region and the many "sportsmen" who spent their free time fishing, purchased Hart Island in 1895 and began a construction boom that was to last for two decades.

George Boldt was born on an island in the Baltic Sea in 1851 and came to the United States at thirteen to work in a New York City hotel. He saved his money and invested in a chicken-and-sheep ranch in Texas. When this venture proved unsuccessful, Boldt returned to the hotel business at Cornwall-on-Hudson, where he soon rose from being the general utility man to the lofty position of steward. He then went to the famous Clover Club in Philadelphia, where he gained the financial support of some club members to convert a large private residence into the Bellevue Hotel.

One night he was asked to find a room for a guest, but there were none available, and without knowing who the guest was, Boldt offered his private quarters. The guest was William Waldorf Astor. This gesture began a relationship with the Astors that led to the building of the Waldorf Hotel on the site of the Astors' New York City home. In 1893 Boldt moved there as manager of the "world's most magnificent" hotel. By 1898 the hotel had expanded with the building of the Astoria. As the manager of the Waldorf Astoria, he had a staff of 1,800 employees. It has been said that George Boldt invented the theory that the public was right: "he trained his employees to give the patron something he would like and he never let a man leave his doors unsatisfied."

Boldt Castle yacht house. — Photograph appearing in picture book published by the Thousand Island House, Alexandria Bay, George J. Walsh, Proprietor

Boldt evidently bought Hart Island with a confrere from the Waldorf, F.W. McCormick, but little is known of the man or his later association with the island. The first summer was spent in the Hart house, but like many who purchase a new home, the Boldts had different tastes and wanted a new home built.

Seth Pope was hired to build a new house on the island. Beautifully designed and constructed, it soon became a landmark. The name of the island was changed to Heart and sea walls were constructed to reshape the island to match the name. The new house was occupied during the summer of 1896, after more than one hundred workmen completed their task. Construction did not cease, though, as Boldt soon had the Alster Tower constructed on the southeast end of the island. This was the recreation complex, complete with a bowling alley and billiard parlour. Other rooms had luxurious furnishings and "incandescent lights" that were positioned to shine through windows, to the delight of the passing boats making their way to and from Alexandria Bay in the night. Power was furnished from the Power House, which was constructed on the north side of the island in 1900.

At the west end of the island, Boldt constructed a lagoon and the Arch of Triumph, through which small launches and skiffs could pass to a safe landing to let off passengers and guests.

Almost immediately after Boldt purchased the island, he began to explore the properties that surrounded Alexandria Bay. He acquired additional acreage on Wellesley Island, and this allowed him to construct a mammoth yacht house to accommodate his newest vessels and guests' boats. The yacht house provided three covered slips. Because of the height of the steamer funnels, the roof was constructed with steel beams and rose some 70 feet above the water. Rooms and living quarters were built for the crew members and caretakers. No cost or expense was spared. George Boldt expected perfection from himself, from his employees and from his surroundings.

By 1900 the Heart Island complex was already a showpiece. Tour boats circled the island — a practice that is still carried on today. But all was not over. In August of that year Boldt announced that he had hired the Philadelphia architectural firm of Hewitt and Hewitt to design a new house. That winter the "old" cottage was moved across the ice to Wellesley Island and converted into a clubhouse for the golf club he had constructed on the island in 1899.

It did not take long before rumors began that the new house would not resemble any in the island region. The plans were to build a stone castle complete with turrets and over one hundred rooms. Hundreds of workmen were hired. Quarry derricks were erected on Oak Island to cut the granite for the foundations and the walls. Columns, blocks and steps were brought to the island and laid in place.

No other home or site in the Thousand islands has been given as much publicity as Boldt Castle. Countless articles have appeared in newspapers around the world showing the castle and telling its romantic story. Boldt and his family were pleased with the construction and by the fall season of 1903 they could see that the end was near. The walls were constructed, the roof was on and many of the major areas were completed. No windows had been installed, but dozens of crates were delivered, containing some of the finishing marble that would be added over the winter of 1904.

On a cold day in January 1904 the foreman received a telegram informing the crew that Mrs. Louise Boldt had died on the night of January 7. Work on Boldt Castle stopped.

George Boldt and his family did not abandon the Thousand Islands altogether; they continued to summer on Wellesley Island. By then several other Boldt properties were developed. In total, more than 1500 acres on the island were purchased and considered part of the Boldt estate. He developed a poultry farm, complete with modern farming techniques and equipment, and a dairy farm that included several hundred dairy cattle. There were horse barns and pasture for the farm's workhorses and the sporting polo ponies and horses. Three polo fields were landscaped, and several houses were built to accommodate guests, including the Swiss Chalet, the Wellesley House, the Birches and the Tennis House.

George Boldt died on December 5, 1916, but to this day his family continues to return to the Thousand Islands.

The castle and most of the Boldt estates were sold to Edward J. Noble in 1916. Noble was born in nearby Gouverneur, New York, and spent his youth summering in the islands. He was the president of Life Savers, Inc., the candy company. In 1940 Noble bought a New York City radio station. This interest grew, and in 1943 he purchased the Blue Network Company from the Radio Corporation of America. In December 1944 the company was absorbed by the American Broadcasting Company and Noble was chairman of the board. The company merged with Paramount Theaters in 1953, and Noble was the largest single stockholder.

In 1940 Noble established the Edward John Noble Foundation to support educational, religious and charitable programs. He founded hospitals in the North Country, including the E.J. Noble Hospital, which was built on the site of the Thousand Island House in Alexandria Bay.

After Noble purchased Boldt Castle, he left it in the hands of a caretaker, and legend has it that when the caretaker died he left a great deal of money that he had collected from curious sightseers. Noble eventually opened the castle for tours; proceeds were given to the E.J. Noble Foundation.

Today the castle is the property of the Thousand Islands Bridge Authority.

HARBOR ISLAND

Historic Name

1816: Owen — Barracouta, Old Friends

Capt. William FitzWilliam Owen assumed command of the *Barracouta* when she arrived in port in India, where he was serving as superintendent of the transports and military equipment. Then he sailed to Java and remained on that coast for eight months, making friends with the ruling sultan of Bantean and various rulers on the coast of Sumatra.

On the voyage the *Barracouta* chased French frigates for six successive days, "sometimes within gun shot, and at times separated by four or five miles." The French outsailed his ship; however, he did capture several small vessels and dispatched information to the Admiralty. He continued to survey the waters of his passage and drew charts of the waters around the Maldives.

The island was also known as Deschler.

Sale

Sold as early as 1855 to Updike Dawson, and afterwards deeded to William T. McCue. It is described in Andrew Cornwall's notebook as "To Wm. T. McCue, Harbor Island or Green Island, 15 1/2 Acres from Stone on the island to Cornwall and Walton Store at Alexandria Bay. Is south 5 1/2 west, Sold for $50 — also called Green Island."

William McCue sold to the Deschler family from Columbus, Ohio, in August 1871.

SUNKEN ROCK LIGHTHOUSE

Names

The island was first called Bush Island.

Island Notes

The original lighthouse was installed in 1847 and refitted in 1855. It was an octagonal white brick tower covered with white painted boards. It stood more than 30 feet tall.

GUSSEY ISLAND

Names

Originally Gussey Island, the name was changed to Netts Island by 1871. Today it is known by both names.

Sale

Andrew Cornwall recorded the sale in his notebook as "1871 . . . to E.A. Kollnyer (Brooklyn) 285 Jay St. . . . An Island called Netts Island (Formerly Gussie Island) is between Deschler Island and Green Island and about North from C & W. Store and the small Island near the Head of Sawmill. [written with another pencil] $30."

ST. JOHN'S ISLAND

Sale

Originally described in the deed as "one of seven islands purchased at the same time." The seven islands include Belle Island and Chicken Island; Three Tree Island; and St. Mary's Island or Reformatory Island; St. John's Island; Stub Island; and Twist Island. These islands were sold to Judge C. Donahue of New York.

THREE TREE ISLAND

One of the seven islands sold to Judge Donahue.

TWIST ISLAND

One of the seven islands sold to Judge Donahue.

STUB ISLAND

One of the seven islands sold to Judge Donahue.

ST. MARY'S ISLAND

Names

Also known as Reformatory Island.

Sale

One of the seven islands sold to Judge Donahue.

BELLE ISLAND

Names

Also known as Chicken Island.

Sale

One of the seven islands sold to Judge Donahue.

MANHATTAN ISLAND

Historic name

1816: Owen — Sea Flower, Old Friends

In 1803 Owen was appointed to command the *Seaflower* (twelve guns) off the coast of France. The ship was used to protect the trade between Falmouth and the Downes. It was demasted in gale-force winds off the coast of France, and Owen barely escaped being taken prisoner.

In 1804 he sailed the *Seaflower* to India, carrying Admiralty dispatches. He arrived three months later, in June, "with the topsides of the vessel separated from the bottom" and the ship taking on water rapidly. When they reached Calcutta they repaired the *Seaflower*, but Owen reported that half the crew was lost from "jungle fever." The ship helped to protect a convoy around the Cape of Good Hope and served in various blockades.

On this voyage Owen began his career as a surveyor by examining the shores of Mauritius, Bourbon and Rodriguez. His sightings enabled sailors to approach Mauritius safely. Owen also examined and found a safe passage through the Maldives, which he called the Sea Flower Straights.

Island Notes

Seth Green, considered one of the first "summer people" wanting to live on an island, bought this small island near Alexandria Bay so he could study the habits of fish.

Green was born in Rochester, New York, in 1817. He was an avid fisherman and sportsman, which resulted in his "making them a life pursuit." He began fishing on Lake Ontario, opening a fish-and-game market near his home. It was so popular that he hired several fisherman and hunters to supply his business. His curiosity led him to scientific research, studying the spawning habits of fish. In 1868 his fish-hatchery experiments on the Connecticut River led to amazing results; over 25 percent of the salmon and trout that he raised lived. His project led to fifteen million eggs hatching in a two-week period, and the next year forty million hatched. He stocked the waters of the Hudson, Susquehannah, Potomac and other large rivers with about fifteen common species of fish. In 1867 he was appointed the fish commissioner for four of the Southern states, and his enthusiasm combined with his scientific acumen led to several other states establishing fish hatcheries and hiring experts, called pisciculturists. Green was the author of a number of books on the subject and invented many hatching boxes. He received prestigious awards before his death in 1888.

STEAMBOAT ISLAND

Historic Name

1816: Owen — Flamer, Old Friends

Beginning in 1797, Capt. William FitzWilliam Owen served as lieutenant-commander of the *Flamer*, seeing action in the North Sea and off the coast of Flanders. The *Flamer* was also ordered to protect the coast of south Wales at Swansea and served as patrol of the coastal trade at Falmouth, England.

The island was also known as Plantagenet Island and Johns Island.

Sale

The sale was recorded in Andrew Cornwall's notebook as "1856. . . to Henry A Brewster, Rochester. Trustee for Robert E. Brewster. . . An island known as Steamboat Island northeast from Green Island and near to it. $40."

CASINO ISLAND

Island Notes

Situated close by the Thousand Island House in Alexandria Bay, Casino Island was considered the entertainment complex for the fashionable hotel. A news release published in 1906 in the *Thousand Islands Sun* describes the last building that took place on the island:

June, 1906. The Casino takes definite form. Roof garden to be featured. The cost $15,000 and ready for occupancy on October 1. . . . The building when completed will be composed of three storeys, the roof garden and a number of provisional rooms for children's nurseries. The building will be equipped with all the latest devises [*sic*] known to pleasure and besides the roof garden and nurseries will also have bathing rooms for both ladies and gentlemen; bowling alleys; billiards; swimming pool; dancing pavilions. . . . Mr. George Walsh, the present manager of the Thousand House, News and Curios Stand will have charge of the new building when finished.

FAIRYLAND ISLAND

Historic Name

1816: Owen — Cornelia, Old Friends

Capt. William FitzWilliam Owen took command of the *Cornelia* in 1812. He was sent to the east coast of Sumatra, a French dependency, to conquer the place and to find an estimated $7 million "hard dollars" that were said to belong to a sultan.

On her last voyage, the *Cornelia*, with Owen at the helm, helped to liberate more than a thousand women and children being held prisoner on a South Sea island and capture almost five hundred pirates. The *Cornelia* eventually made its way back to England. Owen discovered that the ship was rotten and irreparable. This was his last voyage before being sent to Canada to do the survey of the lakes.

Island Notes

The island was sold in 1873 to Peter Hayden, who came to Alexandria Bay to find a summer retreat. He hired a river guide to take him around the region in pursuit of a perfect setting for an island home.

Hayden found his island off Alexandria Bay and soon divided it into three sections. He built on one end, while his two sons, Charles and William, built in the middle of the island and on a small island on the east end, called Estrillita. The island was called Fairyland by a visitor who exclaimed that the island was a "like a fairyland." The property remained in the Hayden family until the 1940s.

Description

2.8 acres

ESTRILLITA ISLAND

Island Notes

The island home of William Hayden was built on this small island as part of the Fairyland estate. The house was described in newspaper accounts as having twenty rooms, two large boathouses capable of housing eight or ten motorboats, docks and extensive shorelines.

Description

0.4 acres

THE HYDROGRAPHERS

One of the specially named groups of islands was called the Hydrographers in honour of the members of the survey team that took part in Capt. William FitzWilliam Owen's survey. The island names were recorded only on the British Admiralty charts and never adopted by their American owners. It is safe to say that the owners were unaware of these first names because the British charts were not widely circulated.

HISTORIC NAME	PRESENT NAME	PAGE
Henderson	Huguenot Island (American)	222
Buchanan	Rob Roy Island (American)	222
Green	Resort Island (American)	223
Owen	Deer Island (American)	223
FitzWilliam	Douglass Island (American)	223
Vidal	Lotus Island (American)	223
Venus	Ina Island (American)	224
Harris	Summerland Island (American)	225
Cranfield	Idlewild Island (American)	224
Amelia	Sport Island (American)	225
Bayfield	Arcadia Island (American)	225
Becher	Hadassah Island (American)	225

HUGUENOT ISLAND

Historic Name

1816: Owen — Henderson, the Hydrographers

Probably named after George Henderson (1783–1855), a lieutenant colonel in the Royal Engineers. He obtained his commission in 1800 and fought for Wellington in the Peninsular campaigns. At the close of the war he was stationed in Ireland until he was sent to Canada. He served on the Canadian Lakes survey with Captain Owen and is credited with surveying the channel around the island of Montreal.

Description

1.5 acres

MARY ISLAND

Historic Name

1816: Owen — Point Vittoria, the Wellington Islands

Sale

Island was purchased by New York State about 1891 as public park land.

Description

12.5 acres

ROB ROY ISLAND

Historic Name

1816: Owen — Buchanan, the Hydrographers

No biographical material is available. It was probably named after a man who served with Captain Owen on the survey team.

Sale

Sold to A.H. Greenswalt in 1885. The sale included Rob Roy and shoals for $300.

Description

1.0 acre

Deer Island.

RESORT ISLAND

Historic Name

1816: Owen — Green, the Hydrographers

No biographical material is available. It was probably named after a man who served with Captain Owen on the survey team.

Known as Walton Island when originally sold in 1872 and probably named after the Walton family from Alexandria Bay.

Sale

Recorded in Andrew Cornwall's notebook as sold in 1872 to the Watertown Club. "An Island East from Picnic and near to it. . . and known formerly as Old Picnic Island now named Walton Island. To Build in 1 year $100, together with a Small Island in the bay at upper or South West end of Main Island."

Description

1.1 acres

DEER ISLAND

Historic Name

1816: Owen — Owen, the Hydrographers

Named after Capt. William FitzWilliam Owen. (See Part I, Capt. William FitzWilliam Owen and the First Survey, 1815–17.)

Locally the island was named Deer Island as early as the 1850s.

Sale

Deer Island was one of the first to be sold as a summer retreat. Recorded in Andrew Cornwall's notebook as "1856, Sept 1. . . to S. Miller (Rochester). . . An Island known as Deer Island situated 3/4 of a mile North of the light house together with the Island nearest to it and North East of it on the head of which is a smooth rock and called Picnic [written with another pen] $175."

Island Notes

The island was first purchased by Samuel Miller in 1856. His son George Douglas Miller gave a fifteen-room stone cottage on the island, known as the "outlook," to Yale University's Skull and Bones Society. The building had stone foundations and walls, with a wooden superstructure. It housed many antiques and library books that were part of the Miller collection. The building and its extensive collection were destroyed by fire in 1949.

Description

50 acres

DOUGLASS ISLAND

Historic Name

1816: Owen — FitzWilliam, the Hydrographers

Named after Capt. William FitzWilliam Owen. (See Part I, Capt. William FitzWilliam Owen and the First Survey, 1815–17.)

The island was locally named Douglass after Douglass Miller, son of the original purchaser.

Description

7.0 acres

LOTUS ISLAND

Historic Name

1816: Owen — Vidal, the Hydrographers

Named after Vice Adm. Alexander Thomas Emeric Vidal (d.1863). Vidal entered the navy in December 1803. He served on the English Channel, on the North Sea, off the coast of Spain and in the West Indies. He was sent to Canada and first served as flag lieutenant to Comdr. Sir Edward Owen in Kingston. The commodore appointed Vidal to his brother William's survey team in February 1815.

In 1822, after completing the work on the Canadian Lakes, Vidal continued to serve under Captain Owen, this time aboard the *Leven* during the survey of the coast of Africa. He also served on the *Barracouta* and was promoted to commander. His service with Owen ended when he returned to England in October 1825.

Following the African survey, Vidal was charged with the task of locating the position of a dangerous rock called the Aitkins' Rock, said to be "small and 4 feet above water." Although Vidal never found the position, he did discover the Vidal Bank, which is located off the west coast of Ireland.

He continued surveying for the British Admiralty until 1845. He was considered "steadily devoted" and praised for his survey efforts. He was promoted to vice admiral and died at seventy-three in Clifton, England.

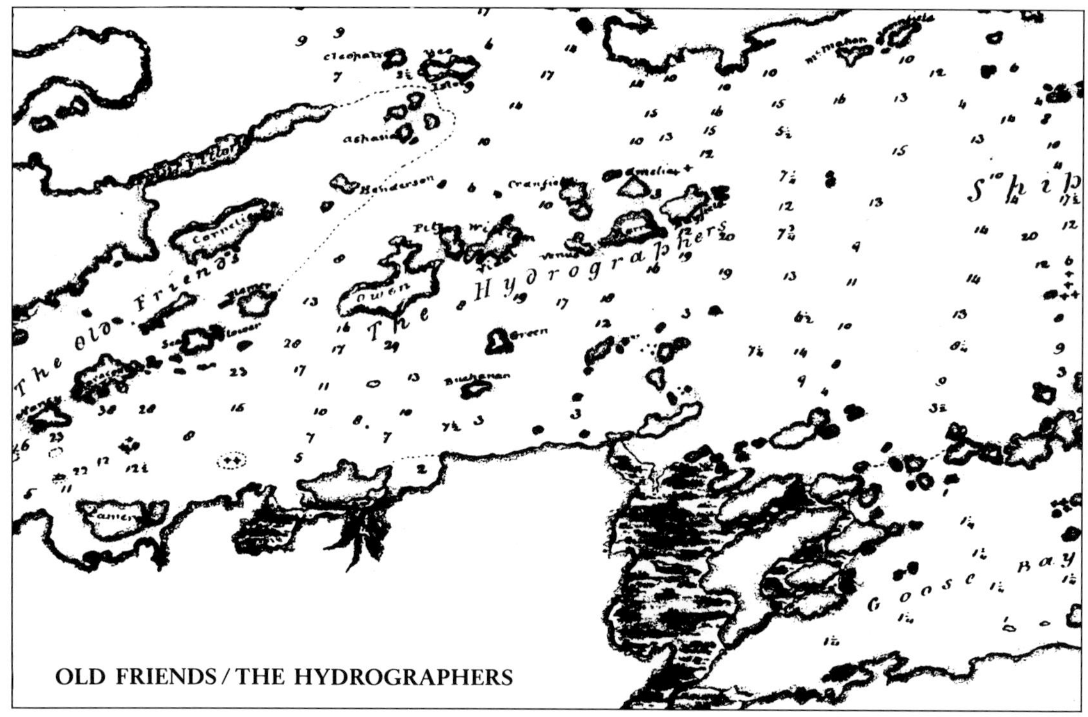

OLD FRIENDS / THE HYDROGRAPHERS

Sale

The island was first sold in 1872 to the Watertown Sportsmen's Club. It was sold again in 1883 to Sarah Robinson, who built her summer house.

Description

0.9 acres

ELEPHANT'S ROCK ISLAND

Sale

The island is recorded in Andrew Cornwall's notebook as being sold in "1871 . . . to Thomas C. Chittendon . . . An Island Called Elephant Rock on the North West side of the American Steam Boat Channel and is about North East from Old Picnic Island and about South West form Summer Land Island and then is a Group of small Islands between Summer Land and the above described Island."

INA ISLAND

Historic Name

1816: Owen — Venus, the Hydrographers

Named after William Venus (d. 1846). He entered the navy in 1800 and served on several ships off the coast of England.

He fought in the Battle of Trafalgar in October 1805. He next served in the West Indies as well as in Halifax on the North American Station; at Walcheren, off the coast of Guernsey; in the Baltic; and finally in the East Indies and Java. Venus returned to England and in 1814 was sent to Quebec and then to Kingston to serve on the *Prince Regent* and the St. Lawrence under both Sir James Yeo and Sir Edward Owen. During the Great Lakes survey, Lieutenant Venus was in command of ships on Lake Ontario and lakes Erie, St. Clair and Huron. He is also credited with surveying around the island of Montreal.

The island was named Ina after Ina Bessie Briggs.

Sale

The island was sold in 1871 to Samuel A. Briggs from Chicago for $150. Briggs also purchased Arcadia Island. Recorded by Andrew Cornwall in his notebook as "Five Islands in a chain one called 'Arcadie' North East of Summerland Land (Island) about 4 rods from it and contains about 3 or 4 acres land the other called 'Ina' and is South West from Summer Land and bout 4 rods from it, and contains about one acres . . . letter from J.W. Pullman on file and Recd his check on West Side Bank N.Y. for $150. [written with another pen] $150."

The island was sold to Mrs. A.T. Hagen in 1896.

Description

20 acres

IDLEWILD ISLAND

Historic Name

1816: Owen — Cranfield, the Hydrographers

Named after Lieut. George Cranfield, a member of the 90th Foot and appointed draftsman for Owen's survey of the Great Lakes and the upper St. Lawrence River. He was transferred to the survey on October 24, 1816, after serving as deputy assistant in the quartermaster department.

A letter in the archives written by Thomas Hurd, British Admiralty hydrographer, states: "A draftsman formed part of the Captain Owen's original outfit from England, but as he did not join in time to embark with the rest of the party on board the vessel appointed to convey them to Canada, the Captain was under the necessity of procuring such an officer on the spot and I consider it very fortunate for the service he was employed on that one so well qualified for such an employment was met with in the person of Lieut. Cranfield, whose works speak for themselves."

He continued to receive his regiment allowance for as long as he was attached to the Royal Navy. There is no other biographical information available.

The island was also called Free and Easy.

Description

Boyd's Illustrated Guide of 1882 notes: "is down the bay and has several cottages, and is one of the most attractive of islands because of its formation, as it possesses sloping banks and rugged bluffs, with tangled brush. It is one and one-half acres in area, and is owned by Robert Packer, Sayre, Pa."

4.3 acres

SUNNYSIDE ISLAND

Names

Also known as Hadassah Island

Description

Boyd's Illustrated Guide of 1882 notes: "is owned by H. Packer, of Mauch Chunk. It comprises one acre."

2.3 acres

SUMMERLAND ISLAND

Historic Name

1816: Owen — Harris, the Hydrographers

Named after Master John Harris (d. 1783), who entered the navy in England in 1803. From 1815 to 1817 he served in Canada, and Comdr. Edward Owen appointed him to the survey team at the same time as Lieutenant Vidal. He married Amelia Ryerse and together they lived in Kingston at the Hydrographer's House. Harris served under Capt. William FitzWilliam Owen throughout his tenure in Canada.

He remained in Canada after the survey was completed and eventually moved to London, Ontario. During the Rebellion of 1837 (see Part I, The Patriot War, 1837–38) he participated in the burning of the *Caroline* near Niagara Falls. He served as treasurer of the London District from 1823 to 1846.

Sale

The island was originally recorded in Andrew Cornwall's notebook as being sold in "1871. . . to Jas M. Pullman, of NY, Almon Gunnison of Brooklyn and Richd. Fisk Sr. of Canton. . . An Island called Summer Land situated in the North West side of the American Steam Boat Channel. . . and Also the Rocks or small Islands that may be common therewith by shoals the water upon which does not exceed one foot in depth at Low Water mark suppose to contain about 10 or 13 acres. [written with another pen] $100."

Island Notes

The island was purchased in 1871 to be used as a summer camp for the families of three Universalist ministers. In 1872 the island guest book had some two dozen guests coming for a holiday. The Summerland Association was formed in 1879 with seven directors: Almon Gunnison, Richmond, Fisk, Sears E. Brace, Joseph A. Stull, George H. Newell, Asa Saxe and Emory B. Chace. The by-laws stipulated that "all building improvements and sanitary regulations subject to approval of directors," and "all deeds and leases shall contain a clause for purpose of restricting nuisances and compelling a uniform system of improvement — forbidding the sale or keeping for sale any spirits or intoxicating liquors." The rules also limited the number of overnight accommodations for members of immediate family "not to exceed 6 except by special permission."

In 1873 a dining hall was built. It was called Gellig Hall, which was decided by placing six letters in a hat and being "juggled into a name." For a few years a boarding-house provided guest accommodations with meals costing $1 for adults and sixty cents for children.

In 1961 Estelle E. Hawley published a history of the island. It contains family photographs and delightful personal memories. (Available in local libraries.)

LITTLE LEHIGH ISLAND

Sale

Described by Andrew Cornwall as being sold in 1872 to: "Solan D. Hungerford. An Island called Island Home and is out side about West from Sport Island and about 4 to 6 Rods from the upper or South West end of Sport Island and North East form five . . . and nearly South from Grenadier Island Light House. to build in two years. [written with another pencil] building clause wavered."

Description

0.8 acres

SPORT ISLAND

Historic Name

1816: Owen — Amelia, the Hydrographers

Named after Amelia Ryerse who married Master John Harris in 1815. During the survey they lived in Kingston at the Hydrographer's House. Amelia was given the title of "Honourary Hydrographer." She traced the soundings on large sheets of paper, and her husband cautioned her to make sure the drawings were accurate because he thought they would be used to set the international boundary line separating Canada from the United States.

Description

Boyd's Illustrated Guide in 1882 notes: "is the property of Mr. H.A. Packer, of Mauch Chunk, Pa. It has an area of one acre, and is being rapidly fitted up with a very fine building which when completed will be one of the finest on the islands."

3.9 acres

ARCADIA ISLAND

Historic Name

1816: Owen — Bayfield, the Hydrographers

Named after Henry Wolsey Bayfield. He entered the Royal Navy in 1806, and six years later he was sent to Canada to serve in the War of 1812. Captain Owen discovered Bayfield on board a ship in

Sport Island. — Photograph appearing in James Bayne Company, *The Thousands Island and the River St. Lawrence*

Quebec and requested that he join the survey crew in Kingston. He served on the survey of Lake Ontario, the Upper St. Lawrence and the Niagara River. He was appointed Admiralty surveyor in June 1817, replacing Captain Owen when he was recalled to London.

Bayfield is considered the "Father of Canadian hydrography" and several biographies have been written. He completed about forty charts of the St. Lawrence Gulf and River.

Sale

The island was originally sold with Ina Island in 1871 to S.A. Briggs.

Island Notes

Samuel Briggs built a house on the bluff at the west end of Arcadia Island. It was torn down in 1925.

Description

5.0 acres

SCHOONER ISLAND

Island Notes

Described in an early river tourist guide as being a 5-acre island, "landscaped with shade trees, gardens and blueberry bushes."

Description

5.0 acres

Boyd's Illustrated Guide, 1882, notes that the island: "is known as Riverhome, is owned by J.H. Whitehouse, of New York."

BIRCH ISLAND

Names

Originally known as Birch Island. When the island was sold to Mary E. Flower, she changed the name to May Flower Island. It was also registered as Pittsburg Island.

Sale

Andrew Cornwall's notebook recorded the sale to "Wm. I. Lewis and Sarah Lewis, from Pittsburgh, Pa. on Sept. 5th, 1874." The deed stipulated that a house be built within five years.

A year later the island was sold and again registered in the Cornwall notebook as "May Flower Island 1875, Sept. 3rd. . .To Mary E. Flower. An Island near the Westerly End of an Island formerly called Burch Island now called Pittsburg conveyed to Wm. I. Lewis and Sarah Lewis 5th Sept. 1875 and is North from the upper end of Island Number Nine and about East from Schooner Island and is named May Flower. $100"

Description

4.6 acres

KRING POINT STATE PARK

Sale

The original Ira Kring homestead was purchased by the New York State government to be a state park. At first, visitors could use the park only if they arrived by boat, but in the 1920s a road was laid out.

LITTLE DELIGHT

No information is available.

Description

0.3 acres

LITTLE ERIN ISLAND

No information is available.

Description

0.3 acres

DIAMOND ISLAND

No information is available.

Description

0.3 acres

MORGAN ISLAND

No information is available.

Description

7.25 acres

CLOUDS NEST ISLAND

Sale

Registered as being sold as early as 1885 to Abraham H. Greenswalt for $300.

See boxed text, Canadian Sector, the British Statesmen, for a full description of islands listed in the British Statesmen.

IRONSIDES

Historic Name

1816: Owen — Liverpool, the British Statesmen Named after Prime Minister Robert Banks Jenkinson, 2nd Earl of Liverpool (1770–1828). This British statesman was in Paris during the storming of the Bastille in 1789. He was elected a member of Parliament, was master of the Mint in 1799, and served in Addington's ministry as foreign secretary. He was home secretary from 1804 to 1806, and again from 1807 to 1809. He was appointed secretary for war and the colonies in 1809 and served until 1812. A firm supporter of Wellington, Liverpool approved the strengthening of the army. He became prime minister in 1812. Liverpool is credited with supporting the war against Napoleon, but his administration of the Canadian colony during the War of 1812 was not considered successful. The last years of his ministry were plagued by domestic and economic problems.

Sale

In the 1960s the island was donated by William Browning to the Nature Conservancy to serve as a rookery for blue herons.

Description

17.9 acres

LITTLE IRONSIDES ISLAND

Historic Name

1816: Owen — Castlereagh, the British Statesmen Named after Robert Stewart, 2nd Marquis of Londonderry, known generally as Viscount Castlereagh (1760–1822). This British statesman was educated at Cambridge and was elected a member of Parliament in 1790. He served as chief secretary for Ireland from 1799 to 1801. He was president of the East India Board of Control in 1802 and was Pitt's war secretary from 1805 to 1806 and again from 1807 to 1809.

He was foreign secretary and leader of the House of Commons during the time of the survey of the Canadian Lakes.

Castlereagh was responsible for choosing St. Helena Island as the place of confinement for Napoleon after the Battle of Waterloo. Castlereagh suffered a breakdown and committed suicide in 1822. He is buried in Westminster Abbey.

HEMLOCK ISLAND

Names

Recorded on an 1872 map as Hemlock Island. The island is also known as Nervina Island and is recorded as such on a deed.

Sale

Recorded as being sold to Dr. J.H. Brownlow of Ogdensburg.

SNIPE ISLAND

Names

Recorded on an 1872 map as Snipe Island. No other information is available.

WATCH ISLAND

Names

Recorded on an 1872 map as Watch Island. No other information is available.

ST. MARGARATES ISLAND

Names

Recorded on an 1872 map as High Island. No other information is available.

HALFWAY ISLAND

Names

Recorded on an 1872 map as Halfway Island.

Sale

The Chapman family bought the island in 1892.

Island Notes

The island was first purchased by Seth Pope of Ogdensburg. It was sold to Frank Chapman in 1892 for $100. The purchase was actually for two islands that were separated by a narrow channel. Chapman had this filled with rock and soil, thus creating one large island. The filled area became a tennis court. The Chapmans also bought a boathouse in Morristown and had it brought upriver on a barge. Several Thousand Islands boathouses were moved this way; in winter, they were brought across the ice by horses.

RABBIT ISLAND

Historic Name

1816: Owen — Norton Island, the Indian Allies Named after John Norton (Teyoninhokarawen). His father was a Cherokee who as a young boy had been taken from North America to Scotland after the British burned his village. He married an Englishwoman and lived near Dunfermline, Scotland. His son John probably first came to Canada as a schoolteacher on the reserve at Deseronto, on the Bay of Quinte. John Norton did not like teaching and eventually went west, but returned to Upper Canada and became an interpreter in the Indian Department at Niagara. He later translated part of the Bible into Mohawk.

In the first year of the War of 1812, Norton assembled and commanded native allied troops. He

THE INDIAN ALLIES

Sir Isaac Brock once said he knew the Indian Allies would be useful for intimidating the enemy. They were so frightening that both British and American troops often turned and ran at the "sight or sound" of enemy natives. Britain relied on these warriors to increase its fighting power.

One of the manoeuvres at Detroit in 1812 saw Tecumseh march his small group past a clearing in view of the American forces. They then doubled back through the woods and passed again — thereby giving the impression of a much larger force!

The Indian Allies aided in capturing Detroit, Fort Dearborn, and helped prevent an early American victory in the West. Many served in the Niagara campaign and on Lake Michigan.

OWEN	PRESENT NAME	PAGE
Norton	Rabbit Island (American)	227
Kate Islands	St. Ann Island and Jug Island (American)	229
Tecumseth (*sic*)	Oak Island (American)	229
Walk-in-the-Water	Brush Island (American)	230
Split Log	Wyanoke Island (American)	230
Prophet	Atlantis Island (American)	231
Blackbird	Manzanita Island (American)	231
John Brandt (*sic*)	Cedar Island (American)	231

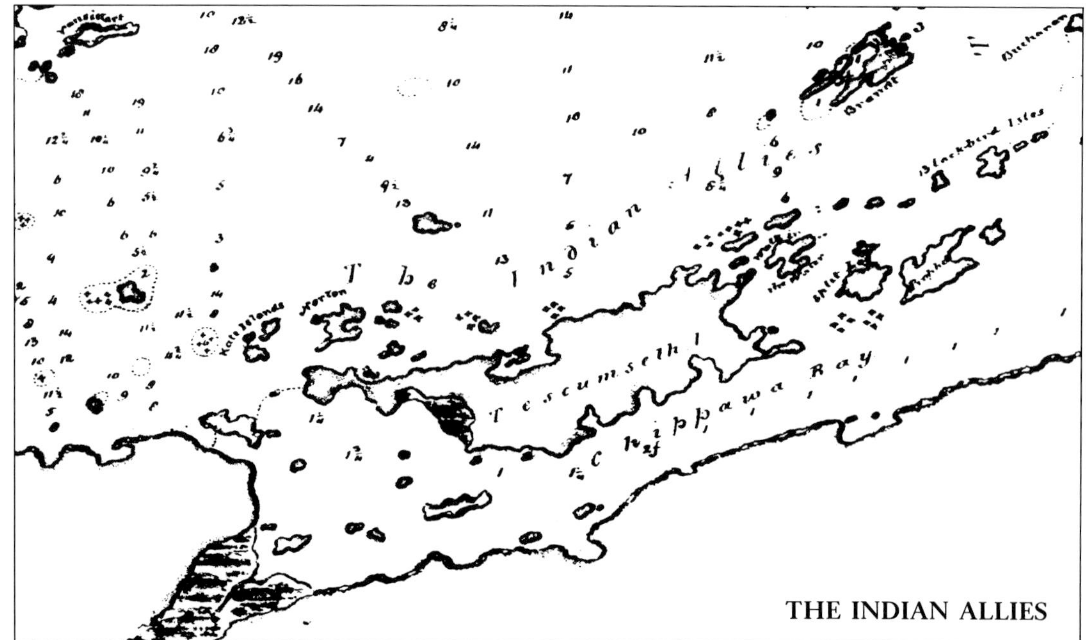
THE INDIAN ALLIES

Major John Norton.
— Mary Ann Knight, Artist, National Archives of Canada C123832

fought at Queenston Heights and is often mentioned in dispatches throughout 1813 and 1814. During the war Norton met and married a woman named Catherine. He received a commission in the British army and was unofficially called Colonel Norton. In 1823 he was convicted of manslaughter for having accidentally killed a young native in a duel, a man he accused of having an affair with his wife. He moved out west and is thought to have died there in 1831.

Description

Boyd's Illustrated Guide, 1882, notes that the island "is the property of Mr. William Littlejohn, of Hammond."

Three islands near Rabbit Island.

ST. ANN ISLAND

Historic Name

1816: Owen — Kate Islands, the Indian Allies Probably named after John Norton's wife, Catherine (Karighwaycagh), who was a Delaware. Norton and Catherine were married in 1813, and she accompanied her husband to England and Scotland in 1815. They remained for a year, and while there she attended school and learned to read and write. In 1823 Norton fought a duel with Catherine's cousin and killed him (see above).

St. Ann Island was also known as Jug Island, Chub Island and Observation Island. Today the adjacent island is known as Jug Island.

SCOW ISLAND

Names

Its name was derived from the scows that came to the island to collect timber for rafting. The timber would have been cut from the islands in Chippewa Bay and along the main shore.

OWATONNA ISLAND

First sold in 1896 to summer residents.
No additional information is available.

OAK ISLAND

Historic Name

1816: Owen — Tescumseth (*sic*), the Indian Allies Tecumseh (c. 1768–1813), was a Shawnee chief also known as Crouching Panther. He united the Western Indians against the Americans and sided with the British during the War of 1812. When Isaac Brock planned his attack on Detroit in August 1812, Tescumseh and his six hundred warriors were eager to assist. The American commander, General Hull, realizing the threat to his troops, surrendered without a fight.

Tecumseh was devastated a year later when the British generals withdrew from the Detroit frontier. He always believed the British would help the

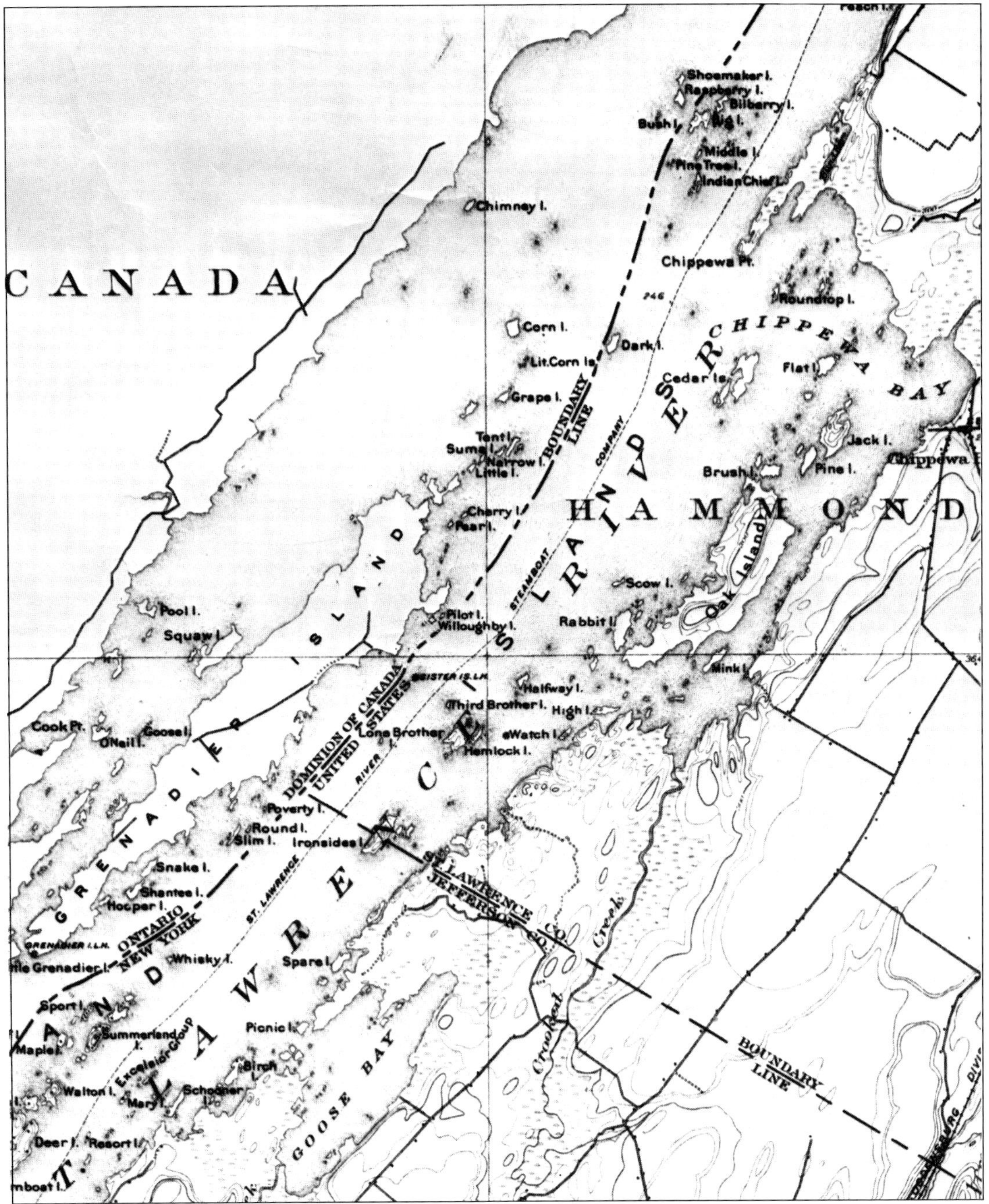

Chippewa Bay. — U.S. Geological Survey, 1903

Tecumseh, a celebrated native chief.
— Metropolitan Toronto Reference Library, J. Ross Robertson Collection T16600

natives maintain their land. By the time the British commanders had moved to safe territory, many of Tecumseh's native forces had withdrawn. When the battle was finally fought at Moraviantown on October 5, 1813, the natives numbered five hundred while the American detachments numbered three thousand. Tecumseh was killed in the battle. It has been said that native resistance south of the Great Lakes ceased with the death of their leader. Colonel Brock wrote to Lord Liverpool in 1812, giving this tribute: "He, who attracted most my attention, was a Shawnee Chief, Tescumseh. A more sagacious or a more gallant warrior does not, I believe, exist. He was the admiration of everyone who conversed with him."

On the 1818 International Boundary survey map the island is identified as Indian Hut Island.

Sale

The Lyon family purchased Oak island in the late 1800s.

Island Notes

In 1907 J.B. Reed, from Alexandria Bay, was hired to build the family home for the Lyons. It was a three-storey house with six bedrooms, living room, dining room, pantry, kitchen and baths. Part of the island was cleared and farmed.

There is a stone quarry on Oak Island. The stone for Boldt Castle was quarried there, as was much of the stone for Jordstat Castle on Dark Island. Some 150 stonemasons worked the quarry under the direction of quarry foreman, William Plimpton. They worked more than four years, taking granite out for Boldt Castle. Evidently the stone cutters followed a precise plan outlined by the architects. The foreman made sure each piece was cut to specifications, so that little had to be done when the stone arrived at the construction site. The granite had to be transported from the quarry walls to the shoreline by railway car, pulled by a horse, then taken by barge to the island. Many large pieces were cut, including some 20-foot-long sections used for steps.

Description

Described as being between "375 and 500 acres." It is the largest island in Chippewa Bay.

MINK ISLAND

Names

Appears on an 1872 map as Mink Island. Also called Treasure Island.

BRUSH ISLAND

Historic Name

1816: Owen — Walk-in-the-Water, the Indian Allies Named after a Wyanot or Shawnee chief who served in the War of 1812.

Also known as Belle Isle, after the Belle family who first purchased the island and built a house. The first house built on the island was destroyed by fire in the 1880s.

Sale

Sold in 1882 to Dr. W.M. Belle.

PRESTON ISLAND

Names

Also known as the Shoal.

Sale

Sold in 1902 to the Preston family.

CHOKE CHERRY ISLAND

Sale

Sold in 1886 to Jas. G. Knap.

TOOTHPICK ISLAND

No information available.

THE ROCK

Names

Also known as Hogs Back or Hogsback Island. It was later called the Rock.

GRANTS ISLAND

No information is available.

WYANOKE ISLAND

Historic Name

1816: Owen — Split Log, the Indian Allies Named after Split Log, a Huron. He served at Frenchtown in January 1813.

Also known as Joe's Island, owned by an old hermit or a runaway slave named Joe. *Wyanoke* is supposed to mean "going around the place."

Sale

Calvin B. Orcutt bought the island some time in the 1890s. He was one of the early guests invited to Atlantis Island to visit the Bailey family. He saw Wyanoke Island and decided it was the perfect place to bring his family.

Daughters of C.B. Orcutt, Commodore of the New York Yacht Club. Boathouse circa 1894, still standing.
— Alan Newell, Wyanoke Island

TEMAGAMI ISLAND

Name

Named Ingleneuk by Frederic Remington and later renamed Temagami by one of the island purchasers, who also owned a tree stand in the Temagami region of Ontario.

Sale

A man named Sheppard sold the island to Frederic Remington, who, after financial problems, sold the island to the Strong family.

Island Notes

Frederic Remington, one of America's great artists, spent ten years on the island, often getting local residents to model for his works. It was not unusual for Remington to ask a group of boys to paddle a canoe by the island for a particular scene in one of his paintings. (The Remington Museum is located in Ogdensburg, New York.)

ATLANTIS ISLAND

Historic Name

1816: Owen — Prophet, the Indian Allies Named after the Shawnee, Tenskwatawa (also called Lolawauchika and Elskwatawa), who was the brother of Tecumseh (see Part II, The American Islands, Tecumseh Island, Chippewa Bay). In 1811 he was defeated in the Battle of Tippacanoe by the American Army under William Henry Harrison. Up until that time he was considered a religious mystic or evangelist, but he lost his prestige when he lost the battle. He lived on a British pension after the War of 1812.

The island appears on an 1872 map as Jack Island, named after a runaway slave who lived there in the late 1860s.

Island Notes

The island was purchased from Cornwall and Walton by Henry Denner, who bought several islands in Chippewa Bay. About 1885, Denner sold the island to Dr. George W. Bailey for use as a summer residence. Bailey named the island Atlantis and was responsible for inviting several guests to the region, many of whom purchased islands for themselves.

TWILIGHT ISLAND

No information is available.

MANZANITA ISLAND

Historic Name

1816: Owen — Blackbird Island, the Indian Allies The name did not appear on the 1816 hand-drawn chart, but was included on the engraved charts that were dated in 1818 and published in 1828.

Named after a Huron called Assiginack, or Blackbird, who defected to the American forces in 1814.

The island appears on an 1872 map as Flat Island. It is also known as Cleared Island. *Manzanita* is the Spanish word for "little apple." The island was named by the Knap family in 1886 after the manzanita bush that grows in California. The owners visited California the winter after they purchased the island and thus adopted a descriptive name for their island.

Sale

In 1886 the island was sold to James G. Knap. It remains in the Knap family.

CEDAR ISLAND

Historic Name

1816: Owen — John Brandt (*sic*), the Indian Allies Named after John Brant (Anyonewaeghe), son of Joseph Brant. He was born in 1794, and his mother was Brant's third wife. He fought at Queenston and in the Battle at Beaver Dam. He died at Mohawk Village in Upper Canada in 1832.

Sale

From 1838 to 1876 Ezra Brockway lived on Cedar Island. In 1885 the island was deeded to Martin Phillips, who built a hotel. In 1905 New York State purchased half the island for the state park system.

Island Notes

From 1838 to 1876 the island was occupied by Ezra Brockway, a so-called hermit who evidently believed he was the son of Napoleon. He remained on the island for almost forty years and made a medicinal salve that he peddled on the mainland to raise money. During the winter of 1876 Brockway died, and his body was discovered by some passing residents who did not see the smoke that usually came from the chimney of his cabin.

Captain John Brant Ahyouwaighs, Chief of the Six Nations.
— Metropolitan Toronto Reference Library, J. Ross Robertson Collection T15499

The "Hunting Lodge" on Dark Island. — National Archives of Canada C27930

DARK ISLAND

Historic Name

1816: Owen — Chatham, the British Statesmen Probably named in honour of William Pitt, Earl of Chatham (1708–78), known as the Elder Pitt, or possibly after his eldest son, Sir John Pitt, the 2nd Earl of Chatham.

In 1818 the International Boundary Commission map recorded the island as Bluff Island.

It also appears on an 1872 map as Round or Dark Island, evidently named because of the many dark green evergreen trees that grew on the island.

Sale

Andrew Cornwall's notebook records the island as being sold in 1892 to "to William H. Harrison Jr & W. Harrison. . . All that Tract Land or Parcel known and described on the old Gov. map made by W.A. Bird as 'Bluff Island' said map being now in the possession of the party of the first part said. Land now recently known as 'Dark Island'. . . Consideration $500."

Sold in 1905 to Comdr. F. Bourne.

Island Notes

Frederick Bourne, a Singer Sewing Machine executive, built a castle on Dark Island, which he described as a hunting lodge. It cost an estimated $500,000 at that time! There are secret passages in the house, including underground passageways from the house to the boathouse. The front reception hall is like those found in European or British hunting lodges, complete with enormous fireplaces and medieval suits of armour standing guard in the hall. One of the unique features of the house is the indoor squash court, added by the second generation of the family.

Bourne was commodore of the New York Yacht Club, one of the most prestigious yacht clubs in North America. He brought many guests to the island and was considered one of the wealthiest men to live in the region. When he died, the island was left to his children. Court battles began as members of the family argued over the value and ownership of the castle. Preys Bourne Thayer, Bourne's daughter, eventually took possession and went to the Thousand Islands for a few weeks every season. In 1962 the property was given to the LaSalle Military College, on Long Island, New York State, with the understanding that Mrs. Thayer would have use of the property during her lifetime. When she died a few years later, the school sold the property to a religious order from the province of Quebec.

IRON ISLAND

Names

So named because the island was used as a depot for storing pig iron that was made inland and transported across the ice during the winter. In the spring the ships would pull in beside Iron Island to pick up loads of iron.

GARDEN ISLAND

Island Notes

Used by Chippewa Bay families for picnics in the late 1800s. The island was purchased in 1915 and a cottage was built. Several aboriginal artifacts were found during excavation.

SNAKEOIL ISLAND

Historic Name

1816: Owen — Buchanan and Shacklock (drawn as two islands), the Amateur Islands

Named after an officer, Buchanan, who along with the other members of his regiment left for England on the same discharge notice. No biographical material is available for Shacklock.

OLIVE ISLE

Historic Name

1816: Owen — Sadler, the Amateur Islands

No biographical information or information about the islands is available.

BLUFF ISLAND

Historic Name

1816: Owen — Jebb, the Amateur Islands

Named after Sir Joshua Jebb (1793–1863), who served in Upper Canada during Captain Owen's survey. He was an artist and a member of the Royal Engineers and served first in Prescott, where he sketched Fort Wellington, and at Brockville, where he examined the courthouse. During the summer of 1816, he was transferred to Kingston. After the survey was completed, Jebb was sent to survey the Rideau Canal system. His most well-known sketch is entitled *Sketch from Nature: Two Ottawa Chiefs who with others lately came down from Mihilimakinac and Lake Huron to have a talk with their great Father the King or his representative.*

After serving in Canada from 1813 to 1820, Jebb returned to England, where he became surveyor general of prisons in Britain from 1837 to 1842. He was appointed inspector general of prisons in 1844. He wrote several reports on prison reform.

Island Notes

This was to be one of three islands purchased by Henry Denner from a native known as Dick. Denner built a seven-bedroom house in 1887. Several aboriginal artifacts have been found along the shores of Bluff Island. Like most of the islands in Chippewa Bay, the region served as a summer campground for native families living in the region long before the white man came to the area.

LONE TREE ISLAND

Historic Names

1816: Owen — Herbert, the Amateur Islands

Named after M.H. Herbert, acting commander of the *Star*. He was appointed to this position by Captain Owen on February 21, 1816. Owen described him as being "fit for the situation."

ELM TREE ISLAND

Historic Name

1816: Owen — Stephenson, the Amateur Islands

The regiment records show that when the 70th Foot was disbanded, Captain Stephenson was being sent to Edinburgh, Scotland, as were a Captain McKay and a Lieutenant Bland.

CHIPPEWA POINT

Historic Name

1816: Owen — Goldfarp, the Amateur Islands

Named after Lieutenant Goldfarp, who was attached to the command of Captain McKay, commander of the 70th Foot.

INDIAN CHIEF ISLAND

Historic Name

1816: Owen — Redigar Island, the Amateur Islands

No biographical information or information about the island is available.

MIDDLE ISLAND

Historic Name

1816: Owen — Smeachman, the Amateur Islands

No biographical information or information about the island is available.

BIG ISLAND

Historic Name

1816: Owen — Ross, the Amateur Islands

Named after John Ross, who was discharged the same day in December 1816 as many of the other members of the regiment listed in the Amateur Group.

Also called Mananna Island.

BILBERRY ISLAND

Historic Name

1816: Owen — Wood, the Amateur Islands

Named after Ensign Wood, member of the 70th Foot.

CROSSOVER ISLAND

Historic Name

1816: Owen — McKay, the Amateur Islands

Named after a member of the 70th Foot. The regiment was formed in the Glasgow lowlands and came to Upper Canada from Ireland in June 1814. The regiment remained in the Kingston region until 1828.

Island Notes

One of the first important lighthouses was built on Crossover Island in the 1840s. The light marked the division of the two main channels through the Thousand Islands.

Scene near Morristown. — Metropolitan Toronto Reference Library, J. Ross Robertson Collection T15324

General Sir Isaac Brock.

— Metropolitan Toronto Reference Library, J. Ross Robertson Collection. T15067

AMERICAN ISLAND

Historic Name

1816: Owen — Brock, the Brock Isles

Named after Sir Isaac Brock, army officer and colonial administrator in Upper Canada when war was declared in 1812. When he was fifteen, he purchased an ensigncy in the 8th Foot. In 1802 Brock was sent to Canada. He was promoted to colonel in 1805, and was responsible for establishing the Provincial Marine, which provided transport service on the St. Lawrence River and the Great Lakes.

Brock was sent to Upper Canada in 1810. His biographers say he often wished to be part of the greater battles that were being fought with Wellington in the Peninsula, but as relations between the United States deteriorated, Brock realized the importance of establishing an army in Upper Canada. By the time Francis Gore, the lieutenant-governor, departed for England on leave in October 1811, Brock was chief administrator for the province.

When war brock out in June 1812, Brock plunged energetically into battle. He was in command at Detroit, using the services of the Indian Allies, under the command of Tecumseh. Then in October Brock realized that the long line between Niagara and Lake Erie would be difficult to defend. At the Battle of Queenston Heights Brock proved his great ability to motivate his troops, but he was killed in action. Four days before, he was recognized for his victory at Detroit by his appointment as knight of the Order of the Bath. He is recognized in Canada by the monument at Queenston and with many streets, towns and public institutions named in his honour.

BOGARDUS ISLAND

Historic Name

1816: Owen — Glegg, the Brock Isles

Named after Capt. John Baskervyle Glegg, a member of the 49th regiment. He served as adjutant-general to Sir Isaac Brock. He was present at Detroit and received a Gold Medal for his actions. He also fought beside Brock at Queenston and fought in the battles at Fort Erie and Lundy's Lane. Glegg died in Cheshire, England, in April 1861.

OLD MAN ISLAND

Historic Names

1816: Owen — Grant, the Brock Isles

Probably named after Col. Lewis Grant, who was an ensign in the 1st Lennox Militia. He served under Colonel Cartwright at Kingston from 1812 to 1813. He was present at the battles of Crysler's Farm, Oswego, Lundy's Lane and Fort Erie. After the war he remained in Upper Canada. He was appointed attorney general in 1837 and was made a judge in 1840. Grant died in May 1874.

The island was also known as Ogden Island.

Island Notes

Always considered the "Hermit's Island" because an elderly man named Henry Graham lived on the island. He died after falling through the ice in 1849. In the later 1880s an article in the Brockville *Recorder and Times* recorded that "Mr. William B.H. Johnson would respectfully inform the inhabitants of Brockville and its vicinity that he has lately bought that island directly opposite the town of Brockville and within a short distance of the American shore, commonly known as the Hermit's Island, and intends laying out as a pleasure garden for the public's accommodation. Refreshments kept always on hand. Picknickers [*sic*] and pleasure parties will receive every attention."

REFERENCES FOR PART II

HISTORIC NAME

Biographical information is recorded in the *Dictionary of National Biography.*

George Smith, founder, *Dictionary of National Biography, From the Beginnings to 1900*. London: Oxford University Press, Smith, Elder and Company, 1903; reprinted 1965.

In some cases, additional information found in books or articles relating to the Peninsular War was added to the biographies.

David G. Chandler. *Dictionary of Napoleonic Wars*. New York: Macmillan Publishers Co. Inc., 1979.

Some of the biographical information relating to the islands lying in the Navy group, the Indian Allies and the Brock Isles can be found in:

L. Homfray Irving. *Officers of the British Forces in Canada During the War of 1812*. Welland, Ont.: Canadian Military Institute, 1908.

Much of the biographical information relating to the Admiralty Islands and the islands lying near Grenadier Island (Rockport) can be found in two volumes:

J.C. Sainty. *Admiralty Officials 1600–1879*, Vol. IV. London: Athlone Press, 1975.

J.C. Sainty. *Treasury Officials 1660–1870*. London: Athlone Press, 1976.

One of the best references for information relating to the Lake Fleet Islands can be found in:

C.P. Stacey. "The Ships of the British Squadron on Lake Ontario, 1812–14," *Canadian Historical Review, XXXIV.*

Military information relating to the battles Wellington fought, commemorated with the naming of prominent points on Wellesley Island, comes from:

Brig. Michael Calvert. *A Dictionary of Battles, 1715–1815*. New York: Mayflower Books, 1979.

EVALUATIONS AND DESCRIPTIONS

The Canadian descriptions and evaluations recorded by John McNaughton (1862), Charles Unwin (1873) and Walter Beatty (1894) can be found in:

John McNaughton. *Schedules and Diary Examination Survey, 1862–63*, Field book: 210A.

NAC, RG10 Volume 2495, Complete volume. Includes *Address of the House of Commons* dated March 30, 1894. Department of the Interior, and the Superintendent General of Indian Affairs.

Canadian Islands in the River St. Lawrence Opposite the Township of Leeds, Landsdowne [sic], Escott and Yonge, 1874, Plans 515–518. Field Notes. Charles Unwin, P.L.S. survey, 1873.

Canadian Islands in the River St. Lawrence Between Townships of Yonge and Gananoque, Map of the St. Lawrence River, Enlarged from Bayfield's Chart, Showing Canadian Islands from Howe Island to Lake Ontario. Walter Beatty, 1893, published 1894, Plan 1464.

ISLAND NOTES

Much of the information quoted from newspaper sources can be found on microfilm in back copies of the *Gananoque Reporter*, the Brockville *Recorder and Times* and the *Thousand Islands Sun*, published in Alexandria Bay. They are found in local libraries. Information from the *Watertown Daily Times* is also quoted.

Gananoque Reporter:

"The Thousand Islands," April 26, 1873

"The Thousand Islands," April 18, 1874

"The Thousand Islands," April 30, 1874

"Fires," September 5, 1874

"Trespass on the Islands," July 13, 1875

"The Islands," May 13, 1876

"Jack Straw Light," April 1881

"The Islands," August 12, 1882

"The Granite Quarries," March 17, 1883

"The Illumination," August 22, 1884

"The Summer Hotel Scheme," August 24, 1885

"Tremont Park," July 2, 1887

"Gananoque's Early Days," June 9, 1888

"The Canoe Club," August 17, 1889

"Chauncey Patterson Drowned," August 30, 1890

"Hay Island House," February 23, 1895

"Twice Told Tales," August 28, 1903

"Twice Told Tales," June 28, 1813
"Died at His Island Home," July 19, 1913
"Soldiers Home on Leek Island," May 9, 1917
"Hospital Deluxe," May 12, 1917

Other references include:

Andrew Cornwall. Hand-written notebook located in the Jefferson County Historical Museum, Watertown, New York.

National Archives of Canada (formerly Public Archives of Canada)
MG21, MMS, B124, Collins to Haldimand, Cateraqui, 1783
RG10, Red Series, Vol. 1879, File 1032, Correspondence, 1873
RG10, Red Series, C11-112, Vol. 1924, File 19127
RG10, Red Series, C11-116 Vol. 1939, File 3813, Correspondence 1872–1874.
RG10, Red Series, Vol. 1971, File 5432
RG10, Red Series, Vol. 1997, File 7093
RG10, Red Series, C11-133 Vol. 2013, File 7944
RG10, Red Series, C11-160 Vol. 2109, File 20131
RG10, Red Series, C11-110 Vol. 2440, File 19127
RG10, Red Series, C11-230 and C11-229 Vol. 2495, File 102438 Pts. 1&2
RG10, Red Series, C11-270 Vol. 2719, File 144,001
The Matheson Notes

Several tour guides and community histories have been used as reference material and are located in local libraries. They include:

J.R. Allan. "The Story of Grenadier Island." Unpublished manuscript, 1971.
E.F. Babbage. *The Phat Boys Racy Description of the St. Lawrence River and its Environs*. Rochester, N.Y., 1887.
Les and Verda Corbin. *The Visgers' World*. Clayton, N.Y.: 1987.
J.D.W. Darling and W.H. Wallace. *Sketch of the Early History of the Front Concessions of Lansdowne and Thousand Islands Group*. Gananoque, Ont.: 1925.
Jno. A. Haddock. *A Souvenir, The Thousand Islands of the St. Lawrence River*. Alexandria Bay, N.Y.: Weed-Parsons Printing Co., 1895.
H. Wm. Hawke. *Miss McCammon's Notes of the Early Days of Gananoque*. Gananoque, Ont.: Gananoque Museum Notebook, 1967.
Helen P. Jacox and Eugene B. Kleinhans, Jr. *Thousand Island Park: One Hundred Years, and Then Some*. Thousand Island Park, N.Y., 1975.
Thad. W.H. Leavitt. *History of Leeds and Grenville*. Brockville, Ont.: Recorder Press, 1879; facsimile edition, Mika Publishing, Belleville, 1972.
Susan Manes, ed. *Who's Up*. Chippawa Bay, N.Y.: 1981.
Margaret Nulty. *Murray Isle*. 1972.
Hugh Reynolds. *History of Rockport*. n.d.
Sagastaweka Island. Finley Family Papers. File of Island History and Photographs.
Susan W. Smith. Eames Collection, Scrapbooks.
Elizabeth P. Stamp. *Glimpses of Grand View*. Spokane, Wash.: 1988.
A.G. Ten Cate. *Brockville: A Pictorial History*. Brockville, Ont.: Besancourt Publishers, 1972.
A.G. Ten Cate and M.B. Fryer. *Pictorial History of the Thousand Islands of the St. Lawrence River*. Brockville, Ont.: Besancourt Publishers, 1982.
E. Visger. *Meandering Among a Thousand Islands*. Watertown, N.Y.: 1882.

BIBLIOGRAPHY

"Among the Thousand Islands," *Scribners Monthly*, Vol. XV, April 1878.

Abler, T.S., D.E. Sanders, and S.M. Weaver, *A Canadian Indian Bibliography, 1960–1970*. Toronto: University of Toronto Press, 1974.

Akenson, Donald Harman. *The Irish in Ontario, a Study in Rural History*. McGill-Queen's University Press, 1984.

Allan, J.R. "The Story of Grenadier Island." Unpublished manuscript, 1971.

All-Round Route and Panoramic Guide of the St. Lawrence, Montreal: International Railway Publishing Co., n.d. (c. 1890s)

Automobile Road Guide. 1912, Don Mills, Ont.: Mussen Book Company, 1971, facsimile edition.

Babbage, E.F. *The Phat Boys Racy Description of the St. Lawrence River and its Environs*. Rochester, N.Y., 1887.

Bachelder, John B. *Popular Resorts and How to Reach Them*. Boston: John B. Bachelder, Publisher, 1876.

Barrett, R.J. *Canada's Century: Progress and Resources of The Great Dominion*. London: The Financier and Bullionist, Limited, 1907.

Bartlett, Richard, ed. *The Gilded Age: America, 1865–1900*. Reading, Mass.: Addison-Wesley Publishing Company, 1969.

Beattie, Judith "Gunboats on the St. Lawrence River, (1763–1839)." Unpublished manuscript, Manuscript Report Number 15, National Historic Sites Service, Department of Indian Affairs and Northern Development, 1967.

Bechard, Henri, S.J. *The Original Caughnawaga Indians*. Montreal: International Publishers, 1976.

Bird, Isabella Lucy. *The Englishwoman in America*, Foreword by Andrew Hill Clark. Madison, Wis.: The University of Wisconsin Press, 1966.

Bishop, Morris. *White Men Came to the St. Lawrence*. Beatty Memorial Lectures, McGill University Press, 1961.

Boehme, Rev. Richard. "Mission of Grape Island," *County*. Vols. 1–3, 1978–79.

Bond, C.C.J. "The British Base at Carleton Island," *Ontario History*. Vol. LII, No. 1, March 1960, 1–16.

Boyd, Marion Calvin. *The Story of Garden Island*. Kingston, 1973.

Bradstreet, John. *An Impartial Account of Lieut. Col. Bradstreet's Expedition to Fort Frontenac: to which are added a few reflections on the conduct of that enterprize* [sic], *and the advantages resulting from its success*. Toronto: Rous & Mann, Ltd., 1940.

Britton, Freeman. *Souvenir of Gananoque and the Thousand Islands with Short Sketch of First Owners, Early Settlement and Other Historical Notes of the Town*. Gananoque: *The Gananoque Reporter*, 1901.

Brown, George W. *The St. Lawrence River*. New York: Weathervane Books, n.d.

Bryce, George. *A Short History of the Canadian People*. New York: Charles Scribner's Sons, 1914.

Burrows, Edmond. *Captain William FitzWilliam Owen of the African Survey: The Hydrographic Surveys of Admiral W.F.W. Owen on the Coast of Africa and the Great Lakes of Canada*. Amsterdam, 1985.

Calvert, Brig. Michael. *A Dictionary of Battles, 1715–1815*. New York: Mayflower Books, 1979.

Calvin, D.D. *A Saga of the St. Lawrence*. Toronto: The Ryerson Press, 1945.

Canada, Indian Treaties and Surrenders, From 1680–1890 in 2 Volumes, 1891. Vol. 1, facsimile edition. Toronto: Coles Publishing Co., 1971.

The Canadian Handbook and Tourist's Guide, 1867. Toronto: M. Longmoore & Co., facsimile edition, Coles Publishing Company, 1971.

Canadian Islands for Sale. Canadian Government Publication, Department of Indian Affairs, 1894.

Canniff, Wm. *The Settlement of Upper Canada*. Toronto: Dudley & Burns, Printer, 1869. Facsimile edition, Mika Publishing Company, Belleville, Ont., 1971.

Carpenter, Cliff. *Cliff Carpenter's Island*. Gannett Rochester Newspapers, 1982.

Chandler, David G. *Dictionary of Napoleonic Wars*. New York: Macmillan Publishers Co, Inc., 1979.

Clark, Ella Elizabeth. *Indian Legends of Canada*. Toronto: McClelland and Stewart, 1960.

Clarke, T. Wood. *Émigrés in the Wilderness*, The Macmillan Company, New York, 1941.

Clow, H. Meribeth, ed. *Leeds & Grenville Bicentennial, 1984*. United Counties of Leeds & Grenville, 1984.

Coleman, Helena. *A History of Halfmoon Bay*. Pitch Pine Island, n.d.

Corbin, Les and Verda. *The Visgers' World*. Clayton, N.Y., 1987.

Costain, Thomas B. *The White and the Gold: The French Regime in Canada*. New York: Doubleday & Company, Inc., 1954.

Coughin, Richard. *St. Lawrence River and the Thousand Islands: History and Legends*. Watertown, N.Y., c. 1920.

Craig, Gerald. *Early Travellers in the Canadas, 1791–1867*. Toronto: The Macmillan Company of Canada Limited, 1955.

——. *Upper Canada, The Formative Years*. Toronto: McClelland and Stewart Limited, 1963.

The Crossman House and the Thousand Islands of the St. Lawrence, By One Who Has Been There. Watertown, N.Y.: Watertown Times and Steam Printing and Publishing House, 1878.

Darling, J.D.W. and W.H. Wallace. *Sketch of the Early History of the Front Concessions of Lansdowne and Thousand Islands Group*. Gananoque, Ont., 1925.

Durham, J.H. *Carleton Island in the Revolution: The Old Fort and Its Builders*. Syracuse: Bardeen, 1889.

Eames, Frank. Family papers, Susan W. Smith purchased 1974.

——. *Briefs — Historic and Prehistoric*. Private publication, 1950.

——. *Toniata*. Private publication, n.d.

——. *Gananoque, The Name and Its Origin*. Gananoque, Ont., 1942.

——. *Robert Forsyth's Plug and Feathermen*. Private publication, Gananoque, Ont., 1936.

Earle, Evelyn Purvis. *Leeds the Lovely*. Prescott, Ont.: St. Lawrence Printing Co. Ltd., 1951.

Eccles, W.J. *Frontenac: The Courtier Governor*. Toronto, 1962.

——. *The Canadian Frontier, 1534–1760*. New York: Holt, Rinehart and Winston, 1969.
Everts, J.H. ed. *History of Jefferson County, New York*. Philadelphia: L.E. Everts & Co., 1878.
Farr, Dorothy. *The St. Lawrence River, Views by Nineteenth Century Artists*. Kingston, Ont.: Agnes Etherington Art Centre, Queen's University, 1981.
Fleming, Roy F. "St. Lawrence River Pirate," *Inland Seas*, Quarterly Journal of the Great Lakes Historical Society. Vol. 17, No. 1, Spring 1976, 47–51.
Flexner, James Thomas. *Lord of the Mohawks*. Boston: Little, Brown and Company, 1959; facsimile edition, 1959.
Franklin, John Hope. *A Southern Odyssey*. Baton Rouge: Louisiana State University Press, 1977.
Fraser, John. *Canadian Pen and Ink Sketches*. Montreal: W. Drysdale & Co., 1890.
Gananoque Reporter
"The Thousand Islands," April 20, 1873
"The Thousand Islands," April 26, 1873
"The Thousand Islands," May 30, 1873
"The Thousand Islands," April 18, 1874
"The Thousand Islands," April 30, 1874
"Fires," September 5, 1874
"Trespass on the Islands," July 13, 1875
"The Islands," May 13, 1876
"The Islands," September 1, 1877
"Lease of the Islands," July 31, 1880
"Jack Straw Light," April 1881
"The Islands," August 12, 1882
"The Granite Quarries," March 17, 1883
"The Illumination," August 22, 1884
"The Summer Hotel Scheme," August 24, 1885
"Tremont Park," July 2, 1887
"Gananoque's Early Days," June 9, 1888
"Hickory Island Attack," June 16, 1888
"The Canoe Club," August 17, 1889
"Chauncey Patterson Drowned," August 30, 1890
"Sale of Islands," July 18, 1891
"Sale of Islands," August 8, 1891
"Hay Island House," February 23, 1895
"Twice Told Tales," August 28, 1903
"Died at His Island Home," July 19, 1913
"Twice Told Tales," June 28, 1913
"Soldiers Home on Leek Island," May 9, 1917
"Hospital Deluxe," May 12, 1917
Garand, Rev. P.S. *Historical Sketch of the Village of Clayton, N.Y. and a Complete History of St. Mary's Parish*. Clayton, N.Y.: G.H. Bates, Printer, 1902.
Golf at the Thousand Islands. Grenadier Island Country Club, Grenadier Island, n.d.
Haddock, Jno. A. *A Souvenir, The Thousand Islands of the St. Lawrence River*. Alexandria Bay, N.Y.: Weed-Parsons Printing Co., 1895.
Hagarty, Col. W.G. "Fort Frontenac," *Historic Kingston*. No. 2, 14–25, October 1953, Kingston Historical Society, Kingston, Ont.
Hawke, H. Wm. *Historic Gananoque*. Belleville, Ont.: Mika Publishing, 1974.
——. *Miss McCammon's Notes of the Early Days of Gananoque*. Gananoque, Ont.: Gananoque Museum Notebook, 1967.
Headley, J.T. *Napoleon and His Marshals*, Vol. I, II. New York: Hurst & Company, n.d. (c. 1890s).
Heritage Kingston. Kingston, Ont.: Agnes Etherington Art Centre, Queen's University, 1973.
Historic Kingston. Transactions of the Kingston Historical Society, Vols. 1 to 10. Belleville, Ont.: Kingston Historical Society, Mika Publishing Company, 1974.
Historic Sackets Harbor. 1000 Islands International Council, n.d.
Hood, George N. "The Federal Government and Land Expropriation: A Case Study of Pressure Group Politics in the Thousand Islands Area," M.A. thesis, University of Western Ontario, 1982.
Hough, Franklin B. *A History of St. Lawrence and Franklin Counties, New York*. Albany, N.Y.: Little & Co., 1853.
——. *History of Jefferson County in the State of New York*. Watertown, N.Y.: Joel Munsell, 1854.
——. *Gazetteer of the State of New York*. Albany, N.Y.: Andrew Boyd, 1853.
Howison, John. *Sketches of Upper Canada*. Edinburgh: Oliver & Boyd, 1921, facsimile edition, Coles Publishing Company, Toronto, 1970.
Hunt, George T. *The Wars of the Iroquois*. The University of Wisconsin Press, 1967.
Hunter, Wm. S., Jr. *Hunter's Panoramic Guide, from Niagara Falls to Quebec*. Boston: John P. Jewett & Company, 1857; facsimile edition, Coles Publishing Company, Toronto, 1970.
Innis, Mary, ed. *Mrs. Simcoe's Diary*. Toronto: Macmillan of Canada, 1971.
Irving, L. Homfray. *Officers of the British Forces in Canada During the War of 1812*. Welland, Ont.: Canadian Military Institute, 1908.
Jacox, Helen P. and Eugene B. Kleinhans Jr. *Thousand Island Park: One Hundred Years, and Then Some*. Thousand Island Park, N.Y,: Thousand Island Park, 1975.
Johnson, Clifton. *The Picturesque St. Lawrence*. New York: The Macmillan Company, 1910.
Johnston, Capt. Henry S. *The Thousand Islands of the St. Lawrence River, with Descriptions of the Scenery, and Historical Quotations of Events, and Reminiscences, with Which They Are Associated*. Boston: Christopher Publishing House, 1937.
Jones, Peter (Kah-Ke-Wa-Quo-Na-By). *Life and Journals of Kah-Ke-Wa-Quo-Na-By*. Toronto: Wesleyan Printing Establishment, 1860.
"Journal of Captain Sherwood, 1783," *Report on Canadian Archives 1884–1889*. Series B., Vol. 169.
Keats, John. *Of Time and an Island*. New York: Charterhouse, 1974.
Landon, Harry F. *The North Country — A History Embracing Jefferson, St. Lawrence, Oswego, Lewis and Franklin Counties, N.Y.* Indianapolis: Historical Publishing Company, 1932.
Lantier, Margaret McCormick. *The Thousand Islands, Vacation Paradise*. Ogdensburg, N.Y.: Ryan Press, 1961.

Leavitt, Thad. W.H. *History of Leeds and Grenville*. Brockville, Ont.: Recorder Press, 1879; facsimile edition, Mika Publishing, Belleville, 1972.
Leggett, Robert. *Rideau Waterway*. Toronto: University of Toronto Press, 1955.
Long, J. *Voyages and Travels of an Indian Interpreter and Trader*. London, England, 1791; facsimile edition, Coles Publishing Company, 1974.
Lord, Walter. *The Dawn's Early Light*. New York: W.W. Norton & Company Inc., 1972.
Mabee, Carleton. *The Seaway Story*. New York: The Macmillan Company, 1961.
Machar, Agnes Maude. *The Story of Old Kingston*. Toronto: The Musson Book Co. Ltd., 1908.
Malkus, Alida. *Blue-Water Boundary, Epic Highway of the Great Lakes and the Saint Lawrence*. New York: Hastings House, 1960.
Manes, Susan, ed. *Who's Up*. Chippewa Bay, N.Y., 1981.
McAlester, Virginia and Lee. *A Field Guide to American Houses*. New York: Alfred A. Knopf, 1984.
McElroy, Robert, and Thomas Riggs, ed. *The Unfortified Boundary: A Diary of the First Survey of the Canadian Boundary Line from St. Regis to the Lake of the Woods, By Major Joseph Delafield*. New York: private publication, 1943.
McKenzie, Ruth. *Admiral Bayfield, Pioneer Nautical Surveyor*. Miscellaneous special publication, #32. Ottawa: Environment Canada, Fisheries and Marine Service, 1976.
——. *Leeds and Grenville: Their First Two Hundred Years*. Toronto: McClelland and Stewart, 1967.
——. "Historical Sketch of Leeds and Grenville," *Illustrated Historical Atlas of the Counties of Leeds and Grenville*. Belleville, Ont.: Mika Publishing.
McNaughton, John. *Schedules and Diary Examination Survey, 1862–63*. Field book 210A.
Mercier, Gilbert B. *Pleasure Yachts of the Thousand Islands*. Clayton, N.Y.: Shipyard Press/Shipyard Museum, 1981.
Mika, N. *Historical Atlas of Leeds and Grenville*. Belleville, Ont.: Mika Publishing, 1973.
Mills, James, C. *Our Inland Seas*. A.C. McClurg & Co., 1910; facsimile edition, Freshwater Press, Cleveland, 1976.
Morgan, Henry James. *The Canadian Men and Women of the Time*. Toronto: William Briggs, second edition, 1912.
Morison, Samuel Eliot. *Samuel de Champlain*. Boston: Little, Brown and Company, 1972.
Morley, William, F.E. *Ontario and the Canadian North, A Bibliography*. Toronto: University of Toronto Press, 1978.
Morris, the Hon. Alexander. *The Treaties of Canada with The Indians of Manitoba and the North-West Territories*. Toronto: Belfords, Clarke & Co., Publishers, 1880; facsimile edition, Coles Publishing Company, Toronto, 1971.
Morris, J.L. *Indians of Ontario*. Ottawa: Department of Lands and Forests, n.d.
National Archives of Canada (formerly Public Archives of Canada) (see References for Part II)
Admiralty 1, Secretary's Department-in-Letters, Captains' Letters "O", Numbers 1–50, 1816, B-2786, Adm. 1, Vol. 2264.
Neilson, J.L.H. "Diary of an Officer in the War of 1812–14" *Queen's Quarterly*, Vol. 2, 1894–95, 318–28; Vol. 3, 1895–96, 23-30.
Nicholson, N.L., and L.M. Sebert. *The Maps of Canada*. Folkestone, England: Wm. Dawson & Sons Ltd., and Hamden, Conn.: Archon Books, 1981.
Nicholson, T.R. *The Age of Motoring Adventure, 1897–1939*. London: Cassell, 1972.
Nulton, Laurie Ann. *The Golden Age of the Thousand Islands, Its people and Its Castles*. Thomas Nulton, 1981.
Nulty, Margaret. *Murray Isle*. 1972.
O'Callaghan, E.B. *Documentary History of the State of New York*, Vols. I–IV. Albany: Weed, Parsons & Co., 1850.
Osbourne, Brian S. *The Thousand Islands Region, 1650–1850*. A study in exploration, settlement and development, St. Lawrence Island National Park, Interpretation Contract, 1976.
Palmer, Richard F. "First Steamboat on the Great Lakes." *Gananoque Reporter*, n.d.
Parkman, Francis. *Count Frontenac and New France Under Louis XIV*. Boston: Little, Brown and Company, 1877.
——. *Montcalm and Wolfe*, Vols. I—III. Boston: Little, Brown and Company, 1901.
Passfield, Robert W. *Building the Rideau Canal: A Pictorial History*. Fitzhenry & Whiteside, Parks Canada and the Canadian Government Publishing Centre, 1982.
Pilcher, Edith. *Castorland, French Refugees in the Western Adirondacks 1793–1814*. Harrison, N.Y., 1985.
Pouchet, M. *Memoir Upon the Late War in North America Between the French and the English, 1755–1760*. Translated and edited by R.B. Hough and W.E. Woodward. Roxbury, Mass., 1866.
Pound, Arthur. *Lake Ontario*. Port Washington, N.Y.: Kennikat Press, 1945.
Powell, Thomas F. *Penet's Square*. Lakemont, N.Y.: North Country Books, 1976.
Preston, Richard A., ed. *Kingston Before the War of 1812, A Collection of Documents*. Toronto: Champlain Society, 1959.
Preston, Richard A., Lamontagne, Leapold. *Royal Fort Frontenac*. Toronto: Champlain Society, 1958.
Queen's Quarterly. Vol. 2, 1894–95.
Read, Colin and Ronald J. Stagg, ed. *The Rebellion of 1837 in Upper Canada*. The Champlain Society in cooperation with The Ontario Heritage Foundation, Carleton University Press, 1985.
Reid, J.H.S., K. McNaught and H.S. Crowe. *A Source-book of Canadian History*. Toronto: Longmans, Green and Company, 1959.
Report on Canadian Archives 1884–1889, Series B, Vol. 169.
Report on Department of Public Records and Archives of Ontario. Ottawa: 1929.
Reynolds, Hugh. "History of Rockport." Unpublished: original held at Sprinfield House, Escott, Ont., n.d.
Robertson, J. Ross. *The Diary of Mrs. John Graves Simcoe, Wife of the First Lieutenant-Governor of the Province of Upper Canada, 1792–96*. Toronto, 1911.

Rome, Watertown and Ogdensburg Railroad Co., Summer Excursion. Oswego, N.Y.: Rome, Watertown and Ogdensburg Railroad, Oliphant's Printing, n.d.

Ross, Don. *St. Lawrence Islands National Park*. Vancouver: Douglas & McIntyre, in association with Parks Canada, 1983.

The St. Lawrence River Pilot Above Quebec. Hydrographic Office, Department of Naval Service, Ottawa, 1920.

Sagastaweka Island. Finley Family Papers. File of Island History and Photographs.

Sainty, J. C. *Admiralty Officials, 1600–1870*, Vol. IV. London: Athlone Press, 1975.

——. *Treasury Officials 1680–1870*. London: Athlone Press, 1976.

Scott, Ina G. *Yesterday's News, Today's History*. Gananoque, Ont.: 1000 Islands Publishers Ltd., 1982.

Segrave, Kerry, and Linda Martin. *City Parks of Canada*. Oakville, Ont.: Mosaic Press, 1983.

Senior, Eleanor Kyte. *From Royal Township to Industrial City, Cornwall 1784–1984*. Belleville, Ont.: Mika Publishing Company, 1983.

Shaw, Robert V. *A Century of Photographs, 1846–1946*. Washington, D.C.: Library of Congress, 1980.

Smith, Donald B. "The Dispossession of the Mississauga Indians: A Missing Chapter in the Early History of Upper Canada." *Ontario History*, Vol. LXXIII, No. 2, 67–87.

Smith, Susan Weston. *A History of Recreation in the Thousand Islands*. Parks Canada, Island Insights, No. 6, 1976.

——. "Historic Resource Inventory, St. Lawrence Islands National Park." Unpublished manuscript, original held at Parks Canada, Eastern Ontario Region, Cornwall, Ont., 1985.

Smith, William Henry. *Smith's Canadian Gazetteer, Comprising Statistical and General Information Respecting All Parts of the Upper Province, or Canada West*. Toronto: Henry Rowsell, 1849.

Souvenir of the Thousand Islands and River St. Lawrence. Grand Rapids: Bayne, 1901.

Stacey, C.P.. "The Ships of the British Squadron on Lake Ontario, 1812–14," *Canadian Historical Review XXXIV*.

Stamp, Elizabeth P. *Glimpses of Grand View*. Spokane, Wash., 1988.

Stanley, G.F.G. *Conflicts & Social Notes: The War of 1812–1814, The Patriot War — 1837/8*. Parks Canada, Island Insights, No. 7, 1976.

Stanton, Junia Fitch. *Links in the Chain, by Solon Massey, 1850–1858*. Watertown, N.Y., 1981.

Summering Among the Thousand Islands. Syracuse, N.Y.: Boyd, n.d.

Sward, Robert. *The Toronto Islands*. Toronto: Dreadnaught, 1983.

Tanney, Donna Spooner. *The Eternal Hills*. Brookfield, N.Y.: Homestead Book, Brookfield, 1973.

Ten Cate, A.G. *Brockville: A Pictorial History*. Brockville, Ont.: Besancourt Publishers, 1972.

Ten Cate, A.G., and M.B. Fryer. *Pictorial History of the Thousand Islands of the St. Lawrence River*. Brockville, Ont.: Besancourt Publishers, 1982.

1000 Islands Area Residents Association, "A Report to the People," Vols. I–IV, Lansdowne, Ont., 1977.

The Thousand Islands of the St. Lawrence River. Carthage, N.Y.: The Great Little Publishing Company, 1983.

Thumm, Eileen, and Wyatt Silver. *Kingston Walk Book*. 1980.

Thousand Island House. *Guide Book of the Thousand Island House, St. Lawrence River, Alexandria Bay, N.Y., O.G. Staples, Proprietor*. c. 1882.

Toye, William. *The St. Lawrence*. Toronto: Oxford University Press, 1959.

Tracy, Frank Basil. *The Tercentenary History of Canada*, Vols. I–III, New York: P.F. Collier & Son, 1908.

Traill, Catherine Parr. *The Backwoods of Canada*. London, 1836; facsimile edition, McClelland and Stewart, Toronto, 1971.

Visger, E. *Meandering Among a Thousand Islands*. Watertown, N. Y., 1882.

Webster's Biographical Dictionary. Springfield, Mass.: G&C Merriam Co., 1943.

Wechsberg, Joseph. *The Lost World of the Great Spas*. New York: Harper & Row, 1979.

Westcott, Allan. "The Thousand Islands and St. Lawrence Border, Their History, Legends and Romance." Unpublished manuscript, n.d.

White, Arthur V. *Long Sault Rapids, St. Lawrence River*. Ottawa: Mortimer Co., 1913.

White, James. *Boundary Disputes and Treaties*. Toronto: Glasgow, Brock and Company, 1914.

Wright, J.V. *Ontario Prehistory, An Eleven-Thousand-Year Archaeological Outline*. Ottawa: National Museums of Canada, National Museum of Man, 1982.

Young, A.G. *Great Lakes Saga*. Toronto: Richardson, Bond and Wright Ltd., 1965.

INDEX (Index of Canadian and U.S. Islands follows)

Index of Historic Names for Canadian and U.S. Islands

Canadian Islands

Numbered Islands

(All Canadian)

U.S. ISLANDS